DEALING
WITH EMPLOYMENT
DISCRIMINATION

Richard Peres

DEALING
WITH EMPLOYMENT
DISCRIMINATION

MCGRAW-HILL BOOK COMPANY
NewYork St. Louis San Francisco Auckland Bogotá
Düsseldorf Johannesburg London Madrid Mexico
Montreal New Delhi Panama Paris São Paulo
Singapore Sydney Tokyo Toronto

Library of Congress Cataloging in Publication Data

Peres, Richard,
Dealing with employment discrimination.

Includes index.
1. Discrimination in employment—Law and legislation—
United States.   I. Title.
KF3464.P47   344'.73'01133   77-9018
ISBN 0-07-049317-0

1234567890   KPKP   7654321098

The editors for this book were W. Hodson Mogan
and Virginia Fechtmann Blair,
the designer was Elliot Epstein, and the production supervisor
was Teresa F. Leaden. It was set in Palatino
by Bi-Comp, Incorporated.

Printed and bound by The Kingsport Press.

To Nanette

Contents

II
HOW TO PREVENT COMPLAINTS

III
RESOLVING COMPLAINTS

Preface

This book is intended to help remedy an apparent lack of practical and realistic works in the field of unlawful employment discrimination. Its purposes are threefold: (1) to provide a concise and useful understanding of an increasingly complex yet vital legal subject, (2) to set forth workable guidelines for the prevention of discrimination complaints in all areas of employment practices, and (3) to give guidance on the effective and rational resolution of existing complaints.

The readership of *Dealing with Employment Discrimination* is not confined to personnel specialists and those in higher management positions, but includes anyone holding a link in the employment practices chain. Although discrimination is discussed here as a legal subject, it has wide applicability to daily occurrences in the employment world. From the receptionist handling job inquiries to the supervisor making job assignments to the administrator setting wage scales—each may be the cause of a discrimination complaint.

Neither good intentions nor moral superiority will be enough to guard against involvement in discrimination lawsuits and costly settlements. Surely the millions of dollars awarded each year to complaining employees bespeaks of something more than a question of morals. This book argues that these troubles are self-inflicted by a misunderstanding of the fundamentals of civil rights law enforcement and the inability to make use of them in preventing complaints. State and federal agencies administering antidiscrimination laws are naturally more disposed toward the investigation of complaints rather than their prevention. Company lawyers and other legal professionals are generally inclined to take an adversary, after-the-fact, courtroom perspective when discussing the subject. But the assumption made in this book is a simple one:

educate and enlighten business people and they will know how to lessen their vulnerability to discrimination-like conflicts.

Part I begins by introducing the reader to the legal terminology of discrimination and the three main ways in which the "law" is defined. The reader is then familiarized with various prohibited employment practices, the several unlawful bases of discrimination, and which employers are covered. In Chapter 3 the all-important proofs of unlawful discrimination are presented. Knowing the proofs enables one to determine whether any practice may be seen as unlawful. Should a complaint occur, Chapter 4 examines how it can be defended and shows what the key factors of a defense are. The last chapter in Part I covers the area of compensatory damages. This material allows one to measure the possible consequences, in both time and money, of a discrimination case. Knowing what is at stake is also essential to sensible decision making on settling a complaint without expensive and drawn-out litigation.

Part II provides guidelines on preventing complaints in the three main areas of employment: hiring, discharge, and the work environment. The emphasis here is on implementing the material of the first part rather than legal theories. In Chapter 6 the reader is shown which management practices are peculiarly suitable to an ongoing strategy of complaint prevention, such as the formulation of policies, the need to supervise the supervisor, and the assets of instituting a viable grievance procedure. The next three chapters give a step-by-step means of stopping complaints before they get started. Twelve different aspects of the hiring process are covered. Chapter 8 provides guidance in the area of discharge, an employment practice which is rarely touched upon in the general literature of personnel management yet represents the most complained about job discrimination issue. Reducing problems in the work environment is facilitated by the material covered in Chapter 9, which separates the relevant issues into those which are supervision related and policy related.

Part III, entitled "Resolving Complaints," deals with an area largely ignored by job discrimination commentators. Yet serious errors are frequently|made in an employer's reaction to a government investigation. Mistakes may make resolution without the expense of legal fees impossible and may greatly enlarge the extent of a back pay award. Therefore, Chapter 10 shows the reader how government agencies handle complaints, and in Chapter 11 guidelines are presented on the best way to handle these investigations and resolve complaints rationally and efficiently.

The intricacies of the legal concept of discrimination, expanding in recent years by numerous court decisions and new statutes, have made unlawful discrimination somewhat like a game whose rules are not well-known. This book attempts to clarify the rules and give guidance on their implementation. All levels of employment will thus find *Dealing with Employment Discrimination* valuable. Competence in the EEO area is quickly becoming a criteria in the evaluation of supervisory employees. This book may certainly be used in an in-house training program on employment discrimination or as an informative text for courses on personnel management, industrial relations, and other similar programs of instruction.

I wish to express my sincere gratitude to those persons who gave me support and confidence in this project, as well as technical assistance: to my colleagues at the New Jersey Division on Civil Rights, notably William T. Landmark and John Blanos, Senior Field Representatives, and Robert W. Gaunt, Chief of the Bureau of Compliance; to Susan Littauer, George Stewart, and Rosemary Fruehling; and to my parents, for their unending encouragement.

RICHARD PERES

DEALING
WITH EMPLOYMENT
DISCRIMINATION

PART

I

UNLAWFUL
DISCRIMINATION

1

Introduction to a Legal Subject

Before we can begin to understand the dynamics of employment discrimination, we must first grasp the true nature of the subject being studied. After all, problems can be solved only when they are first properly identified. Although most people seem to think they know what discrimination is, costly legal actions against employers continue to reverberate throughout the American business scene. Note, for example, the 130,000 complaints presently pending before the Equal Employment Opportunity Commission! What is the problem? One answer is that employers are mistakenly confusing the conventional usage of the term "discrimination" with its legal definition.

THE NEED FOR A LEGAL, OBJECTIVE APPROACH

Our concern here is strictly with the legal concept of employment discrimination. And to study this subject we must be rational, objective, and free from the emotions and feelings associated with the conventional view.

Admittedly, an objective approach to this emotion-charged topic is sometimes difficult. In spite of our long history of discrimination against minority groups and women, discrimination is still commonly thought of as a moral wrong. The general notion is that a company that discriminates is "bad." Therefore, when an employer is accused of discrimination, the reaction is often explosive. A legal complaint is turned into a moral indictment, and the decision-making process that follows does not accurately consider the particular legal realities of the matter at hand. This approach is typical of the employer who will eventually end up on the losing side of a case. (I recall the corporate president who

3

fought a state agency's finding of discrimination by bringing in a trophy he received from the Spanish community. His lawyer argued that this was not the sort of person whose company would violate a fair employment law. But the response to the charge had one small oversight: the company was being accused of sex discrimination.)

Perhaps the conventional definition of employment discrimination should be "a civil violation committed occasionally by *other* employers." According to the conventional approach, the 130,000 complaints do not exist. The standard phrase is "my company would never discriminate against anyone."

But essentially, unlawful discrimination is a complex of legal principles, laws, theories, and proofs that may be applied to the daily practices of people in the employment world. Because actions toward personnel by a manager, supervisor, corporate president, or even a receptionist may cause a valid complaint to be filed, today's employer cannot afford to be unaware of the legal realities of the subject. The first step toward learning about discrimination, then, is to disassociate ourselves from the conventional way in which the subject has been approached.

An objective approach to this topic will be greatly enhanced by a strong dose of honesty and introspection. Before entering the "real world," we must first cut through a maze of illusions we have about ourselves. Let us realize that we are only human and therefore far from perfect. When sex discrimination in employment became unlawful across the land in 1965, the people of America did not suddenly awake free from bias and with halos around their heads. That sort of change, assuming it does occur, is hardly so rapid. Like it or not, we all have our biases, and they can easily manifest themselves in unlawful acts. Only when our vision is clear can we become practical.

While machines and computers are an integral part of industrial America, people still make up its key determining elements. Employers must take an open look at what they do and consider the legal ramifications of their actions. No American employer operates in a vacuum. The burdens *are* great. We must seek to understand civil rights laws just as we would attempt to learn about federal and state tax regulations. Yet there is one essential difference: discrimination relates to the human element in all of us—a fact which emphasizes the need for a well-disciplined, objective approach to the subject.

SOME IMPORTANT TERMS

Civil laws are most often enforced in court. However, an important aspect of laws which prohibit employment discrimination is that complaints are initially handled through agencies responsible for administering the laws. For example, the Equal Employment Opportunity Commission was set up by Congress to enforce Title VII of the Civil Rights Act of 1964, the section prohibiting employment discrimination. Many states have set up similar enforcement agencies relating to state laws. This facilitates the filing of a discrimination complaint against an employer as compared with the more typical lawsuit, which requires the hiring of an attorney and an outlay of money.

The person who files a complaint is called a *complainant*, and the employer and/or persons against whom the complaint is filed are the *respondents*. Other terms for these are *plaintiff* and *defendant*. Should John Doe charge X Company with discrimination, the *case* would be called *John Doe v. X Company*.

A *complaint* of discrimination is a legal document which *alleges* that the employer violated a fair employment law by being responsible for certain acts against the complainant. Note that a complainant need not *prove* a case to make a complaint, but only allege that certain unlawful acts were committed. Figure 1 illustrates a typical EEOC charge form.

A *class action complaint* is one that is representative of several complaints. Most individual charges have the potential of becoming class actions. This is because civil rights laws were enacted to protect certain groups of persons who historically have suffered widespread discrimination. Therefore, most individual complaints are potentially damaging for employers. Class actions frequently originate from one person's charge of unfair, and unlawful, treatment, and may result in millions of dollars in liability.

There is a strong legal foundation which facilitates administrative agencies' and individual complainants' filing of class actions. Section 706(a) of Title VII permits an EEOC member to file charges. In *Bowaters Southern Paper Corporation v. EEOC,* the Sixth Circuit Court of Appeals stated that "there is no constitutional prohibition to Congress permitting investigations of corporate behavior based upon nothing more than official curiosity . . . ."[1] In *Graniteville Company v. EEOC,* the Fourth Circuit Court of Appeals approved of Edward Price's right to initiate an EEOC investigation by alleging various discriminatory practices:

> The allegation by Price in the case at hand that he personally and the class he represents are subject to defendant's discriminatory employment policy is more than sufficient to establish his standing to initiate EEOC proceedings though he makes no claim that the policy has been applied to him in a specific instance.[2]

---

[1] 2 Empl. Prac. Dec. ¶10,240 (1970).
[2] 3 Empl. Prac. Dec. ¶8109 (1971).

(PLEASE PRINT OR TYPE)

CHARGE OF DISCRIMINATION	EEOC CHARGE NO. 5-0000	FORM APPROVED OMB NO. 124-R0001

INSTRUCTIONS

If you have a complaint, fill in this form and mail it to the Equal Employment Opportunity Commission's District Office in your area. In most cases, a charge must be filed with the EEOC within a specified time after the discriminatory act took place. IT IS THEREFORE IMPORTANT TO FILE YOUR CHARGE AS SOON AS POSSIBLE. *(Attach extra sheets of paper if necessary.)*

CAUSE OF DISCRIMINATION

[X] RACE OR COLOR   [ ] SEX

[ ] RELIGIOUS CREED

[ ] NATIONAL ORIGIN

NAME (Indicate Mr. or Ms.) **John Doe**

DATE OF BIRTH **1-23-47**

STREET ADDRESS **80 2nd Ave.**   COUNTY

SOCIAL SECURITY NO. **148-00-9560**

CITY, STATE, AND ZIP CODE **Hamburg, Maine**

TELEPHONE NO. (Include area code) **999-0000**

THE FOLLOWING PERSON ALWAYS KNOWS WHERE TO CONTACT ME

NAME (Indicate Mr. or Ms.) **Amy Doe**

TELEPHONE NO. (Include area code) **888-8888**

STREET ADDRESS **10 30th Street**   CITY, STATE, AND ZIP CODE **Hamburg, Me.**

LIST THE EMPLOYER, LABOR ORGANIZATION, EMPLOYMENT AGENCY, APPRENTICESHIP COMMITTEE, STATE OR LOCAL GOVERNMENT WHO DISCRIMINATED AGAINST YOU *(If more than one, list all)*

NAME **Any Company**

TELEPHONE NO. (Include area code) **777-7777**

STREET ADDRESS **20 Any town St.**   CITY, STATE, AND ZIP CODE **Any town, U.S.A.**

OTHERS WHO DISCRIMINATED AGAINST YOU *(If any)*

CHARGE FILED WITH STATE/LOCAL GOV'T. AGENCY [X] YES [ ] NO

DATE FILED **9-1-77**

AGENCY CHARGE FILED WITH *(Name and address)* **State Human Rights Agency**

APPROXIMATE NO. OF EMPLOYEES/MEMBERS OF COMPANY OR UNION THIS CHARGE IS FILED AGAINST **110**

DATE MOST RECENT OR CONTINUING DISCRIMINATION TOOK PLACE *(Month, day, and year)* **6-15-77**

Explain what unfair thing was done to you and how other persons were treated differently. Understanding that this statement is for the use of the United States Equal Employment Opportunity Commission, I hereby certify:

On 6-15-77, I was fired from my job when I asked my boss why he said it was because of my high absenteeism. I know several white employees who have been absent more than me and were not fired. I am black.

I swear or affirm that I have read the above charge and that it is true to the best of my knowledge, information and belief.

DATE **9-1-77**   CHARGING PARTY (Signature) **John Doe**

Subscribed and sworn to before this EEOC representative.

DATE **9-1-77**   SIGNATURE AND TITLE **Richard Doe E.O.S.**

NOTARY PUBLIC

SUBSCRIBED AND SWORN TO BEFORE ME THIS DATE *(Day, month, and year)*

SIGNATURE (If it is difficult for you to get a Notary Public to sign this, sign your own name and mail to the District Office. The Commission will notarize the charge for you at a later date.)

EEOC FORM JUN 72 5   Previous editions of this form may be used.   GPO 885-959

Figure 1   Sample EEOC Charge Form

In the federal court system, there are four requirements for turning a complaint into a class action. First, the size of the class makes it impractical for each member to file individually. Second, there are common questions of law and fact. Third, the claims made by those filing the complaint are typical of the class. Fourth, those filing the complaint will fairly represent the interests of the class.

For example, during March of 1966 Richard Johnson, Jr., was discharged from Georgia Highway Express, Inc. By the time the case got to district court, Johnson not only charged race discrimination in his termination, but also alleged that he was representative of "Negroes seeking equal employment opportunities without discrimination on the grounds of race or color who are so numerous as to make it impracticable to bring them all before this court."[3]

The court for the Northern District of Georgia ruled that Johnson was limited to representing only the class of discharged Negro employees. However, the United States Court of Appeals, Fifth Circuit, reversed this ruling, stating that a class action representing all Negro employees in "hiring, firing, promotion, and maintenance of facilities"[4] was permissible, and sent the case back to the district court for reconsideration. On March 3, 1972, the district court ordered extensive changes in the respondent employer's promotion, transfer, and recruitment practices; took other remedial action; and invited all previously fired Negro employees to take part in the class action.[5] On August 8, 1972, the district court awarded the complainants $13,500 for attorneys' fees, thus ending a case which had begun more than six years before with the discharge of one black employee![6]

Minority group is a popular civil rights term that needs little explanation. However, from a legal standpoint it causes much confusion. In a sense, it refers to all groups except women (who are in the majority). A related and more relevant term is *protected class*. A protected class member is one of a group of persons who historically have suffered discrimination. Blacks, women, Hispanics, Orientals, and American Indians are all protected classes.[7]

Other minority groups have voiced their concern over the special rights of protected class members. Actually, the rights are identical.

---

[3] 1 Empl. Prac. Dec. ¶9950 (1968).
[4] 2 Empl. Prac. Dec. ¶10,119 (1969).
[5] 4 Empl. Prac. Dec. ¶7753 (1972).
[6] 5 Empl. Prac. Dec. ¶8444 (1972).
For two other early cases which show the ability of individuals to file broad class actions, see *Jenkins v. United Gas Corporation,* 1 Empl. Prac. Dec. ¶9908 (1968), and *Bowe v. Colgate Palmolive,* 2 Empl. Prac. Dec. ¶10,090 (1969).
[7] In 1976 the EEOC revised its nomenclature for protected classes. *Hispanic* replaced *Spanish-surnamed American* and includes all people of Mexican, Puerto Rican, Cuban, Central American, and South American origin, regardless of race. *Asian or Pacific Islander* replaced *Oriental* and includes people of Far Eastern, Southeastern Asiatic, and Pacific Island descent. The *American Indian* category was replaced by *American Indian or Alaskan Native* to include Eskimos and Aleuts.

Under Title VII anyone may file a complaint based, for example, on national origin, religion, race, color, or sex. However, there is a major difference between the two groups in the way unlawful discrimination is proved. This point will be expanded in Chapter 3. Nevertheless, it may be worthwhile to take note at the start that antidiscrimination laws were enacted with the intent of eliminating the traditional unfair treatment of certain groups in our society. After all, the civil rights movement of the 1950s and 1960s was not a response to the persecution of white males. And in the world of civil rights law enforcement, this is a well-understood fact.

An important distinction to keep in mind is that between *violating the law* and being *guilty of discrimination*. While in a strict legal sense there is no difference between the terms, the latter evokes the kinds of feelings that are detrimental to rational decision making on the part of employers. *Guilt* connotes that conventional approach mentioned before which clouds our vision, distorts the facts, and causes us to ignore legal realities. This is not to say that no moral overtones exist in the area of civil rights. But state and federal agencies and the courts are not concerned with moral determinations, but with law enforcement. The factors which separate those who violate the law from those who do not usually relate to things other than moral righteousness.

HOW THE LAW IS DEFINED

To many, the "law" appears as a mysterious subject. When legal problems arise, our natural tendency is to let a lawyer take over. And although we must guide our actions to be in line with the law, a true understanding of the subject is often perceived as beyond our reach.

However, the approach here is largely preventive and therefore founded on the employer's ability to grasp and utilize a working knowledge of civil rights laws and interpretations. The law, in reality, is not all that mysterious, and the ways in which employers' day-to-day actions have legal ramifications *can* be understood. That big area which we call the law is actually a conglomeration of statutes, court decisions, and guidelines. Each deserves our attention.

Statutes

The most obvious way a law is defined is by the statute itself. State statutes are laws passed by the state legislatures; federal laws are passed by Congress.

Title VII. The most comprehensive and significant Federal legislation dealing with employment discrimination is Title VII of the Civil Rights

Act of 1964, as amended by the Equal Employment Opportunity Act of 1972.[8] The law prohibits job discrimination on the basis of race, color, religion, sex, or national origin and is administered by the EEOC. (See Appendix 1.)

There is a long legislative history to Title VII. The Civil Rights Act of 1964 represented a departure from the government's haphazard and inconsistent efforts toward eliminating discrimination over the last hundred years. It was a direct result of a politicized social movement that dominated the domestic scene during the late 1950s and early 1960s, as well as one of the longest and intense congressional debates on record. And despite the protections which the law provides for women and ethnic and religious groups, the enactment of Title VII was primarily motivated by 300 years of persecution of black people in America. In fact, the inclusion of the prohibition of discrimination on the basis of sex was an afterthought.

The historical foundations of Title VII are worth recalling, for they provide insight into the interpretive decisions by the courts and the enforcement efforts of government agencies and interest groups. Some seem to feel that there is no longer a civil rights movement in this country, that the incident rate of discrimination has substantially lessened. Actually, the movement is alive and well and can easily be located in courtrooms and government agencies throughout the country rather than in the streets.

Because of the importance of Title VII as compared with all other federal and state laws, it will receive much of our attention here. As will be seen, court decisions rendered in Title VII cases will have a bearing on the interpretation and enforcement of similar antidiscrimination laws.

Age and Equal Pay Acts.   Two other relevant federal laws are the Age Discrimination in Employment Act of 1967[9] (see Appendix 2) and the Equal Pay Act of 1963[10] (see Appendix 3); both are amendments to the Fair Labor Standards Act and are enforced by the Wage and Hour Division of the U.S. Department of Labor. The first prohibits age discrimination for applicants and employees in the 40 to 65 category; the second prohibits unequal compensation for equal work based on sex and was revised in 1972 to cover professional and management occupations.

Civil Rights Act of 1866.   This statute was originally enacted with the intent of enforcing the provisions of the Thirteenth Amendment of the

---

[8] 42 U.S.C. §2000(e) *et seq.*
[9] 29 U.S.C. §621.
[10] 29 U.S.C. §206(d).

U.S. Constitution, which banned slavery. In part, the act states that "All persons within the jurisdiction of the United States shall have the same right in every State and Territory to make and enforce contracts . . . as is enjoyed by white citizens. . . ."[11] This law has generally been interpreted to prohibit race discrimination and, occasionally, discrimination on the basis of national origin. Although not enforced by any agency of the government, it has been used in many court actions because it is not subject to some of the limitations imposed by Title VII.

Civil Rights Act of 1871. This statute originates from the enabling provisions of the Fourteenth Amendment, It states:

> Every person who, under color of any statute, ordinance, regulation, custom, or usage of any State or Territory, subjects, or causes to be subjected, a citizen . . . to the deprivation of any rights, privileges or immunities secured by the Constitution and laws, shall be liable to the person injured. . . .[12]

Like the 1866 act, this statute is not administered by any agency. It has been interpreted as prohibiting sex, race, and national origin discrimination, but only on the part of someone who acts under state authority or law. This restriction generally excludes private employers.

Fourteenth Amendment. Several employment discrimination complaints have also been filed in the federal courts under this amendment to the U.S. Constitution.

State Statutes. Many states have enacted antidiscrimination statutes relating to employment. Those state agencies which have substantial enforcement power and administer laws similar to Title VII are listed in Appendix 4. Employers should contact the agency they are subject to for more detailed information.

These state statutes and the agencies that enforce them are often highly significant. Many small employers will find that while they are not covered by Title VII, they will fall within the jurisdiction of a state law. Local state laws may be more inclusive than Title VII and prohibit discrimination based on marital status, physical handicap, age (beyond the 40 to 65 limitation), and various other factors. The question frequently asked by employers is: Which law takes precedence? The an-

---

[11] 42 U.S.C. §1981.
[12] 42 U.S.C. §1983.

swer is, essentially, that the employer will be subject to the *stricter* law. Section 708 of Title VII states the following:

> Nothing in this title shall be deemed to exempt or relieve any person from liability, duty, penalty, or punishment provided by any present or future law of any State or political subdivision of a State, other than any such law which purports to require or permit the doing of any act which would be an unlawful employment practice under this title.

Further, Section 706(c) of Title VII requires that charges filed with the EEOC must first be filed with the appropriate state or local agency should that agency also prohibit the alleged unlawful practice and have the power to "grant or seek relief from such practice." At present, there are 36 so-called 706 agencies which investigate and act on EEOC deferrals. They are listed in Appendix 4.

The EEOC has entered into various agreements of cooperation with these agencies and often pays them for the services they perform. It is not uncommon for the EEOC deferral to be with the local or state agency for more than 60 days before the EEOC begins its investigation of the complaint. Or the EEOC may be working on a complaint at the same time that the state agency is carrying out its investigation. Although the EEOC gives substantial weight to most of the investigations done by these agencies, this is not always the case. At any rate, complainants will generally be able to have their allegations investigated on both the state *and* federal level.

The EEOC deferrals to state and local 706 agencies take on even greater significance when one realizes that the state enforcement procedures are usually more effective than those available to the EEOC. When the EEOC cannot settle a case with an employer whom they feel has probably violated Title VII, the complainant is told that he or she may file a complaint in Federal District Court. While the EEOC can go to court themselves, they rarely do. The state agencies, on the other hand, frequently have the ability to hold public hearings on cases that fail conciliation and issue cease and desist orders that can be enforced (and appealed) in state courts. Instead of having to obtain and pay an attorney, complainants who file with state agencies may often have their cases litigated free of charge.

Other Statutes.   There are other federal statutes and executive orders that prohibit employment discrimination. The U.S. Department of Health, Education, and Welfare enforces Title IX of the Higher Education Act, which outlaws sex discrimination by educational institutions receiving federal funds. Executive Order 11246, as amended by Executive Order 11375, prohibits federal contractors from discrimination and requires them to recruit and promote women and minorities where necessary. The Rehabilitation Act of 1973 prohibits discrimination on the basis of a mental or physical handicap by all federal contractors. Generally, where federal funds are given over to state and local programs, there are also federal restrictions on employment discrimination—the violation of which could result in a withdrawal of the funding.

Court Decisions

The meanings of the laws are shaped and delineated by court decisions. While Congress and the state legislatures enact statutes which prohibit job discrimination, the courts ultimately interpret such statutes through the cases which work their way through the court system. The body of written decisions by the courts is called *case law*. Because judges are influenced in their opinions by past decisions, or precedents, made in cases having similar fact situations, one must know the case law to truly know the law.

Each law has its accompanying set of relevant cases and decisions. For example, the Commerce Clearing House, Inc., of Chicago publishes a multivolume set called Employment Practices Decisions. These volumes report the text of all significant decisions relating to unlawful employment discrimination on both the state and federal levels. Commerce Clearing House also issues, as do some other publishers, weekly reports on recent decisions and new developments in the field. Such publications are an important source of information for state and federal law enforcement agencies, as well as employers who wish to stay abreast of a subject that is constantly being redefined and reexamined by the courts.

Court decisions in the area of civil rights have been of monumental significance, not only affecting the interpretation of those laws but also influencing the course of American history. The modern-day civil rights movement was predated almost one hundred years by sit-ins, demonstrations, and court actions during the post-Civil War period. The Civil Rights Act of 1866 and the Fourteenth Amendment were indicative of a strong intent on the part of Congress to eliminate the discriminatory vestiges of slavery. Provisions similar to those in Title II of the Civil Rights Act of 1964, prohibiting discrimination in public accommodations, were part of the Civil Rights Act of 1875. Blacks across the country gained access to hotels, railroad cars, theaters, restaurants, and other public accommodations, while at the same time reconstruction legislatures in the South eradicated laws which had previously eliminated black rights. However, several infamous decisions by the United States

Supreme Court thoroughly destroyed the intent of these laws and delayed their restitution for almost a century. On October 15, 1883, the court ruled 8 to 1 (John Marshall Harlan dissenting) that the public accommodation sections of the 1875 act were unconstitutional, and Congress was therefore unable to implement its intentions. Further, the Republican Party, which up until that time had been a strong advocate of black rights, no longer made them an issue. Southern Democrats gained political support by attacking the equal rights of blacks. And in the 1896 case of *Plessy v. Ferguson,* the Supreme Court drove home the final nail in the civil rights coffin by upholding new laws passed by Southern states which required railroads to segregate passengers by race.

Case law relating to employment discrimination has been critically important in determining what kinds of evidence are necessary to prove unlawfulness, how charges of discrimination can (and cannot) be defended, and what remedies can be ordered for violations. References to case law are made throughout this book. Employers who feel they can interpret the law by themselves by taking a "reasonable" look at what is conventionally called "discrimination" will normally be in for a surprise. Do you think an employer can lawfully refuse to hire women who have small children at home? Can a company lawfully recruit new workers by word-of-mouth referrals if most of its employees are white? Is it legally proper to generally use arrest records as a criterion for denying employment? Can women be fired after they are seven months' pregnant even if they are still physically able to perform their jobs? A straight reading of Title VII does not provide clear answers on these subjects. The courts, on the other hand, have given definite "no's" to all the above questions.

Federal and State Court Systems. Cases dealing with federal laws are naturally decided in the federal court system, which has three levels: district courts, courts of appeals, and the Supreme Court. Most state court systems also have three such levels. In deciding the relative importance of cases on the state and federal level, Supreme Court decisions obviously rank the highest. The federal court system will be bound by the precedents set by the Supreme Court, and the state courts will be highly influenced by federal decisions where the questions of law are similar.

Yet the majority of federal court decisions do not occur on the Supreme Court level. This means that circuit court of appeals decisions hold great significance. Some employers seem to think that legal precedents hold little weight when they are not decided at the highest level. This thinking is absolutely wrong unless the employer can guarantee a precedent-setting decision at the highest level. Without a Supreme

Court clarification of an issue, the circuit courts will look to each other for guidance. It is rare for two circuit courts to disagree on legal questions relating to similar fact situations.

While the guidance one obtains from case law is not exact, it does exist. One can often determine how a particular set of circumstances will be viewed by the courts by taking into consideration the thrust of decisions on the court of appeals level, as well as EEOC and Department of Labor policy guidelines. The ability of an employer to go against the grain of the general case law on an issue will therefore be determined by the importance of the issue to the employer as well as his resources. Supreme Court decisions are costly and not a viable option for the vast majority of private employers.

State courts and civil rights agencies are also very much guided by the federal case law, which is larger and encompasses more types of issues than the case law of individual states. Some state agencies, however, may have their policy-making discretion somewhat altered by decisions in their own courts. To the extent that state laws are dissimilar from the provisions of Title VII and other federal laws, state judges will be less influenced by federal case law. Further, state courts may be more autonomous in their decisions relating to issues that are not clearly decided by the federal courts. Nevertheless, complainants who feel limited by restrictive court decisions in their states may easily resolve this problem by filing their complaints with the EEOC or the Department of Labor.

An Example.   Let us look at an example of how a case may run its course through the federal court system and the importance of court interpretation. On July 9, 1968, in the case of *Phillips v. Martin Marietta Corporation*, the United States District Court, Middle District of Florida, Orlando Division, ruled that Ida Phillips' denial of employment by the Martin Marietta Corporation on the basis of her having preschool age children was not a violation of Title VII. The court sided with Marietta's position, noting that most of the applicants and employees for the position in question, namely assembly trainee, were women. There was, therefore, no sex discrimination. The fact that Marietta employed males with preschool age children in the position of assembly trainee was seen as

> . . . irrelevant and immaterial to the issue before the Court. The responsibilities of men and women with small children are not the same, and employers are entitled to recognize these different responsibilities in establishing their hiring policies.[13]

---

[13] 1 Empl. Prac. Dec. ¶9906 (1968).

On May 26, 1969, the United States Court of Appeals, Fifth Circuit, ruled as follows:

> The evidence presented in the trial court is quite convincing that no discrimination against women as a whole or the appellant individually was practiced by Martin Marietta. The discrimination was based on a two-pronged qualification, i.e., a woman with preschool age children. It is the coalescence of these two elements that denied her the position she desired. In view of the above, we are convinced that the judgment of the District Court was proper, and we therefore affirm.[14]

Thus, the circuit court strongly upheld the district court's ruling.

However, on January 25, 1971, the U.S. Supreme Court decided an appeal by Ida Phillips of the Fifth Circuit's decision. They stated that the court of appeals "erred" in interpreting Title VII "as permitting one hiring policy for women and another for men—each having preschool age children." In an important concurring opinion, Justice Marshal wrote:

> When performance characteristics of an individual are involved, even when parental roles are concerned, employment opportunity may be limited only by employment criteria that are neutral as to the sex of the applicant.[15]

Traditional roles would no longer be successfully used as an argument in Title VII cases.

A recurring theme throughout this book is the obvious need for employers to be familiar with the relevant case law. There are several series of law books which contain copies of court decisions. Wherever possible, citations of cases in this book will refer to *Employment Practices Decisions*, published by Commerce Clearing House, Inc., Chicago. This series covers all the significant decisions in the area of employment discrimination on both the state and federal court levels. For example, in a case cited 3 Empl. Prac. Dec. ¶8088 (1971), 3 refers to the volume number, ¶8088 signifies the case number, and (1971) is the year of the decision.

Guidelines

Employment discrimination "law" is also defined by guidelines. Governmental agencies empowered to enforce laws have issued guidelines

---

[14] 2 Empl. Prac. Dec. ¶10,012 (1969).
[15] 3 Empl. Prac. Dec. ¶8088 (1971).

which interpret various provisions and set specific policies. Such regulations have the power of law unless they are overturned by the courts. The guidelines and interpretive bulletins in the appendices have generally been upheld in the courts. There are some, but few, exceptions. In a case involving employment testing, *Griggs v. Duke Power Company*, the U.S. Supreme Court stated the following:

> The Equal Employment Opportunity Commission, having enforcement responsibilities, has issued guidelines interpreting 703(h) to permit only the use of job-related tests. *The administrative interpretation of the Act by the enforcing agency is entitled to great deference.* See, e.g., *United States v. City of Chicago*, 400 U.S. 8 (1970); *Udall v. Tallman*, 380 U.S. 1 (1965); *Power Reactor Co. v. Electricians*, 367 U.S. 396 (1961). Since the Act and its legislative history support the Commission's construction, this affords good reason to treat the guidelines as expressing the will of Congress.[16] *[Emphasis added.]*

Note that the court cited three other Supreme Court cases in supporting the EEOC guidelines.

The EEOC has issued guidelines on discrimination involving sex, national origin, religion, and the testing and selecting of employees. The Wage and Hour Division of the Department of Labor has issued interpretive bulletins on the Age Discrimination Act and the Equal Pay Act. These and other regulations appear in the appendices.

Statutes, court decisions, and regulations all comprise the "law" which prohibits discrimination in employment. Many of the legal principles and perspectives which will guide the employer throughout this book are a combination of these three important elements.

---

[16] 3 Empl. Prac. Dec. ¶8137 (1971).

2

General Prohibitions

Employment discrimination is illegal in America. Included in that general prohibition is virtually every type of employment practice. Although it is impossible to list every possible employment situation that may prove to be unlawful—there have been 15,000 pages of court decisions since Title VII was enacted—we *can* draw some familiar outlines of legal liabilities. The purpose of Chapter 2 is therefore threefold: (1) to acquaint the reader with the more typical issues of discrimination, (2) to discuss some of the bases of discrimination, and (3) to detail the coverage and exemptions of private employers pursuant to federal law.

Section 703(a) of Title VII combined with Section 4(a) of the Age Discrimination in Employment Act reads as follows:

It shall be unlawful employment practice for an employer

(1) to fail or refuse to hire or to discharge any individual, or otherwise to discriminate against any individual with respect to his compensation, terms, conditions, or privileges of employment, because of such individual's race, color, religion, sex, national origin, or age (40 to 65); or

(2) to limit, segregate, or classify his employees or applicants for employment in any way which would deprive or tend to deprive any individual of employment opportunities or otherwise adversely affect his status as an employee, because of such individual's race, color, religion, sex, national origin, or age (40 to 65).

Section 6(d) of the Fair Labor Standards Act of 1938, which is the Equal Pay Act, reads as follows:

No employer having employees subject to any provisions of this section shall discriminate, within any establishment in which such employees are employed, between employees on the basis of sex by paying wages to employees in such establishment at a rate less than the rate at which he pays wages to employees of the opposite sex in such establishment for equal work on jobs the performance of which requires equal skill, effort, and responsibility, and which are performed under similar working conditions, except where such payment is made pursuant to (i) a seniority system; (ii) a merit system; (iii) a system which measures earnings by quantity or quality of production; or (iv) a differential based on any other factor other than sex: *Provided,* That an employer who is paying a wage rate differential in violation of this subsection shall not, in order to comply with the provisions of this subsection, reduce the wage rate of any employee.

These represent the general prohibitions of the three major federal laws. Let us look at the issues they represent in more detail.

ISSUES OF DISCRIMINATION

Title VII has been interpreted to cover the broad spectrum of employment practices. The following are the most common.

Discharge

Complaints of discrimination relating to discharge occur more frequently than those involving any other single issue charged against private employers.[1] Some employers seem to think that the hiring of a woman, black person, or other protected class member precludes a discrimination complaint relating to their discharge. The typical reaction is, "If we wanted to discriminate against her, then why did we hire her in the first place?" The fact that most complaints relate to discharge should dispel the curious, and invalid, logic of this defense. All persons fired obviously had to have been hired at one time or another!

In a way, the reverse of this thinking has been applied by civil rights agencies to cases in which long-standing employees have been discharged. The line of attack becomes "If he was such a bad worker, why wasn't he fired 12 years ago?" The burden to justify discharge in these cases becomes even greater.

Reasons for Discharge.   Unlawfulness is found when the reasons for a protected class member's discharge did not result in the discharge of

---

[1] This issue occurs more than any other in race and national origin complaints; it is second in sex complaints. See Ninth Ann. Rep. EEOC (CCH) 99, at 36 (1976).

others outside of the class. For example, a black is fired for not calling in sick while whites, who also did not call in when sick, are only given a warning. Although there might be a company rule on calling in when sick, the standard has been differentially applied, with the difference being race. The discharge is therefore seen as race discrimination.

Similarly, reasons for discharge that appear neutral on the surface may affect certain groups differently, and may therefore be viewed as illegal unless justified by business necessity. Reginald Wallace, a black man, was discharged by the Debron Corporation because garnishment proceedings were brought against him more than once in a 12-month period, violating a company rule.[2] The Eighth Circuit Court of Appeals ruled that despite the neutral application of a standard for discharge, the rule had a disproportionate effect on blacks, who have their pay garnished more than whites. Since the rule could not be shown as necessary to the operation of the employer's business, the discharge of Wallace, based on garnishments, was found to be unlawful race discrimination. This theory of "disparate effect" will be discussed in detail in the next chapter.

Manner of Discharge. Many discrimination complaints relating to discharge evolve more from the way the discharge occurred rather than the reason behind it. A worker—any worker—who is fired without explanation and is told by the boss to "immediately leave the plant and never come back" will more than likely make his or her way to a civil rights office to file a complaint. And based on certain circumstances, the complaint may just hold up. Company policy may state that "all discharges are not to be carried out until reviewed by the personnel department." When company policy is violated and someone is treated differently, the discharged person may find cause to file a complaint, i.e., charge that the differential treatment was related to race, color, sex, age, religion, or national origin. The variables are many. Whether or not the complaint has validity, the employer should be interested in preventing it from getting started.

Constructive Discharge. The person who resigns or otherwise quits employment because of unbearable circumstances will be able to make a complaint of *discriminatory constructive discharge.* The Fifth Circuit Court of Appeals defined this term when deciding the case of *Young v. Southwestern Savings and Loan Association:*

> The general rule is that if the employer deliberately makes an employee's working conditions so intolerable that the employee is forced

---

[2] *Wallace v. Debron Corporation,* 7 Empl. Prac. Dec. ¶9246 (1974).

into an involuntary resignation, then the employer has encompassed a constructive discharge that is as liable for any illegal conduct involved therein as if it had formally discharged the aggrieved employee.[3]

The court further stated that constructive discharge applies to "a case in which an employee involuntarily resigns in order to escape intolerable and illegal employment requirements." The conversion of a resignation to another form of discharge due to working conditions is not peculiar to civil rights law and is also found in many other labor cases. This form of complaint often comes as a big surprise to employers.

Failure to Hire

The failure or refusal to hire an individual encompasses several related areas.

Recruitment.   According to Section 704(b) of Title VII and Section 4(e) of the Age Act, it is unlawful for an employer to indicate a discriminatory preference in any advertisement relating to employment except where religion, sex, or national origin is a *bona fide occupational qualification.* [This *bona fide* occupational qualification (BFOQ) requirement will be discussed in Chapters 3 and 4.] In addition, employers may be in violation of Title VII if their method of recruitment has the effect of discrimination on certain groups. In *United States v. Georgia Power Company,* the Fifth Circuit Court of Appeals ruled that the respondents' form of recruitment by referrals from present workers had the effect of excluding blacks because it perpetuated the generally all-white makeup of its employees. Georgia Power Company was also found to have sought skilled personnel only from white educational institutions. The court stated:

> Word-of-mouth hiring and interviewing for recruitment only at particular scholastic institutions are practices that are neutral on their face. However, under the facts of the instant case, each operates as a "built-in-headwind" to blacks and neither is justified by business necessity.[4]

This is another disparate effect case. In-house job referrals are standardly viewed as unlawful when they have the effect of excluding a protected class from employment opportunities.

---

[3] 9 Empl. Prac. Dec. ¶9995 (1975).
[4] 5 Empl. Prac. Dec. ¶8460 (1973).

Interviewing.　Subjective interviews frequently form the basis for a discrimination charge and make an employer vulnerable to the bias of the interviewer. The Sixth Circuit Court of Appeals noted in the case of *EEOC v. Detroit Edison* that "the use of racial coding of applications and heavy reliance on subjective judgments of interviewers were found to discriminate against black applicants."[5] In a case that was similar, although it involved sex discrimination, the Sixth Circuit Court also cited the use of vague interview standards:

> The decision to hire males before appellant was based, according to testimony of Ford's warehouse supervisor, on his 'subjective appraisal' that they were 'better qualified'. His appraisal at the time was that appellant was not qualified, but he was unable to point to specific items in her application or interview, other than general lack of experience, upon which to base his appraisal.[6]

While interviewing may not blatantly reveal bias, the courts have viewed subjective hiring interviews as unlawful when they can be shown to have the effect of denying employment to protected class members.

Interviewers who *do* reveal their biases will, of course, cause a lot of problems for employers. Improper attitudes are often revealed when women applicants are questioned. The question "Do you have small children at home and, if so, how will you be able to care for them while working?" is an example of discriminatory questioning. It was such a line of questioning that resulted in the *Phillips v. Martin Marietta* decision by the U.S. Supreme Court. Interviewers who attempt to elicit information from women which is not sought of men, such as marital status, spouse's occupation, intentions on raising a family, etc., will be viewed as carrying out unlawful practices relating to hiring.

Testing.　Section 703(h) of Title VII states in part:

> . . . nor shall it be an unlawful employment practice for an employer to give and to act upon the results of any professionally developed ability test provided that such test, its administration or action upon the results is not designed, intended or used to discriminate because of race, color, religion, sex or national origin.

The EEOC has issued guidelines on "testing and selecting employees" (located in Appendix 1) which have been upheld by two highly

---

[5] 9 Empl. Prac. Dec. ¶9997 (1975).
[6] *Causey v. Ford Motor Company*, 10 Empl. Prac. Dec. ¶10,321 (1975).

significant Supreme Court decisions. Sections 1607.2 and 1607.3 of those guidelines are particularly noteworthy. First, the term "test" is very broadly defined:

> The term "test" includes all formal, scored, quantified or standardized techniques of assessing job suitability including . . . specific qualifying or disqualifying personnel history or background requirements, specific educational or work history requirements, scored interviews, biographical information blanks, interviewers' rating scales, scored application forms, etc.

This definition includes written examinations as well as other criteria and methods for employee selection. Further, the guidelines relate not only to hiring, but also to testing used to measure eligibility for "transfer, promotion, membership, training, referral or retention." All such methods for evaluating employees are encompassed by the guidelines.

Second, there is the definition of discrimination:

> The use of any test which adversely affects hiring, promotion, transfer or any other employment or membership opportunity of classes protected by Title VII constitutes discrimination unless: (a) the test has been validated and evidences a high degree of utility as hereinafter described, and (b) the person giving or acting upon the results of the particular test can demonstrate that alternative suitable hiring, transfer or promotion procedures are unavailable for his use.

The primary question, therefore, is whether or not a test has been validated; that is,

> . . . predictive of or significantly correlated with important elements of work behavior which comprise or are relevant to the job or jobs for which candidates are being evaluated.

In layman's terms, a test which is failed to a greater degree by, say, blacks as compared with whites, would be unlawful unless it is (1) statistically job-related and (2) the only suitable means of selection available.

Test validation is a complex subject. An employer cannot simply "look at" the test, taking one question at a time, and determine whether or not it "appears valid." The first step toward test validation is a thorough and detailed analysis of the various dynamics of the job in question. Second, test validation can only be done by trained professionals.

Guidelines for proper test validation comes from three areas. First, there are the EEOC guidelines mentioned above. In *Griggs v. Duke Power Company*, the Supreme Court cited them as "expressing the will of Congress."[7] In *Albemarle Paper Company v. Moody*, the court also relied upon the EEOC guidelines in its decision.[8] Second, there are the writings and comments that stem from the educational and psychological testing professions. This literature is for the most part represented by publications of the American Psychological Association. Third, several federal court decisions have delineated proper procedures for test validation.

Qualifications. Differential treatment of protected class members with regard to the qualifications for employment is unlawful. For example, a black is told she lacks experience to be a salesperson, but a white with no experience is hired for the same position. There are many examples of such cases, though often they are more complex. However, the question of who is "more qualified" is not always so simple.

Similar to testing, a qualification for employment may be unlawful if it is not job-related and has a disparate impact on a protected class. In *Gregory v. Litton Systems, Inc.*, the Ninth Circuit Court of Appeals upheld a lower court ruling that questions regarding an applicant's arrest record were unlawful since they "showed no reasonable business purpose" and also operated to bar employment to a far greater number of blacks than whites.[9]

Placement. Employers who generally place blacks, Hispanics, and women in lower paying, less responsible, dead-end jobs as compared with others will be in violation of Title VII. The term used to describe a discriminatory pattern of job assignments is *channeling* and commonly gives rise to serious class action complaints. Women tend to be placed into clerical positions or assembly trainee jobs; men with similar qualifications become management trainees or semiskilled workers.

Terms and Conditions

The phrase "terms and conditions of employment" applies to several issues of discrimination, many of which deserve mention.

Wages. The Equal Pay Act was specifically intended to eliminate discrimination in compensation for employment because of sex, with the

---

[7] 5 Empl. Prac. Dec. ¶8017 (1972).
[8] 9 Empl. Prac. Dec. ¶10,230 (1975).
[9] 5 Empl. Prac. Dec. ¶8089 (1972).

understanding that women have historically been paid less than men for the same work. (Men have won some equal pay cases, but rarely.) Title VII is more broadly prohibitive with regard to wage discrimination than the Equal Pay Act. It prohibits more than just sex discrimination and may cover several tangential areas, such as channeling, that cause unequal wages. And while equal pay sex charges may be deferred by the EEOC to the Wage and Hour Division, they may be brought under both laws at the same time.[10]

The Interpretive Bulletin in Appendix 2 details the criteria of skill, effort, responsibility, and similar working conditions used in determining whether the act has been violated. "Skill" refers to such things as education, training, ability, and experience that are related to the performance of the job. "Effort" refers to the physical or mental exertion required to perform the job. Occasional heavy lifting by men or different kinds of exertion will normally not justify a wage differential. "Responsibility" deals with the relative importance of the job to the employer's operation. Should the skill, effort, and responsibility of two jobs be substantially similar (rather than exactly equal) and performed under similar working conditions, there should be no difference in compensation.

It is important to understand that equal work does not mean "identical work," but, rather, equal in terms of the above criteria. The classification or title of the job is not as important as the content of the job. For example, in *Hodgson v. Allied Supermarkets, Inc.*, the court found that female checkers should be paid the same amount as male checker-stockers:

> Defendant's reliance upon heavy stocking performed by checker-stockers as a basis for the pay differential here in question is insufficient to support its pay practices since only insubstantial amounts of heavy stocking were done by checker-stockers. Moreover, the overall physical effort exerted by checkers has been substantially equal to any heavy work performed by checker-stockers. Furthermore, the greater mental effort exerted by the grocery checkers results in more effort than that brought about by the work performed by the checker-stockers. It is well settled that the Act's equal pay provisions apply to jobs which are substantially equal in terms of skill, effort, and responsibility, and working conditions, and that minor or insubstantial differences in such substantially equal jobs do not render them unequal.[11]

According to the Equal Pay Act, a wage differential may be justified if "based on any other factor other than sex." Guidelines on this broad

---

[10] See for example, *Laffey v. Northwest Airlines, Inc.*, 6 Empl. Prac. Dec. ¶8930 (1973), in which violations under both laws in equal pay were cited.

[11] 4 Empl. Prac. Dec. ¶7843 (1972).

exemption are found toward the end of the Interpretive Bulletin in Appendix 3. The use of a training program as a pretext for discrimination in wages will be closely scrutinized by the courts. Male-dominated training programs have not been able to justify a wage differential.[12] Nor can the use of a merit system be used to justify differences in salaries when there are many deficiencies and inequalities in the application of such a system.[13]

Let us not leave the impression that wage complaints relate only to sex discrimination. As mentioned, all types of wage complaints alleging unequal compensation based on one or more of the prohibitions covered by the law may be filed under Title VII. A difference relating to race or national origin, etc., in pay may also be seen as unlawful.

Promotion. Differentially applying standards for promotion is also an unlawful employment practice. As with interviewing, the use of subjective standards which have a disparate effect on blacks and other protected groups may bring a violation. An important subjectivity/promotions case was decided by the Fifth Circuit Court of Appeals in *Rowe v. General Motors.* The court found

> . . . a great disparity in employment opportunities for blacks which, at least so far as promotions/transfers to non-hourly jobs is concerned, show that Blacks—perhaps in less numbers than the pre-1962 100%—do not get the same advances as Whites."[14]

This disparity resulted from the way promotions were conducted, allowing discrimination to occur:

> [We] think it clear that the promotion/transfer procedures as applied violate Title VII in several particulars which can be briefly capsulated:
>
> (i) The foreman's recommendation is the indispensable single most important factor in the promotion process.
>
> (ii) Foremen are given no written instructions pertaining to the qualifications necessary for promotion. (They are given nothing in writing telling them what to look for in making their recommendations.)
>
> (iii) Those standards which were determined to be controlling are vague and subjective.

---

[12] *Hodgson v. Behrens Drug Co.,* 5 Empl. Prac. Dec. ¶8452 (1973); *Hodgson v. Security National Bank of Sioux City,* 4 Empl. Prac. Dec. ¶7847 (1972); *Hodgson v. Fairmont Supply Co.,* 4 Empl. Prac. Dec. ¶7644 (1972).

[13] *Brennan v. Goose Creek Consolidated Independent School District,* 5 Empl. Prac. Dec. ¶8621 (1973).

[14] These and succeeding quotes from the Rowe case can be found in 4 Empl. Prac. Dec. ¶7689 (1972).

(iv) Hourly employees are not notified of promotion opportunities nor are they notified of the qualifications necessary to get jobs.

(v) There are no safeguards in the procedures designed to avert discriminatory practices.

The court explained that testimony at the trial indicated that

> . . . under the social structure of the times and place, Blacks may very well have been hindered in obtaining recommendations from their foremen since there is no familial or social association between these two groups. All we do today is recognize that promotion/transfer procedures which depend almost entirely upon the subjective evaluation and favorable recommendation of the immediate foreman are a ready mechanism for discrimination against Blacks much of which can be covertly concealed and, for that matter, not really known to management. We and others have expressed a skepticism that Black persons dependent directly on decisive recommendations from Whites can expect nondiscriminatory action.

Drawing upon the decision in *Griggs v. Duke Power Company*, the court stated the following:

> The only justification for standards and procedures which may, even inadvertently, eliminate or prejudice minority group employees is that such standards or procedures arise from a non-discriminatory legitimate business necessity.

Just as a test having a disparate effect on certain protected groups is unlawful unless validated, other personnel practices which also affect such groups disproportionately are unlawful unless justified by business necessity. This exception will be dealt with in more detail in the chapters that follow.

Training. Section 703(d) of Title VII specifically prohibits an employer from discrimination because of race, color, religion, sex, or national origin relating to "admission to, or employment in, any programs established to provide apprenticeship or other training."

Discipline. Included in terms and conditions of employment are all personnel practices relating to disciplinary actions, including reprimands, demotions, and suspensions.

Harassment. Employers who harass workers for reasons relating to the prohibitions of the law will be in violation of Title VII. In addition, employers are also prohibited from allowing such harassment of employees by coworkers.[15]

Issues Relating to Sex.   There are a whole series of unlawful practices which relate especially to women in terms and conditions of employment. Such prohibitions are covered by the EEOC guidelines on sex discrimination found in Appendix 1. The more relevant court cases refer to the following practices as unlawful: compulsory maternity leave after a fixed, arbitrary date; lesser life insurance benefits for women; different retirement ages for men and women; failure to provide maternity leave; and mandatory maternity leave despite medical considerations.

Benefits.   All groups are entitled to equal treatment in the fringe benefits of employment, including those relating to hospital and medical coverage, leave benefits, disability, meals, company store discounts, employee housing, vacations, holidays, etc. An exception is exclusion of pregnancy benefits in a disability benefits plan.[16]

Seniority.   Section 703(h) of Title VII states that

> [I]t shall not be an unlawful employment practice for an employer to apply different standards of compensation, or different terms, conditions, or privileges of employment pursuant to a bona fide seniority or merit system. . . .

However, some seniority provisions have been ruled unlawful by the courts. One example is separate lines of seniority that are based on race or sex.

More notably, in situations where black employees and women, because of past discrimination, have been relegated to segregated, lower-paying departments, the use of departmental seniority may be held unlawful. An exemplary case is *U.S. v. Lee Way Motor Freight, Inc.*:

> Where, as here, a company has in the past operated a racially segregated system of employment in which assignments to particular job classifications were restricted on the basis of race or national origin, the continued reliance on a seniority system which requires an employee to give up his seniority for all purposes except company fringe benefits if he transfers to a traditionally white job classification covered by another collective bargaining agreement (or another such job classification covered by the same agreement), perpetuates the effects of past discrimination and constitutes a present pattern or practice of dis-

---

[15] *Johnson v. Ryder Truck Lines, Inc.,* 10 Empl. Prac. Dec. ¶10,535 (1975).
[16] *General Electric v. Gilbert,* 12 Empl. Prac. Dec. ¶11,240 (1976).

crimination against black employees, depriving them of employment opportunities and adversely affecting their status as employees because of their race or national origin within the meaning of [Title VII].[17]

The courts have consistently held that in such post-1964 circumstances, departmental seniority is in violation of Title VII.

Similarly, a seniority requirement for promotion where there has been a history of discrimination is also unlawful.[18]

By far the most controversial question regarding seniority is, "Are plant-wide seniority systems which call for layoffs on a 'last-hired first-fired' basis unlawful?" The answer is "no," but it depends. In *Jersey Central Power and Light Company v. Local Unions, IBEW,* the Third Circuit Court of Appeals ruled that layoffs by reverse seniority were not unlawful despite the disproportionate effect such layoffs would have on minority group members and women. The conflict arose due to allegedly contrary provisions of the union contract and an EEOC agreement which called for Jersey Central to increase minority and female employment over the next five years. Although the EEOC agreement was somewhat deficient in that it did not contain provisions relating to layoffs, the court was unequivocal in its decision:

> We believe that Congress intended a plant-wide seniority system, facially neutral but having a disproportionate impact on female and minority group workers, to be a bona fide seniority system within the meaning of 703(h) of the Act.[19]

In *Watkins v. United Steelworkers of America, Local 2369,* the Fifth Circuit Court of Appeals, recognizing the disproportionate effect of seniority-based layoff, did not see the layoff as unlawful employment discrimination. The court emphasized throughout its decision that none of the complainants—black employees laid off by the Continental Can Company in Harvey, Louisiana—had been personally discriminated against:

> All but one were under the age of legal employment when the Company commenced equal hiring. No plaintiff has alleged that he applied for employment with the Company prior to 1965 and was rejected for discriminatory reasons or that he would have applied for employment but for the discriminatory hiring practices of the Company. During the

---

[17] 7 Empl. Prac. Dec. ¶9066 (1973).
[18] See for example, *Afro American Patrolmen's League v. Duck,* 7 Empl. Prac. Dec. ¶9207 (1973), *aff'd* 6th Cir.
[19] 9 Empl. Prac. Dec. ¶9923 (1975).

working lifetime of these plaintiffs, there has been no history of discrimination, and none of them has suffered individual discrimination at the hands of the Company.[20]

Black employees now laid off by the employer could not be given preferential treatment, for they themselves had not been subject to any discrimination, such as being locked into lower-paying positions because of departmental seniority or denied previous employment: "Each has his rightful place in the employment hierarchy without regard to race. This is important. Each is treated equally with white persons who have places equal to his in the hierarchy." Such preferential treatment, the court added, is specifically prohibited by Section 703(j) of Title VII, and any award of seniority to those who did not suffer discrimination would be "fictional." The court added that even if "the seniority system was somehow discriminatory, we think it would be exempted from being an unlawful employment practice under Title VII by Section 703(h) . . . ."

In *Southbridge Plastics v. Local 759, Rubber Workers*, the District Court for the Northern District of Mississippi ruled that the seniority/layoff provisions of a union contract could be modified by an EEOC agreement that gave preference to females. However, the court noted that the facts of this case were different from those of *Watkins* cited above:

> The court conceives the situation before it to be precisely that contemplated but undecided by the court in *Watkins*. The employer here has a very recent history of employment discrimination and the female employees who are here seeking relief from the last-hired first-fired policy contained in the bargaining agreement are among the first females hired by the employer when the policy of complete exclusion of females was terminated in April of 1974. In the mind of the court, it is beyond question that the female employees here failed to obtain earlier employment because of Southbridge's previous policy of total exclusion of women from its work force in the job classifications here in issue.[21]

Since in *Southbridge* it was adjudged that the complainants personally lost seniority rights because of past discrimination, the seniority/layoff provisions of the union contract could lawfully be modified to remedy those acts. The court therefore stated, and it is agreed here, that the *Watkins* and *Southbridge* decisions do not conflict with each other.

On March 24, 1976, the Supreme Court entered its decision in the case of *Franks v. Bowman Transportation Co.* Though not touching directly on

---

[20] 10 Empl. Prac. Dec. ¶10,319 (1975).
[21] 10 Empl. Prac. Dec. ¶10,556 (1975).

the question of layoffs relating to seniority, the court ruled that retroactive seniority could be awarded to "the victims of hiring discrimination."[22] This and the other cases cited above indicate that at this juncture in the interpretational development of the law, the general application of the last-hired first-fired rule with regard to layoffs is not an unlawful employment practice as defined by Title VII. However, changes in contractual provisions or the awarding of retroactive seniority may be court-ordered—to the extent that individuals or a class of complainants can show how they were personally subjected to past discrimination by the employer.

Reprisal. Section 704(a) of Title VII prohibits discrimination by an employer against any individual

> . . . because he has opposed any practice made an unlawful practice by this title, or because he has made a charge, testified, assisted, or participated in any manner in an investigation, proceeding, or hearing under this title.

Most state laws prohibiting employment discrimination contain such a reprisal prohibition as well.

In *EEOC v. Kallir, Phillips, Ross, Inc.*, the court ruled that an employer who fired a woman shortly after she had filed a charge of discrimination with the New York City Commission on Human Rights had violated Section 704(a). The court further stated that terminating the complainant because she discussed her discrimination charges with coworkers also constituted an unlawful reprisal action.[23] In *East v. Romaine*, the Fifth Circuit Court of Appeals ruled that an employer also violated Section 704(a) by denying a woman employment because she had filed two previous EEOC complaints: "A person cannot be penalized for resorting to the legal procedures that Congress has established in order to right congressionally recognized wrongs."[24]

BASIS OF DISCRIMINATION

Some people tend to believe that "fair employment" laws prohibit unfairness in employment. They do not. Discrimination laws were not enacted for such a broad general purpose, but rather to rectify a long history of discrimination against certain groups in our society. Knowing the particular nature and significance of the basis of discrimination

---

[22] 11 Empl. Prac. Dec. ¶10,777 (1976).
[23] 10 Empl. Prac. Dec. ¶366 (1975).
[24] 10 Empl. Prac. Dec. ¶10,383 (1975).

will therefore greatly assist the reader in dealing with the subject matter as a whole. As the Supreme Court stated in *Griggs v. Duke Power Company:*

> The objective of Congress in the enactment of Title VII is plain from the language of the statute. It was to achieve equality of employment opportunities and remove barriers that have operated in the past to favor an identifiable group of white employees over other employees.[25]

After all, it was not the persecution of white men that motivated Congress to enact Title VII. Those employers who do not fully acknowledge this past and present purpose of the law will have difficulty in seeing how many common personnel practices may be viewed as unlawful.

Race, Color

Chairman Hannah: I would like to ask Mr. Ladd if I understood him correctly to say that Southern Bell has not as yet opened up its employment to Negroes in either the operators or mechanical or clerical?

Mr. Ladd: That is correct, sir, here in Memphis.

Chairman Hannah: That is based on the assumption that the Negroes are not able to perform these services?

Mr. Ladd: No, sir. That's based on the assumption that local traditions and customs have not changed to the point that we feel it is the thing to do in our company at this time.[26]

The attitudes revealed in this 1962 conversation have not disappeared 15 years later. Race discrimination in the American employment world is a common phenomenon.

If social and cultural patterns are any indication, our society is largely race segregated. Stable integrated housing has not been achieved. The black and white experiences are still basically separate—the highways bypassing the urban ghettos, the schools resisting orders of integration, the suburbs maintaining their predominantly white composition. The changes in the last 15 years have been mostly cosmetic. Blacks continue to hold lower-paying, less desirable jobs, suffer higher rates of unem-

---

[25] 3 Empl. Prac. Dec. ¶8137 (1971).

[26] Testimony of Paul S. Ladd, Division Personnel Manager, Southern Bell Telegraph and Telephone Co., *Hearings Before the United States Commission on Civil Rights, Memphis, Tennessee*, 326–327 (June 26, 1962).

ployment, receive less education, and have lower incomes than whites. (See Figure 2.)

This social fragmentation inevitably causes whites, who generally hold positions of employment power, to perceive blacks differently. The courts have recognized this, as the decision in *Rowe v. General Motors* previously mentioned illustrates: "Blacks may well have been hindered in obtaining recommendations from their foremen since there is no familial or social association between these two groups." This lack of family and social ties, along with a perception of blacks as being something less than equal, obviously *results* in discrimination. However, proving discrimination, as will be seen in the next chapter, is not so obvious. Since the enactment of Title VII and similar state laws, race discrimination has increasingly become covert. This is so not only because it is unlawful, but also because most whites in America do not readily identify their own prejudices. Despite the fact that race cases far outnumber all others combined,[27] the American employer still tends to ignore the possibility that race may have affected an employment decision. This more than any other single factor has prevented the manager, supervisor, personnel person, affirmative action officer, and executive from knowing what race discrimination is all about.

Race prejudice outside of the South seems to lie deeper within the American subconscious mind. There is a natural tendency away from conflict and confrontation. The liberalism of the 1960s that fought urban decay, high crime rates, and racism has lost and retreated to the suburbs, with industry following not far behind. The well-integrated character of the civil rights movement has given way to the realization that "civil rights" could bring confrontation at home and at work. Encroachments in the neighborhoods by busing has brought violence. It is an indication of the latent feelings whites have for blacks. These are not accusations of moral turpitude, but rather observations of fact.

Sex

[W]hile pseudoscientific justifications of racist policies directed against black and brown people seem to be of relatively recent origin—not earlier, certainly, than the 17th century—the subjugation of women has been accepted as both scientifically and morally justified since the dawn of Western civilization. Accordingly not only do many men accept unquestioningly the limited role women are restricted to in our society, but so do many women. Women have been conditioned not only to accept a secondary role, but enjoy it was well.[28]

---

[27] Ninth Ann. Rep. EEOC (CCH) 99, at 35 (1976).

[28] This statement was made by William H. Brown III, then Chairman of the EEOC, *Hearings Before the Special Subcomm. on Education, Comm. on Education and Labor,* 625 (1971).

Percent distribution	Total		White		Black	
	Male	*Female*	*Male*	*Female*	*Male*	*Female*
Total employed, 14 years old and over	100.0	100.0	100.0	100.0	100.0	100.0
Professional, technical, and kindred workers	13.5	14.8	14.2	15.3	5.2	10.3
Managers and administrators, except farm	10.6	3.5	11.4	3.8	2.7	1.3
Sales workers	6.8	6.9	7.3	7.5	1.8	2.2
Clerical and kindred workers	7.2	32.9	7.2	34.8	7.2	18.4
Craftsmen, foremen, and kindred workers	19.7	1.7	20.4	1.8	13.2	1.3
Operatives, except transport	12.7	12.8	12.3	12.5	17.2	14.2
Transport equipment operatives	5.5	0.4	5.2	0.4	8.8	0.4
Laborers, except farm	6.1	0.9	5.4	0.9	13.6	1.3
Farmers and farm managers	2.7	0.2	2.9	0.2	0.7	0.1
Farm laborers and farm foremen	1.6	0.5	1.5	0.4	3.1	0.8
Service workers, except private household	7.6	15.2	6.9	14.2	13.8	22.5
Private household workers	0.1	3.6	0.1	2.1	0.4	15.3
Occupation not reported	5.9	6.8	5.3	6.1	12.3	11.9

Source: U.S. Bureau of the Census, *General Social and Economic Statistics*, Fiscal Report PC(1)-C1 United States Summary, 1972.

Figure 2 Major Occupations of Employed Persons By Race and Sex

Preconceptions of women's roles in our society, though changed somewhat since the above statement was made, can easily be seen with a flick of the television switch. Women are normally viewed as domestic creatures, subservient and incapable, flighty, emotional, and very much preoccupied with things like laundry detergent, meal selection, and the husband's choice of coffee. The feminine swearword that the American businessman can't seem to get out of his mouth is "girl," a word which refers to a female who is not an adult, but rather a child and therefore not equal to a "man." The use of that term has been used as evidence in sex discrimination cases, particularly those that allege differential treatment in promotion.

The courts do not assign any lesser degree of importance to sex discrimination cases as compared with others. As Thurgood Marshall stated in the *Phillips v. Martin Marietta* case:

> By adding the prohibition against job discrimination based on sex to the 1964 Civil Rights Act Congress intended to prevent employers from refusing "to hire an individual based on stereotyped characterizations of the sexes."

Sex bias, stereotypes, and preconceptions about women explain the disparities in the statistics of Figure 2. One can see the typical nationwide pattern of women in employment: underrepresentation in the managerial category and overrepresentation in the clerical category.

Some employers contend that they should not have to accept the entire responsibility for the results of society's conditioning women to choose limited employment roles. They prefer to blame it on the secretarial schools, the news media, the misguided guidance counseling, the long legacy of women having to take second place to men in the employment world. And what is more, they continue, women are *not* equal; look at their average height and weight, strength, home responsibilities, reduced capabilities when pregnant, etc. Unfortunately, this type of reasoning has a way of perpetuating itself. Men who generalize about women's capabilities will often play a part in preventing women from fulfilling their potential. Men who talk of physical standards tend to leap into other areas like personality and brain power. The purpose of Title VII is to eliminate the traditional roadblocks that have restricted women in the past so that their progression may be uninhibited. Allowing generalizations and stereotypes to affect the decision making of employers is the root of unlawful job discrimination.

Just as companies do not operate in a legal vacuum, nor do they operate in a societal vacuum. When people come to work, the sex biases of society naturally spill over into the work environment. While it is realized here that people cannot easily eliminate their biases, they can surely make *attempts* at eliminating them; they can begin to move in the right direction, trying continually to deal with people on an *individual basis*. Further, there are several management steps that can be taken to structure employment practices better so as to lessen the chance that bias will interfere.

National Origin

On a hot and humid day during the summer of 1971, a Puerto Rican man entered the neighborhood center where I was then working and related to me how he was unable to apply for an apartment just outside of town. He stated that he was told by the superintendent that no apartments were available in spite of a sign outside to the contrary. As part of an investigation by the New Jersey Division on Civil Rights, I went to "test" the apartment by applying for it myself. I had no problem. The next day I went back to the rental office to sign the lease but this time brought the Puerto Rican man with me, hoping he would be allowed to rent the apartment. The superintendent looked at me point-blank and said, "I never saw this guy in my life." "I didn't say you could have the apartment," he said, looking at me, "You must have misunderstood."

It is always a misunderstanding.

There are over 9 million persons of Hispanic origin or descent living in the United States.[29] However, the two groups most often subject to discrimination are Puerto Ricans and Mexican-Americans.

The Puerto Rican population of the United States numbers about 1½ million and is almost totally located in urban areas of the Northeast. Most of the 1.6 million Mexican-Americans can be found in the urban areas of the Southwest. While disadvantaged Hispanics provide a steady source of cheap labor for many American factories, their complaints of discrimination refer generally to discharge and terms and conditions of employment. Employers seem to make unfair use of their lack of familiarity with English and their lack of knowledge of the protections given to them by the law.

The EEOC guidelines on discrimination because of national origin (see Appendix 1) state that discrimination based on citizenship has the effect of discrimination based on national origin and is therefore prohibited. It also states that all state laws which prohibit the employment of noncitizens are superseded by Title VII. However, these guidelines

---

[29] U.S. Bureau of the Census, *General Social and Economic Characteristics*, Table 86 (1972). These and the following figures are from the 1970 census.

were somewhat modified by the Supreme Court's decision in *Espinoza
v. Farah Manufacturing Company:*

> The EEOC's guideline, though perhaps significant in a wide range of
> other situations, does not apply here or support the premise that dis-
> crimination on the basis of citizenship is tantamount to discrimination
> on the basis of national origin, since there is no showing that respon-
> dent (96 percent of whose San Antonio division employees are
> Mexican-Americans) discriminated against persons of Mexican
> origin.[30]

The court did not rule out, though, the general validity of the EEOC's
position, or the possible use of a citizenship requirement as a pretext for
national origin discrimination. In the *Farah* case, the disparate effect of
the alienage ban on national origin was simply not demonstrated. With
regard to the EEOC's guidelines on state laws, the *Farah* decision will
obviously have a similar bearing. It is worth noting that the Supreme
Court, *in Sugarman v. Dougall,* ruled that New York's ban on the employment of aliens in the competitive classified civil service was unconstitutional because the ban in that case had "little, if any, relation to a
State's legitimate interest . . . ."[31] This case did not, however, relate to
any such ban or to questions under Title VII.

There are about 24 million persons of foreign or mixed parentage
living in America. Still, many of us react negatively toward the particular ethnic identities and cultures of others. Such bias may allow for an
employer to treat an employee or applicant in a differential manner, thus
leading to a discrimination complaint. While Hispanics are more often
the targets of unfair treatment because of national origin than any other
ethnic group and are therefore a protected class, the potential for a wide
variety of national origin discriminations is great.

Age

To Whom It May Concern:
January 23, 1974. Too depressed to go on any longer haven't worked
since March 1973. Worked five nights for [grocery store] and they told
me what I was worth—they laid me off for being too old (48). Company
policy on that job is age 30. I should have killed myself 18 years ago. If
I'm too old to stock shelves what am I good for. I can't let my family
starve. Let [grocery store] provide for them—I can't.

---

[30] 6 Empl. Prac. Dec. ¶8944 (1973).
[31] 6 Empl. Prac. Dec. ¶8682 (1973).

This suicide note was written by a man who had filed an age complaint. Statistics sometimes lose their meaning, and the singular experience dramatized by this note perhaps provides us with a greater understanding than an array of figures. This note represents all relevant statistics on age discrimination.

Religion

In 1972 Section 701(j) was added to Title VII:

> The term "religion" includes all aspects of religious observance and practice, as well as belief, unless an employer demonstrates that he is unable to reasonably accommodate to an employee's or prospective employee's religious observance or practice without undue hardship on the conduct of the employer's business.

This section incorporated the language of the EEOC religion guidelines because they had formerly not been supported by the courts.[32]

The employer's duty to make reasonable accommodation to religious beliefs without "undue hardship" has been defined by several court decisions. In a recent case, the Sixth Circuit noted that an employer does not demonstrate undue hardship "merely by showing that an accommodation would be bothersome to administer or disruptive of the operating routine."[33] The complaints of fellow employees, for example, do not represent an undue hardship. Nor do arguments about "hypothetical hardships" hold well with the courts: "The employer is on stronger ground when he has attempted various methods of accommodation and can point to hardships that actually resulted."[34] While each case will be decided on its individual merits, an employer should carefully consider this reasonable accommodation clause and the EEOC guidelines before discharging or not hiring a person because of religious observances or practices.

The other type of religious discrimination case involves direct bias against a person's religion. Such cases are rare compared with those involving all other bases of discrimination. In particular, cases alleging anti-Semitism stand out among the rest. Offhanded comments by em-

---

[32] See for example, *Kettell v. Johnson & Johnson*, 4 Empl. Prac. Dec. ¶7740 (1972), in which the district court stated: "The EEOC regulation imposing a duty to so accommodate unless there is an undue hardship on the employer goes beyond the Congressional mandate . . . . If such an affirmative duty were intended to be imposed, Congress could easily have so provided."

[33] *Draper v. United States Pipe and Foundry Co.*, 10 Empl. Prac. Dec. ¶10,546 (1975).

[34] Ibid.

ployers which are derogatory to Jewish persons have been observed as leading to serious and damaging discrimination complaints.

Physical Handicap

Thirty-one states now have amended their fair employment laws to prohibit discrimination based on physical handicap. This fact represents a low-keyed but growing civil rights movement in America. The view is that persons should not be denied employment for a physical handicap if they can perform the job in question. In cases handled by the New Jersey Division on Civil Rights, the reason of increased insurance liability should a disabled employee become totally disabled has not been viewed as a valid defense to such denials. Since these amendments are quite recent and most complaints are settled without long and costly litigation, there are few court decisions in the various states which provide guidance in their interpretation.

The Rehabilitation Act of 1973 is the only federal law relating to this type of discrimination. It was established to

> . . . provide a statutory basis for the Rehabilitation Services Administration and to authorize programs to promote and expand employment opportunities in the public and private sectors for handicapped individuals and to place such individuals in employment.[35]

The Act prohibits such discrimination and requires that affirmative action be taken to recruit qualified handicapped individuals. However, the Act only applies to employers who hold federal contracts or subcontracts of more than $2,500 and all programs receiving federal grants. Handicapped individuals who believe they have been denied employment in violation of this law may file complaints with the U.S. Department of Labor.

During 1977 the Department of Health, Education, and Welfare published a total of 85 pages of rules for HEW aid recipients, 12 of which relate to physical handicap discrimination in employment. They may be obtained from the Office of Civil Rights, Department of HEW, P.O. Box 1909, Washington, D.C. 20013.

COVERAGE OF EMPLOYERS

The only employers not covered by laws prohibiting discrimination are those with fewer than 15 employees (Title VII) or fewer than 20 (Age Act and Equal Pay Act) and those located in one of these nine states: Alabama,

---

[35] 88 U.S.C. §1619.

Arkansas, Georgia, Louisiana, Mississippi, North Carolina, Tennessee, Texas, and Virginia. The state laws vary in the scope of their coverage. Some have several exemptions; others cover all employers regardless of size. Forty-three states prohibit sex discrimination, forty-two outlaw religious discrimination, and thirty-seven have prohibitions regarding age.

There are a number of exemptions in the federal laws that should be mentioned.

Religious Employers

This exemption does not apply to employers having good church attendance. Rather, Section 702 of Title VII exempts "a religious corporation, association, educational institution, or society with respect to the employment of individuals of a particular religion" for performing work relative to that employer's activities. This exemption is limited to religious discrimination. It is also cited in Section 703(e)(2) with regard to educational institutions which are run by a religious organization.

Bona Fide Occupational Qualification (BFOQ)

Section 703(e) of Title VII states that it is not unlawful to deny someone employment

> . . . on the basis of his religion, sex, or national origin in those certain instances where religion, sex, or national origin is a bona fide occupational qualification reasonably necessary to the normal operation of that particular business or enterprise.

The BFOQ has been used most often in trying to justify restrictions based on sex. Misunderstandings of the narrow interpretation given to the BFOQ exemption, by both the EEOC sex discrimination guidelines and the courts, continue to cause serious problems for employers. The BFOQ will, therefore, be dealt with more thoroughly in Chapter 4.

Section 703(h)

This section of Title VII relates to some exemptions already covered in this chapter and defined in other areas of the book. The first allows an employer

> . . . to apply different standards of compensation, or different terms, conditions, or privileges of employment pursuant to a bona fide seniority or merit system, or a system which measures earnings by quantity

or quality of production or to employees who work in different locations, provided that such differences are not the result of an intention to discriminate because of race, color, religion, sex, or national origin.

As stated earlier, however, some practices involving seniority, such as departmental seniority in formerly segregated departments, have been found to be discriminatory.

The second exemption under 703(h) relates to the use of testing so long as tests are not "intended or used to" discriminate. This subject is also given considerable comment throughout.

The third approves of differential pay based on sex so long as it is authorized by the provisions of the Equal Pay Act.

None of these exemptions should be taken at face value, but rather viewed within the context of court decisions and administrative guidelines.

Indian Reservations

Section 703(i) allows for the preferential treatment of Indians by an employer both of whom are located "on or near a reservation."

Employment Imbalance

Section 703(j) is another one of those legal clauses which should never be considered in isolation. It states that *nothing* in Title VII

> . . . shall be interpreted to require any employer . . . subject to this title to grant preferential treatment to any individual or any group on account of any imbalance which may exist with respect to the total number or percentages of persons of any race, color, religion, sex, or national origin employed by any employer . . . in comparison with the total number or percentage of persons of such race, color, religion, sex, or national origin in any community, State, section, or other area, or in the available work force in any community, State, section, or other area.

However, what the law says and what is seen as a just remedy for violating the law must be distinguished. Section 703(j) appears to outlaw "reverse discrimination." But the concept of affirmative action to remedy past discrimination, including percentage hiring goals of minorities and women, has consistently been upheld by the courts in Title VII cases. Chapter 5 will deal more specifically with the subject of remedies.

Other Exemptions

Title VII also exempts discrimination based on membership in the Communist party of the United States or on individuals not meeting requirements "imposed in the interest of national security."

Exemptions under the Age Act

There are four main exemptions to discrimination based on age in the 40 to 65 category; they are covered in detail in the Interpretive Bulletin in Appendix 2: (1) where age is a BFOQ, (2) where differential treatment relates to a *bona fide* seniority system or employee benefit plan, (3) where discharge or discipline is for good cause, and (4) where differential treatment is based on factors other than age.

While there is not much case law under the Age Act as compared with Title VII decisions, some comments may be made on the above exemptions. With regard to the BFOQ, the courts may be more lenient than in a Title VII case. In *Hodgson v. Greyhound Lines, Inc.*, the refusal to consider driver applicants who are over 35 years of age was seen as lawful by the Seventh Circuit Court of Appeals.[36] Taking into consideration that the body undergoes "degenerative changes due to the aging process" and substantial statistics showing the strenuous aspects of the job in question, age was ruled a *bona fide* occupational qualification in this case. The *Greyhound Lines* decision runs counter to the Interpretive Bulletin, which states that each case must "be determined on an individual case-by-case basis, not on the basis of any general or class concept . . ." [860.103(d)]. However, this decision is not viewed as applying to all jobs. The job requirements in *Greyhound Lines* were demanding, sometimes requiring 12 hours of driving daily, and were also directly related to public safety. According to the BFOQ exemption at Section 4(f)(1) of the Age Act, age was seen as "reasonably necessary to the normal operation of the particular business," and therefore not unlawful. Future cases will delineate further the parameters of this exemption in other situations.

It is also not unlawful under the Age Act to

> . . . observe the terms of a bona fide seniority system or any bona fide employee benefit plan such as a retirement, pension, or insurance plan, which is not a subterfuge to evade the purposes of this Act, except that no such employee benefit plan shall excuse the failure to hire an individual.

This means that mandatory termination under 65 is permissible, but only when pursuant to a *bona fide* retirement plan. Otherwise, forced

---

[36] 7 Empl. Prac. Dec. ¶9286 (1974).

retirement would be unlawful. The National League's mandatory umpire retirement at age 55, for example, was not held to be age discrimination because it was part of a *bona fide* plan. Nor was it seen as a "subterfuge" to evade the Act since it was established long before age discrimination became unlawful.[37] On the other hand, when New York City was contemplating the early retirement of employees to save money, Peter J. Brennan, then Secretary of Labor, spoke to Mayor Beame and the matter was quickly dropped.

The other exemptions to the Act are discharge for cause and treatment relating to reasonable factors other than age. The factual questions involved in "discharge for cause" are clear, and can only be answered on a case-by-case basis. As for "other factors," business conditions may be a valid defense to the layoff of a protected employee. However, should age be a "determining factor," as stated in the Interpretive Bulletin, the act may be viewed as unlawful. For example, in one case the court found that reductions in force were "predominantly of older employees for no apparent, rational reason other than age."[38]

---

[37] *Steiner v. National League of Professional Baseball Clubs,* 8 Empl. Prac. Dec. ¶9800 (1974).

[38] *Bishop v. Jelleff Associates,* 7 Empl. Prac. Dec. ¶9214 (1974).

3

How Unlawful Discrimination is Proved

Knowing about unlawful discrimination means knowing the proofs; that is, understanding how employment practices are found to be unlawful by the courts and enforcement agencies. How else can violations be prevented if not by realizing the conditions under which they occur? How can the employer assess alleged violations without the ability to determine their legal validity? Notwithstanding the fact that proofs are the key to an employer's recognition of what is and what is not "against the law," ignorance still abounds concerning this important area. The result of ignorance is usually mismanagement and costly blunders.

Because unlawfulness is actually defined by proofs, the employer who adequately grasps their several implications will be far ahead of others in dealing with discrimination. Memorizing a list of important cases, reading up on the most recent regulations and guidelines, and studying the law are all helpful to our endeavors. What makes the knowledge of proofs so essential, however, is that it represents the most *efficient* way of comprehending a difficult and far-reaching subject matter. It provides flexibility in meeting problems as they develop and in evaluating an infinite variety of employment situations.

Assuming you are now convinced by what has been said, the following question logically may be asked: "Why are proofs not presented more often by those who make such information their business, such as state and federal agencies, their lawyers, and their officials?" The answer is not clear, but some speculations may be advanced. Accepting the age-old maxim that knowledge is power, it seems that institutions, including those of the "legal profession," do not readily relinquish the expertise which justifies their existence. All institutions are inherently biased this way. Just as doctors are not overly inclined toward the area

43

of preventive medicine, law enforcement agencies prefer to hold back just a little on what they know and how they know it. It is analogous to one team being more familiar with the rules of the game than the other. Why divulge them? The proofs of unlawful discrimination get at the heart of the matter *too well* to be thoroughly disseminated. At any rate, law enforcement agencies are just that—those responsible for resolving problems after they occur are not necessarily interested in their prevention.

THE NATURE OF EVIDENCE IN DISCRIMINATION CASES

It is universally realized that the evidence in cases of unlawful discrimination is almost never obvious. The whole judicial-governmental civil rights network is well aware of this fact. Discrimination is by its very nature covert and hidden. For these reasons, then, it is now uniformly accepted that the evidence presented in such cases will be circumstantial in nature. This point was well articulated by Judge Knox in *Johnson v. University of Pittsburgh:*

> It is obvious that in a case of sex discrimination, as in a case of race discrimination, we very seldom find a resolution of a board of directors or a faculty committee agreeing to engage in sex discrimination any more than we would expect to find the same in a conspiracy to violate the antitrust laws. The existence of such discrimination must therefore be found from circumstantial evidence and inferences from the circumstances.[1]

This comparison of a Title VII case with conspiracy is noteworthy. The assumption that evidence will most likely have to be inferred "from the circumstances" is standard in the thinking of those who investigate and litigate discrimination charges against employers. The employer who does not recognize the evidential character of circumstances suffers from a common and costly misunderstanding of what it takes to make a case proving discrimination.

Another key aspect of evidence in discrimination cases—and one that is also well understood by those who enforce the law—is that discrimination need not be the only determining factor in order for an employer's actions to be seen as unlawful. In the often-quoted case of *King. v. Laborers, Local 818,* the Sixth Circuit Court of Appeals stated:

> But where it can be shown that discrimination on the basis of race, color, religion, sex or national origin was, *in part,* a causal factor in a

---

[1] 5 Empl. Prac. Dec. ¶8660 (1973).

discharge or refusal to hire the aggrieved party, the aggrieved party is statutorily entitled to damages of lost compensation.[2] [*Emphasis added.*]

It is significant that the discriminatory element need not be the more substantial reason for the employer's actions for those actions to be violative of the law. It need only be shown that discrimination had played some part in what took place.

In a similar, more recent case, the EEOC found itself on the wrong end of a court order. Despite the fact that the complainant was not the most qualified applicant for the job in question, race was a factor in the selection. As the district court stated:

> Where selection is based on a subjective appraisal and race plays a part, *no matter how weighed,* in the total factors said to govern choice, the selection is tainted and the rejected party must be made whole.[3] [*Emphasis added.*]

However, on appeal this decision was reversed.

In summary, the evidence in these cases is normally circumstantial in nature, and proving unlawfulness does not require that discrimination be the only determining element in an employment decision.

SCOPE AND KINDS OF EVIDENCE

The scope of circumstantial evidence scrutinized as part of the investigation of a complaint may be very far-reaching. In *Rich v. Martin Marietta Corporation*, the Tenth Circuit Court of Appeals reversed a lower court ruling which limited the amount of information sought by the plaintiffs (complainants). The court stated:

> We think it plain, therefore, that the plaintiffs had a right to the information and statistics from which they *could have compiled trends and policies* on the numbers of white persons receiving promotions during the relevant time periods *in the departments and throughout the plant* opposed to the number of blacks, Hispanics and women who received promotions.[4] [*Emphasis added.*]

Note that the court referred to trends which "could" have been compiled by the complainants, as well as allowing for the discovery of information relating to the "entire" plant.

---

[2] 3 Empl. Prac. Dec. ¶8198 (1971).
[3] *Rogers v. EEOC,* 10 Empl. Prac. Dec. ¶10,416 (1975).
[4] 10 Empl. Prac. Dec. ¶10,339 (1975).

All employment practices of an employer may be examined as a result of one or two complaints. A notable case in this regard is *Sanchez v. Standard Brands, Inc.*, which justified a charge of sex discrimination, prompting an investigation which found evidence of national origin discrimination: "It is only logical to limit the permissible scope of the EEOC investigation which can reasonably be expected to grow out of the charge of discrimination."[5] And it is reasonable, according to the courts, for a charge of national origin discrimination to lead to an investigation of race and sex discrimination, or vice versa.[6] This liberal interpretation of the scope of evidence allowed in a case is part of the courts' inclination toward the "liberal construction" of civil rights laws generally.[7]

The kind of evidence permitted is also liberally interpreted. All personnel files may be reviewed by investigatory agencies in order, for example, to obtain documentation regarding evaluations, promotions, demotions, warnings, reprimands, salaries, transfers, requests for personnel action, complaints, interoffice communications, absenteeism, tardiness, applications for employment, terminations, company policies, etc. Interoffice memorandums of seemingly minute importance may have a substantial bearing on the merits of a complaint. For example, an unanswered request by a female employee for a promotion, coupled with a lack of women in the applicable job category, will surely appear to be sex discrimination (and for good reason!).

In addition to evidence in written form, statements made by co-workers and company personnel are also pertinent. During trials and at public hearings these statements will take the form of direct testimony. However, hearsay evidence on what was said by others may also have a bearing. Because complaints are first investigated by employees of state and federal agencies, the statements made to investigators by company personnel will be important to the agency's findings. Unlike criminal matters, employers will not be warned that such statements can and will be used against them. Again, we are discussing circumstantial evidence. Enunciations by all sorts of company personnel—such as a supervisor's references to "women's jobs" or a manager's comments on "unwritten company policy"—will be viewed as indications of the employer's policies and practices. Policies may also be oral and exist outside the confines of the personnel manual.

---

[5] 2 Empl. Prac. Dec. ¶10,252 (5th Cir. 1970).

[6] *EEOC v. Raymond Metal Products, Inc.*, 9 Empl. Prac. Dec. ¶9883 (1974); *EEOC v. Kroger Company*, 11 Empl. Prac. Dec. ¶10,717 (1976).

[7] For but one example, see *Parham v. Southwestern Bell Telephone Company*, 3 Empl. Prac. Dec. ¶8021 (8th Cir. 1970).

WHERE PROOFS COME FROM

Congress's enactment of Title VII was concerned with prohibiting by law enforcement the practice of discrimination rather than setting forth the parameters of its legal definition. The job of determining what it takes to prove unlawful discrimination was left to the courts, as well as agencies responsible for the administration of the law. Because there were few governmental efforts at enforcing prohibitions against discrimination, the courts only recently have provided us with guidance. As an illustration, volume 1 of Commerce Clearing House's Employment Practices Decisions contains 31 years of cases—from 1937 to 1968. However, in the years immediately following the new law, the number of court decisions has greatly increased; so that at present it takes two employment practices decisions volumes to cover just one year of decisions. As the cases make their way through the appellate courts and some, eventually, to the Supreme Court, the legal outlines of discrimination become clearer and more specific. As decisions continue to emerge from our judicial system, the process of defining what constitutes unlawful discrimination will also continue.

THE BURDEN OF PROOF

Who has to prove what in a discrimination case? In *McDonnell Douglas Corporation v. Green*, the Supreme Court dealt with the important question of "the proper order and nature of proof in actions under Title VII."[8] Initially, the burden of "establishing a *prima facie* case" rests with the complainant. This burden is not met simply by making a charge with certain allegations. Evidence must also be presented which establishes, or proves, at "first appearance" that discrimination took place. These proofs of discrimination will be covered in more detail later.

Once such a *prima facie* case has been presented, the burden then shifts to the employer to "articulate some legitimate, nondiscriminatory reason" for the alleged acts. In the *McDonnell Douglas* decision the court noted that the employer met this burden by showing how Green had carried out unlawful conduct against McDonnell Douglas. This answered the *prima facie* evidence that Green had not been rehired after a strike because he was black. However, the burden then shifts again. In the court's words:

> [Employer's] reason for rejection thus suffices to meet the prima facie case, but the inquiry must not end here. While Title VII does not,

---

[8] 5 Empl. Prac. Dec. ¶8607 (1973).

without more, compel rehiring of [complainant], neither does it permit [employer] to use [complainant's] conduct as a pretext for the sort of discrimination prohibited by 703(a)(1). On remand, [complainant] must, as the Court of Appeals recognized, be afforded a fair opportunity to show [employer's] stated reason for [complainant's] rejection was in fact pretextual.

In other words, the burden of presenting proof of a *prima facie* case of discrimination rests with the complainant. Once this burden has been met, it then shifts to the employer to adequately defend the charges. Once this is done, however, the complainant has an opportunity to examine and possibly rebut the employer's defense, discrediting it as a pretext or excuse for discrimination. What the Supreme Court said, basically, is that Percy Green should be given this additional opportunity.

THE THREE MAIN PROOFS OF UNLAWFUL DISCRIMINATION

The three main proofs of a *prima facie* case of discrimination which, when successfully argued, will result in a violation of the law are evil intent, differential treatment, and disparate effect. Taken in order, they represent two decades of attempts by the judicial system at resolving what is acknowledged to be a national social problem.

Identifying a problem is always easier than resolving it. In 1964 Congress recognized the plight of certain groups in our society—mainly blacks—who suffered from a pervasive social conspiracy of the highest order. Employment discrimination may have seemed subtle, at least in the Northern states, but it was surely a significant force that undermined the aspirations of millions of Americans.

Similarly, in *Brown v. Board of Education*, the Supreme Court identified another aspect of this problem—namely education—and found such discriminatory practices in education to be in violation of the equal protection clause of the Fourteenth Amendement. Educational facilities separated by race were found to be inherently unequal. The problem was summarized in this way:

> To separate [blacks] from others of similar age and qualifications solely because of their race generates a feeling of inferiority as to their status in the community that may affect their hearts and minds in a way unlikely ever to be undone.[9]

But solving the problem has not been so easy. The reaction to busing as a remedy for segregated schools indicates, at the very least, that social

---

[9] 347 U.S. 483 (1954).

problems are not conducive to being remedied by law enforcement. It is within this context that we view the Herculean task of the courts in *effectively* applying the prohibitions of Title VII to the activities of employers. The proofs that have ultimately been developed *are* quite effective. They have understandably evoked some stiff reactions from employers. It is hoped here that this hostility will be lessened by an understanding of the reasons for their development.

Evil Intent

In the years immediately following World War II, and when Title VII took effect in 1965, there were few court decisions relating to employment discrimination. The cases that did appear, filed under constitutional prohibitions or state laws, provided little help on what discrimination meant. Therefore, in order to make a case during these early years, a complainant had to demonstrate the evil motive or intent of those who allegedly committed the unlawful acts. In most instances such a demonstration was impossible. As the New York Court of Appeals admitted back in 1954:

> One intent on violating the Law Against Discrimination cannot be expected to declare or announce his purpose. Far more likely is it that he will pursue his discriminatory practices in ways that are devious, by methods subtle and elusive . . . .[10]

And so, proving discrimination by proving evil intent becomes almost impossible.

In *Buford v. Morganton City Board of Education,* a complaint filed by nine black teachers who were not rehired by a school system, we can see the way the evil intent concept was applied to an individual case. Out of 26 black teachers in the school system, a total of 14 were not rehired. All of these teachers had been confined to two all-black schools. One of those schools had been virtually eliminated and the other integrated due to desegregation orders. This sudden decline in black teachers, coinciding with the integration of formerly all-black schools in Morganton, is what prompted the charge of race discrimination. The federal district court, however, ruled against the teachers:

> Counsel for the teachers and the Teachers Association stated in oral argument that it is impossible to probe the minds of the members of the School Board to determine their motivation in making decision with respect to reemployment. If this be true, then it seems to me that

---

[10] *Holland v. Edwards,* 1 Empl. Prac. Dec. ¶9634 (1954).

plaintiffs cannot prevail . . . . Unless the evidence establishes that failure to reemploy was *because of race*—regardless of what else it may establish—the plaintiffs have failed to prove their case. There is not one scintilla of direct evidence of wrongful purpose in the failure to reemploy any of the plaintiffs or members of their class.[11]

In contrast to the absence of *direct* evidence of considerations relating to race, the court cited the respondent superintendent's good faith and experience in evaluating teacher applicants. It is obviously easier for a respondent employer to show good faith in support of his actions than for a complainant to demonstrate his evil intent. Accordingly, few employers could be found to have violated antidiscrimination laws when evil intent was the required proof. The search for evidence that would reveal the state of mind of the accused employer was often a failure, even in the more blatant cases.

In a case similar to, and cited by, the *Buford* decision, the Eighth Circuit Court of Appeals found no discrimination by a school district that had not reemployed seven black teachers. Some excerpts from that decision are enlightening:

It is conceded that some of the Negro teachers had a greater number of college credits than some of the white teachers, and it is likewise true that some of the plaintiffs had more years of experience in teaching than some of the white teachers who were employed . . . . We concede that the result is unusual and somewhat startling. In the usual situation, considering the number of applicants involved, one would suppose that a fair application of standards would result in the reemployment of some of the Negro teachers. However, we cannot say with certainty here that there was no substantial evidence to support the trial court's finding and conclusion that the Board acted honestly pursuant to its rule in awarding the teacher contracts . . . . There was not the slightest inference in the testimony of these men that the race or color of any teacher entered into his recommendations.[12]

The continuing failure of state agencies to administer fair employment laws by means of the evil intent proof is what provided the impetus toward the development of more productive and realistic proofs. Nevertheless, the evil intent proof can be extremely detrimental to a respondent's case if it is present, such as in the form of admissions or motivational evidence. A slip of the tongue by a supervisory employee may act to discredit any subsequently raised defense. This is exemplified by the *Rogers v. EEOC* district court decision cited above.

---

[11] 1 Empl. Prac. Dec. ¶9719 (1965).
[12] *Brooks v. School District of City of Moberly, Missouri*, 267 F.2d 733 (8th Cir. 1959).

Investigations by civil rights agencies will rarely seek to uncover such evidence, but should direct evidence be revealed, it will place a difficult burden of defense on the employer.

Cases in which evil intent is the proof of discrimination do not often make their way into the state and federal courts; most are apparently settled without further litigation. An exception is *U.S. v. Lee Way Motor Freight, Inc.* In that case the district court noted several intentional examples of race bias: "Throughout the years blacks have been denied employment by Lee Way because of their race. Some were directly informed by Lee Way hiring officials that they could not be considered for traditionally white jobs at the company because of their race." One black man who applied for a mechanics job was told "what the colored do out here is porter work." A black porter who asked the superintendent of drivers if Lee Way was going to hire any black road drivers was told that "Lee Way wasn't ready to trust them."[13]

Admissions by employers of bias are rare, though many times those who have stereotyped notions about other groups of persons cannot avoid revealing them. This is notably true of men exhibiting sex prejudices. Not long ago it was common for a male company official to pass on to me his views about women, indicating the restricted role he thought they should play in society, while I was investigating a complaint. Needless to say, I would write down these comments soon after the conversations, and the notes would be used as important evidence of evil intent. Such statements that directly demonstrate bias by employers are highly damaging and make the defense of complaints that much more difficult.

Differential Treatment

The person who fills out an EEOC charge form answers the following question: "Explain what unfair thing was done to you and how other persons were treated differently." (See Figure 1.) The differential treatment of a protected class member as compared with the treatment of a similarly situated nonmember is a *prima facie* case of unlawful discrimination. The burden then shifts to the employer, who must adequately explain the treatment by citing improper behavior on the employee's part or show that standards were not in fact differentially applied. The underlying assumption in a differential treatment case is that it demonstrates overt discrimination.[14] Fully realizing that states of mind will

---

[13] 7 Empl. Prac. Dec. ¶9066 (1974).

[14] See for example, the Eighth Circuit Court of Appeals decision in *Rogers v. International Paper Co.*, 9 Empl. Prac. Dec. ¶9865 (1975): "Overt discrimination may be demonstrated by the production of qualified minority applicants for past vacancies who were rejected for a less qualified white person."

rarely be revealed, the differential treatment proof applied the equal protection concept to the definition of discrimination. There is, therefore, no need to directly show intent. The motivation behind the treatment is assumed.[15]

It should be emphasized here that all differential treatment which is based on one or more of the prohibitive reasons is unlawful. However, in order to *prove* that such treatment was unlawful in cases where members are not of a protected class, it will be necessary to show some direct evidence of evil intent. For example, the Greek who is discharged for reasons that did not result in the discharge of a non-Greek coworker would have to show something more than just differential treatment in order to demonstrate a violation. The Supreme Court has recently ruled that whites may file race complaints just as blacks have in the past.[16] However, the burden of proof on the white complainant will surely be greater. (Obviously, blacks are subjected to race bias immeasurably more than whites.)

Complaints alleging differential treatment are by far the most common. When one considers the almost limitless varieties of employment practices covered by the law and the six general prohibitive reasons for discrimination—race, color, religion, sex, national origin, and age—the potential of an employer being charged with such a complaint is great indeed. Even if the reason for discharge is unlawful activity, it must be applied in a nondiscriminatory manner.[17] Several examples of the differential treatment proof were mentioned in Chapter 2 and appear as examples at the end of this chapter.

Disparate Effect

The first Title VII case to be decided by the Supreme Court and by far the most influential in its affects on the American employment scene was *Griggs v. Duke Power Company*. In the words of Chief Justice Burger, the questions raised were:

> . . . whether an employer is prohibited by the Civil Rights Act of 1964, Title VII, from requiring a high school education or passing of a standardized general intelligence test as a condition of employment in or transfer to jobs when (a) neither standard is shown to be

---

[15] "The word 'intentional' in the Act has been interpreted as meaning the defendant intended to do what it did." *Johnson v. University of Pittsburgh*, 5 Empl. Prac. Dec. ¶8660 (1973).

[16] *McDonald v. Santa Fe Transportation Co.*, 12 Empl. Prac. Dec. ¶10,997 (1976).

[17] In the *McDonnell Douglas v. Green* case cited earlier, the Supreme Court stated: "Petitioner may justifiably refuse to rehire one who was engaged in unlawful, disruptive acts against it, but only if this criterion is applied alike to members of all races."

significantly related to successful job performance, (b) both requirements operate to disqualify Negroes at a substantially higher rate than
white applicants, and (c) the jobs in question formerly had been filled
only by white employees as part of a longstanding practice of giving
preference to whites.[18]

There was no question of whites not doing considerably better than
blacks with regard to the diploma and testing requirements. The Duke
Power Company was located in North Carolina where 34 percent of
white males were high school graduates as compared with 12 percent of
black males. And the passing rate of whites on the test of general intelligence, used by the company, the Wonderlic and Bennet, was far better
than that for blacks. According to the EEOC, the success rate of whites is
almost 10 times better on those standardized tests. The Court's explanation of this disparity is central to the disparate effect theory of proof:

> Basic intelligence must have the means of articulation to manifest itself
> fairly in a testing process. Because they are Negroes, petitioners have
> long received inferior education in segregated schools and this Court
> expressly recognized these differences in *Gaston County v. United
> States,* 395 U.S. 285 (1969). There, because of the inferior education
> received by Negroes in North Carolina, this Court barred the institu-
> tion of a literacy test for voter registration on the ground that the test
> would abridge the right to vote indirectly on account of race.

Because of society-wide discrimination against blacks in other areas,
such as education, the imposition of these job requirements was tan-
tamount to race discrimination:

> What is required by Congress is the removal of artificial, arbitrary, and
> unnecessary barriers to employment when the barriers operate invidi-
> ously to discriminate on the basis of racial or other impermissible clas-
> sification.

Regardless of the intent of the employer, such "barriers" could only be
allowed if they were essential:

> The Act proscribes not only overt discrimination but also practices that
> are fair in form, but discriminatory in operation. The touchstone is
> business necessity. If an employment practice which operates to ex-
> clude Negroes cannot be shown to be related to job performance, the
> practice is prohibited.

---

[18] See 3 Empl. Prac. Dec. ¶8137 (1971) for this and other quotes.

On the record before us, neither the high school completion requirement nor the general intelligence test is shown to bear a demonstrable
relationship to successful performance of the jobs for which it was used.

Perhaps the most significant sentences of the *Griggs* decision are the
following:

> But Congress directed the thrust of the Act to the *consequences* of em-
> ployment practices, not simply the motivation. More than that, Con-
> gress has placed on the employer the burden of showing that any given
> requirement must have a manifest relationship to the employment in
> question.

Job requirements which have a disparate effect on groups protected by
Title VII are a *prima facie* proof of discrimination. The burden then falls
on the employer to show that they are job-related and justified by business necessity. If such job requirements involve the use of tests, their
validity must comply with the EEOC guidelines on testing and selecting
employees.

The *Griggs* case is quoted at length here because of its monumental
influence on the legal definition of discrimination. Although the disparate effect concept has not been held to invalidate tests along constitutional grounds,[19] its application pursuant to Title VII and laws which
expressedly forbid employment discrimination is clear. There have been
several other cases in which the disparate effect proof has been used to
prohibit job qualifications that can be related to certain groups. The
following are some examples:

In *Gregory v. Litton Systems, Inc.*, the Ninth Circuit Court of Appeals
ruled that the refusal to hire a black because of his arrest record was
unlawful since it operated to bar employment to blacks in far greater
proportion than to whites and no reasonable business purpose for the
requirement could be shown.[20]

In *Wallace v. Debron Corporation*, the Eighth Circuit Court of Appeals
ruled that the discharge of a black based on his having more than one
garnishment per year, in violation of a company rule, was unlawful
because of its disparate effect on blacks and lack of evidence that the rule
fosters employee productivity.[21] In *Bailey v. DeBard*, however, a district
court ruled that prehire inquiries by the Indiana State Police relating to

---

[19] *Washington v. Davis*, 11 Empl. Prac. Dec. ¶10,958 (1976).
[20] 5 Empl. Prac. Dec. ¶8089 (1973).
[21] 7 Empl. Prac. Dec. ¶9246 (1974).

arrest records and credit ratings were lawful because they were job-related, even though the findings disparately affected blacks.[22]

In *Meadows v. Ford Motor Company*, the district court ruled that a minimum weight requirement of 150 pounds was unlawful in that it disparately affected women. Although the jobs in question involved strenuous effort, the requirement could not be shown to be directly related to job performance. The court ordered that "each woman applying for a job on the production line must be given the same opportunity to qualify for employment on said production line as the men . . . ."[23]

In *Brown v. Gaston County Dyeing Machine Co.*, the Fourth Circuit Court of Appeals found that the lack of objective standards for hiring, pay increases, and promotions had the effect—as shown by statistics—of discrimination.[24]

Two cases decided by the Fifth Circuit Court of Appeals, as well as several other decisions, also point to the obvious disparate effect of subjective standards.[25]

Recruitment of employees by word of mouth is another apparently neutral employment practice which may disparately affect certain groups. An all-white and/or all-male work force will be perpetuated by such recruitment practices to the obvious detriment of minorities and women.[26]

The *Griggs* case has also been cited in several decisions that have found so-called neutral seniority systems unlawful. These cases have generally fallen into two categories: (1) cases in which departmental seniority rules have the effect of freezing the advance of minorities and women because of past discriminatory practices,[27] and (2) cases in which seniority requirements for promotion present a barrier to minorities because of discrimination in previous denials of employment.[28]

---

[22] 10 Empl. Prac. Dec. ¶10,389 (1975).

[23] 5 Empl. Prac. Dec. ¶8468 (1973).

[24] 4 Empl. Prac. Dec. ¶7737 (1972).

[25] The most important case, discussed in Chapter 2, is *Rowe v. General Motors*, 4 Empl. Prac. Dec. ¶7689 (1972). See also *Baxter v. Savannah Sugar Refining Corp.*, 7 Empl. Prac. Dec. ¶9426 (1974); *EEOC v. Detroit Edison*, 9 Empl. Prac. Dec. ¶9997 (6th Cir. 1975); and *Newman v. Avco Corp.*, 7 Empl. Prac. Dec. ¶9117 (1974).

[26] *Clark v. American Marine Corporation*, 2 Empl. Prac. Dec. ¶10,084 (1969); *Parham v. Southwestern Bell Telephone Company*, 2 Empl. Prac. Dec. ¶10,055 (1969); *United States v. Georgia Power Company*, 5 Empl. Prac. Dec. ¶8460 (1973).

[27] *United Papermakers, Local 189 v. United States*, 2 Empl. Prac. Dec. ¶10,047 (5th Cir. 1969); *United States v. Bethlehem Steel Corporation*, 3 Empl. Prac. Dec. ¶8257 (2d Cir. 1971); *Robinson v. Lorillard Corporation*, 3 Empl. Prac. Dec. ¶8267 (4th Cir. 1971).

[28] *Afro-American Patrolmen's League v. Duck*, 8 Empl. Prac. Dec. ¶9697 (6th cir. 1974); *Gates v. Georgia-Pacific Corporation*, 7 Empl. Prac. Dec. ¶9185 (9th Cir. 1974).

Finally, one notes that there have been a multitude of court decisions similar to *Griggs* wherein tests[29] and educational requirements[30] have been ruled unlawful.

On June 25, 1975, the Supreme Court went somewhat beyond the *Griggs* decision with *Albemarle Paper Company v. Moody*, another testing case. Referring to the *McDonnell Douglas v. Green* decision discussed above in reference to burden of proof, the court indicated that an employer may have to show more than job-relatedness should the tests have a disparate effect:

> If an employer does then meet the burden of proving that its tests are "job-related," it remains open to the complaining party to show that other tests or selection devices, without a similarly undesirable racial effect, would also serve the employer's legitimate interest in "efficient and trustworthy workmanship." Such a showing would be evidence that the employer was using its tests merely as a "pretext" for discrimination.[31]

The employer may therefore have the burden of demonstrating that other, nondiscriminatory means of employee selection are not available. In addition, the court reaffirmed its previous decision that the EEOC testing guidelines should be given great deference.

In summary, then, a complainant can make a *prima facie* case of unlawful discrimination by showing that a respondent's policy, though neutral on its face and in application, has adversely affected the complainant as a member of a class protected by the law. The burden on the respondent employer is one of showing that the practice is justified by business necessity.

STATISTICS: AN IMPORTANT ELEMENT OF PROOF

Various numerical measurements pertaining to the presence of minorities and females in an employer's work force are potentially important elements of proof in any discrimination case. Numbers are easy to look at and hard to dispute. It is, therefore, normal procedure for a state or federal investigation of a race, sex, national origin, or age com-

---

[29] See, for example, *United States v. Jacksonville Terminal*, 3 Empl. Prac. Dec. ¶8324 (5th Cir. 1971); *United States v. Georgia Power Co.*, 5 Empl. Prac. Dec. ¶8460 (5th Cir. 1973); *Boston Chapter, N.A.A.C.P., Inc. v. Beecher*, 8 Empl. Prac. Dec. ¶9678 (1st Cir. 1974); and *Albemarle Paper Company v. Moody*, 9 Empl. Prac. Dec. ¶10,230 (U.S. 1975).

[30] For example, in *United States v. Lee Way Motor Freight, Inc.*, 7 Empl. Prac. Dec. ¶9066 (1973), it was found that the college degree requirement for management trainee positions discriminated against blacks.

[31] 11 Empl. Prac. Dec. ¶10,230 (1975).

plaint to examine statistical data and use them accordingly. Such statistics are highly relevant in both individual and class action complaints.

EEO-1 Report

The most popular compilation of employment data is the EEO-1 report (Figure 3), which is required by all employers of 100 or more employees by the EEOC. State civil rights agencies also require this format of information as a standard part of their investigations.

There are several ways of statistically analyzing an employer's EEO-1 profile. The most common method is to apply the concept of "underutilization" to the data. Generally, minorities and women are underutilized when their representation in various levels in the employer's work force is not comparable to their presence in the surrounding population and/or work force.

Let us now look at Figure 3 and evaluate the data. A quick calculation shows that about 19 percent of the employees are black and a little more than 12 percent are Hispanic. Assuming these percentages are representative of the population that surrounds the facility, or the *standard metropolitan statistical area* within which the plant is located, we can say that little underutilization exists. Because there is not much disparity between the two groups of percentages, there seems to be little "statistical liability" from this viewpoint.

However, another key perspective is the location of minorities and women in the work force. There are no blacks, women, and Hispanic individuals in the officials and managers category. Blacks are concentrated in the semiskilled and unskilled jobs. And while 19 percent of the company are black, only 4 percent of them are found in the professional group, which contains a total of 74 employees. With regard to women, 89 percent of them are found in the office and in clerical and unskilled positions. There are no female salesworkers at all. While there are many women in the unskilled category, few have been able to move one step up to the semiskilled category. Most of the Hispanic job holders are women, performing unskilled jobs. In general then, minorities and women appear underutilized in the company's work force, not when their overall presence is considered but when viewed from the perspective of individual job categories.

Other Statistics

In addition to an analysis of the EEO-1 report, an investigation may require the furnishing of various other data which can be compiled into statistics. Agencies seek this data by means of interrogatories, which are questions that must be answered in writing and under oath or by re-

Section D — EMPLOYMENT DATA

Employment at this establishment--Report all permanent, temporary, or part-time employees including apprentices and on-the-job trainees unless specifically excluded as set forth in the instructions. Enter the appropriate figures on all lines and in all columns. Blank spaces will be considered as zeros.

JOB CATEGORIES	OVERALL TOTALS (SUM OF COL B THRU K)	MALE					FEMALE				
		WHITE (NOT OF HISPANIC ORIGIN)	BLACK (NOT OF HISPANIC ORIGIN)	HISPANIC	ASIAN OR PACIFIC ISLANDER	AMERICAN INDIAN OR ALASKAN NATIVE	WHITE (NOT OF HISPANIC ORIGIN)	BLACK (NOT OF HISPANIC ORIGIN)	HISPANIC	ASIAN OR PACIFIC ISLANDER	AMERICAN INDIAN OR ALASKAN NATIVE
	A	B	C	D	E	F	G	H	I	J	K
Officials and Managers	31	29	1	1							
Professionals	72	61	3				8				
Technicians	9	7	1	1							
Sales Workers	15	12	2		1						
Office and Clerical	96	7					75	14			
Craft Workers (Skilled)	31	26	4				1				
Operatives (Semi-Skilled)	82	48	16	5			9	4			
Laborers (Unskilled)	104	6	4				10	36	48		
Service Workers	3	3									
TOTAL	443	199	30	7	2		103	54	48		
Total employment reported in previous EEO-1 report	406	179	30	7	2		94	50	44		

(The trainees below should also be included in the figures for the appropriate occupational categories above)

Formal On-the-job trainees	White collar										
	Production										

1. NOTE: On consolidated report, skip questions 2-5 and Section E.
2. How was information as to race or ethnic group in Section D obtained?
   - 1 ☐ Visual Survey   3 ☐ Other — Specify ....
   - 2 ☐ Employment Record   ....
3. Dates of payroll period used –   6/76 to 6/77

4. Pay period of last report submitted for this establishment   6/75 to 6/76

5. Does this establishment employ apprentices?
   - This year? 1 ☐ Yes 2 ☑ No
   - Last year? 1 ☐ Yes 2 ☑ No

Section E — ESTABLISHMENT INFORMATION

1. Is the location of the establishment the same as that reported last year? 1 ☑ Yes 2 ☐ No 3 ☐ last year 4 ☐ Reported on combined basis / Did not report

2. Is the major business activity at this establishment the same as that reported last year? 1 ☑ Yes 2 ☐ No 3 ☐ No report last year 4 ☐ Reported on combined basis

OFFICE USE ONLY

3. What is the major activity of this establishment? (Be specific, i.e., manufacturing steel castings, retail grocer, wholesale plumbing supplies, title insurance, etc. Include the specific type of product or type of service provided, as well as the principal business or industrial activity.

Manufacturer of clothing

e.

Section F — REMARKS

Use this item to give any identification data appearing on last report which differs from that given above, explain major changes in composition or reporting units, and other pertinent information.

Section G — CERTIFICATION (See Instructions G)

Check one
1. ☐ All reports are accurate and were prepared in accordance with the instructions (check on consolidated only)
2. ☐ This report is accurate and was prepared in accordance with the instructions.

Name of Certifying Official	Title	Signature		Date
Name of person to contact regarding this report (Type or print)	Address (Number and street)			
Title	City and State	ZIP code	Telephone Area Code	Number Extension

All reports and information obtained from individual reports will be kept confidential as required by Section 709 (e) of Title VII
WILLFULLY FALSE STATEMENTS ON THIS REPORT ARE PUNISHABLE BY LAW, U.S. CODE, TITLE 18, SECTION 1001

Figure 3   Sample EEO-1 Report

view of personnel records. The areas most dealt with are hirings, discharges, and promotions. For example, blacks may have been discharged at a greater rate than whites or hired at a lesser rate. A greater percentage of whites as compared with minorities or men as compared with women may have been promoted.

Statistics and Individual Cases

Statistics may lend considerable support to an individual complaint, indicating that the employer's actions "conformed to a general policy and practice of discrimination . . . ."[32] For example, data of the sample EEO-1 report would very much help the case of a black, female, or Hispanic person who was denied employment as an official and manager or the woman and/or Hispanic individual who was unable to gain a promotion from an operative position to a semiskilled job. Statistical evidence becomes particularly crucial to a charge of discrimination when the employer's actions can only be justified by subjective, arbitrary, and vague responses. Statistics which reveal underutilization relative to a specific complaint will place an added burden on the employer to account for the alleged act of discrimination.

Statistics and Class Action Complaints

Statistics which show an underutilization of women and minorities as evidence in class action cases shift the burden of proof to the employer:

> [S]tatistical and specific disparities between white and black employees must be "justified" by proper "business necessity" or a Title VII violation has occurred. See *Griggs v. Duke Power Company*, 401 U.S. 424, 91 S.Ct. 849, 28 L.Ed.2d 158 (1971); *Rowe v. General Motors Corporation, supra; United States v. Jacksonville Terminal Company, supra.* Murray [Corp.] did not meet the business necessity burden. The only evidence which might justify the disparate results were conclusory statements by Murray that race was no consideration in job assignment and that their policy of immediately placing a new employee in whatever opening is available is racially neutral. This is no explication of a "business necessity" but is only a declaration that facially neutral policies have been used.[33]

This burden of demonstrating business necessity, a concept which will be detailed in the next chapter, may require employers to explain virtually every aspect of their employment procedures and practices and prove their legal validity.

THE PERCY GREEN PROOF

In *McDonnell Douglas v. Green*, the Supreme Court made some interesting assessments of what may be proof in a Title VII case. The Court's position was prompted by the particular facts of the Green case, and the

---

[32] *McDonnell Douglas v. Green*, 5 Empl. Prac. Dec. ¶8607 (1973).
[33] *Bolton v. Murray Envelope Corp.*, 7 Empl. Prac. Dec. ¶9289 (5th Cir. 1974).

Court added in a footnote that it would not necessarily be applicable to all factual situations. Nevertheless, the Court set a precedent by specifying some guidelines on proving an individual complaint:

> The complainant in a Title VII trial must carry the initial burden under the statute of establishing a prima facie case of racial discrimination. This may be done by showing (i) that he belongs to a racial minority; (ii) that he applied and was qualified for a job for which the employer was seeking applicants; (iii) that, despite his qualifications, he was rejected; and (iv) that, after his rejection, the position remained open and the employer continued to seek applicants from persons of complainant's qualifications.[34]

This standard of proof has wide application for situations in which protected class members are rejected for employment despite, they may allege, their qualifications for the job in question. These criteria may be especially significant for cases in which complainants meet the minimal qualifications of the job or where the job is generally a low-level one. However, it may be applied to all such rejections. Following this standard, a black woman named Jeannette Gates made her case against Georgia-Pacific Corporation when she was rejected for an accounting position despite her qualifications. The defense of the employer was preference for promotion from within the corporation. This defense was not seen as valid by the court because it had a disparate effect on blacks in that the work force was predominantly white.[35] In the language of *McDonnell Douglas,* the employer did not show "some legitimate, non-discriminatory reason for the employee's rejection."[36]

Another court decision applied the Percy Green standard of proof to an age discrimination complaint. Although the court noted some "factual dissimilarities between *McDonnell* and the present case," the influence of the decision can be seen in the court's judgment:

> We simply state that in the particular procedural framework within which this case is presented, a showing that the Appellant was within a protected class, was asked to take early retirement against his will, was doing apparently satisfactory work, and was replaced by a younger person, will not permit dismissal at such an early stage of the trial proceeding. A minimal showing of these analogous *McDonnell* factors justifies some explanation on the part of the employer.[37]

---

[34] *McDonnell Douglas v. Green,* 5 Empl. Prac. Dec. ¶8607 (1973).
[35] 7 Empl. Prac. Dec. ¶9185 (9th Cir. 1974).
[36] *McDonnell Douglas v. Green,* 5 Empl. Prac. Dec. ¶8607 (1973).
[37] *Wilson v. Sealtest Foods,* 8 Empl. Prac. Dec. ¶9691 (1974).

And so the standard of proof found in *McDonnell Douglas v. Green* was used in a termination case as well. Further, I can see no reason for it not being also applicable to a promotion situation. This means of making a *prima facie* case is important and seems to have vast implications. At the very least, it places the burden of proof once more on the shoulders of the employer, and without the need for a showing of evil intent, differential treatment, disparate effect, or a statistical pattern of discrimination. At the very most, isolated incidents of unfair treatment to protected class members may be viewed as unlawful. For these reasons then, the "Percy Green" standard should not be forgotten.

QUESTIONS OF CREDIBILITY

Any argument that has more than one side will involve a dispute over facts. Many disagreements in civil rights cases touch on the inferences which can be made from the circumstantial evidence that is presented, such as memoranda, personnel records, etc. However, many questions also relate to incidents and practices which are not well documented, but instead are evidenced by the testimony of witnesses. When the observations of persons differ over similar questions of fact, the conflicting testimony raises questions of credibility.

In our legal system, judges and juries resolve questions of credibility by viewing them within the context of other evidence as well as by making judgments on the demeanor and performance of those giving testimony. However, the majority of complaints must first be filed with state and federal enforcement agencies which handle their initial investigation. The findings of these agencies are pivotal to the future of a complaint. Most state organizations will seek monetary damages and other remedies to settle cases where they have found "probable cause" to credit the allegations. Should the case not be settled, the state might commence public hearings on the matter. Similarly, federal investigations that lead to a finding of discrimination will more likely result in court actions. An important question, then, is how these initial investigations resolve questions of credibility.

Two contradictory statements, such as "I was told by Mr. X that women could not become managers" and "I never made any such statement" cannot be directly resolved. Circumstantial evidence, on the other hand, will certainly lend credibility to one statement or the other. For example, a total lack of any female managers in the employer's work force might decide the issue in favor of the person who made the statement charging Mr. X with discrimination. The point is that investigating field representatives for government agencies do not make determinations on who is telling the truth and who is lying. Statements are taken at face value and evaluated solely within the context of other evidence. On the other hand, statements allegedly made to investigating field representatives which are supportive of the complainant's allegations will likely be given substantial weight on the administrative level.

SOME TYPICAL CASES

Because most cases are first decided by state and federal investigations, the following examples reflect the standard application of the proofs outlined here to the workings of government agencies. Such investigations naturally go a little beyond the establishment of a *prima facie* case and seek to evaluate the defenses of the employer. Although we have discussed the proofs separately, it will be realized that more than one proof, in various combinations, may be utilized to establish the existence of a violation. The examples are organized in four parts: (1) the initial interview of the complainant at the civil rights agency, (2) the employer's response to the complaint, (3) the evidence obtained by the agency, and (4) the agency findings.

Failure to Hire: Sex

The Complaint.   In an interview at the EEOC office Sarah recounted her inability to get a sales trainee position with Electronics Company. She had responded to an advertisement which read: "Sales trainee, m/w, no experience required, looking for an aggressive, career-minded individual." Sarah alleged that she was asked several questions during her interview which were prejudicial toward women and discouraging, such as "What are your plans on marriage?" and "Are you really intent on making a career with Electronics Company?" and "You know there aren't too many women in the electronics field?" After the interview, she was told that the company would give preference to someone with a background in electronics, which she did not have, and would let her know in a few days about the status of her application. The very next day Sarah was informed by letter of her rejection. She then charged the employer with sex discrimination in their failure to hire her.

The Employer's Answer.   When questioned by an "equal opportunity specialist" of the EEOC, the personnel director of the company gave several responses to Sarah's charge of sex discrimination: Electronics Company has a firm policy of no discrimination and has an affirmative action program to recruit minorities and women. The charge had no merit because the person chosen was more qualified in that he had taken electronics in high school. Also, Sarah displayed a negative attitude during the interview as evidenced by her refusal to answer questions about her personal plans for the future. These questions were not unlawful, for all applicants are queried on their attitude toward a career. The interviewer was not trying to discourage Sarah, but merely to inform her of some factual observations for her own information. Finally, the company stated that there were several male applicants who were also not qualified for the job. And, if the EEOC would send Electronics Company a qualified female trainee, she would be hired as soon as a job became available.

The Investigation. Further investigation by the EEOC revealed that there were presently no women employed by Electronics Company as sales trainee or sales representative—out of 7 trainees and 28 representatives. Significantly, the person hired had taken an electronics course in high school. But four persons presently employed as trainees and more than half of the representatives had no electronics background at all. Accordingly, the in-house training program for sales trainees was very extensive and lasted over a year. The investigation sampled half of the 21 other applicants for the position and found that all were men and none had been asked questions relating to their marriage.

The Findings. In a Letter of Determination, the EEOC found reasonable cause to believe that Sarah had been unlawfully denied employment because of her sex. The EEOC's findings were based on four factors. First, no women had ever been hired by Electronics Company as sales trainee. Second, the employer admitted that Sarah's refusal to answer an inquiry on marriage counted against her. But such inquiries were not asked of male applicants, not justified by business necessity, and showed bias against women. Third, it was found that the complainant was qualified for the job as evidenced by the "no experience required" qualification of the advertisement, the lack of related experience by male workers then employed in trainee positions with the company, and the extensive training program that those employees were provided. Finally, the statements made to the complainant have the obvious effect of discouraging women for employment, revealing bias. In view of the above factors, the electronics-course background of the man hired for the position must be viewed as a pretext for denying the complainant employment.

Failure to Hire: Race

The Complaint. Robert, a black man, told a state civil rights worker that he could not understand his rejection for employment with Power Company since he was obviously qualified. He therefore claimed race discrimination. Referred by a state employment agency, Robert related to the civil rights worker his four years of experience as a mechanic, his good references, and apparently good performance on the company's examinations as evidence that he should have gotten the job.

The Employer's Answer.   The company's response to the complaint of discrimination was simply that Robert was not as qualified as the employee selected and that race was, therefore, in no way, shape, or form a factor. In a detailed letter to the state agency, the Power Company's legal staff replied to the complaint as follows. There are five criteria utilized in evaluating all applications for the company. They are (1) length of related experience, (2) quality of related experience, as indicated by references, (3) performance on job-related, validated examinations, (4) record of absenteeism, and (5) personnel interview by the applicant's supervisor. The company attorney wrote:

> When one takes into consideration the sum total of the complainant's performance in these five significant areas, one finds that the employee finally selected was considerably more qualified. The selected applicant had more years of experience, had a better record in regard to absenteeism, and was highly recommended by the person to whom he would be reporting.

The Investigation.   The state's investigation obtained all applications and made the following comparison between the black complainant, Robert, and the person who got the job, a white man. The black complainant had four years of experience as a mechanic. The variety of the tasks he performed and the depth of his technical expertise ranked him highest among the applicants. Robert also came in first on the mechanics examination. However, he had been absent an average of 10 days per year during the whole of his work experience. Further, the supervisor who interviewed him reported that "his attitude was poor, he seemed disinterested in the job, his answers were short and arrogant, and he slouched in his chair the whole time of the interview."

The successful white applicant had seven years experience as a mechanic. The quality of his work was satisfactory as reported by his past employer's personnel department. He did well in the examination, finishing in the top third of all the applicants, was absent only an average of six days per year, and was seen as "highly motivated" and portraying "good attitude" during his interview with the supervisor.

When questioned by a state field representative as to the relative worth of the five criteria, the personnel director stated that "they were all important" and none was given priority. During further questioning the personnel director admitted that no applicant had been successful who was not approved by the interviewing supervisor. The director stated that "this is understandable since the guy will be his boss and they will have to be able to get along."

Statistics showed that 11 percent of Power Company's employees were black. According to the 1970 U.S. census, the company was located in a standard metropolitan statistical area that is 34 percent black. There are four other mechanics in the plant where Robert had applied for work, one of whom was black. All but three supervisory persons in the plant were white, which is about 4 percent of the total.

The Findings. The state agency found that Power Company had denied Robert employment as a mechanic because of his race. First, Robert appeared to be the more qualified candidate. In the two most important job-related areas—the validated examination and the quality of work experience—he ranked the highest. The longer experience of the white person selected and the better absenteeism record were not seen as justifying the selection. Second, the least job-related criterion was used by the company as the most important: the interview with the supervisor. The structure of the interview is entirely subjective. Because of the mostly white makeup of the plant's supervisory staff, such interviews worked to the obvious detriment of blacks and other minorities. The great statistical disparity between the number of blacks in the company's work force and the number of blacks in the general population surrounding the company was evidence that the company's selection procedures had a disparate impact on blacks. Third, the absence of any definite priorities in the criteria used for selection, with the exception of the subjective interview, allowed for continued discrimination against minorities and exclusion of them from the company's work force.

Discharge: Race

The Complaint. Samuel came to the civil rights office the day after he had been fired. Samuel was black and felt that this was the cause of his sudden discharge. He angrily stated:

> I've been working for them for eight years. So now one day I come to work and my timecard is missing and there's a note there instead that says to come to the office. So I went to the office and they tell me I'm fired. Period. I haven't seen any whites fired the whole time I've been working there.

The Employer's Answer. At first, the employer's response to the government's investigation was only that Samuel was "fired for cause." However, in answers to interrogatories the employer was more specific:

The complainant was terminated because he threatened his supervisor with physical violence. Rule number 43 of the personnel manual, of which every employee has a copy, states that such actions may result in termination. The complainant also had a record of absenteeism that is one of the worst, if not the worst, in our company's history. Further, the complainant was previously given a reprimand for other actions which violated company policy.

The Investigation. The government investigator assigned to Samuel's case looked through files of company records (particularly the complainant's personnel folder), spoke with witnesses by phone after working hours, and spoke several times with the complainant. Most of the witnesses agreed that Samuel and his white supervisor, Bill, had not gotten along ever since Bill began working for the company eight months ago. The argument which precipitated the discharge evolved when Bill ordered Samuel to unload a truck during his lunch hour, which is customarily not done with any employee. Samuel was heard to have said, "You leave me alone or I'll break your neck into little pieces." Samuel did not dispute this.

A review of company records indicated that the complainant's rate of absenteeism was satisfactory during his last two years of employment as compared with his coworkers'. The company plant manager pointed out that during Samuel's first three years of work he was absent more times than anyone else, but that the company had kept him on *because* he was black. During that three-year period the complainant had also been given a reprimand for leaving his work area to make a phone call without authorization. This reprimand was dated almost six years before his discharge. A review of other personnel folders revealed that two other present employees, both white, had been given reprimands and suspended one week without pay for fighting with a supervisor. The company's position was that these employees were not terminated because "their overall record was better than Samuel's."

Statistics showed that there was a fair representation of minorities, including blacks, in the company's work force.

During the investigation the company's president sent additional correspondence to the civil rights agency stating:

> In order to properly and effectively operate our business we must necessarily give support to our supervisory staff and respect their judgment. The complainant's attitude toward his supervisor and the remarks made can in no way be tolerated by management without a substantial loss of employee respect for the authority of supervision.

The Findings. The recommendations of the state investigator, which were approved by the civil rights agency, were as follows:

There is good reason to believe that complainant Samuel was discharged from Employer for reasons relating to his being black. The complainant was employed by the Employer for eight years. He was shown differential treatment in his termination in that he was discharged for reasons which had not been cause for the discharge of white coworkers. The complainant had allegedly threatened his supervisor while white employees were suspended for a week without pay for the more serious act of fighting with their supervisors. The employer's justification of the discharge in light of the complainant's past record is not a valid defense since the reprimand and absenteeism occurred several years previous to the incident. Further, race was a causal factor in the discharge in that the argument was apparently a result of unfair treatment on the part of the supervisor. There is no record of any other such behavior by the complainant in regard to supervision throughout his entire work record with the Employer.

Discharge: Age

The Complaint.   One day Frederick received the following note in his pay envelope:

> We regret to inform you that due to recent declines in sales, Consumer Products Company has found it necessary to streamline its operation by eliminating your position. We thank you for your good service and wish you luck in your future endeavors.

Frederick did not feel so lucky. At age 57 he felt he was being discriminated against, and he filed an age complaint with the fair employment practices commission of his state.

The Employer's Answer.   Consumer Products Company's chief personnel manager responded to Frederick's complaint in writing:

> Frederick was unfortunately one of 70 persons whose jobs were either eliminated or consolidated in order to get the company out of the red. His job of "statistics coordinator—marketing research" was eliminated by having that function taken over by marketing research assistants. His work performance had been satisfactory. Management's position is that his age complaint has little validity since Frederick's discharge was directly related to this business necessity. In that regard, the company emphasizes that the complainant was hired at age 54, three years ago, a fact which surely precludes the validity of any age discrimination complaint.

The Investigation.   The state's investigation revealed that the company's work force was indeed cut by 70 persons. However, in the nine months since the cutback Consumer Products Company hired 65 persons, only three of whom were in the group terminated with Frederick. It was also revealed that 58 of the 70 were between the ages of 50 and 60; the company's retirement age was 63. Of the 65 newly hired persons, only 4 were over the age of 50.

The complainant further stated to the state field representative that while his job may have been eliminated, he was not considered for any other marketing research position despite his 22 years of experience in the field. Investigation did not discover any evidence that Frederick was so considered. In fact, it was found that the complainant's two assistants, both in their twenties, were not terminated but offered other positions in the marketing research department.

The Findings. The Consumer Products Company was therefore found to have discharged the complainant for reasons relating to his age. Although the cutback of employees may very well have been justified by business necessity, the manner in which Frederick was terminated while other, younger employees were kept on, and evidence which suggested that his termination was part of a pattern of eliminating older employees from the company, all pointed to unlawful discrimination.

Promotion: Sex

The Complaint. It was not easy for Karen to complain against her employer of seven years. But her inability to be promoted to the position of assistant branch manager in any of 14 offices of Big Bank during the last three years led her to the civil rights office of her state. In an interview Karen stated that she had progressed rather well during her early years with the bank, starting as assistant teller and then advancing to teller, senior teller, loan officer trainee, and loan officer. Upon hearing rumors that several vacancies existed in the other offices for the position of assistant branch manager, she sent letters to management indicating her desire to be considered for any such openings. For three years she watched men occupy the vacancies, and her chances for promotion continually appeared to lessen.

The Employer's Answer. Big Bank was certainly upset by Karen's complaint. The board of trustees decided that a noted expert in civil rights law should carry out an independent investigation and answer the charge. In correspondence to the state division against discrimination, she stated:

> In each and every instance in which a person has been promoted to, or otherwise hired into, the position of assistant branch manager the qual-

ifications of those persons were in accordance with the standards set by Big Bank and not met by the complainant. These qualifications are: (1) the attainment of a master's degree in business administration, (2) three years' experience in banking, and (3) good job references. The complainant did not meet the degree requirement.

The Investigation. The vice president in charge of personnel provided the division against discrimination with Big Bank's personnel manual which, he said, "should answer any of your questions regarding our personnel practices and policies." However, there was no mention of promotional procedures or qualifications in the manual. Investigation did ascertain that every branch manager and assistant branch manager did possess the M.B.A., as Big Bank's attorney had implied.

The state agency sought more specific information from Big Bank, particularly the reasons for the M.B.A. requirement, the ability of the complainant to be an assistant branch manager despite her lacking the degree, and their apparently unwritten procedures for promotion. The attorney responded that:

> My client strongly feels that every management person in the bank should possess the M.B.A., since it is needed for flexibility in handling the multifaceted exigencies that daily occur in the business world. While Karen is familiar with Big Bank's operations and might get by for a while, she was not the kind of person my client is looking for.

As to procedure, he stated, "Occasionally management will let it be known that we are considering making a promotion, yet our procedure does not depend on employee initiative."

Conversations with several assistant branch managers disclosed that their main functions were to assist in the supervision of the branch and that most important policy decisions were made by the central office. More than half of those persons interviewed had at one time held a job identical to one of the complainant's, such as teller and loan officer.

When the bank was questioned by interrogatories on the reason for not communicating to Karen after she made her desire for promotion known, the attorney responded:

> The bank did not think it was required to respond to Karen's indicating to us her desire for promotion. We heard what she was saying and did consider her but found that she did not meet the degree requirement.

It was also divulged that all but 2 out of a total of 14 assistant branch managers were male. All management positions above that level were filled by men.

The Findings.   In a finding of probable cause the division against discrimination credited Karen's complaint of sex discrimination. The following is an excerpt:

> The M.B.A. requirement for promotion to the assistant branch manager's position has an obvious disparate impact on women since the majority of persons holding that degree are men. What is more, the requirement cannot be found to be justified by business necessity. The "strong feelings" of management and their preference for those attaining this degree are not sufficient to justify discrimination. The fact that many persons holding the position sought by the complainant have a similar background of work experience also acts to discredit the need for this qualification. In addition, the failure of respondent Big Bank to answer the complainant's correspondence and the almost total lack of women employed by the respondent employer in management positions also lend credibility to the complaint of sex discrimination.

Promotion: Hispanic National Origin

The Complaint.   Gustavo had been a machine operator for Plastics Company for three years. Several times during the last two years he had applied for the foreperson positions on his shift as they became vacant. Finally, when the plant manager remarked that he would have to improve his accent before he got promoted, he came to the EEOC to file a complaint.

The Employer's Answer.   A letter from the president of Plastics Company was received by the EEOC a month after the charge form had been signed. It stated in part:

> Plastics Company absolutely denies that it has discriminated against anybody because of their national origin or for any other reason. This company, in actuality, has received numerous awards of good service from the Hispanic community in virtually all our plant locations, and the percentage of Spanish-surnamed individuals employed by us is twice as great as their presence in the population. I trust this will have at least some bearing on your investigation. In regard to the complainant, Gustavo, not being promoted for discriminatory reasons, this is entirely false. Although Gustavo is an excellent individual worker this does not mean that he has the ability to supervise others. Also, in that regard, the complainant's difficulties with English and the inability of others in understanding him should be considered by the EEOC. Feel free to come to our plant and speak with the plant manager about this at your convenience.

The Investigation.   Taking the advice of Plastics Company's president, the investigator for the EEOC decided to speak with the plant manager.

After the investigator introduced herself, the plant manager said, "You mean to tell me that a sweet little girl like you is going to investigate my company?" The investigator replied in the affirmative, and the questioning eventually began.

It was stated that two main factors blocked Gustavo's promotion. The first was his overall "lackadaisical attitude" toward the employer's concept of supervision. He was extremely friendly to almost everyone he worked with and did not seem to have the right "bent" to tell other people what to do. Second, many commented about his accent, often mimicking it and making it a topic for jokes. The plant manager was afraid this would continue even when Gustavo got a supervisory position. It was added that "there aren't too many Spanish persons on his shift, which is where we could least utilize him, and Gustavo has told me that he doesn't want to change shifts."

Further questioning disclosed that the complainant's work record was excellent. He received merit increases as frequently as possible, and his evaluations were among the highest in the company. There were no problems with absenteeism. The EEOC investigator then questioned many of Gustavo's non-Spanish coworkers by calling them at home at night. While all indicated that Gustavo had a heavy accent, none stated that they had difficulty understanding him.

The Findings. In a Letter of Determination the EEOC found reasonable cause to credit Gustavo's charge of discrimination in promotion based on national origin:

> It is undisputed that the complainant's work record was excellent and that the main reason for his not being promoted was his accent, which directly related to his national origin. There was no business justification on the part of Plastics Company for this position. The employer provided no evidence whatsoever that other employees had problems understanding the complainant, and investigation of coworkers showed the contrary. Plastics Company's position that the complainant was too friendly with coworkers and did not have the correct attitude desired by employer for a supervisor cannot be viewed as valid. Not only is it highly subjective, it also contradicts the plant manager's statements that the complainant might be "utilized" on another shift made up of predominantly Spanish-surnamed individuals. Nevertheless, where discrimination is a causal factor in failure to promote—in this case the factor which relates to the accent of the complainant—the employer's actions must be viewed as violative of Title VII.

Reprisal

The Complaint. Helen had been working for Truck Company for one year as the personnel manager when she was suddenly fired. She felt her termination was an act of reprisal. Title VII makes it unlawful for an employer to discriminate against an employee "because he has opposed any practice made an unlawful employment practice by this title, or because he has made a charge, testified, assisted, or participated in any manner in an investigation, proceeding, or hearing under this title."[38] Helen told her story this way:

> I had been working for them for one year and there had been no complaints. Then one day a friend of mine, who happens to be black, told me that he was looking for a job. I then referred him to our shipping supervisor because I knew that there were at least two openings there. But my friend was told that there were no openings at present. I went straight to the president of Truck Company and shortly afterward he fired me, stating that I had been disruptive to the company and was therefore no longer needed.

The Employer's Answer. The following was stated by the company's president:

> Helen was not fired as a reprisal for complaining about discrimination. She was fired because she had a history of disruptive behavior in reference to the company generally and me specifically. The most recent incident was but the last straw. Previously Helen had made vociferous comments to me, many times interrupting phone conversations and meetings, about the way *she* thought the accounting department should be run, or her problems with this supervisor or that manager, or even her opinions on the overall ways which *I* should follow in running *my* company. These comments from her were highly disruptive and were surely not solicited by me or anyone else. The last incident was just too much for me to take. She runs into my office almost screaming about how Phil, the head of shipping, was racist and that I should immediately do something about him. I told her that I had had it with her bothersome, harassing actions, but she continued to behave in this manner for two days. I had no choice but to let her go. Her complaint of reprisal discrimination has little merit and I trust it will be disposed of accordingly.

The Investigation. In response to further questioning by a government investigator, the president stated that Helen said she knew for a fact that Phil had told false information to a black friend of hers who had tried to get a job with shipping. He thought her claim "was purely ridiculous and did not merit an investigation because I've known Phil for years and I knew it wasn't true."

---

[38] §704(a).

Conversations with the black applicant verified what Helen had said. When Phil was asked about the incident, he denied misleading the applicant and said, "I just told him what the salary and hours were, and what the job was like, and he said 'thanks' and left, that's all." Both Phil and the applicant agreed to the date of the incident, March 1. The complainant had been fired on the morning of March 4.

Questioning of several other office workers produced very little. None knew of any past conflicts between Helen and her boss or of his lack of satisfaction with her.

The Findings. The civil rights agency made an initial finding that Helen was probably discriminated against because of reprisal in that she was fired for opposing practices forbidden under the act. There were admittedly questions of credibility as to the nature of the incident and the complainant's record of employment with Truck Company. However, a key factor in the agency's findings was the total lack of investigation of Helen's charges that race discrimination had occurred. There was no indication from any source that Phil had ever been questioned on what happened, regardless of what did actually happen. Had the employer done an objective investigation of the matter and found it baseless, and the complainant continued to complain, Truck Company might have been justified in letting her go. But this was not the case. Instead, her complaint of discrimination brought about her discharge and, therefore, the finding of unlawful reprisal.

Terms and Conditions: Sex

The Complaint. Susan stated to a state human rights commission worker that she had worked almost until her eighth month of pregnancy, at which time her doctor recommended she stop. Susan planned on taking a year's maternity leave, in line with company policy. The problem which caused her to file a sex discrimination complaint had occurred a month before, when she asked the personnel director of Toy Company if she could use what sick days she had accumulated before beginning the maternity leave. The response was a definite "no." It was contrary to Toy Company policy to grant sick leave based on pregnancy.

The Employer's Answer. There was no dispute as to the factual allegations of the complainant. However, the employer felt that Toy Company's sick leave policy was not unlawful sex discrimination. There were several reasons for their position: First, the sick leave policy was part of a *bona fide* contract between the Toy Company and the Toy Workers' Union, of which the complainant is a voting member and was a voting member at the time of contract negotiations. Second, the employer's policy did not discriminate against all women, but only against women who were pregnant. All women could use their sick time toward all illnesses and other disabilities. Third, pregnancy is a voluntary condition and should not be considered along with nonvoluntary illnesses. Fourth, pregnancy is not an illness. Company policy allows use of sick days "for illness or illness-related disabilities only." And, finally, to allow the use of sick days for pregnancy-related disabilities would put an unreasonable financial burden on Toy Company. The employer's policy was therefore justified by "any concept of business necessity."

The Investigation. Because there was no disagreement over factual questions, and the employer's answer had been complete, there was no need for further investigation.

The Findings. Despite a recent U.S. Supreme Court decision, the state human rights commission found that the denial of sick leave for pregnancy-related disabilities was unlawful sex discrimination. The following is excerpted from those findings:

> The respondent employer's defense that the sick leave policy is part of a *bona fide* contract between Toy Company and the employee's union is not valid. The rights of the complainant are statutory in nature and cannot be abrogated by contractual ones. Not to force private contracts to yield to a public right would make the law worthless. If the Toy Company's defense in this regard were valid, they could lawfully exclude black employees by means of a contractual provision. Second, the employer argues that the policy does not apply to women but merely pregnant women. However, the courts have consistently ruled that when groups protected by the statute are disproportionately disadvantaged by an employer practice, that practice is unlawful. Accordingly, this defense was raised in *Phillips v. Martin Marietta Corporation,* in which the U.S. Supreme Court reversed a lower court ruling that the discrimination was proper because it was based on sex *plus* having preschool-age children.
>
> Third, Toy Company argues that pregnancy is a voluntary condition and should not be considered with nonvoluntary illness. Pregnancy is not entirely voluntary, when one considers the possible role played by religious convictions or the fact that contraception is not always sure. Further, voluntariness relates to many other nonpregnancy conditions which are brought about by smoking, drinking, driving, and athletics. Voluntariness is therefore not a valid basis for discrimination. Fourth, respondent states that pregnancy is not an illness or illness-related disability in line with company policy. The distinction is invalid. Pregnancy is like any other temporary disability in that it results in loss of income, hospitalization, and convalescence. According to company policy a nonpregnant person with the complainant's physical symp-

toms during her last month of pregnancy would have been able to make use of the sick leave policy. Finally, Toy Company states that to change their policy would cause an unreasonable financial burden. However, the legal requirement for such a defense is that the policy not be just convenient, but rather necessary to the safe and efficient operation of the business. Such an overriding, legitimate business purpose has not been demonstrated by the respondent.

In summary, the human rights commission finds that Toy Company's policy of denying use of sick days for pregnancy-related disabilities has the effect of discrimination against women generally, and against the complainant specifically, and is therefore unlawful sex discrimination.

Terms and Conditions: Race

The Complaint. Donald was an electronics engineer for Computer Company and felt that he was being treated differently because of his race in the terms, conditions, and privileges of his employment. Specifically, one Wednesday morning during April his white supervisor allegedly told him, "You will be taking your two weeks' of vacation starting Friday." Donald had planned on taking a vacation during August, but the employer was inflexible in response to his requests for other dates. In addition, the complainant alleged that he was given more difficult and time-consuming work assignments, which necessitated overtime, than other employees, who worked normal hours. And unlike other employees, Donald was given no assistance in the completion of his work.

The Employer's Answer.

Donald's race complaint is totally without merit. Pursuant to Computer Company policy, he was assigned vacation dates. That policy, as stated in our personnel manual, is "vacation dates will be assigned by the employee's supervisor so that each department's work is properly coordinated." Donald's supervisor simply carried out this company policy. If Donald needed to work overtime to complete his assignments, why should the company be blamed? The nature of this complaint very much resembles Donald's attitude in other areas; he always seems to think the world is out to get him and that he's something special.

The Investigation. Donald is the only black employee in the engineering department. Questioning of the complainant's coworkers revealed that Donald's supervisor had been generally willing to alter vacation schedules and often arranged them solely by employee requests. It was also found that all engineers at the complainant's level had been given help by supervisory staff in problem areas involving their special expertise and experience. It was also generally agreed that Donald had performed his work reasonably well with regard to both quality and quantity, yet his assignments were such that he frequently spent weekends and holidays in the office. Not one engineer in the department could recall such overtime work being done by anyone else.

The Findings.   The above investigation concluded that the complainant has been shown differential treatment in vacation schedules, work assignments, and supervisory assistance because of his race. The defense of Computer Company was negated by a clear preponderance of the evidence presented in the statements of coworkers.

Constructive Discharge

The Complaint.   Richard's problems began when he took off from work for the Jewish holidays. It was then that his coworkers started making derogatory comments to him, such as "Jew-baby" and "Cheapy." Richard was proud of his religious and cultural heritage, and after several months of such harassment despite protests to management, he quit. He charged his employer with constructive discharge based on religion.

The Employer's Answer.   In a formal answer to the charges the company's lawyer stated:

> The employer laments that alleged harassment by fellow employees resulted in the complainant leaving his employment voluntarily. Assuming for the sake of argument that such harassment did occur, how is the employer responsible? The complainant has not presented even an allegation that members of supervision or management were in any manner responsible for discriminatory treatment. Without such evidence, the employer cannot be held responsible for unauthorized treatment by coworkers. As to authority for this conclusion, one should note the decision by the District Court in *Howard v. National Cash Register Company,* 9 Empl. Prac. Dec. ¶10,177 (1975), in which the Court stated: "We have not yet reached the point where we have taken from individuals the right to be prejudiced, so long as such prejudice did not evidence itself in discrimination . . . . The defendant in this case is charged by law with avoiding all discrimination; the defendant is not charged by law with discharging all Archie Bunkers in its employ." I await your reply and shall assume the charge will be withdrawn.

The Investigation.   Personnel records revealed that the complainant had made more than a dozen written complaints to management and eight of these referred to his religion. Questioning of coworkers and management revealed no efforts whatsoever by the company to discipline or at least question the coworkers alleged to have carried out the harassment activities. An excerpt from the *Howard* case, cited by the respondent attorney, emphasizes this important distinction:

> We are not confronted with a situation in which an individual was subjected to a concerted pattern of harassment by workers which the company knew about and did not attempt to stop.

In *Howard*, the employer disciplined one employee and transferred the complainant in an effort to deal with the problem. The respondent employer in this case had made no such efforts.

The Findings. The employer was found to have committed an unlawful employment practice by allowing the harassment of the complainant because of his religion to result in the forced termination of his employment.

4

How Complaints Are Defended

Considering the variety and complexity of the proofs just presented in Chapter 3, is it possible for the employer charged with discrimination to respond with an effective defense? The odds certainly appear to be in favor of the complainant when one ponders the liberal definitions given discrimination by the courts. First, regardless of whether the employer has directly revealed bias or prejudice, there is a big *assumption* that the differential treatment of a protected class member is the result of an intention to discriminate. This assumption permeates the decisional law relating to civil rights. Second, the disparate effect proof has the potential of placing a heavy burden of justification on every facially neutral job requirement imposed by the employer. Third, the number and location of women and minorities in the work force shift the burden of proof to the employer and will help the case of an individual complainant. Finally, the criteria expounded by the Supreme Court in *McDonnell Douglas v. Green* may make the unfair treatment of a woman or protected class member—without having to show differential treatment—an indication of unlawful discrimination.

In each of the 10 examples presented at the end of the last chapter, the employers failed at defending the charges against them. At first glance, their responses to the complaints appeared credible and convincing. But they were easily discredited by the more experienced and knowledgeable government investigators. Had those employers been given another chance of rebuttal after hearing the government's reasons for finding against them, the result might have been different. But that second chance usually comes during a public hearing or court proceeding, thus making the defense of a complaint prolonged and costly.

We reiterate that knowledge is power. Just as one cannot discuss discrimination without conveying its proofs, one cannot adequately respond to complaints without a thorough understanding of not only the proofs, but also the legal limitations and management factors involved in an adequate defense. Obviously, not all complaints are equally defendable; some discrimination charges will be upheld no matter what the response of the employer, simply because of the nature and facts of the given case. The ability to recognize such cases is important in order to alleviate the need for an expensive and futile court battle. On the other hand, the ability to defend a complaint varies greatly among employers and is a major determinant in the outcome of many cases. Later on, in Part III, we will examine the more specific means of resolving complaints, through defense as well as settlement. This chapter aims at providing the employer with a legal framework which is essential for sensible and productive decision making in the process of responding to complaints.

WHATEVER HAPPENED TO PERCY GREEN?

After seven court decisions, Percy Green lost his case against the McDonnell Douglas Corporation. A review of the decisions is a lesson in what may be required to defend a complaint.

Background of the Case

Percy Green began his employment with the McDonnell Douglas Corporation in 1956. He was laid off on August 28, 1964, more than 10 months before Title VII took effect (on July 2, 1965).

During the late 1960s, Green was involved in several civil rights protests and activities. As a means of protesting his own layoff, he took part in a "stall-in" outside McDonnell Douglas during October of 1964 with other members of the Congress on Racial Equality. According to the district court, "He refused to move his car voluntarily. Plaintiff's car was towed away by the police, and he was arrested for obstructing traffic. Plaintiff pleaded guilty to the charge of obstructing traffic and he was fined."[1] Green was also chairman of a civil rights organization that was responsible for a "lock-in" of employees on July 3, 1965.[2] On July 26, 1965, Green applied to be rehired at McDonnell. Although he was qualified for the job, he was not hired. The company based its rejection of Green on his participation in the "stall-in" and the "lock-in" demonstrations.[3]

---

[1] 3 Empl. Prac. Dec. ¶8014 (1970).
[2] Ibid.
[3] Ibid.

Five Decisions

Green went to the EEOC and charged that he was denied employment unlawfully because of his race and involvement in civil rights activities. The EEOC found reasonable cause to believe that Green was refused employment because of the civil rights activities—a form of reprisal—but made no finding on the race complaint. After conciliation efforts by the government failed to bring a settlement, Green filed a complaint in district court making the same allegations.

On May 13, 1969, the court issued its first ruling on the matter. It granted a motion to strike the race allegation of Green's complaint, stating as its reason that Green could not file a complaint in district court unless the EEOC had found reasonable cause on those specific allegations.[4] On September 25, 1970, the district court issued its ruling on the merits of the case. It found that (1) Green did not show that McDonnell Douglas was motivated by racial prejudice or his involvement in "legitimate" civil rights activities, (2) Title VII does not protect "activity which blocks entrance into or from an employer's plant or office," and (3) the employer's refusal to rehire Green was justifiably based on his misconduct.[5]

On March 30, 1972, the Court of Appeals for the Eighth Circuit made its ruling in the matter, later modifying its decision on May 12, 1972. Initially, the appellate court agreed with the lower court that the stall-in demonstration was not the kind of activity protected by Title VII. However, it was not agreed that Green was prevented from making a claim based on race discrimination simply because the EEOC had not found reasonable cause on that issue. While the district court may have found no basis for that claim, Green had not been allowed to present evidence on it. It was therefore ordered that the case should again be tried by the district court:

> Of the several civil rights protests which Green directed against McDonnell, the employer selected two, the "lock-in" and the "stall-in," as reasons for its refusal to rehire Green. Green should be given the opportunity to show that these reasons offered by the Company were pretextual, or otherwise show the presence of racially discriminatory practices by McDonnell which affected its decision. The district court did not use appropriate standards in determining whether McDonnell's refusal to hire Green was racially motivated. On remand, both parties will have the opportunity to present evidence on this matter.[6]

---

[4] 2 Empl. Prac. Dec. ¶10,009 (1969).
[5] 3 Empl. Prac. Dec. ¶8014 (1970).
[6] 5 Empl. Prac. Dec. ¶8102 (1972).

McDonnell Douglas appealed this ruling to the Supreme Court, which agreed to render a decision in the matter. Generally, the ruling by the appellate court was upheld. It was affirmed that Green should have been allowed to make a race discrimination claim in district court and was not barred from doing so because the EEOC had not credited that allegation. More importantly, the Court found that although McDonnell Douglas had apparently been successful in rebutting Green's claim of discrimination, Green should be allowed to show that the reason was "pretextual or discriminatory in its application." It then detailed what kinds of evidence would possibly discredit the employer's defense:

> Especially relevant to such a showing would be evidence that white employees involved in acts against petitioner of comparable seriousness to the "stall-in" were nevertheless retained or rehired . . . . Other evidence that may be relevant to any showing of pretextuality includes facts as to the petitioner's treatment of respondent [Green] during his prior term of employment, petitioner's reaction, if any, to respondent's legitimate civil rights activities, and petitioner's general policy and practice with respect to minority employment. On the latter point, statistics as to petitioner's employment policy and practice may be helpful to a determination of whether petitioner's refusal to rehire respondent in this case conformed to a general pattern of discrimination against blacks.[7]

By its decision, the Supreme Court legitimized Green's ability to raise several other issues in attacking McDonnell's defense and, in a sense, widen the battleground of the debate. McDonnell Douglas's attempt to narrow the issues of the case to one—the legality of denying employment because of unlawful activity—had failed. As part of its defense, McDonnell would have to respond to some of the major circumstantial proofs of discrimination, namely differential treatment and statistics, in order to justify its denial of employment to Green. The case was therefore remanded, or sent back, to the district court for a decision on these factual questions.

The Circumstantial Evidence

According to the instructions of the Supreme Court, the district court now heard testimony in several areas to determine if race was a factor in Percy Green's not being rehired. From four main perspectives the lower court once more ruled against Green.

First, it was found that Green had been laid off, along with seven

---

[7] 5 Empl. Prac. Dec. ¶8607 (1973).

white men, because of a necessary reduction in force. Green might have averted this had he not refused to take tests to determine his eligibility for other positions or agree to a reduction in status. At any rate, the court found no record of past discrimination against the complainant while employed by McDonnell Douglas.

Second, although Green had been involved in various civil rights activities throughout the early 1960s, "Defendant's management never reprimanded plaintiff, reduced his job status, or did anything which would interfere with his work because of his legitimate civil rights protests or because of his race."[8]

Third, Green tried to show by statistics that his rejection was part of a "general pattern of discrimination against blacks." In 1960 the St. Louis metropolitan area contained 14 percent nonwhites, but in 1964 and 1965 the employer's nonwhite work force was 5.4 percent and 6.4 percent, respectively. However, other evidence presented by the company negated these figures:

> The McDonnell work force is drawn from a much broader area than the St. Louis metropolitan area, and the percentage of non-white decreases outside the St. Louis metropolitan census area. In 1965, 11 percent of all persons hired by McDonnell were non-white, and in 1966, 22 percent of those hired were non-white.[9]

The statistics were, therefore, in the company's favor.

Fourth, Green could not show that he had been treated differently than whites involved in acts of "comparable seriousness":

> There is nothing in this record to show that the conduct of the persons involved in any of the slowdowns concerning traffic by members of the union, on which occasions as many as 18,000 employees had walked out because there was no contract, was comparable to locking employees in a building.[10]

And so ten years after Green's initial rejection, he had again lost his case in the district court. Because he was denied employment for a job despite his qualifications, Green had made a *prima facie* case of discrimination against McDonnell due to the fact that he was black and had been active in civil rights protests. On the other hand, McDonnell had

> . . . shown by a preponderance of the evidence that the reason for plaintiff not being reemployed was because of his participation in the

---

[8] 9 Empl. Prac. Dec. ¶10,087 (1975).

[9] Ibid.

[10] Ibid.

illegal stall-in and lock-in and not because of his race or his legitimate civil rights activities. The defendant has shown that its stated reasons were not mere pretext, but the real reasons, and these reasons are adequate under the law for defendant not to rehire the plaintiff.[11]

The employer had finally met the burden of defense.

Finally, on January 28, 1976, the Eighth Circuit Court of Appeals once more decided an appeal by Green of the district court's ruling. This time, however, the lower court ruling was upheld after a thorough reexamination of the evidence. The level of scrutiny of the evidence by the court indicates the extent to which an employer may have to go in order to adequately make a defense. In this case, the employer had to show that Green was not treated differently, because the other employees were not similarly situated, as well as provide other evidence that its refusal to hire Green was not discriminatory.

> Green contends that the labor strikers' violence, threats, mass picketing and traffic tie-ups were at least as unlawful and disruptive as his own "stall-in" and "lock-in" activities. Several employees were arrested in connection with these labor disputes. However, those arrested were not discharged by defendant, because as a part of subsequent strike-settlement negotiation, all strikers were granted amnesty. The arrested workers were white. Green argues that since he, a black man, was disciplined by defendant for similar activity and white strikers were not discharged, a case of racial discrimination had been shown. We disagree . . . .

> First, the evidence reveals that the labor strikes were participated in by both black and white employees. Whites and blacks were treated alike. Defendant's decision not to discipline striking employees was a bargained-for agreement with the labor unions involved. In return, defendant received the union's promise to return to work immediately. It was a business decision motivated by a desire to resume production and not by any racially discriminatory reasons. . . .

> Furthermore, the striking employees were attempting to improve their bargaining position with the defendant. Appellant's activities, on the other hand, were by a *non-employee* with the sole purpose of harassing the defendant. Appellant had no bargaining leverage. The record reveals no instances where defendant offered employment to a non-employee who had previously engaged in unlawful demonstrations against it.[12]

The appellate court also discredited the statistical proofs presented by Green. Although 6.4 percent of the employer's work force was nonwhite

---

[11] Ibid.
[12] 11 Empl. Prac. Dec. ¶10,663 (1976).

as compared with the figure of 14 percent for the St. Louis metropolitan area,

> . . . no showing was made indicating what percentage of job appli-
> cants qualified for positions with defendant were black. . . .
>
> Also persuasive is the district court's finding, supported by the record,
> that in 1965, of the trainees hired to fill the type of position appellant
> applied for, 15 percent were black.[13]

The case of *Green v. McDonnell Douglas Corporation* should be quite instructive. First, it provides some important case law on the shifting burdens of proof in a civil rights case. Second, it sets forth guidelines on another form of proof of discrimination: unwarranted adverse actions by an employer against a protected class member. Finally, it reveals in detail how an employer can defend a discrimination charge and the variety of issues that will necessarily be part of such a defense. The narrowing of issues to one or more of the reasons for the adverse action of the employer was impossible.

KEY FACTORS OF A DEFENSE

No matter how intent an employer is on successfully defending, and thereby disposing of, a complaint, there must be an impersonal consideration of three key factors before defensive actions can begin.

What Are the Facts?

The first necessary step toward the fashioning of a defensive posture is a calm and thorough look at the factual questions raised by the complaint. Too often the employer will disregard important bits of evidence after being accused of discrimination and immediately assume that the company is right and the complaint has no merit, and proceed to gather facts to support this position. The results of such partial self-investigations are unfortunately decided before they begin and consequently are neither objective nor helpful to the employer. A prerequisite to any defense is some honest information on the relevant facts of the case.

But how are facts determined? Who is to differentiate between fact and fiction? What about contradictory opinions over what really happened and whether or not race, sex, or other bases were motivations for the alleged acts? Well, these types of questions actually cannot be answered. When we speak of obtaining the relevant facts of a given case, the sole criteria for their scrutiny are the proofs outlined in Chapter 3.

---

[13] Ibid.

This means that questions of credibility are not directly decided, but are taken at face value. This means that all aspects of possible differential treatment are pondered. In light of the Percy Green case, adverse employment actions are looked at to see if they can be justified. A true gathering of the facts entails a realistic search for evidence which may be damaging *or* helpful to the respondent employer. This realism must be founded on a legal perspective, and must go beyond the so-called intent of those involved in the alleged acts to the all-important *circumstances* which surround the complaint. The question should be, "What is the sum total of circumstantial evidence, from the point of view of the defendant *and* from the point of view of the prosecutor?"

Discrimination is a matter of proofs, and it is within that context that defenses are viewed and the facts gathered. Employers might well keep this in mind before giving their responses. As exemplified by the man who defended a finding of sex discrimination by a state agency with trophies given to him by members of the Hispanic community, instinctive and emotional reflexes are no substitute for a practical and thought-out defensive posture. A mind works best with a clear head, not a hot head. The employer who lets passions and principles get in the way of legal realities poses the most difficult problem of defense.

Can the Facts Be Documented?

A fact is not a fact unless it can in some manner be documented to others. For this reason the ability of the employer to support a defense with credible evidence is another important determining element of its success. Several variables will affect this ability to document.

Subjectivity. One maxim is that employment decisions will not lend themselves to documentation to the extent that they are based on criteria which are subjective in nature. As the Eighth Circuit Court of Appeals has stated:

> Our prior decisions make clear that, in cases presenting questions of discriminatory hiring practices, employment decisions based on subjective, rather than objective, criteria carry little weight in rebutting charges of discrimination.[14]

The more subjective the defense, the less credible it will be. In Chapter 3, several examples of the disparate effect of subjective standards were cited (see page 55) with the result of findings of unlawful discrimination

---

[14] *Green v. McDonnell Douglas Corporation*, 5 Empl. Prac. Dec. ¶8102 (1972).

by the courts. Accordingly, such standards have little value as a defense.

Of course, there is a realistic limit on the number of quantifiable and specific factors which may comprise a management decision. Employment practices can hardly be characterized as scientific, regardless of the professional qualifications and training of supervisory personnel. Along with this notion, there is the universal sentiment that "management prerogative" permits an employer to hire, fire, promote, and carry out various other duties at will. This capability is based on management's long experience in recognizing the presence or absence of certain intangible attributes in their employees or applicants, such as attitude, initiative, potential, quickness, and a host of other factors. This is all fine and good, but intangibles are rather difficult to grasp, especially when viewed from the point of view of legal proofs. This means that although subjectively based decisions may very well be warranted and valid, they are simply more difficult to defend later on.

When a complaint is filed against a company based on what was generally an unstructured decision-making process, there is frequently a lot of scurrying about to determine just what happened and what were the reasons for the decision. When the person was fired, there was little thought that the reasons for termination would have to be detailed pursuant to a government agency's investigation. Had the termination been in accordance with a definite procedure and guideline, the scurrying about would not have been necessary. Statements like "Well look, the guy just wasn't able to do the work" or "I've been in this business 15 years and she just didn't have what it takes to be a manager" are not very convincing. Accountability is not supported by *ad hominem* arguments such as "I'm the employer and therefore I know that person wasn't qualified for the job." Subjective decisions based on vague ideas of qualifications and misbehavior will be viewed with great skepticism and will probably be unable to counter other evidence, such as statistics showing underutilization of women or minorities or perhaps examples of differential treatment.[15]

---

[15] Perhaps it should be clarified that subjective decisions by themselves are not necessarily violations. However, when combined with other evidence, such as examples of differential treatment or statistics showing that a greater percentage of minorities or women are affected by the subjective standards, they carry almost no weight as a defense. For a case in which the Fifth Circuit Court of Appeals found that subjective standards are not in and of themselves unlawful, see *James v. Wallace*, 12 Empl. Prac. Dec. ¶11,001 (1976). Also, in *Alexander v. Gardner-Denver Co.*, 10 Empl. Prac. Dec. ¶10,254 (1975), the Tenth Circuit Court of Appeals stated: "Before we can condemn the subjectivity of the standards applied by the foreman [the trial court found those standards to be subjective], we must determine that discriminatory results occurred."

Policies.   The employer who has a policy to "hang his defense on" will at least have some foundation for his arguments. The absence of a policy which relates to the particular charge makes explanation that much more difficult. What is your company's policy on promotions, hiring, firing, reasons for discipline, transfers, salaries, layoffs, job duties, etc.? Is the policy written down? If the policy is not written down, how, when, where, and by whom is it communicated to employees? Obviously, the absence of a written rule or job requirement that is widely known by employees will work to discredit a defense that is based on a so-called "company policy."

Practices.   What a company does, or did in the past, will carry more weight than what it says it does. Policies are nothing more than statements of intention and can be refuted by evidence of past practices. For example, a company policy may require two years of in-house service for a promotion, but this will not help as a defense against discrimination should it be revealed that someone other than the complainant has been promoted without the requirement. Indeed, a policy that is discredited by actual practices may only serve to strengthen the complainant's allegation of differential treatment. The ability of an employer to document a defense will therefore require a thorough look at what the employer actually has done in the past in similar circumstances. Following the example cited, the employer would have to be concerned with a record of those who were promoted in the past and their qualifications. Agencies will normally seek evidence of past practices to determine whether discrimination has taken place.

Records.   An employee is fired after six years of mediocre job performance. Are there any reprimands, warnings, memos, evaluations, disciplinary reports, or other documents to support this fact? The complainant says that his work has been fine; to "prove" it, he says he has not been reprimanded or even criticized once in the whole duration of his employment. Are there any documents to counter this evidence? An investigator will listen to a company's story and then ask to see the personnel file, that is, the documentary evidence of what really happened. The written evidence reflective of what occurred at the time it occurred certainly is viewed with more importance than a subsequent verbal justification.

Moreover, records should be accurate and honest if they are to support the company's position. An investigation which revealed dozens of reprimands for minor latenesses for a black employee written by a white supervisor—far beyond what any other employee received—was viewed with great skepticism and eventually worked against, instead of for, the employer. It was seen as a clear case of harassment. Accordingly, records which are not valid "records," but exaggerated and somewhat fictional accounts of past actions, may also backfire as evidence for a defense. The common method for creating such documentary memoranda, used often by bureaucrats and lawyers alike, goes something like this: "This will confirm our conversation of October 10, at which time you indicated to me that you understood your work was not up to par and would strive for improvement." A denial by the person alleged to have made the statements, or perhaps the absence of a confirming signature, will all but invalidate such "documentary" evidence.

Statements. Particularly when other evidence is lacking, an investigator will seek out the statements and testimony of others who were involved in the employment practice. The ability of those persons to recall what occurred, as well as the substance of the testimony, will affect the employer's ability to document a defense. Some persons just may not be available to give statements due to death or termination of their employment. Also, persons who are no longer employed by the company may not be so disposed toward making statements which are in the company's favor. In fact, they may be strong witnesses for the complainant.

What Are the Legal Limitations of a Defense?

In addition to knowing the facts of a given case and having the ability to document them, a defense will definitely be tempered by the legal precedents of past court decisions and other legal limitations. An employer may begin to construct a defense which long ago has been found invalid by the courts. To do so will simply be a waste of time and effort. Therefore, many of these legal limitations will be outlined, where applicable, in this chapter.

DISPROVING THE PROOFS: THE FIRST LINE OF DEFENSE

The foremost consideration of a defense will be to discredit or otherwise invalidate the *prima facie* evidence of the charging party, which supposedly places the burden of proof on the respondent employer. This initial defense therefore centers on an attack of the evidence which appears to substantiate one or more of the proofs described in the previous chapter. To prevent the burden of proof from shifting in the first place is obviously of prime importance, for it essentially kills the complaint and precludes the need for other defenses. After all, the person who files with a state agency or makes out an EEOC charge form is doing nothing more than making an allegation. The initial burden is on the complainant to obtain evidence which credits the allegation, thus placing on the shoulders of the employer the need to explain away the differential treatment, disparate effect, or whatever else the complaint alleges.[16] The first line of defense aims at refuting the initial basis of the allegation. Let us then look at five main proofs of discrimination and the manner in which they may be successfully disputed.

Evil Intent

The complainant states, "I was told by the personnel director that women could not be promoted to management positions because they might become pregnant." How can such a statement, which may surely be used as a crucial bit of evidence by a civil rights agency, be attacked? The most obvious method, and perhaps the least effective, is to deny that such a statement was ever made. This would cause a question of credibility to exist on the matter which could only be resolved by a look at other evidence.

Another possible defense to a statement that indicates direct bias would be a demonstration that the person who made the statement was in no way authorized to do so by the employer and played no role in the actual employment practice. In regard to authorization, the defense is a tenuous one. If a personnel assistant denies a woman an application for employment stating that "women don't work in the plant," the employer is responsible for what the personnel assistant did and said, no matter what the intent or past policy of the company. A more effective defense to statements revealing evidence of evil intent would be a showing that the person who made them played no part at all in the employment decision.

A third avenue of defense rests in the discrediting of the particulars of the statement; for example, showing that a substantial number of women are in management will counter a statement that they are not promoted to those positions. This manner of response has the greatest potential of success. Of course, there may be statements which cannot be substantively rebutted by factual evidence and are simply derogatory of women, blacks, or other groups. In other words, a company's entire pattern of employment practices may act to credit or discredit an allegation.

Differential Treatment

The most common form of complaint alleges differential treatment because of one or more of the prohibited bases of discrimination. A workable defense must demonstrate that the complainant was not differen-

---

[16] *Long v. Ford Motor Company*, 7 Empl. Prac. Dec. ¶9290 (1974).

tially treated. Naturally, many variables exist in the factual situations which surround such complaints.

The main rebuttal to a claim of differential treatment is that the alleged treatment was not different, but actually the same as shown to others in similar situations. For example, the complaint of a black discharged due to tardiness alleging that whites were not so treated would entail a defense showing that whites with similar records were in fact also discharged. Of course, the facts will have to be with the employer.

Although the purpose of such a defense is clear, the defense itself may be rather complicated under certain circumstances. Some of the reasons for adverse personnel actions, such as incompetence, insubordination, quality of work performed, and others, are not so easily comparable. An argument which declares that treatment was similar might require an in-depth analysis of several aspects of job performances in these more complex cases.

In fact, when a protected class member alleges differential treatment in a discharge, virtually every aspect of the complainant's employment history may be examined—from the location of the complainant's desk and his salary to opportunities for advancement and training. Because a complaint of discharge often alleges differential treatment in terms and conditions of employment as support of the complaint, the employer should be prepared to detail at length the similar treatment of the complainant. This was successfully done by the Pillsbury Company during their defense of a charge by a woman alleging sex and race discrimination in her discharge. But many issues were raised by the complainant:

> The principal specific claims of plaintiff in support of her allegations of discrimination and wrongful discharge on account of race and sex are that she did not receive adequate training or supervision in her work, was not furnished meaningful job description of the work expected of her, did not receive compensation comparable to that received by others in similar occupations in Pillsbury, was not provided office, telephone and secretarial facilities equal to other employees similarly situated, was discouraged and obstructed in her assigned work of dealing with problems of minorities and women employees, was not afforded language training to qualify her for work in the International Department and was wrongfully discharged because she was a black and a woman.[17]

Although the complainant lost her case, the employer was required to present testimony and other evidence to counter each allegation of differential treatment with a showing of similar treatment.

---

[17] *Donaldson v. Pillsbury Company,* 11 Empl. Prac. Dec. ¶10,653 (1976).

Another argument to a claim of differential treatment asserts that the comparisons made are not valid because those used for comparison are not similarly situated. Accordingly, the illegal stall-in and lock-in alleged to Percy Green were distinguished from the legitimate demonstrations of employees during a strike action. McDonnell Douglas argued that although both involved disruptive acts, they were not similar in their nature or in degree. Another example is two persons having the same yearly absenteeism record in terms of days out, but not in terms of excused absences. The defense must therefore establish that the performance of the complainant was notably different from others and justified the more adverse action by the employer.

Disparate Effect

A job requirement which disproportionately affects certain protected groups, such as blacks and women, when compared with others is unlawful unless justified by "business necessity." Several examples of such cases were cited in Chapter 3; they related to requirements such as high school diploma, weight, arrest record, garnishments, etc. The burden of showing the disparate effect is with the complainant. The employer will not have to deal with the business necessity question if it can first be shown that the requirement did not disparately affect the complainant as a member of a protected class.

An example of a case in which the burden was not met is *Robinson v. City of Dallas,*[18] recently decided by the Fifth Circuit Court of Appeals. Willie L. Robinson was a black man who was suspended without pay for five days by his employer, the City of Dallas, because of "failure to pay just debts." In light of prior court decisions ruling that the discharge of blacks due to garnishments had a disparate effect on blacks as a class and was therefore unlawful,[19] Robinson argued that the Dallas rule of suspension for credit problems "had a discriminatory effect on minority employees." While the relationship between minorities and credit problems seems obvious, the burden was still on the complainant to demonstrate, within the confines of the particular circumstances of the case, the unlawful consequence of the "just debts" rule. Robinson could not meet the burden in this case.

Robinson's first argument was that a greater proportion of blacks as compared with whites had been disciplined by the rule. Three out of seven disciplined employees between 1965 and 1973 were black; three of

---

[18] See 10 Empl. Prac. Dec. ¶10,245 (1975) for the excerpts that follow.

[19] *Johnson v. Pike Corporation of America,* 4 Empl. Prac. Dec. ¶7517 (1971); and *Wallace v. Debron Corporation,* 7 Empl. Prac. Dec. ¶9246 (1974).

five from 1968 to the present were black. However, the court ruled that "such small numbers are insufficient to support any conclusion as to whether the rule has a discriminatory effect."

Second, Robinson argued that a "disproportionately large portion of the poor people in Dallas" are black and that "people who do not tend to pay their just debts are poor people." The complainant supported the first assertion with statistics, but provided no evidence to support the second. Yet, even had Robinson proved the second assertion, according to the court,

> [P]utting the two premises together does not compel his conclusion. It may be that although Negroes comprise a disproportionately large percentage of the poor, they do not comprise a disproportionately large percentage of the poor who do not pay their just debts.

Furthermore, the court noted that statistics relating to the population of Dallas would be relevant in a hiring case, but not in regard to Robinson's complaint:

> In the present case the employment practice is applied only to employees of the City of Dallas. Thus the question is whether black *employees* of the City of Dallas fail to pay their just debts more frequently than white *employees* of the City of Dallas. The statistics offered by plaintiff are not helpful in answering this question.

Finally, the complainant attempted to cite the other court decisions relating to the disparate effect of garnishments to help make his case. But the court found that in those cases the discriminatory effect was "either proved by adequate evidence or was stipulated," and the evidence in those cases "is not a substitute for that required in this case."

The message of *Robinson v. City of Dallas* is clear: the discriminatory effect of certain job requirements may seem obvious in some cases, but it is a question of fact, and courts are not generally disposed toward the assumption of factual arguments. Accordingly, neither should such allegations be assumed or stipulated by employers. An effective initial defense in such cases can be found by scrutinizing the statistical proofs of disparate effect for both relevance and applicability to the particular allegations and facts of the complaint. A thorough analysis may reveal that the complainant does not meet the required burden of proof.

Statistics

Numbers seem difficult to dispute. In class action cases, statistical disparities of women and minorities in the employer's work force place the burden of proof on the company and may make a case. In individual cases, statistics may similarly place the burden on the employer when it can be shown that job requirements have a disparate effect on members of protected classes. And in *McDonnell Douglas v. Green*, the Supreme Court affirmed the use of statistics in deciding certain individual complaints. Yet the *City of Dallas* case at least demonstrates that not all statistical proofs have the same degree of significance and that some can successfully be discredited.

One determinant of statistical relevance is the actual number of persons being statistically analyzed. For example, it may appear meaningful to proclaim that "half of all the black applicants to X company were rejected for employment whereas only one-fourth of the white applicants were rejected" and "the failure rate of blacks in obtaining employment was twice that of whites." But if the figures supporting the rejection rates were one out of two for black applicants and one out of four for whites, the statistical disparities between blacks and whites would have no significance whatsoever. In *Ochoa v. Monsanto Company*, the complainants argued that discrimination in hiring against Mexican-Americans was evidenced by the fact that the local Mexican-American population was about 10 percent of the total and respondent's work force was less than 1 percent Mexican-American.[20] However, the actual number of Mexican-American applicants over a one-year period was only 11 as compared with a total of 684 applicants. Relevant hiring statistics would compare the disposition of those 11 Mexican-Americans to the success rate of others, but in the case in point the extremely small number of Mexican-American applicants made such statistics irrelevant.

The *Ochoa* case reveals another possible defense to statistical proofs, and that is applicability to the complaint. The court here found that statistical disparities between the population and the employer's work force did not directly apply to *hiring* practices as would the actual percentages of those hired. As stated by the Fifth Circuit Court of Appeals in *Hester v. Southern Railway Company*:

> The most direct route to proof of racial discrimination in hiring is proof of disparity between the percentage of blacks among those applying for a particular position and the percentage of blacks among those hired for the position.[21]

However, in most cases the disparity between the presence of minorities and women in a job and their presence in the general popula-

---

[20] 4 Empl. Prac. Dec. ¶7739 (1971); and 5 Empl. Prac. Dec. ¶8437 (5th Cir. 1973).
[21] 8 Empl. Prac. Dec. ¶9582 (1974).

tion will be a relevant factor.[22] In *Jones v. Tri-County Electric Cooperative,* the Fifth Circuit Court of Appeals, perhaps the most experienced appellate court in employment discrimination cases, stated:

> The statistics which the Courts have always considered is the composition of the employer's work force as compared to the percentage of the minority population in the employer's service area. Here the three counties served by the defendant had a population which was approximately 40 percent non-white; before the suit was filed there was one black employee, at no time following the filing of this suit did the employer ever maintain a work force of more than about 10 percent non-white.[23]

There are two main ways to defend this type of statistical disparity. The first argues that population statistics should not be utilized in determining work force disparities because they are unrealistic and do not really determine the availability of minorities and women. For example, while the general population may be 51 percent female, a lesser percentage of women work as compared to men. What is more, in several professional and skilled job categories, minorities and women are simply not represented as they are in the population. The presence and location of women and minorities in a company's work force should therefore be compared with work force availability figures.

The second argument concerns the recruiting area of the employer. Companies located in suburban areas lacking in minority population normally try to have their local area, perhaps their county, as the area for comparison. The general criterion, however, is the standard metropolitan statistical area in which the company is located as measured by the Census Bureau, which is likely to have higher percentage figures for minorities. And attempts by employers to limit the recruiting area when the facility is within commuting distance of urban populations have not been very successful.

Another defensive strategy states that statistics do not make an individual case by themselves and can be countered with other evidence. For example, let us assume that a black who alleged discrimination in her discharge can show that a comparatively greater percentage of blacks than whites were fired by the employer during the last two years and that the numbers involved are great enough to be statistically relevant. The employer may still be able to offset the statistical proof with other evidence showing that the discharge was justified and that the

---

[22] *Chance v. Board of Examiners,* 4 Empl. Prac. Dec. ¶7600 (1971); and 4 Empl. Prac. Dec. ¶7756 (1972).
[23] 9 Empl. Prac. Dec. ¶10,120 (1975).

complainant was neither differentially treated nor disparately affected by the employer's termination standards.

Once more, it is reiterated that this ability to justify an adverse employment action enough to counter such statistics will relate to the amount of structure and objectivity in the employer's decision-making process, that is, the ability to document and explain a decision. It is in this manner that statistical proofs can be overcome, especially in individual cases. For one example, note that in *Labat v. Board of Higher Education, City of New York*, a black professor was not able to show denial of tenure because of race, despite the fact that a greater percentage of whites as compared to blacks had tenure. The court noted that the defendant employer has rebutted this statistical evidence well:

> The overwhelming weight of the evidence on the entire case establishes that the decision to deny tenure was made in good faith based upon criteria fairly applied to plaintiff and all other candidates for the position of associate professor with tenure, and that the plaintiff's race played no part in the judgment of the defendants.[24]

Lastly, it should be mentioned that employers may use favorable statistics to their advantage in defending a complaint. The plaintiff in *Faro v. New York University*, who held a Ph.D. in anatomy, tried to support her charge of sex discrimination in being denied a teaching position with the department of cell biology by showing that women faculty members of the medical school were concentrated in the pediatrics and pathology departments. But the employer pointed out that the percentage of female faculty members, 9 percent, was more than the 7.1 percent national figure for women doctors. This was an important bit of evidence which helped the employer prevail in the case.[25]

The Percy Green Proof

Briefly stated, a *prima facie* case of discrimination occurs when a protected class member applies for a position for which he or she is qualified and is rejected for employment, and the employer continues to seek applicants with the protected class member's qualifications. This type of proof, which may also be applied to promotion and discharge complaints and is explained in more detail in Chapter 3, may be sufficiently rebutted initially in two main ways: (1) showing that the complainant was not qualified, and/or (2) showing that the job was not available.

---

[24] 10 Empl. Prac. Dec. ¶10,563 (1975).
[25] 6 Empl. Prac. Dec. ¶8940 (1973).

Should the employer be able to show that the complainant was not qualified for the position in question, the complainant will then have the opportunity to demonstrate that the employer's position is actually a pretext for discrimination. To this end, the complainant may use evidence of statistics or the differential application of the company's standards. Furthermore, the employer's basis for rejecting the applicant will be scrutinized as to the disparate effect proof, for it may have the *effect* of unlawful discrimination.

A showing of lack of qualifications may therefore be a difficult task. The reasons given by the employer will surely be a target for analysis by the complainant or whatever government agency is investigating the case. The ability of the employer to prevail on this point will thus depend on (1) the absence of subjective reasoning in the employer's position, (2) the amount of uniformity, as shown by past decisions, in the application of the employer's reasoning, (3) the possible disparate effect on the complainant's class of the employer's job requirements, (4) the presence of job-related elements in the employer's reasoning, and (5) the absence of arbitrariness in the reasons.

The question of whether the job was available is factually a lot easier to answer. The presence of advertising or posting will of course be important. In addition, the employer who recruits or promotes by word of mouth, or even without any notification to employees, will have to contend with statements, indications, or promises on job availability made by persons involved in employee selection.

SOME COMMON DEFENSES: THE SECOND LINE OF DEFENSE

Should proofs establish a *prima facie* case of discrimination without successful rebuttal by the employer, there is a second line of defenses to thwart the complaint. These proofs are called "common" because they have been repeatedly raised by employers and adjudicated by the courts; so their limits in effectively countering the *prima facie* evidence have been spelled out by court decisions. By becoming familiar with these precedents, an accurate prediction can be made of their probable effectiveness in the case at hand. Admittedly, their usefulness is in most instances negligible. Yet they deserve mention if only for this very reason. The continual unsuccessful attempts by employers to give many of these defenses great credence make their discussion noteworthy.

Business Necessity

Several times in Chapter 3 it was mentioned that a job requirement which has a disproportionate effect on protected classes is unlawful unless justified by "business necessity." This doctrine was created by

the courts and first received substantial recognition in the Supreme
Court decision of *Griggs v. Duke Power Company:*

> The Act proscribes not only overt discrimination but also practices that
> are fair in form, but discriminatory in operation. The touchstone is
> business necessity. If an employment practice which operates to ex-
> clude Negroes cannot be shown to be related to job performance, the
> practice is prohibited.[26]

Several other court decisions have elucidated this doctrine more
specifically. Perhaps the most cited definition is found in the Fourth
Circuit Court of Appeals' ruling in *Robinson v. Lorillard Corporation:*

> [T]he applicable test is not merely whether there exists a business pur-
> pose for adhering to a challenged practice. The test is whether there
> exists an overriding legitimate business purpose such that the practice
> is necessary to the safe and efficient operation of the business. Thus, the
> business purpose must be sufficiently compelling to override any racial
> impact; the challenged practice must effectively carry out the business
> purpose it is alleged to serve; and there must be available no acceptable
> alternative policies or practices which would better accomplish the
> business purpose advanced, or accomplish it equally well with a lesser
> differential impact.[27]

The fact that a business practice is convenient or practical is not sufficient to allow for its discriminatory effect and meet the test of business
necessity. And as stated above, necessity implies that there be no alternative to the business requirement. Nor does the burden of additional
expense to the employer, because of extra training or other costs,
brought on by the elimination of the requirement adequately meet the
business necessity test.[28] Or, as stated in *U.S. v. Bethlehem Steel Corporation* by the Second Circuit Court of Appeals: "Necessity connotes an
irresistible demand."[29]

Have any employers been able to defend an unlawful employment
practice by the business necessity defense? It would seem that once the
burden has shifted to the employer, a defense based on this doctrine
becomes almost perfunctory. There are few examples of its successful
use. In *Richardson v. Hotel Corporation of America,* the discharge of a
black bellman because of his having been previously convicted of theft

---

[26] 3 Empl. Prac. Dec. ¶8137 (1971).

[27] 3 Empl. Prac. Dec. ¶8267 (1971).

[28] See for example, *Jones v. Lee Way Motor Freight,* 2 Empl. Prac. Dec. ¶10,283 (1970);
United States v. Bethlehem Steel Corporation, 3 Empl. Prac. Dec. ¶8257 (1971).

[29] 3 Empl. Prac. Dec. ¶8257 (1971).

was found to be lawful, despite the possible disparate effect of the rule on blacks. The court found, and the Fifth Circuit Court of Appeals upheld, that the respondent employer met the business necessity test:

> It is reasonable for management of a hotel to require that persons employed in positions where they have access to valuable property of others have a record reasonably free from convictions for serious property related crimes.[30]

(However, in another case the blanket denial of employment because of conviction records could not be justified.)[31]

In *Waters v. Furnco Construction Corporation*, experience and skill requirements and the absence of a training program all met the business necessity requirement due to the great potential of serious safety hazards should work be done improperly. However, no disproportionate impact was demonstrated because of these stringent qualifications.[32]

Despite the cases cited above, however, the business necessity defense is not viable for most cases in which the disparate effect proof is present.

BFOQ

The BFOQ defense, as provided for by Section 703(e) of Title VII, allows for discrimination based on religion, sex, or national origin where such factors are "a bona fide occupational qualification reasonably necessary to the normal operation of that particular business or enterprise." The requirements for a BFOQ closely resemble those of the "business necessity" doctrine.

Religion may be a BFOQ in regard to religious organizations or societies that require their employees to be of a particular religion. This obviously does not apply to almost all private employers. Also, educational institutions that are run by a particular religion may also have religion as a job requirement. National origin may be a BFOQ in the case of those organizations and groups who are identified with a particular culture or national origin.

But the BFOQ defense is most commonly raised in reference to sex discrimination. During the Stone Age of Title VII, about ten years ago, it was generally thought that some jobs were simply "not for women" and that with a little showing of good faith by the employer, the BFOQ

---

[30] 4 Empl. Prac. Dec. ¶7666 (1971); 5 Empl. Prac. Dec. ¶8101 (1972).

[31] See for example, *Green v. Missouri Pacific Railroad Company*, 8 Empl. Prac. Dec. ¶9831 (1974), *reversed* 10 Empl. Prac. Dec. ¶10,314 (8th Cir. 1975).

[32] 9 Empl. Prac. Dec. ¶9968 (1975).

exemption could be used with success. The few cases decided during those early years seem to be in accord with a traditional view of women's roles.[33] Indeed, few people realized that sex discrimination in employment was unlawful way back in 1965. Yet it eventually became clear, in the words of Justice Thurgood Marshall, that "the exception for *'bona fide* occupational qualification' was not intended to swallow the rule.'"[34] The EEOC guidelines on sex as a BFOQ, found in Appendix 1, have been upheld by the courts and should therefore be referred to for guidance in this area. They narrowly limit the use of the BFOQ as a defense.

Several early cases against large employers have defined the limitations of making sex a BFOQ such that the defense is rarely seen in contemporary decisions. In *Weeks v. Southern Bell Telephone and Telegraph Company,* the denial of a switchman's job to a woman because it was "strenuous" and required the regular lifting of 30 pounds was found unlawful. The Fifth Circuit Court of Appeals stated:

> We conclude that the principle of nondiscrimination requires that we hold that in order to rely on the bona fide occupational qualification exception an employer has the burden of proving that he had reasonable cause to believe, that is, a factual basis for believing, that all or substantially all women would be unable to perform safely and efficiently the duties of the job involved . . . .
>
> While one might accept, *arguendo,* that men are stronger on the average than women, it is not clear that any conclusions about relative lifting ability would follow . . . .
>
> What does seem clear is that using these class stereotypes denies positions to a great many women perfectly capable of performing the duties involved.[35]

The Seventh Circuit Court of Appeals issued a similar decision in *Bowe v. Colgate-Palmolive Company,* the issue being whether women could be restricted from jobs that required the lifting of more than 35 pounds. The court found that restrictions should be on an individual basis:

> Accordingly, we hold that Colgate may, if it so desires, retain its 35-pound weight-lifting limit as a general guideline for all of its employees, male and female. However, it must notify all of its workers that each of them who desires to do so will be afforded a reasonable opportunity to demonstrate his or her ability to perform more strenuous jobs on a

---

[33] See *Ward v. Firestone Tire & Rubber Company,* 1 Empl. Prac. Dec. ¶9754 (1966).
[34] *Phillips v. Martin Marietta,* 3 Empl. Prac. Dec. ¶8088 (1971).
[35] 1 Empl. Prac. Dec. ¶9970 (1969).

regular basis. Each employee who is able to so demonstrate must be permitted to bid on and fill any position to which his or her seniority may entitle him or her.[36]

The message is clear: to restrict women on the basis of stereotypes and generalizations about their abilities is unlawful and does not meet the requirements of the BFOQ defense.[37] Sex must be essential to the performance of the job for the qualification to be *bona fide*. In another example, sex was not found to be a BFOQ for the position of probation and parole officer.[38] And, in another, the restriction of a female employee due to contact with male prisoners was also found to be unlawful.[39]

Can sex be a BFOQ? There are some examples. In *City of Philadelphia v. Pennsylvania Human Relations Commission*, a Pennsylvania state court found that the BFOQ exemption should be granted to the position of youth center supervisor. Because supervisors shared housing with juveniles and took part in such activities as monitoring showers and carrying on personal searches, it was lawful that they be the same sex as those supervised.[40] In an uncommon complaint filed by a man, the female sex was found to be a BFOQ by the New York State Supreme Court for state troopers who carried out the following activities:

. . . (1) search, transportation and interrogation of female prisoners; (2) interview of female complainants and witnesses, particularly in cases where the presence of a male trooper might cause embarrassment or lack of cooperation; (3) undercover assignments in the field of major crimes; (4) special investigations, particularly in the fields of child abuse or neglect, sex crimes, or unlawful abortion.[41]

These are the kinds of situations where the BFOQ defense has worked. Other jobs justifiably restricted to one sex are restroom attendant and wet nurse (hardly a common job title).

Client Preference

The Fifth Circuit Court of Appeals, in *Diaz v. Pan American Airways, Inc.*, found that customer preference was not an adequate defense to

---

[36] 2 Empl. Prac. Dec. ¶10,090 (1969).

[37] See also *Rosenfield v. Southern Pacific Company*, 3 Empl. Prac. Dec. ¶8247 (9th Cir. 1971); *Long v. Sapp*, 8 Empl. Prac. Dec. ¶9712 (5th Cir. 1974).

[38] *Tracy v. Oklahoma Department of Corrections*, 8 Empl. Prac. Dec. ¶9713 (1974).

[39] *Reynolds v. Wise*, 8 Empl. Prac. Dec. ¶9778 (1974).

[40] 5 Empl. Prac. Dec. ¶8535 (1973). For a similar case, see *Long v. State Personnel Board*, 8 Empl. Prac. Dec. ¶9745 (Cal. App. 1974).

[41] *Button v. Rockefeller*, 6 Empl. Prac. Dec. ¶8835 (1973).

maintain an all-women policy for flight attendants. The court cited the EEOC guidelines, which state that a BFOQ should not be based on "the refusal to hire an individual because of the preferences of coworkers, the employer, clients or customers . . . ." The court added:

> Indeed, while we recognize that the public's expectation of finding one sex in a particular role may cause some initial difficulty, it would be totally anomalous if we were to allow the preferences and prejudices of customers to determine whether the sex discrimination was valid. Indeed, it was, to a large extent, these very prejudices the Act was meant to overcome. Thus, we feel that customer preference may be taken into account only when it is based on the company's inability to perform the primary function or service it offers.[42]

Nor could customer preference pass the business necessity test in the *Diaz* case:

> No one has suggested that having male stewards will so seriously affect the operation of an airline as to jeopardize or even minimize its ability to provide safe transportation from one place to another.[43]

The use of customer preference as a defense to discrimination will generally fail unless it strikes at the heart of an employer's business and is essential to its operations. Restaurants which prefer to use waiters exclusively (or waitresses, as the case may be) have been consistently unable to meet this requirement. It is doubtful that any employer will. To allow for a discriminatory practice based on customer preference is "anomalous" to the intent of civil rights law in general and will likely not be accepted by the courts. For a further understanding of this view, note the statements by the Southern Bell representative on page 31 regarding local traditions and customs affecting the hiring of blacks.

Intent

Just as evil intent was once a required proof of unlawful discrimination, good intent was once an adequate defense. Both proofs and defenses have since changed, and the good intent defense has consequently lost its significance. Bluntly put, an employer will suffer from indications of evil intent, but demonstrations of the opposite will carry little weight, if any, to counter proofs of discrimination.

Yet the average employer's ignorance of this rather elementary fact causes innumerable problems. Although protestations of good faith and

---

[42] 3 Empl. Prac. Dec. ¶8166 (1971).
[43] Ibid.

lack of intention to discriminate have practically no evidentiary value, employers continue to misallocate their defensive efforts in this direction. Some speak of black roommates in college, lifetime memberships in the NAACP, and make statements such as, "Look, I have nothing against women, I'm married to one." Another common cry is that the company has an affirmative action program and employs many minorities and women. Some lawyers play the same role and relate how many years they have known their client, stating, "He doesn't care if you're white, black, green, or blue." Other employers point out that their company has a black manager or a female personnel officer. But employers take note: these defenses do not work.

In the famous *Griggs* decision, the Supreme Court noted the following:

> The Company's lack of discriminatory intent is suggested by special efforts to help the undereducated employees through Company financing of two-thirds the cost of tuition for high school training. But Congress directed the thrust of the Act to the *consequences* of employment practices, not simply the motivation.[44]

Griggs was a case in which job requirements had a disparate effect on blacks. But indications of an employer's good intentions are of similarly little value in other cases. "Intention" has simply been interpreted to mean that the employer intended to do what it did.[45]

State Laws

Many states have enacted laws which set maximum limits on weights that can be lifted and number of hours that can be worked by women. Laws which restrict opportunities for women are unlawful and in violation of Title VII. However, in most states those laws have already been appealed or struck down by the courts. The states which have at least one kind of female protective law still in effect are Idaho, Indiana, Maine, New Hampshire, and Texas. Although employers who rely in good faith on these laws will be found to have violated Title VII, several courts have not ordered back pay in those instances.[46]

Union Contracts

Many elements of a company's employment policies and practices are integrally tied with the terms of a union contract. Several of these con-

---

[44] 3 Empl. Prac. Dec. ¶8137 (1971).
[45] *Johnson v. University of Pittsburgh*, 5 Empl. Prac. Dec. ¶8660 (1973).
[46] *Williams v. General Foods Corporation*, 7 Empl. Prac. Dec. ¶9365 (7th Cir. 1974).

tractual provisions may be the target of a discrimination complaint, such as those relating to seniority, wages, promotion procedures, bidding, insurance benefits, sick leave policy, and other terms and conditions of employment. A commonly invoked employer defense to complaints relating to these areas is that the contract is binding and prevents, or prevented, the employer from taking corrective actions. The defense further argues that even if the employer had desired to make contractual alterations, union threats of severe opposition, perhaps in the form of strikes and other disruptive actions, make modifications a practical necessity.

But this defense has no validity. The employer is obligated to the law first and therefore has the legal authority to do away with practices that are violative of civil rights law. For example, in *Savannah Printing Specialties Local 604 v. Union Camp Corporation*, a company's refusal to have a union's complaint about seniority provision modifications decided by arbitration was upheld by the district court. The modifications were part of an affirmative action agreement approved by the Office of Federal Contract Compliance. The court's explanation was as follows:

> If arbitration can result in obstructing or thwarting the eradication of racial discrimination in employment, an employer is not forced to go through with it. The new seniority provisions in question were entered into under the laws of the United States and pursuant to its public policy and cannot be diluted by private negotiation or arbitration. Union Camp cannot obey both the Government and an adverse arbitration award. The Agreement with Local 604 recognizes that there is no liability on its part for failure to comply with any provision "when such non-compliance is occasioned by circumstances beyond its control." A contractual duty is excused in cases where intervening government regulations render performance impossible.[47]

This legal authority to take unilateral action for compliance with civil rights laws therefore precludes the use of the union contract by the employer as a defense. As stated by the Fifth Circuit Court of Appeals in *Carey v. Greyhound Bus Company, Inc.*, "Union contracts grant no immunity on the subject of racial discrimination. Neither can the employer use the union or unions for a shield."[48]

While legal issues are clearly given priority over contractual conflicts, the employer may still have considerable problems with unions relating to unlawful discrimination. For one thing, being in the right legally may not always assuage the opposition of labor unions. A lack of union cooperation may make life rather difficult, and it is hardly feasible to

---

[47] 5 Empl. Prac. Dec. ¶8551 (1972).
[48] 8 Empl. Prac. Dec. ¶9698 (1974).

settle such conflicts by court decisions. On the other hand, the ability to determine unlawfulness in employment practices is far from an exact science. The answers to many questions (to say the least) will not be easily agreed upon. What is more, several employment practices—such as subjective criteria for evaluations, lack of job duties and descriptions, absence of policy guidelines—are not necessarily illegal, but make employers more *vulnerable* to complaints of discrimination. They too may be tied to union contracts.

Arbitration

Does an adverse arbiter's decision on similar issues prevent an employee from also filing a discrimination complaint? The answer is "no." This issue was decided by the Supreme Court in 1974:

> We think, therefore, that the federal policy favoring arbitration of labor disputes with the federal policy against discriminatory employment practices can best be accommodated by permitting an employee to pursue fully both his remedy under the grievance-arbitration clause of a collective-bargaining agreement and his cause of action under Title VII. The federal court should consider the employee's claim *de novo*. The arbitral decision may be admitted as evidence and accorded such weight as the court deems appropriate.[49]

This means that in addition to an avenue of relief by means of arbitration, a complainant may also take his or her chances on the federal and state levels pursuant to a civil rights law. However, the arbitor's decision, as the court indicated, does carry some weight. Although in the *Gardner-Denver* case the arbitration was not very important—it did not consider the question of racial discrimination in Alexander's discharge—it may be important in other cases. The court's thoughts on the effect on discrimination cases of prior arbitrations is noteworthy:

> Relevant factors include the existence of provisions in the collective-bargaining agreement that conform substantially with Title VII, the degree of procedural fairness in the arbitral forum, adequacy of the record with respect to the issue of discrimination, and the special competence of particular arbitrators. Where an arbitral determination gives full consideration to an employee's Title VII rights, a court may properly accord it great weight. This is especially true where the issue is solely one of fact, specifically addressed by the parties and decided by the arbitrator on the basis of an adequate record. But courts should ever be mindful that Congress, in enacting Title VII, thought it neces-

---

[49] *Alexander v. Gardner-Denver Co.*, 7 Empl. Prac. Dec. ¶9148 (1974).

sary to provide a judicial forum for the ultimate resolution of discriminatory employment claims. It is the duty of courts to assure the
full availability of this forum.[50]

In light of these guidelines of the Supreme Court, an arbiter's decision
favorable to the company in basically the same complaint may be useful
as a defense. But it will not prevent the complainant from proceeding
with a discrimination complaint with a government agency or by means
of court action. It is perhaps ironic that despite Alexander's having won
this point, he eventually lost his case.[51]

---

[50] Ibid.
[51] 10 Empl. Prac. Dec. ¶10,254 (1975).

5

What the Employer Stands to Lose

Why be concerned about becoming embroiled in matters of unlawful discrimination?

The most common responses to this question are couched in terms which are both unspecific and intangible. "Should the public find out about this, it would be disastrous," one company official told me. "My whole professional reputation is on the line," said another. "I have never discriminated against anyone," said the plant owner who was far removed from those who took part in the alleged discrimination, "and there's an important principle here that I intend to fight no matter what."

What is the important principle? We are concerned here with violations of a law that is both complex and rather liberally interpreted by those who enforce it, a law that relates to the ways in which employers interract with their employees on many levels and from many different perspectives. At the very least, the previous chapters demonstrate that the lines of principle are not clearly drawn. Indeed, a company official may be held responsible for unlawful discrimination without any showing of an intent to discriminate on the part of the company or those involved in the alleged acts. Nor does the argument of disgrace in the public's eyes seem to hold much weight. This concern over public image, which is usually expressed by those companies producing consumer goods, does not justify the writing of this book.

What employers really stand to lose most by discrimination complaints' being filed against them is money. It is a matter of dollars and cents. Even complaints which have little merit may be expensive because their resolution will mean the expenditure of time, legal fees, and court costs. Furthermore, complaints with seemingly little merit may be given merit by government agencies and even the courts. All those involved in the management side of employment practices must therefore be aware of the potential monetary liabilities of their actions. This awareness should provide the motivation to take corrective, preventive actions, and, more importantly, it should enable the employer to resolve complaints pragmatically and sensibly.

PRINCIPLES OF COMPENSATORY DAMAGES

Awards for damages in discrimination cases are compensatory in nature and are therefore directly related to making up the losses incurred by the complainant. Section 706(g) of Title VII typically provides for the payment to complainants for damages incurred:

> If the court finds that the respondent has intentionally engaged or is intentionally engaging in an unlawful employment practice charged in the complaint, the court may enjoin the respondent from engaging in such unlawful employment practice, and order such affirmative action as may be appropriate, which may include, but is not limited to, reinstatement or hiring of employees, with or without backpay (payable by the employer, employment agency, or labor organization, as the case may be, responsible for the unlawful employment practice), or any other equitable relief as the court deems appropriate.

In reading Section 706(g), just ignore the word "intentionally," for as the law has been interpreted it has little, if any, significance.

In a very important recent decision by the Supreme Court, *Albemarle Paper Co. v. Moody,* the standards to be followed by the lower courts in awarding back pay were clarified. The most important standard is "making the complainant whole":

> Title VII deals with legal injuries of an economic character occasioned by racial or other antiminority discrimination. The terms "complete justice" and "necessary relief" have acquired a clear meaning in such circumstances. Where racial discrimination is concerned, "the [district] court has not merely the power but the duty to render a decree which will so far as possible eliminate the discriminatory effects of the past as well as bar like discrimination in the future." *Louisiana v. United States,* 380 U.S. 145, 154. And where a legal injury is of an economic character, "the general rule is that when a wrong has been done, and the law gives a remedy, the compensation should be equal to the injury. The latter is the standard by which the former is to be measured. The injured party is to be placed as near as may be, in the situation he would have occupied if the wrong had not been committed." *Wicker v. Hoppack,* 6

Wall. 94, at 99. The "make whole" purpose of Title VII is made evident by the legislative history.[1]

The principles of "relief" to the complainant are set apart from the nature of the complaint and the basis of discrimination. Either there is a "legal injury" or not; either the complainant is to be made whole or not. The issues are not ones of degree but are absolute.

And just as the good intentions of the employer will have little effect on the merits of the case, they should not prevent the awarding of damages. This was frequently not the posture of the appellate courts before the *Albemarle* decision. For example, back pay had been denied in class action cases where the employer had shown efforts to recruit and promote minorities and women or had taken corrective actions to eliminate discriminatory practices. But in *Albemarle* the Supreme Court was clear on this "good faith" defense:

> If backpay were available only upon a showing of bad faith, the remedy would become a punishment for moral turpitude, rather than a compensation for workers' injuries. This would read the "make whole" purpose right out of Title VII, for a worker's injury is no less real simply because his employer did not inflict it in "bad faith." Title VII is not concerned with the employer's "good intent or absence of discriminatory intent" for "Congress directed the thrust of the Act to the *consequences* of employment practices, not simply the motivation." *Griggs v. Duke Power Co.*, 401 U.S., at 432.[2]

Once more it appears that the intent of the employer has no bearing on the matter at hand—in this case, what the employer stands to lose. The only exceptions may be situations in which the employer relied upon the provisions of a state law, such as in sex discrimination cases, which are violative of federal law. As noted in Chapter 4, most of these state laws have been repealed.[3]

Although this book emphasizes individual rather than class action complaints because the latter are less common than the former, it deserves mention that an individual complaint may easily turn into a class

---

[1] 9 Empl. Prac. Dec. ¶10,230 (1975).

[2] Ibid.

[3] It can surely be said that the use of the good faith defense by employers to deny monetary awards was diminished by the *Albemarle* decision. Subsequent cases bear this out. However, since many areas of unlawful discrimination are truly complex, one cannot completely disregard the good faith argument. Of note is a case in New York in which the district court denied an award of back pay although the employer's testing methods violated the EEOC guidelines and had the effect of discrimination [*Rios v. Enterprise Association Steamfitters Local 638*, 10 Empl. Prac. Dec. ¶10,273 (1975)].

action *complete with the awarding of damages on a class basis*. Such awards might be in the millions-of-dollars category. What greatly increases the employer's vulnerability to these potentially very costly complaints is the well-established principle that only one person need file charges for all members of the class to be entitled to compensation. Thus, in *Albemarle* the Supreme Court noted:

> The petitioners also contend that no backpay can be awarded to those unnamed parties in the plaintiff class who have not themselves filed charges with the EEOC. We reject this contention. The courts of appeals that have confronted the issue are unanimous in recognizing that backpay may be awarded on a class basis under Title VII without exhaustion of administrative procedures by the unnamed class members.[4]

The *Albemarle* decision will likely increase the frequency of class back pay awards in future cases.

The importance of familiarizing oneself with the principles of compensatory damages and the various ways in which they may be applied to individual cases is central to dealing with discrimination. Compensation for injuries incurred is the aim of most complainants and government agencies. The amount of monetary awards obtained by state and federal civil rights commissions is often used as a measurement of their effectiveness. The underlying assumption in their actions is that employers who have to pay for violating the law will be less inclined to violate it again. Since antidiscrimination laws are civil in nature rather than criminal and there are no real fines or penalties for breaking them, the concept of "making the complainant whole" is seen as a major enforcement weapon against employers. In *Albemarle* the court readily admitted to this:

> If employers faced only the prospect of an injunctive order [that is, to cease unlawful acts], they would have little incentive to shun practices of dubious legality. It is the reasonably certain prospect of a backpay award that "provides the spur or catalyst which causes employers and unions to self-examine and to self-evaluate their employment practices and to endeavor to eliminate, so far as possible, the last vestiges of an unfortunate and ignominious page in this country's history."[5]

REINSTATEMENT, INSTATEMENT, AND PROMOTION

The logical remedy to an unlawful discharge, refusal to hire, or denial of promotion will be the reinstatement, instatement, or promotion of the

---

[4] 9 Empl. Prac. Dec. ¶10,230 (1975).
[5] Ibid.

complainant to the job in question. For many employers this is a tough pill to swallow. The presence of an employee who was fired but has returned to work due to a court order is seen as a living symbol of company error. From the employer's vantage point such a situation is detrimental to the company's management capabilities. Not only did an employee successfully win his or her case by going *outside* of the company, it is feared that other employees also may be inclined to use the laws against job discrimination to their advantage. In a word, what the employer stands to lose here is authority.

If we assume that the complainant still desires to fill the job, there appear to be two arguments which might prevent that from occurring. The first states that the person is not qualified for the job; the second asserts that the job is no longer available.

In cases where the issue of relative qualifications controls the merits of the decision, the qualification defense will obviously not work. In other cases, the burden of demonstrating lack of qualifications will be on the employer, assuming the complainant has made a *prima facie* case. In an important case decided by the Fifth Circuit Court of Appeals, the difficult standards of such a defense were outlined:

> [T]he employer must demonstrate by clear and convincing evidence that any particular employee would have never been advanced because of that individual's particular lack of qualifications . . . . The court on remand will have to deal with probabilities. Any substantial doubts created by this task must be resolved in favor of the discriminatee who has produced evidence to establish a prima facie case. The discriminatee is the innocent party in these circumstances.[6]

The "clear and convincing" criterion is often cited in other court decisions. Also, note from the above that the benefit of the doubt that arises in determining the proper award for damages is resolved in favor of the complainant.

Nevertheless, the lack of qualifications defense has been used successfully. In *Cooper v. Allen* the employer demonstrated that a black man would not have been hired because of his lesser qualifications despite a discriminatory testing requirement.[7] And just as a showing of lack of qualification may preclude a back pay award,[8] it logically follows that it may preclude a reinstatement order as well.

On the other hand, the issue may not be "most qualified" but rather

---

[6] *Baxter v. Savannah Sugar Refining Corp.*, 7 Empl. Prac. Dec. ¶9426 (1974). See also *Harkless v. Sweeny*, 2 Empl. Prac. Dec. ¶10,235 (1971); and *Jinks v. Mays*, 4 Empl. Prac. Dec. ¶7922 (1972).

[7] 7 Empl. Prac. Dec. ¶9361 (5th Cir. 1974).

[8] *United States v. Georgia Power Co.*, 3 Empl. Prac. Dec. ¶8318 (1971).

"minimally qualified." In *Rogers v. EEOC* the complainant was awarded complete relief, in spite of the court's admission that he was not the most qualified person for director of EEOC's Philadelphia District Office. Yet Rogers was not unsuitable for the position and had met the standards of the Percy Green proof, as outlined in Chapter 3 (see page 60). The following rationale presented by the Court in this case makes the denial of compensation based on qualifications virtually impossible, especially where there is any evidence of evil intent:

> EEOC argues that even if the Court finds some evidence of discrimination plaintiff should not recover because he was not the best qualified applicant for the job. The purpose of Title VII cannot be so easily turned aside, even by an agency charged with special responsibility to enforce the statute. Race played a part in the challenged selection decision. To accept EEOC's view that if this factor is one of two mixed motives governing the selection but is less than the controlling one it should be ignored would be to allow race prejudice again to raise its ugly head. Those who suffer from its effects would again face the constant refrain of "unqualified" so often used in the past to conceal the subtle effect of race bias. Where selection is based on a subjective appraisal and race plays a part, no matter how weighed, in the total factors said to govern choice, the selection is tainted and the rejected party must be made whole.[9]

In summary then, it appears that a clear demonstration by the employer that the complainant is unable to perform the job will be necessary to prevent the reinstatement or an award of damages in lieu of reinstatement. To convincingly argue that the complainant was not as qualified as others will be much more difficult. Others in the employer's work force with similar qualifications will negate such an argument. And also, the controlling factors will be the particular circumstances of the case and those key ingredients of a defense as outlined in Chapter 4 (see pages 85 to 89).

The second defense to a reinstatement, instatement, or promotion states that it is plainly impossible because the job is presently occupied. Such a defense makes the assumption that the person who now occupies the position in question cannot be ejected to remedy another person's discrimination complaint. For all intents and purposes, this assumption is correct. Title VII does not have the broad reinstatement powers found under the National Labor Relations Act.[10] However, in such situations the courts have not stood still and taken an "okay, let's forget it" at-

---

[9] *Rogers v. EEOC*, 10 Empl. Prac. Dec. ¶10,416 (1975).

[10] Grimsley, *Front Pay—Prophylactic Relief Under Title VII of the Civil Rights Act of 1964*, 29 Vand. L. Rev. 1 (1976). Also note that reinstatement is discretionary, not mandatory. Also see *Brito v. Zia Co.*, 5 Empl. Prac. Dec. ¶8626 (10th Cir. 1973).

titude. Instead, they have sought alternatives to bumping or firing an innocent employee. The most common remedy ordered has been that the injured party be given the next available position. However, other courts, especially in cases involving large companies, have not accepted the "no vacancy" argument[11] or have ordered that the complainants be able to share the positions in question with present employees.[12]

Another remedy that is increasingly gaining acceptance as an equitable way to deal with the problem of a filled position is *front pay*. The complainant not only receives monies for wages lost in the past but continues to be compensated in the future until such time as the reinstatement *is* possible. For example, in *Rogers v. EEOC* the district court not only ordered that Rogers be given back pay but also stated the following:

> The annual salary rate of George T. Rogers provided for in this paragraph shall continue until the next district directorship in the Philadelphia Region is filled or Mr. Rogers is offered and accepts a position with equal or better pay.[13]

Similarly, in *Cross v. Board of Education, Dollarway, Arkansas School District* the court ordered the employer to promote the complainant

> . . . to the position of head high school football coach and athletic director of the Dollarway School District or to pay him a salary equal to that paid to any other person employed as head high school football coach and athletic director of the District.[14]

In such court-imposed situations, employers will obviously be motivated to solve the reinstatement problems themselves rather than needlessly pay the complainant. For these reasons then, it can generally be stated that even if the job in question is no longer available, the employer may be forced to employ the complainant or be held liable for the complainant's future loss of earnings. And while the likelihood of this occurring cannot now be viewed as probable, it is certainly a possibility worth noting.

BACK PAY

By far the most common form of monetary compensation to complainants is back pay. It is often the most important objective of a complaint and represents the major way in which an employer's monetary liability

---

[11] See *Gamble v. Birmingham Southern Railroad Co.*, 9 Empl. Prac. Dec. ¶10,223 (1975).
[12] See *Wade v. Miss. Cooperative Extension Service*, 7 Empl. Prac. Dec. ¶9186 (1974).
[13] 10 Empl. Prac. Dec. ¶10,416 (1975).
[14] 10 Empl. Prac. Dec. ¶10,469 (1975).

is determined. Knowing what back pay is, how it is computed, and the ways in which it may be lessened are therefore an essential part of dealing with discrimination.

Recent back pay settlements in class action cases have been big news. In *United States v. Allegheny-Ludlum Industries, Inc.*, the settlement established "a back pay fund of $30,940,000, to be paid to minority and female employees injured by the unlawful practices alleged in the complaint."[15] There have been many other settlements over the million-dollar mark. And as stated earlier in *Albemarle v. Moody*, the ability of unnamed class members to obtain back pay awards was affirmed by the Supreme Court. The concern here, however, will be with individual complaints, which far outnumber class actions. Although in class action cases the principles of back pay are more difficult to apply, they are nevertheless the same.

If it is found that an employer has practiced unlawful employment discrimination, is an award of back pay mandatory? The courts have not given a "yes" answer to this question, but the *Albemarle* decision and the legislative history of Title VII make back pay awards almost a certainty. Section 706(g) of Title VII was modeled after the back pay provisions of the National Labor Relations Act, which has been affirmed by several U.S. Supreme Court decisions. It was stated in *Albemarle* that although the courts have the discretion to award back pay, "such discretionary choices are not left to a court's 'inclination, but its judgment; and its judgment is to be guided by sound legal principles.' " And the court added:

> It follows that, given a finding of unlawful discrimination, backpay should be denied only for reasons which, if applied generally, would not frustrate the central statutory purposes of eradicating discrimination throughout the economy and making persons whole for injuries suffered through past discrimination.[16]

Computing Back Pay

Back pay restores to the complainant the amount of wages he or she would have earned but for the discrimination. In determining back pay, one must first know the beginning and end of the back pay period and the standards used to approximate the wages that would have been earned.

Start of the Back Pay Period. In failure-to-hire cases, the back pay period would start on the date the complainant would have begun em-

---

[15] 10 Empl. Prac. Dec. ¶10,368 (1975).
[16] 9 Empl. Prac. Dec. ¶10,230 (1975).

ployment. In promotion cases, the date would be whenever the promotion would have become effective. In cases of unlawful discharge, the start of back pay would obviously be the day after termination.

However, in many cases the act of discrimination is seen as continuing over a period of time. This is particularly true in situations where certain practices, such as departmental seniority, have had the effect of discrimination for several years in preventing the promotions of minorities and women. Another example would be a person who has been unlawfully paid less than others for doing the same work over a long period of time. Under Title VII, the Equal Pay Act, and the Age Discrimination in Employment Act, back pay awards in cases of continuing discrimination are limited to two years prior to the filing of a charge with the federal agency. The Equal Pay and Age acts also allow for a three-year limitation in cases of willful violations.

Complaints which are filed under other laws will be subject to their particular limitations. But in the Civil Rights Act of 1866,[17] which has been used in several recent law suits, there is no such limitation provision; therefore, the appropriate *state* statute of limitations would ordinarily be referred to by the courts.[18] In *Waters v. Wisconsin Steel Works* this resulted in a five-year limitation on back pay.[19] State fair employment laws which do not contain provisions limiting the recovery of back pay will probably be subject to similar statutes of limitations.

End of the Back Pay Period. The back pay period ends when the unlawful employment practice is remedied, such as when the complainant is reinstated, instated, or promoted; salaries are adjusted; benefits are restored; etc. Some courts have ended the back pay period at the date of their judgment, despite the time between the decision and its effective date.

But what if a government agency takes a long time in investigating and processing a complaint, resulting in delays of one, two, three years or more? Considering the backlog of charges with the EEOC and state civil rights commissions, such delays are highly likely. They can stretch the back pay period to a point where the potential monetary liability of a case is great indeed and far beyond what the employer thought it would be. This is especially true in times of high unemployment when persons formerly discharged or denied a job cannot find work. (Interim earnings act to lessen the amount of awardable back pay.) Employers and their attorneys argue that because of unreasonable delays in the processing of a complaint, further action by the complainant should not be allowed,

---

[17] 42 U.S.C. §1981.

[18] *Johnson v. Railway Express Agency, Inc.*, 9 Empl. Prac. Dec. ¶10,149 U.S. 1975).

[19] 2 Empl. Prac. Dec. ¶10,206 (1970).

for it would place the employer at a distinct disadvantage. The legal term to describe such an inappropriate delay is *laches*.

Unfortunately for employers, this argument of laches on the part of government agencies will probably not succeed. In *Chromcraft Corp. v. EEOC*, it was held that an agency which had not served a complaint on the employer for more than a year after the charge was filed was not barred by laches since the EEOC is "a governmental agency acting to vindicate a public right."[20] In a footnote the Fifth Circuit Court of Appeals cited several Supreme Court decisions to support this view, as well as the following:

> The rule *nullum tempus occurrit regi*—the statute of limitation does not run against the sovereign—is explained historically as a vestige of the privileges of the English King. Its survival in this country has been attributed to the policy that the public interest should not be prejudiced by the negligence of public officers. As recently as 1940 the Supreme Court termed the exemption of the United States from the bar of statutes of limitations or from the defense of laches as a "well settled" rule of law. [*Citations omitted.*][21]

It will be important, then, to remember that the end of the back pay period may be long in coming because of the slowness of those government agencies that initially process a complaint. This is doubtlessly one of the most painful dimensions of back pay (to employers) and will have a direct bearing on when and how to settle a complaint.

Standards of Computation.   Because the general principle used to compute damages is making the complainant whole, an award of lost wages would include not only straight time pay but also overtime pay, shift differentials, raises, or promotions that would have been earned by the complainant, and even lost insurance benefits as well. Determining the correct amount may not always be so easy, particularly in cases where no set policy exists on wages and promotions or when such decisions are subjectively made. One means of computation looks at the salary and progression of the person who replaced the complainant. In other cases, one might use the rates of similarly situated employees to project what the complainant's salary might have been. The method used will of course depend on the nature of the particular case.

Difficulty in determining with certainty the amount of back pay will not be to the advantage of the employer. The courts have generally ruled that the benefit of the doubt must go to the complainant. For example, in

---

[20] 4 Empl. Prac. Dec. ¶7925 (5th Cir. 1972).
[21] Ibid.

Bowe v. Colgate-Palmolive Co. the district court awarded the complainants back pay based upon "the minimum rate of pay which they would have made had they worked during the period when they were laid off" because the rate of pay could not be determined with any "mathematical accuracy."[22] However, the Seventh Circuit Court of Appeals reversed this standard of computation and ordered that the complainants be compensated at the "highest rate of pay."[23] Similarly, in *Evans v. Sheraton Park Hotel* the court asserted that the complainant "may not be penalized because of the uncertainties of proof [of damages]."[24] And in *Meadows v. Ford Motor Co.*, the Sixth Circuit Court of Appeals reversed a lower court ruling which denied back pay due to the difficulties in its computation, stating:

> In addition to the injustice to the victims of illegal discrimination, such a policy prohibiting back pay because of the difficulty of computing it actually would encourage employers who had the inclination to disregard this act to do so with impunity, knowing that in the end the worst that could happen to them is that they might be ordered to hire women wholly prospectively.[25]

Reducing Back Pay

There are several factors which may have the effect of reducing, or even eliminating completely, the back pay award. Every employer should therefore be familiar with their application.

The two most significant deductions of back pay are found in Section 706(g) of Title VII and would apply in any case, whether state or federal: "Interim earnings or amounts earnable with reasonable diligence by the person or persons discriminated against shall operate to reduce the back pay otherwise allowable."

Interim Earnings. If a complainant's interim earnings are equal to the amount he or she would have made had there been no discrimination, the back pay liability would be zero. If they are less, then the back pay would be lessened by that amount.

It should be emphasized that interim earnings are only deducted to the extent that they replace the previous employment. Earnings from

---

[22] 1 Empl. Prac. Dec. ¶9804 (1967).
[23] 2 Empl. Prac. Dec. ¶10,090 (1969).
[24] 5 Empl. Prac. Dec. ¶8079 (1972).
[25] 9 Empl. Prac. Dec. ¶9907 (1975). Note: Under the Equal Pay Act and the Age Discrimination in Employment Act complainants may recover twice the amount of back pay in cases of willful violations. (See Appendixes 2 and 3.)

employment outside of regular working hours which could have been earned while previously employed are not deducted.[26]

Employers frequently assert that unemployment benefits which may have been collected by the complainant during the period of back pay liability should be deducted as interim earnings. The issue is not well settled; some courts have deducted such monies[27] and others have not.[28] The authority cited by the latter cases, the Supreme Court decision in *National Labor Relations Board v. Gullet Gin*, would seem to carry the most weight, especially if the issue is ever decided by the Supreme Court. The NLRB's remedial powers were the model for those of Title VII, and it has long been the policy of the NLRB not to deduct unemployment compensation from back pay awards. In *Gullett Gin* such compensation was seen as "collateral" income rather than earnings because "the payments to the employees were not made to discharge any liability or obligation of respondent, but to carry out a policy of special betterment for the benefit of the entire state." The court then stated:

> To decline to deduct state unemployment compensation benefits in computing back pay is not to make the employees more than whole, as contended by respondent. Since no consideration has been given or should be given to collateral losses in framing an order to reimburse employees for their lost earnings, manifestly no consideration need be given to collateral benefits which employees may have received.[29]

It is also noted that in some states persons who receive back pay awards may have to return the unemployment benefits to the state. If back pay awards were offset by these benefits, the complainant may still have to pay back the state because the back pay would make void the previously paid unemployment compensation. This would run counter to the "make whole" principles stated above.

Another reason not to deduct such benefits would be found in those cases where the compensation fund was at least partially financed by employee contributions. This is the case in many state plans for unemployment compensation and of course applies to other programs, such as social security. Conversely, severance pay is viewed as deductible interim earnings.[30]

---

[26] See for example, *Horton v. Lawrence County Board of Education*, 4 Empl. Prac. Dec. ¶7559 (5th Cir. 1971); *Laugesen v. Anaconda Co.*, 9 Empl. Prac. Dec. ¶9870 (6th Cir. 1975).

[27] *Bowe v. Colgate-Palmolive Co.*, 2 Empl. Prac. Dec. ¶10,090 (7th Cir. 1969); *Diaz v. Pan American World Airways, Inc.*, 5 Empl. Prac. Dec. ¶8473 (1972); *Newman v. Avco Corp.*, 8 Empl. Prac. Dec. ¶9769 (1974).

[28] *Mabin v. Lear Siegler, Inc.*, 4 Empl. Prac. Dec. ¶7768 (1971), *aff'd* 6th Cir.; 4 Empl. Prac. Dec. ¶7742 (1972); *Tidwell v. American Oil Co.*, 4 Empl. Prac. Dec. ¶7544 (1971).

[29] 340 U.S. 361 (1951).

[30] *Laugesen v. Anaconda Co.*, 9 Empl. Prac. Dec. ¶9870 (1975).

Amounts Earnable with Reasonable Diligence. The complainant who sits idly by while back pay liability accumulates without making efforts to find a job will not be entitled to an award. The complainant therefore has an obligation to mitigate, or lessen, the damages if possible. Although the burden of proving that damages could have been mitigated is on the employer,[31] this burden is easily shifted by detailed questioning of the complainant.

To the extent that damages are not reasonably mitigated by the complainant, the award will be reduced. For example, a back pay award by the New York State Division of Human Rights was lessened by five months' wages because for the time period the complainant made no attempt to obtain other employment.[32] Similarly, one complainant had back pay reduced from $10,505 to $3,100 and another from $9,996 to $2,200 because they "should have and could have exercised greater diligence in seeking other employment."[33] And in another case the complainant was awarded no back pay whatsoever for lack of mitigation efforts, even though he managed to receive unemployment benefits during the time he was out of work.[34] In that case the judge noted that "it is a settled rule of damages that recovery may not be made for losses which the injured party might have prevented by reasonable efforts."

As evidenced by the above, employers should take special note of complainants' mitigation efforts, the absence of which may act to considerably reduce or even eliminate a back pay award. The criteria of "reasonableness" is, of course, subject to the discretionary powers of the courts. And although judgmental questions may be decided either way, employers should nevertheless be aware of how the standards have been applied and the relevant issues. For example, if a person refuses employment during the back pay period, there should be no award for losses from that point onward.[35] On the other hand, it has been argued that the complainant need not accept employment which would "degrade or lower his calling or usual means of support"[36] or require him (or her) to move to another location.[37] One court severely limited back

---

[31] *Hegler v. Board of Education,* 3 Empl. Prac. Dec. ¶8337 (8th Cir. 1971).

[32] *Broadway Realty v. New York State Division of Human Rights,* 9 Empl. Prac. Dec. ¶10,238 (N.Y. Sup. Ct. App. Div. 1975).

[33] *Brito v. Zia Co.,* 5 Empl. Prac. Dec. ¶8626 (10th Cir. 1973).

[34] *Bradford v. Sloan Paper Co., Inc.,* 8 Empl. Prac. Dec. ¶9744 (1974).

[35] See for example, *Williams v. Albemarle City Board of Education,* 6 Empl. Prac. Dec. ¶8870 (1973); *Horton v. Lawrence County Board of Education,* 4 Empl. Prac. Dec. ¶7590 (1970).

[36] Davidson, *"Back Pay" Awards Under Title VII of the Civil Rights Act of 1964,* 26 Rutgers, citing 11 *Williston Contracts* 1359 (3d ed. 1968), from *Canning v. Star Publishing Co.,* 130 F. Supp. 697, 700 (D. Del. 1955).

[37] Davidson, *supra,* noting *Hegler v. Board of Education,* 3 Empl. Prac. Dec. ¶8337 (1971).

pay when the complainant quit interim employment;[38] however, another court did not view the voluntary termination of seven interim jobs as unreasonable.[39] In this case the complainant continued to search for permanent work and was justified, according to the court, in leaving the interim jobs because they were unsuitable. Of course, if a complainant is fired for cause during the interim employment rather than being laid off due to a reduction in the work force, the back pay liability should end at that point.

Another factor affecting "amounts earnable with reasonable diligence" is the availability of the complainant for work during the period of unemployment. Decisions pursuant to the National Labor Relations Act have held that unavailability due to school, jail, or military service will cause a deduction from a back pay award for that period.[40] Illness would also cause a deduction from a back pay award unless perhaps such unavailability would have been compensated by the respondent employer or was caused by an injury during interim employment.[41]

Union Liability. Unions, as well as employers, may be required to share the liability of a back pay award to the extent that unions are responsible for the unlawful employment practices.[42] The question then arises, "Can an employer file a complaint against a union for its prohibiting the employer from complying with antidiscrimination laws and thereby force the union to share the back pay liability?" The answer is "no" if such actions are to be filed pursuant to a civil rights law. Such laws are for employees and not employers.

In *Brennan v. Emerald Renovators, Inc.*, the District Court for the Southern District of New York specified the alternative of an employer who felt inhibited by a recalcitrant labor union:

> Section 8(b)(3) of the National Labor Relations Act, 29 U.S.C. 158(b)(3), makes it unfair labor practice for a labor organization or its agents to refuse to bargain collectively with an employer. Section 8(d) of the NLRA, 29 U.S.C. 158(d), requires the parties to collective bargaining to meet and confer in good faith. Either party's insistence upon the inclusion of illegal contract provisions within the collective bargaining agreement amounts to a refusal to bargain collectively in good faith within the meaning of Sections 8(b)(3) and (d).[43]

---

[38] *McLaughlin v. Mercury Freight Lines, Inc.*, 5 Empl. Prac. Dec. ¶8560 (1972).

[39] *Lowry v. Whitaker Cable Corp.*, 5 Empl. Prac. Dec. ¶8440 (1972).

[40] Davidson, *supra*, p. 763.

[41] Ibid.

[42] In *Guerra v. Manchester Terminal Corp.*, 8 Empl. Prac. Dec. ¶9584 (5th Cir. 1974), the union was held partially liable for back pay because of its insistence on unlawful contractual provisions.

[43] 9 Empl. Prac. Dec. ¶10,178 (1975).

The other alternative to the above filing of an unfair labor practice would be a request by the employer to include the union as a codefendant. This strategy might meet with some success, since it may make the complainant's or government's actions more effective and seems to be within their best interests.

Qualifications.   Back pay awards may be reduced completely if it can be shown that without the unlawful discrimination, the complainant would not have been hired, fired, or promoted anyway. This argument was covered above in reference to reinstatement (see page 111) and applies here as well.

Intent.   As outlined above (see page 109), the good intentions of the employer or lack of evil intentions will not weigh heavily, if at all, in preventing a back pay award. The main exception has been where the employer had relied on a state law which was violative of Title VII.

Laches.   Although government delay in taking an employer to court has not been found to reduce back pay liability, unreasonable delay by a complainant may be subject to the doctrine of laches.

The doctrine of laches is to be distinguished from a statute of limitations. The latter refers to a certain time period within which the complainant must file a complaint, the period commencing with the act of discrimination. Should the act be continuing, so would the period for filing. The doctrine of laches, on the other hand, is meant to protect respondents or, as applied here, employers. It asserts that the delay of the complainant in filing a court action is unexcusable and unfair to the respondent. In such cases it is said that the complainant "sat on his rights." And laches has been used successfully as a defense to back pay in employment discrimination cases.[44]

AWARDS FOR PAIN AND HUMILIATION, AND PUNITIVE DAMAGES

Some courts have made monetary awards to complainants to compensate their suffering pain and humiliation or as punitive damages punishing the employers for highly unreasonable behavior. However, the vast majority of awards have been only for actual monetary losses.

In *Humphrey v. Southwestern Portland Cement Co.*, a Title VII case, the district court concluded that "the purposes of the Act will best be served

---

[44] *Stallworth v. Monsanto Co.*, 9 Empl. Prac. Dec. ¶10,045 (1975); *Franks v. Bowman Transportation Co.*, 7 Empl. Prac. Dec. ¶9401 (5th Cir. 1974); *Guerra v. Manchester Terminal Corp.*, 8 Empl. Prac. Dec. ¶9584 (5th Cir. 1974); *United States v. Georgia Power Co.*, 5 Empl. Prac. Dec. ¶8460 (5th Cir. 1973).

if all of the injuries which are caused by discrimination are entitled to recognition."[45] It therefore awarded the complainant $2,500 for losing "a chance to learn and gain experience" and $1,200 for suffering "emotional distress." In *Evans v. Sheraton Park Hotel* the district court awarded the complainant $500 for the harrassment she received after filing a complaint, also pursuant to Title VII.[46] And in *Rogers v. Exxon Research & Engineering Co.*, a case filed under the Age Discrimination in Employment Act, a jury awarded the complainant's estate $750,000, later reduced by the court to $200,000, as compensatory damages for pain and suffering.[47] In addition, some state agencies have been empowered by their state courts to award monies to complainants for these types of remedies.

However, in *EEOC v. Detroit Edison Co.*, the Sixth Circuit Court of Appeals reversed a lower court ruling that had awarded $4 million to the complainants for punitive damages. The court rejected the notion that such damages were awardable under Title VII or under the Civil Rights Act of 1866 in employment cases.[48] Because the *Detroit Edison* decision appears to be the controlling authority at this time, it is highly unlikely that such awards will be made under Title VII in the future, particularly in class action complaints. The possibility of such awards being made in individual complaints is also slim, although the situation may be entirely different under state laws.

ATTORNEY'S FEES

A potentially very costly loss to the employer is the payment of the complainant's attorney's fees. Section 706(k) of Title VII provides for the awarding of reasonable attorney's fees to the prevailing party,[49] and such awards have been made pursuant to the Civil Rights Act of 1866 also.[50]

The imposition of having to pay for the complainant's attorney's fees is not given much attention and may be called a "sleeper" for that

---

[45] Empl. Prac. Dec. ¶8501 (1973).

[46] 5 Empl. Prac. Dec. ¶8079 (1972).

[47] 10 Empl. Prac. Dec. ¶10,494 (1975).

[48] 9 Empl. Prac. Dec. ¶9997 (1975).

[49] "In any action or proceeding under this title the court, in its discretion, may allow the prevailing party, other than the Commission or the United States, a reasonable attorney's fee as part of the costs, and the Commission and the United States shall be liable for costs the same as a private person." The reason for awarding attorney's fees under Title VII is to encourage attorneys to enforce Congress' expressed policy against discrimination. See *Newman v. Piggie Park Enterprises*, 2 Empl. Prac. Dec. ¶9834 (1968).

[50] *Fowler v. Schwarzwalder*, 7 Empl. Prac. Dec. ¶9427 (8th Cir. 1974); *Chance v. Board of Examiners*, 11 Empl. Prac. Dec. ¶10,631 (1975).

reason. Yet consideration must be given to everything that an employer stands to lose by a prolonged court fight, and attorney's fees are certainly a big factor. For example, in *United States v. United States Steel Corp.* the respondent employer and union not only had to pay over $200,000 in back pay but also were liable for $102,500 due the six attorneys who handled the case for the complainants.[51]

Naturally, such awards are apart from what the employer will have to pay for his or her own legal representation.

ALTERATION OF EMPLOYMENT POLICIES

In addition to the compensation of complainants for monetary loss, an employer may be forced to correct or eliminate some of its employment practices which are deemed to be unlawful. The range of remedial relief ordered by the courts is quite extensive. Sometimes it is viewed as "reverse discrimination."

Is it correct to label these alterations of policies and practices as something the employer stands to lose? Perhaps the loss cannot be measured in dollars and cents, yet it can certainly be gauged in terms of authority. No employer likes to be told how to operate the business, or have its personnel practices monitored by a government agency. Indeed, many court-imposed remedies are carried out over a period of years and often require progress reports and compliance checks.

Section 703(j) of Title VII states that nothing in the law requires an employer to "grant preferential treatment to any individual or to any groups" in comparison with their presence in the local population or work force. However, courts have continually affirmed the right to "order such affirmative action as may be appropriate" [Section 706(g)], including preferential treatment for minorities and women, as a *remedy* for past discrimination. Many people seem to think that "reverse discrimination" is a heated legal issue across the nation. But it seems to have been uniformly decided by the courts that employers may be required to restructure their employment practices and take several steps to assure that future discrimination will not occur. Similarly, many federal contractors are required to develop and carry out affirmative action programs in order to do business with the government.

Recruitment of Minorities and Women

Employers whose recruitment practices have resulted in the general exclusion of minorities and women will be required to actively seek out

---

[51] 6 Empl. Prac. Dec. ¶8790 (1973). For a comprehensive examination of the relevant factors considered by the courts in computing reasonable attorney's fees, see *Johnson v. Georgia Highway Express, Inc.*, 7 Empl. Prac. Dec. ¶9079 (1974).

minority and women applicants. The following excerpt from a district court's order is exemplary:

> In order to insure that the Company's policy of nondiscriminatory hiring is communicated to minority groups, the Company shall establish contacts with high schools, technical and vocational schools and organizations which specialize in minority employment in the Detroit area . . . . In addition, whenever the number of black applicants among all applicants being considered for employment is less than 50%, the Company shall advertise opportunities in mass media which are directed primarily to the black community.[52]

The employer would normally be required to develop an affirmative action file, based on the gathering of applicants from special schools and referral organizations, which would be given first consideration as job vacancies occurred.

Numerical Goals and Quotas

Just as statistics have been used as a standard by which discrimination may be proved, they have also been used to determine the specific objectives and requirements of a class action remedial order. Although for the most part these remedial orders have been against public employers and labor unions, the following examples are illustrative of the goals and quotas which have been imposed on private employers.

In *United States v. Masonry Contractors Association of Memphis, Inc.,* the Sixth Circuit Court of Appeals upheld a lower court ruling that the association "employ sufficient black bricklayers, permitmen and/or apprentices so that at least 5% of the total bricklayer manhours worked would be worked by black workers."[53]

In a case dealing with promotions, *United States v. N.L. Industries,* the court first considered giving complete preference to blacks until the goal was reached; however, the court ultimately decided that a black-to-white promotion ratio of one-to-one should be utilized until the goal was reached. The ruling in this case is noteworthy because it typifies the rationale behind the imposition of numerical remedies and the disclaimer that a permanent quota system is being ordered:

> In *Carter v. Gallagher* this court, sitting *en banc,* extensively discussed appropriate remedies for discriminatory practices. We stated that, although we acknowledge the legitimacy of erasing the effects of past racially discriminatory practices, an absolute preference for qualified

---

[52] *Stamps v. Detroit Edison Co.,* 6 Empl. Prac. Dec. ¶8890 (1973).
[53] 8 Empl. Prac. Dec. ¶9445 (1974).

minority persons would operate as an infringement on those nonminority group persons who are equally or better qualified for the position in question. We concluded that to accommodate these conflicting considerations, a reasonable hiring ratio between minority and nonminority persons, rather than an absolute hiring preference, would more appropriately assure minority persons fair representation in a particular position and presently eliminate the effects of past discriminatory practice. . . . However, in determining an appropriate minority-nonminority hiring ratio, we think that the number of qualified blacks available is an important factor and the evidence indicates that a substantial number of blacks already working in the plant possess the necessary qualifications for promotion to supervisory positions. Thus, we conclude that a one-black-to-one-white ratio is appropriate here until 15 blacks have been promoted to front line foreman positions. We do not think that 15 black foremen out of 100 is an unreasonable initial goal in light of the fact that blacks represent approximately 25 percent of the Company's production workers. As we stated in *Carter*, this procedure does not constitute a quota system, because upon complete implementation of this order, all future promotions will be on a nondiscriminatory basis and the racial composition of a job classification may contain a percentage of blacks which may be more or less than the percentage of blacks in the other areas of the plant or in the community at large.[54]

Similarly, in *EEOC v. Detroit Edison Co.* the court modified an order for preferential hiring "to make its provision subject to the availability of qualified applicants and provide a time or maximum percentage at which this obligation ceases."[55]

Undoubtedly, numerical goals and quotas will continue to be used as a remedy against private employers. However, it should be reiterated that such orders are more commonly found in cases relating to the public sector, such as police and fire departments. And while much attention has been given to them, along with charges of "reverse discrimination," the widespread implementation of numerical goals as part of the affirmative action responsibilities of federal contractors has made goals and quotas less newsworthy. At any rate, numerical goals are but one form of remedy in class action complaints. The emphasis at present seems to be shifting more toward demands for class back pay awards rather than affirmative action.

Changes in Seniority Provisions

Seniority provisions which have the effect of discrimination may obviously be eliminated. The most common remedial action has been to

---

[54] 5 Empl. Prac. Dec. ¶8529 (8th Cir. 1973).
[55] 9 Empl. Prac. Dec. ¶9997 (6th Cir. 1975).

allow minorities and women to compete on the basis of company-wide rather than job or department seniority.[56] Included in such cases has been the requirement that those members of the class who transfer between departments will retain their former salary in spite of salary provisions to the contrary. In at least one case, job seniority requirements for promotions were modified so as to facilitate the eventual promotions of newly hired minorities.[57]

It is well established that tests and other job requirements which have a disparate effect on protected class members may be eliminated by court order.

Changes in Personnel Procedure

Certain personnel practices which have been found to have the effect of discrimination may be eliminated or otherwise altered. In *Rowe v. General Motors Corp.* this meant that promotions could not be denied consideration because the immediate supervisor's recommendation was lacking and that training opportunities and job qualifications had to be posted.[58] For another example, in *United States v. N.L. Industries, Inc.* the following order was issued:

(1) The Company shall promulgate in writing and publish throughout the plant reasonably objective standards for its selection of foremen.

(2) The Company shall develop a roster of plant personnel eligible for promotion to foreman.

(3) All plant personnel who deem themselves qualified shall be entitled to submit an application for this roster.

(4) The Company shall evaluate and rate candidates for the position of foreman without regard to race and upon reasonably objective standards.

(5) Foremen shall be selected without regard to their race and without regard to whether predominantly black or predominantly white crews are to be supervised . . . .

(1) The Company shall promulgate job descriptions and qualifications for clerical, secretarial, and laboratory personnel.

---

[56] See for example, *United States v. Bethlehem Steel*, 3 Empl. Prac. Dec. ¶8257 (2d Cir. 1971); *United States v. Jacksonville Terminal*, 3 Empl. Prac. Dec. ¶8324 (5th Cir. 1971).

[57] *Bridgeport Guardians v. Bridgeport Civil Service Commission*, 8 Empl. Prac. Dec. ¶9514 (2d Cir. 1974). In *Franks v. Bowman Transportation Co.*, 11 Empl. Prac. Dec. ¶10,777 (1976), the U.S. Supreme Court affirmed the awarding of retroactive seniority when required to make complainants "whole."

[58] 4 Empl. Prac. Dec. ¶7689 (5th Cir. 1972).

(2) It shall list qualifications on job orders submitted to employment agencies for these vacancies.

(3) When seeking to fill vacancies, the Company shall circularize job orders to appropriate employment services to ensure equal notice to potential black and white applicants.

(4) Job vacancies shall be filled on the basis of qualifications as evaluated under reasonably objective criteria.

(5) To ensure equal consideration of black applicants, the Company shall record the reasons for its choice in filling a vacancy and for rejecting any applicant and shall notify the referring agency of its reasons for rejection.[59]

The theme that seems to run through these remedial orders is that employers who are found to have violated the law will be forced to account objectively for what they do in the future. The assumption is that nebulous standards and weak management allow for discrimination and this can be prevented by effective, structured management practices.

TIME

Time and money are closely related, and when complaints are filed against employers, the process of investigation and possible court action will be very time-consuming.

Many state agencies have the power of subpoena and interrogatories, which are questions which must be answered under oath. Since the proofs are often circumstantial in nature, a wide variety of information is sought, including the race, sex, national origin, names, addresses, and phone numbers of persons terminated or promoted, as the case may be. In *General Motors Corp. v. Blair* a state court upheld a civil rights agency's procedures which called for a default procedure if interrogatories were not answered by the employer. Should the employer be in default, the agency has the power to hold a public hearing without the employer's participation in a defense.[60]

Regardless of the outcome of a complaint, inquiries by state and federal agencies may be quite burdensome to the normal operations of a business. When personnel conflicts are resolved by state and federal law enforcement agencies rather than management participation, employers will find themselves involved in a highly inefficient, time-consuming, and costly way of doing business.

---

[59] 5 Empl. Prac. Dec. ¶8529 (1973).
[60] 8 Empl. Prac. Dec. ¶9654 (1974).

II

HOW TO PREVENT
COMPLAINTS

6

The Strategy of Prevention

Some employers are considerably freer from the entanglements of discrimination complaints than others. Why? The conventional explanation is that some employers are simply "good" while others are "bad." But this assumption is not valid for several reasons. In the first place, it is an unrealistic view. How can one ascribe to employers the individual attributes of one person when employers are actually a group—a large number of people involved in several interrelated business functions? Further, unlawful discrimination is a complex legal principle, as illustrated by the material covered in Part I. Many managers, corporate executives, and even personnel directors are often an integral part of unlawful discrimination without any intention whatsoever. This is evidenced by the many employers who honestly believe an unlawful act has not been committed when, in fact, there is sufficient evidence to *prove* unlawfulness.

And putting the law into practice is no easy matter. After having absorbed the basics the reader might ask, "Now what do I do?" There is no simple answer. The application of the complicated set of legal concepts and proofs involved in the realities of business—production requirements, past discrimination, high unemployment, union-management conflicts—often appears perplexing. State and federal agencies are concerned with law enforcement, and they actually provide little guidance in the area of complaint prevention. It is also unfortunate that lawyers are sometimes part of this problem rather than its cure because they play an integral role in our adversary, after-the-fact legal system.

Yet complaints of discrimination *are* preventable. One obvious means

131

is to apply the lessons of Part I to one's own personnel practices to ensure that unlawful discrimination does not occur. Chapters 7, 8, and 9 try to do just that, setting forth guidelines in three key areas: hiring, firing, and terms and conditions of employment.

But there exists another way of complaint prevention, for the boundary which separates discrimination complaints from others is not always so clear. As stated earlier, "discrimination" is also a conventional term used by many to characterize the type of unfair treatment they have seemingly received. The people who file complaints do not always have legal principles in mind. Some employers seem to think that people who complain of discrimination at work are just troublemakers rather than persons seeking the vindication of a legal right. Well, I think the motivation most often falls somewhere between these two views. The people who walk into the offices of the Equal Employment Opportunity Commission to make out a charge against an employer may *know* something of the law, but more often than not they *feel* that something wrong has been done. Instead of saying, "I have been differentially treated because of my race," complainants are more likely to say, "I have been treated unfairly" or "I wasn't given a chance to explain my side of it." The thought that an alleged act may relate to one's race, sex, national origin, etc., frequently comes later, after this perception of unfairness has occurred.

The important point to be made here, and one that cannot be overemphasized, is that these complaints may be given legal credibility by government agencies empowered to enforce the law, as well as by the courts. In other words, what motivates people to file complaints with the EEOC or a state civil rights commission may have little to do with their ultimate legal outcome. Civil rights laws today cover many prohibitions and, as will be seen later, complaints are easily filed.

The strategy of prevention, then, is essentially an attitude—and one that emanates from sound management principles. Indeed, if there is one answer to the alleviation of personnel complaints, whether tied to unlawful discrimination or not, it is good management. This is especially true in situations where there is a charge of differential treatment or where bias may have been a factor in an employment decision. Employers can therefore lessen their vulnerability to complaints not only by applying the material covered in the first five chapters, but also by implementing a general "posture" that tends to eliminate people-related conflicts.

Several management principles apply directly to the prevention of complaints and deserve mention here. Of course, these management practices are central to the efficient and effective operation of any personnel organization and have wide applicability in other areas.

ASSERTING CONTROL

"No one in my company would discriminate," said the vice president of a rather large corporation. Would you make such a statement? Could you guarantee that no employee would cheat on his or her income tax or drive while "under the influence"? If assurances cannot be made that felonies will not be committed, how then can this executive state that not one employee would partake in violating a complex civil law for which the company would ultimately be responsible? Obviously, employment practices cannot be left up to any "one in my company." Instead, prevention of complaints entails control, the ability to effectively manage and direct all involved employees. Such persons may not only include personnel assistants, but also the supervisory staff and even the receptionist who answers job inquiries on the telephone.

FORMULATING POLICIES

The absence of a policy in a particular personnel area may repeatedly be a source of difficulties. Nothing starts a complaint quite as well as the lack of a rule, guide, or procedure with which to assess an employment decision. For example, think of the problems that normally arise in the area of wages. A common practice for employees is to look over another's shoulder to compare earnings. The typical statement is, "I have *more seniority* or *more education* or *more experience* or *a better work record*, but I'm getting less money; this is discrimination." A uniform employee compensation plan would end practically all such disgruntlements.

There is another major advantage to the existence of an applicable policy. Should a complaint arise in an area where no policy exists, the charge of discrimination becomes tough to defend. In Chapter 4 it was stated: "The employer who has a policy to 'hang his defense on' will at least have some foundation to an argument. The absence of a policy which relates to the particular charge makes explanation that much more difficult." Similarly, the lack of a policy weakens the employer's ability to justify what it does to its own employees, thus greatly increasing the probability of a complaint.

It is also necessary that these policies be as specific and objective as possible, as well as widely known by the work force. Policies which are vague and subjective and open to anyone's interpretation have little value. Of course, there are a certain amount of intangible standards which are not so conducive to preciseness. The term "unsatisfactory performance," for example, may incorporate many significant concepts that *are* vague and subjective. But objectivity should always be the goal in mind when setting policies. Regarding unsatisfactory performance, there may be several related guidelines against which judgments may be made such as the period of time during which unsatisfactory performance can be tolerated and criteria for measuring the quality and quantity of work performed. Setting firm policies is all part of good management, and good management is part of preventing complaints.

ENSURING UNIFORMITY IN POLICY IMPLEMENTATION

Beyond the setting of policies, the way they are implemented is crucial to the strategy of prevention. Uniformity is therefore the key. It is a principle against which the average employee measures unfairness and against which civil rights agencies and the courts often measure unlawfulness. Complaints of differential treatment are by far the most common. When one considers the myriad of potential issues, combined with the broad coverage of the law, the possibilities of this type of conflict occurring are high indeed.

Uniformity in *effect* is, of course, of relevance here, too. For example, the policy of refusing employment to anyone under 5 feet 6 inches tall, while uniform on the surface, has an obvious discriminatory impact on women (who are generally shorter than men). Unless such a policy could be justified by a strict definition of business necessity, this qualification for employment would be unlawful when used to deny a woman a job. Disparate effect is a major proof of unlawfulness, as discussed in Chapter 4. Uniformity in policy implementation is therefore essential from these two perspectives: treatment *and* effect.

SUPERVISING THE SUPERVISOR

Managing the supervisor, particularly at the lower management levels, is an important element of prevention. It may be said that personnel policies are manifested by what the boss does, for many practices are in the hands of those at the first line of supervision. People who charge discrimination might complain about the company, but they talk about their supervisor: "He harassed me and made me work harder than others." "My forelady wouldn't give me a promotion, but she did for people who weren't Spanish." "My boss told me he didn't think women belonged in sales because they'd have to travel." "My shift foreman said that if I didn't like it, I should quit." First-line supervisors can frustrate higher management's attempts to comply with the law in many ways, depending on the extent of their involvement in management decisions. In addition, many complaints relate to an incident between an employee and an immediate supervisor.

It is necessary, then, for the employer to realize where "the buck stops" in discrimination cases. As in most other matters, it stops at the top. The supervisor who inappropriately fires a worker is not liable for the back pay which may be incurred against the company. The employer pays the attorney's fees, court costs, and damages. The employer takes the time to comply with an investigation, meet with government officials, go to public hearings, etc. An incident with a supervisor may result in an incredible amount of expensive involvement with civil rights agencies and even provide the catalyst to a class action or pattern and practice investigation of the employer's entire operation.

It is understandable that employers are generally reluctant to overrule the personnel decisions of lower management. Any time the decisions of supervisors are altered or discredited by those higher up the management ladder, their authority deteriorates. This may seriously affect their other important functions such as seeing that production deadlines are met or monitoring quality control. But suffering the responsibility for the actions of lower management gives the employer the authority necessary to direct and control what they do. It is an authority that should be assumed without any hesitation whatsoever.

This means that the daily actions of supervisors should never be totally accepted without an objective review. This review must also be open-minded. The employer should not be unwilling to reverse incorrect actions or recommendations. For one thing, employees actually seem to respect employers who are willing to correct deficiencies in supervision for the sake of fairness. Corrected mistakes now may mean fewer complaints later. Further, management has an obligation to consistently train and improve supervisory personnel at all levels of management, and correcting errors is basic to improving their performance.

In order to develop control and uniformity in policy implementation, the employer must determine the various roles played by supervisory personnel in employment practices and make changes where necessary. Do they set wage rates? Do production supervisors interview applicants for employment? Does the personnel department control the ways in which employees are evaluated? Are supervisors' recommendations a prerequisite for promotion? To what extent do they make job assignments, grant overtime, and discipline workers? Are the roles played by supervisors uniform and consistent? These are questions that must be answered.

Supervisor participation in employment practices should be structured by written guidelines that spell out the role of supervisors and specifically what is expected of them. Vague procedures, as noted earlier, are bad for communication and bad for complaint prevention. For example, what criteria are used when a supervisor evaluates the performance of an employee? Management, after all, should be able to state what is expected of their employees, what they are being paid for. Standards such as "overall performance," "initiative," and "attitude" should be replaced, where possible, by criteria such as "quantity of work produced," "frequency in meeting production deadlines," and "days absent." Difficult issues of credibility appear more frequently when the standards are not specific. They also permit more latitude in the charge of differential treatment by employees, and they allow bias to interfere more often in the decision-making process of supervisors as well.

Some corporate managers locate their "policy of equal employment opportunity" by looking through drawers and shuffling papers. But an effective, workable policy is one that is part of the general obligations of those who play a role in personnel practices. This means that one of the standards used in evaluating supervisors and other such persons should be performance in the equal employment opportunity area. However, the supervisor's role can only be evaluated in conjunction with a training program in the fundamentals of unlawful discrimination and the ways in which legal concepts are applied to everyday work situations. Also, evaluation can occur only after supervisor participation is formally structured.

STRIVING FOR JOB RELATEDNESS

Nothing seems to cause as many problems as the consideration of irrelevant and unjustifiable factors when making personnel decisions. This is not to say that the absence of job relatedness in employment practices is by itself unlawful. No, it is not unlawful. Employers ostensibly have the right to impose job requirements that are in no way related to the performance of the job, or admire qualifications that are based more on fiction than fact. But the complaints that will follow are almost inevitable.

First, job requirements which have a disparate effect on certain groups and cannot be justified by business necessity are unlawful. Many examples of this type of violation were covered in Chapter 3. Second, the use of criteria which have no direct bearing on predicting job performance will not have a convincing, positive effect on present employees. Unjustifiable employment decisions bring employee discontent. Third, the use of non-job-related criteria in personnel decisions allows for the intrusion of bias into decision making.

As an example, let us look at the personal characteristic known as "accent." Everybody has one. During a recent excursion to Tennessee, everybody seemed to know that I was from New York or thereabouts—and I could easily tell who was Tennessean!

Now many of us have accents that do not prevent the routine performance of our occupations. I seriously doubt that one's accent would slow down an assembly line. Nor did it seem to prevent Henry Kissinger from becoming Secretary of State. But accent sometimes has a disturbing effect on people. Instead of looking at the job and the applicant's ability to perform that job based on certain qualifications, people make subjective, often idiosyncratic judgments of the person's general suitability. For example, in a recent case a black Haitian was denied the job of x-ray technician by a hospital because "his accent would make it difficult for him to communicate with our Spanish-speaking patients." The rejection was made in the face of the applicant's educational background and excellent four-year work record in a hospital whose patients are mostly Spanish-speaking. Based on job-related criteria, the rejection was unfounded and, in fact, unlawful, for it directly related to the applicant's national origin.

Striving for job relatedness in employment practices may be no easy task, however. Many employers have historically stayed with traditional concepts of qualifications for employment that are not well supported by facts but well founded by theories. Some interviewers, therefore, tend to evaluate factors which make many assumptions as to applicants' psychological influence on qualifications. Some of these factors are: financial background; attitude; maturity; motivation; other personality traits; outside hobbies and activities; spouse's occupation, activities, interests, and attitudes; parents' background; mental stability; socioeconomic status; etc. Clearly some of these factors do influence job performance, but the ability to make accurate predictions of success based on them is often tenuous. It is difficult, if not impossible, to establish a direct link between these so-called qualifications and job performance, and employers will find it tough to defend and justify what they do when the bases of their actions are nebulous and subjective. Once more it is stated that employers do not operate within a vacuum. This means that the need to show a clear relationship between the job and what it takes to perform the job is mandatory.

STRIVING TO ELIMINATE UNFAIRNESS

Arbitrary and unreasonable management decisions are also not unlawful, but they do cause similar problems. For example, an unfair employment action which adversely affects a protected class member may be construed as unlawful discrimination. And even when it cannot, it may be the catalyst to a complaint and all those costly elements that go along with it.

Unfair practices resulting in discrimination complaints pose real problems for the defendant employer because of that same old problem: justification. What then occurs is an attempt to apply hindsight in developing a half-decent explanation for the alleged discriminatory act. Because there is no need to show evil intent to prove a violation, employer protestations that the unfairness was not related to any of the impermissible bases of discrimination will ordinarily be viewed with great skepticism.

One of the more noteworthy unfair practices is the carrying out of an employment action without explanation. During more than five years of employment with a state civil rights agency, I have listened to the complaints of many persons who were simply given no reason, even after requesting it, for what was done to them. If you went to work one day and your boss just stated that you were no longer employed by the company, how would you feel? What would you do? How long would it be before you thought that your "civil rights" had been violated?

DEALING WITH BIAS

When people go to work, they naturally carry with them the feelings, perceptions, and values of the outside world. Although bias may not reveal itself on the surface, it affects employment practices in various ways and may well frustrate an employer's prevention efforts.

The most obvious effect is to cause acts of overt discrimination. They do occur, particularly against women. For example, "I don't think you'd be interested in a position in sales; the men would object," said the branch manager to the secretary inquiring about promotion. One New Jersey firm laid off women on the basis of seniority principles while retaining men because the men had "families to support." A fast-food chain refused to hire women as cooks because "their skin is too soft and would be burned by grease." A movie house manager told a woman, "We don't hire usherettes, just ushers." A factory's personnel officer once told me, "We just can't hire a female welder."

Evidence of overt discrimination, or "evil intent," is highly damaging in any case. Denial is not easy, particularly if statistics and other circumstantial evidence give added credibility to the charge. Allegations of statements showing bias are difficult to defend and may be especially damaging to companies that manufacture consumer products.

Quite apart from cases involving admission of bias or other direct motivational evidence, bias can work its way into employment practices if standards are differentially applied. The examples are numerous: a Hispanic worker is discharged for an absenteeism record that is no worse than similarly situated non-Hispanic coworkers'; a woman is not hired for a position, but a man, with poorer qualifications, is hired; the procedure for giving warnings and reprimands has not been applied to a discharged black as it has been to white coworkers; etc. Any person involved in an employer's personnel activities may be to blame for lack in uniformity. If the allegation related to a "protected class member" such as blacks, women, or Spanish-surnamed persons, the treatment will be viewed as unlawful.

Bias commonly enters employment decisions that are subjectively based. As detailed in Chapter 4, the circuit court ruled in *Rowe v. General Motors* that subjective methods of promotion having a disparate effect on blacks are unlawful. It is noteworthy that one key witness in that case rejected being called biased, stating he did not "hold any grudge against anybody." However, in his later testimony he admitted, "I have never had occasion to mix and mingle among colored people." The court significantly recognized that white supervisors' lack of "familial or social association" with blacks when combined with subjective criteria of performance causes a measurable disparity in the promotions of blacks as compared with whites.[1] Even when the effect may not be statistically or lawfully proved, actions based on vague and otherwise unclear standards are certainly more vulnerable to bias.

Bias itself cannot be eliminated, but steps can be taken to reduce its influence on employment practices.

First, develop objective standards and procedures for all important employment practices. The management advice given above has direct relevance here as well. As stated by the court in the *Rowe* case, there should be "safeguards in the procedure designed to avert discriminatory practices."

Second, the employer should take a generally rational, emotionless attitude toward the resolution of work-related conflicts. This means that in-house investigations of bias charges should be done without reluctance and with open-mindedness. Employers are too quick in making the *big assumption* that a bias charge is "of course" not true. This leads to the defensive attitude of explaining away the allegedly discriminatory act. The better way is to view all such complaints solely as they relate to compliance with certain objective standards and not to make some sort of moral determination. These should be the parameters of any in-house investigation.

Of course, these investigations will not always be a simple matter. Deciding issues of credibility are difficult and, admittedly, sometimes impossible. Continuous monitoring of employment decisions and actions so as to detect small examples of supervisory negligence may be needed so that bigger discriminatory acts like a discharge are prevented before they happen. The alternative is to stumble and grope for hints of who is telling the truth. The following two documents, taken from an EEOC case, illustrate this type of dilemma.

---

[1] 4 Empl. Prac. Dec. ¶7689 (1972).

MEMO FROM MANAGER TO VICE PRESIDENT OF HOME OFFICE

At the conclusion of a one-hour discussion Mrs. X was terminated with the understanding that she would receive full pay for the balance of this week and, in addition, severance pay amounting to two weeks' salary. It should be noted that Mrs. X expressed considerable regard for the company and its management, but was disappointed when the demands of her position exceeded in volume and responsibility that which she felt she was able to handle or willing to assume; therefore, the termination came about in an atmosphere of mutual agreement and understanding.

STATEMENT OF COMPLAINANT ON EEOC CHARGE FORM

I feel the manager is prejudiced. He has been pressuring me to leave for the past couple of months. He has made statements to me that indicate he does not care for minority groups. When the assistant manager tried to straighten things out, he claimed that I didn't like him and did not want me working under him. Also, I had asked for a meeting with the vice president of our home office to discuss the manner I was being treated and was told he would come out to our office to see me, but instead I was terminated before having this meeting.

The race bias charge above is in direct contradiction to her boss's version that the "termination came about in an atmosphere of mutual agreement and understanding." Should the complainant demand reinstatement as part of settling her case and the employer acquiesces, the manager's authority in future disagreements will be severely damaged. Fighting the case may mean, on the other hand, a prolonged and costly court battle. But the entire conflict could have been prevented had consistent management practices been in force, such as objective criteria in employee evaluations and review of supervisory actions. Then there would have been no need to answer those hard credibility questions.

Third, remember the need for self-realization. Bias is often deeply buried, a product of our individual backgrounds and cultures. The conventional law enforcement efforts in civil rights are aimed at altering behavior, not changing attitudes. But strong, underlying feelings about other groups surely affect behavior and should not be ignored. Getting those innermost feelings out in the open is a good idea that may eventually be beneficial. Some employers periodically practice sensitivity training, often using outside professional consultants in these areas, to educate supervisory personnel. Inasmuch as race and sex discrimination charges far outweigh all others,[2] these types of bias should receive the most consideration.

Finally, a key principle that needs to be reiterated to all those taking part in personnel activities is that applying generalizations to individuals just does not work. The concept of individual identity and worth is central to preventing discrimination complaints, as well as the big management asset of good morale. While each of us may have a race, sex, religion, national origin, and age, none of us likes to be confined by a label or classification. Everyone seeks to be recognized because of his or her own efforts. More importantly, stereotypes about human behavior are historically limiting and blatantly lacking in validity. Indeed, they were the basis for enacting antidiscrimination laws in the first place and have no place in today's employment world.

CARRYING OUT AFFIRMATIVE ACTION

An affirmative action program aims at recruiting and upgrading minority and female employees and eliminating discriminatory employment practices.

Affirmative action programs generally come in three forms. First, they may be court-ordered to remedy a finding of unlawful discrimination. Some of these remedies may be found in the previous chapter under "Alteration of Employment Policies." Second, affirmative action may be required of an employer doing business with the federal government. These programs are overseen by the Office of Federal Contract Compliance. Third, an affirmative action program may be voluntary on the part of the employer. It is this type of program which deserves our attention here.

Much can be said about the means and methods of implementing an affirmative action program. Interested employers may obtain an excellent free publication entitled *Affirmative Action and Equal Employment—A Guidebook for Employers* by writing to the Office of Voluntary Programs, Equal Employment Opportunity Commission, 1800 G Street, N.W., Washington, D.C. 20506. The following is taken from that publication and presents a good summary of the major elements of affirmative action.

AFFIRMATIVE ACTION = RESULTS

The most important measure of an Affirmative Action Program is its RESULTS.

---

[2] Ninth Ann. Rep. EEOC (CCH) 99, at p. 35 (1976).

Extensive efforts to develop procedures, analyses, data collection systems, report forms and fine written policy statements are meaningless unless the end product will be *measurable, yearly improvement in hiring, training and promotion of minorities and females in all parts of your organization*.

Just as the success of a company program to increase sales is evaluated in terms of actual increases in sales, the only realistic basis for evaluating a program to increase opportunity for minorities and females is its actual impact upon these persons.

The essence of your Affirmative Action Program should be:

· Establish strong company policy and commitment.

· Assign responsibility and authority for program to top company official.

· Analyze present work force to identify jobs, departments and units where minorities and females are underutilized.

· Set specific, measurable, attainable hiring and promotion goals, with target dates, in each area of underutilization.

· Make every manager and supervisor responsible and accountable for helping to meet these goals.

· Re-evaluate job descriptions and hiring criteria to assure that they reflect actual job needs.

· Find minorities and females who qualify or can become qualified to fill goals.

· Review and revise all employment procedures to assure that they do not have discriminatory effect and that they help attain goals.

· Focus on getting minorities and females into upward mobility and relevant training pipelines where they have not had previous access.

· Develop systems to monitor and measure progress regularly. If results are not satisfactory to meet goals, find out why, and make necessary changes.

The Office of Voluntary Programs will also provide personal assistance in the establishment of an affirmative action program.

The assets of affirmative action should be clear at this point, and much of the advice given in the following three chapters may be called affirmative action. But certainly one of the major assets of a program, and one that directly relates to the measurement of its success, is a statistical change in the amount and location of minorities and women in the employer's work force. In Chapter 3, we discussed statistics as an important element of proving unlawfulness; Chapter 4 detailed some of the ways statistical disparities may be defended when they are part of the complainant's case. Yet surely the most effective way to deal with statistics is to change them. Numbers are important not only in defending a complaint, but also in filing one. The fact that minorities or women are underrepresented in a particular job category may provide the substance necessary to make out a complaint.

The concept of affirmative action has increasingly been attacked as "reverse discrimination." Recently the Supreme Court upheld the right of whites to file race complaints pursuant to Title VII, a decision which is not contrary to the position of the EEOC.[3] Some have voiced an opinion that because of such attacks, affirmative action may soon become a thing of the past.

Until recently, court-ordered affirmative action has been one of the most consistently upheld legal principles in the federal judiciary. From a *legal* standpoint, then, it is not that controversial.

On the other hand, blatant discrimination is unlawful, and affirmative action programs which are carried out in an inappropriate manner will produce complaints and probably substantial headaches. Absolute preference for minorities and women without any consideration of other groups has not been approved by the courts. As stated by the Eighth Circuit Court of Appeals in *Carter v. Gallagher*, "We hesitate to advocate implementation of one constitutional guarantee by the outright denial of another.[4] Employers who deny applications because of one of the prohibited bases of discrimination will have violated the law. Accordingly, employers who set rigid minority hiring and promotion goals when in fact there is no indication that minorities or women are being underutilized may also be vulnerable to a successful suit of reverse discrimination.[5] This may be the case even when such goals are a result of the requirements of the Office of Federal Contract Compliance.[6]

In one startling case, an employer was found to have committed sex discrimination against a man while complying with a court-approved agreement to give certain preferences to women. District Court Judge Gerhard Gesell ruled that the complainant, Daniel McAleer, was "an innocent employee who had earned promotion but was disadvantaged when AT&T rejected his application in order to rectify its past discrimi-

---

[3] *McDonald v. Sante Fe Transportation Co.*, 12 Empl. Prac. Dec. ¶10,997 (1976), as noted in Chapter 3 under "Differential Treatment."

[4] 4 Empl. Prac. Dec. ¶7616 (1972).

[5] *Brunetti v. City of Berkeley*, 11 Empl. Prac. Dec. ¶10,804 (1976); *Weber v. Kaiser Aluminum and Chemical Corp.*, 12 Empl. Prac. Dec. ¶11,115 (1976).

[6] *Brunetti, supra; Cramer v. Virginia Commonwealth University*, 12 Empl. Prac. Dec. ¶10,968 (1976).

nation against women."[7] The district court did not decide to grant McAleer's promotion, but did indicate that damages would be awarded. Citing *Lee v. Bowman Transportation Co.*, Gesell stated that the Supreme Court "agreed that courts should attempt to protect innocent employees by placing this burden on the wrong-doing employer whenever possible."[8]

Additionally, several courts have been reluctant, or even averse, to ordering strict minority quotas and have sometimes opted instead for flexible goals to be achieved by a "good faith effort." State courts especially have taken this more conservative position when reviewing lower court remedial orders. Recently, for example, the New Jersey Supreme Court approved a reversal of a division on civil rights directive to have one qualified black promoted for each qualified white promotion in a municipal police and fire department.[9]

What ramifications do these cases have for voluntary affirmative action? Can preference be given to minority groups and women without risking reverse discrimination complaints from innocent employees or job applicants? Some recent decisions suggest that an employer must "speak out of both sides of the mouth" by giving preference to certain groups on the one hand while not affecting the rights of others. In one case, *Cramer v. Virginia Commonwealth University*, this did not work, and the district court ordered the university to cease giving special preferences to female applicants. The court noted:

> The objectives underlying the Virginia Commonwealth University Affirmative Action Plan are best typified by the "sleight-of-hand" wording of the policy statement which precedes the detailed plan. It reads: "Fully qualified minorities and women will be given equal consideration for employment as best qualified male Caucasians." This policy statement can be interpreted but one way—that minorities and women with minimum job qualification will be considered for competitive positions on an equal basis with white males even though the actual credentials of such males might surpass those of their female or minority competitors for a given position. Females are not merely to be considered "first among equals." They are to be considered and hired ahead of better qualified applicants who happen to be males.[10]

Indeed, the economic "pie" can only be sliced in a limited number of ways. Although some courts have ruled that nonprotected classes are only losing the privileged position they never should have had in the

---

[7] *McAleer v. AT&T*, 12 Empl. Prac. Dec. ¶10,994 (1976).

[8] Ibid.

[9] *Lige v. Town of Montclair*, 12 Empl. Prac. Dec. ¶11,258 (1976).

[10] 12 Empl. Prac. Dec. ¶10,968 (1976).

first place, recent complaints demonstrate that the loss is not fictional but real. At the very least, employers carrying out affirmative action may have to balance recruitment and promotion goals with the resentment and opposition of others.

The recommendations of this writer are as follows. First, affirmative action programs must be properly implemented. The task should not be oversimplified. In order to justify the remedying of past underutilization of women and minorities, it is necessary that practices and procedures be carefully examined so that goals and objectives are accurate and reasonable. Second, if goals are established, they must be flexible. They do not mandate the recruitment or hiring of unqualified persons, and this is especially so in voluntary programs. Third, goals are just one part of affirmative action. Employers would do more toward developing a preventive strategy by concentrating on those neutral job requirements and practices which have a disparate effect on minority groups and women: subjective evaluations of employees and applicants, word-of-mouth recruiting, height and weight requirements, arrest records, language requirements, etc. Many of these factors are grounds for a complaint and may lead to a finding that civil rights laws have been violated. Fourth, employers should keep in mind how the success of an affirmative action program is statistically measured. The relative absence of protected class members from a company's work force will often contribute to the filing of a complaint and also, as reviewed in Chapter 3, be an important element in proving unlawful discrimination. Therefore, changing statistics whenever possible is certainly beneficial from these perspectives.

HAVING A VIABLE GRIEVANCE PROCEDURE

In 1974 the Supreme Court ruled in *Alexander v. Gardner-Denver* that an employee has the right to file a formal complaint of unlawful discrimination and argue his or her case even if the matter has been adversely decided by union arbitration. Why then have a grievance procedure?

The foremost reason is to prevent small internal complaints from becoming long and complex civil rights or labor disputes. A good in-house procedure for resolving personnel disputes may settle a complaint before it begins. Indeed, it should not be forgotten that large class actions are often started by small and relatively innocuous individual disagreements. In spite of the *Alexander* decision, most internal complaints can be settled to the satisfaction of the complainant without any need to advance the case down the road of litigation, incurring all the costs and aggravation that go along with it.

Second, should the grievance go to formal arbitration (for those employees operating under a union contract) and the decision be in management's favor, the employer may later refer to the decision as a defense to the extent that the arbiter dealt with the issue of discrimination. The results of an arbitration hearing do carry some weight in court.

A third reason for supporting the internal resolution of employee complaints is the age-old management counsel of good communication. A complaint procedure acts as a message carrier between employee and employer. The upset employee is saying something, and it could be important. Internal complaints may assist management in identifying problem areas where policies are being inappropriately or inconsistently applied to personnel. It may also assist the employer in recognizing where and how practices should be altered or eliminated. In other cases, a workable grievance procedure acts as a safety valve, allowing the employee to let off some steam or just have someone to complain to.

Yet a grievance procedure must be *viable*. Essentially, this means that the employee should perceive the procedure as fair and workable, and regard it as an alternative to filing charges with a government agency outside of the company. Viability is therefore the key to the successful resolution of internal complaints. It requires that management be receptive, open-minded, and objective when reacting to complaints. Management should respond promptly and not let the process of resolution drag on. There should be a thorough investigation of the factual issues without accepting secondhand and hearsay evidence. All statements, facts, and documents should be examined. The inquiry should not be determined by an early predisposition on the merits of the complaint; judgments are to be saved for last, *after* the relevant questions have been answered.

The conclusion of a grievance procedure is a written, rational explanation of the employer's decision that is given to the complaining employee. If the decision indicates that management was arbitrary and unfair and did not listen in good faith to the complaint, the whole procedure will have been a waste of time. On the other hand, an impartial and honest judgment may in all probability resolve the matter, even if the decision is not in the complainant's favor.

7

Hiring

What steps can employers take to lessen the chance that refusal-to-hire complaints will occur? This chapter offers some suggestions for establishing a preventive hiring process.

THE HIRING PROCEDURE

The first step the employer should take is to ascertain whether or not there is, in fact, a hiring procedure. If not, a written set of hiring guidelines should immediately be set forth. As stated previously, the existence of a policy vacuum in any given area is definitely a liability to the employer. It seriously weakens the ability to justify and defend employment practices, as well as maintain control and uniformity in the application of company policies.

People

Who is involved in the hiring procedure? Who has the final word and ultimate responsibility on the selection of prospective employees? Who determines the hiring standards to be utilized and what the qualifications should be for each job? Who has the obligation to advertise and recruit, screen out unqualified applicants, and conduct job interviews? Who develops the tests to be used and sets the physical requirements? Who decides where new employees are to be placed? People make up the hiring procedure, so the answers to these questions must be provided and disseminated to all involved personnel.

One person should be responsible for the whole process of employee selection and that person should be able to delegate authority downward to others. This responsibility calls for centralized control and review. This means that the person who directs and decides all aspects of employee selection must be knowledgeable in the area of personnel matters in general and the area of unlawful discrimination in particular. That may seem to go without saying, but it is surprising how many employers assign the wrong person to the responsibilities of personnel activities. A lot of companies have no separate personnel department, using a plant manager or production chief to direct such vital practices as hiring and firing. In such situations, it is incumbent on that person to be fully aware of the legal ramifications of the job.

Each person involved in the hiring procedure must be informed specifically of his or her functions. A hiring procedure specifies the duties of all those involved and contains understandable guidelines on their proper roles. All must be so instructed, for many at even the lowest level of personnel management have caused complaints. One example is the receptionist who answers the phone with "I don't think they're hiring women for that job." This sort of thing happens a lot, and so the procedure should indicate how phone inquiries are to be handled. For example, they may be answered directly or by referral to another person.

This may seem to be simple advice, but many complaints originate because of the ways in which the applicant's initial contacts are managed. To illustrate, suppose a minority individual comes in and is told, "There are no job openings at present." A nonminority person comes in and is told the same thing, but is also told, "You can fill out an application if you want, and we'll consider you if something becomes available." This sort of differential treatment may very well lead to a complaint.

Elements

Any hiring procedure must contain policies and guidelines for the following areas: unlawful hiring standards, qualifications, recruitment, screening, application forms, interviews, tests, physical exams, training, placement, and the rejection of the applicant.

UNLAWFUL AND/OR TROUBLESOME HIRING STANDARDS

Several criteria by which applicants for employment are evaluated are obviously unlawful; others may possibly have the effect of unlawful discrimination under certain circumstances. Thus, employers should not use the following standards in judging prospective employees, and inquiries relating to these standards should also be avoided except where tempered by *bona fide* job-related requirements.

Race, Color. This is never a lawful hiring standard.

Religion. Religious discrimination is unlawful, the only exception being cases in which "reasonable accommodation" of an employee's religious beliefs is impossible without undue hardship to the employer's operations. Accordingly, inquiries relating to the applicant's ability to work during days which may be prohibited by certain religious observances and practices, such as during weekends, should not be used unless the employer can demonstrate the hardship that would result. Under Title VII the only other exception to the use of this standard occurs when the employer is a "religious corporation, association, educational institution, or society."

Sex. Sex may only be a requirement in those extremely rare instances in which it is a *bona fide* occupational qualification for the job in question, such as restroom attendant or actress.

National Origin, Ancestry. Except for those scarce instances in which the employer's aim is promoting the interests of a particular national group, this is an unlawful hiring standard.

Age. The Age Discrimination in Employment Act prohibits age discrimination in the 40 to 65 category. Many states prohibit discrimination based on any age whatsoever. Age may be used for compliance with state or federal child labor laws.

Marital Status. Marital status discrimination is not prohibited under Title VII, although in some states it is unlawful. However, since this standard has historically been differentially applied to women, it should not be used.

Citizenship. Using citizenship as a standard may have the effect of national origin discrimination. Its use should be avoided.

In-House Referral. Some employers may wish to give preference to those applicants recommended by present employees or friends and relatives of present employees. A nonminority work force would tend to be perpetuated by such a policy, and the policy may therefore be viewed as having the effect of unlawful discrimination.

Height and Weight Requirements. These requirements have a disproportionate effect on women and certain minority groups and may therefore be unlawful unless justified by the strict doctrine of business necessity.

Credit.   Employee selection based in whole or in part on the applicant's credit background may have the effect of discrimination against several minority groups and women, who are more subject to credit difficulties than others. Employers disposed to using credit as a hiring standard have requested credit references, done a credit check, and made inquiries on car and home ownership. Since credit is not a job-related criteria and may have obvious discriminatory implications, it should not be used in employee selection.

State Protective Laws.   Restrictions in hiring for compliance with state protective legislation, such as those laws which prohibit the employment of women on night shifts or for longer than 40 hours per week, violate Title VII.

Spouse's Background.   Implausible as it may seem, some employers are very interested in the occupational status, attitudes, and even interests of the applicant's spouse. One reason for this has been the tendency by some to deny women employment if their husbands are also working, the assumption being that it would be unfair to unemployed male breadwinners. Therefore, the use of this standard is very suggestive of sex discrimination. And because its overall value in terms of job relatedness is quite difficult to justify, there should be no inquiries made in this area.

Care of Children.   Judgments regarding the applicant's ability to care for children while employed have notably been used to deny women employment, as the Supreme Court noted in *Phillips v. Martin Marietta Corporation.*

Arrests.   This standard should not be used because of its disproportionate effect on some minority groups. Since arrest records do not indicate whether a crime has been committed, use of this standard can rarely be justified.

Convictions.   The use of conviction records may, like arrests, have a disparate impact on certain minority groups. But since conviction is a valid indication of guilt, this standard may be used in disqualifying applicants in situations where the conviction is directly related to the reliable performance of the job. For example, an employer may justifiably disqualify an applicant for a security position if he or she has been convicted of theft.

Garnishments.   In some cases, the garnishment history of employees has been used as a standard of employment selection and evaluation to the disproportionate detriment of certain minority groups.

Bonding. Because of its potential disparate effect, the requirement that employees be bonded should only be imposed when actually necessary.

English Language Requirement. There are several unskilled and operative positions in which extensive abilities in speaking and writing English are not essential to the performance of the job. Therefore, to impose such requirements when not *bona fide* may have the effect of unlawful national origin discrimination against Hispanics and other minority groups.

Dress, Appearance. The employer has a right to impose standard neatness and dress requirements on its employees, particularly in those cases where there is direct dealing with the public. The imposition of length-of-hair regulations depending on sex has not been found to be unlawful sex discrimination since hair is not an immutable (unalterable) characteristic. However, rejections based on appearance may be viewed as unlawful discrimination when they relate to the particular dress and styles distinctive of certain groups such as blacks' wearing afros and dashikis. Also, a rejection based on appearance may be viewed as a pretext for discrimination if it applies to a protected class member and is not a *bona fide* requirement.

References. The references and recommendations of the applicant's past employers may certainly be a valid indicator of future performance, or at least the employer may be justified in basing hiring decisions on such references. However, it is worth noting that the use of references has given rise to at least one complaint, the allegation being that the standard was applied differentially to blacks. The complainant in that case failed because an equal number of blacks and whites presently in the respondent's work force had been hired in spite of bad references. Had it been otherwise, the complainant might have been able to make her case.[1] Another possible liability involved in using job references occurs when the reference made is knowingly biased.

Antinepotism Rule. In one case, a woman was able to show that an employer's ban on the hiring of spouses of present employees had a disparate effect on women. The rule appeared neutral on the surface, but actually had excluded 71 women and 3 men from the respondent's work force—an obvious disproportionate impact. When such a *prima facie* case is made, the employer then has the burden of showing that the policy is justified on the grounds of business necessity and "there is no

---

[1] *EEOC v. National Academy of Sciences,* 12 Empl. Prac. Dec. ¶11,010 (1976).

equally effective alternative available with a lesser discriminatory impact."[2]

Veteran's Preference. In one case involving a constitutional issue, the absolute use of a veteran's preference in hiring was found to have an unlawful discriminatory effect on women.[3] However, this type of criterion is rarely used by nonpublic employers. And Section 712 of Title VII protects the "special rights or preference" of veterans.

Whether or not the use of the above standards for employee selection are patently unlawful or may be unlawful when applied to a protected class, it makes good sense to generally avoid their use during the hiring process. Even when, in fact, these standards are not used in an unlawful manner, inquiries relating to their use may also suggest unlawful discrimination and provide the basis for a complaint. Their liabilities seem to far outweigh their assets. Their value in predicting job performance is dubious at best, and there are far better qualification standards available.

THE ISSUE OF QUALIFICATIONS

Naturally, the biggest issue that arises in refusal-to-hire complaints is qualifications. The often cited excerpt from the Supreme Court's decision in *McDonnell Douglas Corp. v. Green* deserves repeating here:

> The complainant in a Title VII trial must carry the initial burden under the statute of establishing a prima facie case of racial discrimination. This may be done by showing (i) that he belongs to a racial minority, (ii) that he applied and was qualified for a job for which the employer was seeking applicants, (iii) that, despite his qualifications, he was rejected, and (iv) that, after his rejection, the position remained open and the employer continued to seek applicants from persons of complainant's qualifications.[4]

But what are "qualifications," and can one applicant be "more qualified" than another?

The primary concern for the employer should be an accurate determination of what it takes to perform the job in question satisfactorily. The

---

[2] *Yuhas v. Libby-Owens-Ford Co.*, 12 Empl. Prac. Dec. ¶11,074 (1976).

[3] *Anthony v. Commonwealth of Massachusetts*, 12 Empl. Prac. Dec. ¶10,991 (1976).

[4] 5 Empl. Prac. Dec. ¶8607 (1973). Of course, this is not the only possible proof of discrimination. For a more detailed discussion of this case and other forms of proof, see Chapter 3.

three factors most often referred to in this regard are skill, effort, and responsibility. Deciding qualifications, therefore, implies an analysis of the various requirements of the job and an evaluation of those indicators which correctly predict the applicant's ability to perform them. Simple as it may seem, managers occasionally have a difficult time in directly connecting requirements with qualifications. Some have their own special ideas of how to make the connection: "I don't look at resumes," one vice president of a small company told me. "If the person is well recommended, I hire him." Other managers convert the hiring procedure into a mathematical equation of test scores and aptitude examinations. And of course, some wish to rely more on their own "business sense" and make heavy use of the personal interview. But once more we say that the need to justify employment actions is central to preventing and resolving complaints, thereby requiring a link between the job and the applicant's ability to perform it that is both convincing and rational.

Let us look at the relationship between requirement and qualification standards in the job of clerk typist. The requirements for the job are: ability to type, answer telephones, take dictation, and file. Qualifications for the job may be: scoring well on typing and dictation tests, satisfactory work experience, and related educational background. Qualification standards which cause problems and are difficult to justify are: proper attitude and personality as exhibited during a personal interview, scores on a general intelligence examination, spouse's occupation, marital status, family obligations, commuting distance to work, police record, pleasantness of telephone voice, and attractiveness. The qualifications on the first list more directly indicate the applicant's ability to meet the skill, effort, and responsibility requirements of the job. The second list takes the roundabout route and increases the possibility of a complaint.

The issue of qualifications is complicated by the tendency to vary the standards of employee selection in response to the availability of applicants. During times of high unemployment, employers may have the luxury of setting higher standards. Aside from obtaining better personnel, an auxiliary purpose in this would be to screen out most applicants, thus facilitating a more efficient hiring procedure.

But unreasonably high standards may not be justifiable in view of the business necessity doctrine, and may have a disproportionate, and therefore unlawful, effect on certain protected classes. Qualifications should instead be set with their original purpose in mind; to do otherwise would cause needless problems. If it is anticipated that there will be a flood of applications for just a few positions, the number that must be processed may be reduced by means of a time limitation or proper screening techniques.

Setting Priorities

The larger the amount of qualification factors examined by the employer, the greater the need to set priorities as to their relative importance. The problem that develops when priorities are formally absent from the hiring procedure is evident in the following typical case.

The job in question was that of quality control supervisor. The qualification factors examined were experience, test results, interview performance, past rate of absenteeism, and education. The rejected black applicant had six years of related experience, finished highest on the test, did satisfactorily during the interview, was absent an average of 12 times per year, and had no formal education in the field. The successful white applicant had only six months' experience, did not do as well on the test, was also satisfactory during the interview, but had six months of formal education and a much better absenteeism record, averaging a little more than three times per year. The employer's response to the rejected black applicant's discrimination complaint was that a good absenteeism record was a prerequisite for this particular job. Fine. But there is no verification of this fact in the job description or list of qualifications for the job on file with the company. On the surface the black applicant surely appears to be the most qualified.

The point here is that the complaint may have been prevented, or at least better defended, had there been a formal statement on the relative worth of the qualification factors; in this case, something was necessary to the effect that a good absenteeism record was a prerequisite which could nullify any other qualification.

The "More Qualified" Problem

Returning once more to the case of *McDonnell Douglas v. Green*, what happens if a minority or female applicant is denied a job although he or she meets the minimal qualification standards because the employer wants to find someone *better* qualified? Is it unlawful discrimination? If the "employer continued to seek applicants from persons of complainant's qualifications," it would appear that the employer's "more qualified" argument has no chance of succeeding. But even if the employer did look for "better qualified" applicants, such a defense is met with great skepticism in civil rights quarters. It is generally suggested that such reasons for denying employment are more often than not an excuse for discrimination, for this has historically been the pattern. So this argument loses its validity, particularly when the job in question is on the entry level. On the other hand, the "more qualified" position gains validity as one progresses to higher level positions. In these cases, the question of qualification is not so absolute and may legitimately be viewed as one of degree. As an example, an appellate court reversed a lower court's finding of discrimination, despite evidence of racial considerations, when it was found that the person hired possessed greater qualifications.[5]

Uniform Application

The absence of uniformity in the application of employment standards brings complaints, and violations as well. Of course, hiring standards cannot be consistently applied unless they are formulated and their relative worth is determined. The employer who utilizes a wide variety of hiring standards with no written formal policy—especially one who makes use of subjective, rather intangible standards—is more apt to be hit with a complaint. The key is control. Management loses control when policies are unclear, thus leaving the operation of personnel practices up to whatever manager happens to be involved at the time.

How is uniformity measured? To the government investigator seeking to establish whether there has been a refusal-to-hire violation, the measurement for uniformity is found by comparison with the employer's present work force. It is the first place an investigator will look; it is an area where the employer might look to see if discrimination is being practiced. For example, a woman is rejected for a sales position because she does not possess a college degree. Yet, of those presently in sales positions, only half meet this requirement, and most or all of them are men. Result: a *prima facie* case of unlawful sex discrimination. The present work force is the best index as to whether a hiring standard has been differentially applied. It is, therefore, a good place to look to establish whether hiring standards are really uniform.

Education

The modern age of civil rights court decisions began with *Griggs v. Duke Power Co.*, in which the Supreme Court found that a high school diploma requirement could be unlawful race discrimination if it disproportionately affected blacks and was not justified by "business necessity." Similarly, in several other cases educational requirements have been struck down. Obviously then, employers should closely examine their educational standards, particularly the college degree, to see if they are necessary and justifiable. In many situations the degree requirement may be replaced by some job-related college courses or, in some cases, on-the-job training. In this respect, it is noteworthy that the federal

---

[5] *Rogers v. EEOC*, 13 Empl. Prac. Dec. ¶11,549 (1976).

government's own hiring standards give substantially less credit to college degrees than other factors, particularly experience.

Work Record

The most important qualification factor is the work record of the applicant; it should receive the most attention.

A thorough examination of prior employment enables management to carry out several key inquiries: What is the nature of the applicant's experience and how does it relate to the position being sought? How well did the applicant perform during the prior employment? Did the applicant have supervisory duties? What was the absenteeism record? Why did the applicant leave the prior job, and does the explanation reveal possible weaknesses? Do the references of immediate supervisors disclose any indexes of his or her ability?

RECRUITMENT

The manner in which recruitment is carried out may also affect the likelihood of a complaint.

The obvious first step is to ensure that civil rights laws are not violated in advertising for job applicants. Title VII makes it unlawful for an employer to place an advertisement or job notice which indicates "any preference, limitation, specification, or discrimination, based on race, color, religion, sex, or national origin" except for the few instances in which religion, sex, or national origin is a BFOQ. Employers most often commit violations in advertising when indicating preferences as to sex. The EEOC guidelines on sex discrimination note:

> The placement of an advertisement in columns classified by publishers on the basis of sex, such as columns headed "Male" or "Female," will be considered an expression of a preference, limitation, specification, or discrimination based on sex.

Employers should also use neutral job categories such as "salesperson" and "foreperson" rather than ones which indicate a preference.

Similarly, advertisements which indicate a preference which would discourage or discriminate against persons in the 40 to 65 age group are unlawful under the Age Discrimination in Employment Act (see Appendix 2). Many states have enacted age discrimination laws which go beyond the 40 to 65 age group, making advertisements indicating any preference also unlawful. Indeed, some states have made it unlawful for newspapers to publish job announcements which reveal a discriminatory preference. Nevertheless, it should be emphasized that discriminatory advertising will be used as evidence against an employer should a related complaint be filed.

A second step is to see that the whole recruitment process does not have the effect of excluding minorities and women. The existence of such a discriminatory process may act as an auxiliary proof in individual failure-to-hire cases, as well as provide substance for major class actions. Perhaps the most common practice having a discriminatory effect is word-of-mouth applicant referrals. Job openings are not publicly announced, but instead are made known by present workers to their friends and relatives. The effect of such a procedure when the work force is predominantly white is obvious—minorities end up left out of the hiring process. Accordingly, in such situations it would be unlawful to give preference to a white over a black applicant mostly because he or she was recommended by a present employee.

Other discriminatory recruitment practices relate to the use of referral sources that themselves are discriminatory, such as employment agencies which for various reasons restrict or limit applicants based on one or more of the impermissible reasons. Other ways of recruiting may exclude the participation of several protected classes, for example, advertising through newspapers with low minority readership or through educational institutions basically white and/or male in their makeup.

A third step is to control the recruitment activities by a well-coordinated—and not haphazard—effort. The absence of coordination is demonstrated by the following familiar example. The newspaper advertisement says "Wanted: Experienced Secretaries and Production Supervisors," but on the same day the receptionist responds to an inquiry with "The job has been filled." It is the kind of thing that arouses a person and provides the necessary stimulus, as well as basis, to go down to the civil rights office and charge discrimination. What is more, should an investigation reveal that no one had in fact been hired up to and including the date of the inquiry (meaning the position had been vacant), the suggestion of discrimination would be great.

This is not to say that the employer under such circumstances may not have a credible defense. Perhaps the advertisement had been placed to run for a week and too many applications had been received. Perhaps the receptionist was simply misinformed or just said the wrong thing about a person who was to be offered the job in the very near future. Perhaps someone was offered the job, but turned it down after the incident. Yet, preventing complaints requires that there be more control over the recruitment process. This may mean that the recruitment period will be specific and made known to the public, or it may even mean that the first person qualified will be hired. Whatever, there should be consistency and openness in the recruitment procedures so that complaints as illustrated above will not get started.

A final note: Never deny a person the opportunity to fill out an application, even when there are no positions available. The refusal of an employer to allow a protected class member to at least have an application kept on file implies discrimination and is difficult to justify.

SCREENING

Screening is often a part of the hiring procedure. It is a method by which the number of applications is lessened, making the hiring procedure an easier one, by filtering out those who are obviously not qualified for the position.

Some employers have admittedly used screening as a way of carrying out unlawful discrimination. As an example, a woman inquiring by phone about a management position may be told that the job is no longer available, or she may be purposely discouraged from pursuing the application by being told of stringent qualification standards which are not in fact required. On the other hand, when a man calls up he is treated differently. He is asked a few pertinent questions and then, if he passes this stage, is told to apply in person. Such differential treatment is of course unlawful and is readily revealed when a male friend of the female applicant cooperates in a "test." He inquires about the job, is treated differently, and writes down what he is told to establish the evidence that will be used later on after a complaint is filed. Such underhanded screening techniques can thus be very risky. And for many it is easy to perceive that the advertisement for a job does not "jibe" with the responses given to their inquiries. The basic flaw of discriminatory screening is its rather easily detected lack of consistency.

The legitimate purpose of screening—reducing to a reasonable number the amount of candidates to be considered—should be accomplished with as much care as any other aspect of hiring. In order to screen properly, the most important task will be to establish which factors are absolutely necessary for the performance of the job. Not only must priorities be set, but also prerequisites. For example, it would be reasonable to require a minimum amount of training and experience for the position of personnel director, or a good driving record and license for truck driver. Valid, job-related, nondiscriminatory requirements are the key to good, lawful screening.

Screening done over the phone seems especially vulnerable to inconsistency and bias. Anyone handling incoming job inquiries should be given a written set of instructions on the minimal qualifications of each job and what is to be said. For example, it might be a good idea to end all such calls with a statement such as, "If you wish to fill out an application, you may do so at the personnel office between the hours of 9:30 A.M. and 4:00 P.M."

APPLICATION FORMS

The relevant application forms in a refusal-to-hire case are given great scrutiny by investigating civil rights agencies. They represent by far the most important piece of evidence in such cases and for this reason should be given substantial attention by the employer, not only with respect to the form being used, but also with regard to how the completed application form reflects the evaluation of prospective employees.

The application form should naturally take into consideration the unlawful and/or potentially unlawful hiring standards mentioned above. And they may vary in relation to the differing needs of various jobs. With this in mind, the following topics are suggested for inclusion in any application form.

- Name, address, social security number, telephone number
- Any physical factors which would prevent performance of the job in question
- Military service record
- Driver's license, if applicable
- Work experience, including dates of employment, job title, nature of duties, salary, immediate supervisor, and reason for leaving
- Education and training
- Reason(s) for interest in the position
- Reason(s) for feeling qualified for the position
- Other experience and background relating to the position
- Objections to traveling, if applicable
- Conviction record, if applicable
- Personal and employment references

Although the application form is not the only basis for selecting employees, it is one which provides easy comparisons with other applicants. For this reason, the employer should be able to justify the selection of a particular job candidate by referring to one or more of the areas covered by it. Selections based on factors not contained in the application form are less justifiable and usually more subjective, thus increasing the probability of a complaint over the reason or reasons for rejection.

INTERVIEWS

Many employers have traditionally relied on the art of interviewing to obtain the correct assessment of a job applicant. To many it is the most important activity in the selection process. The assumption made is that application forms and paper qualifications can never equal the personal interview for establishing the many intangibles, such as character, attitude, personality, and motivation, so necessary for a proper evaluation. One must see the way the applicant responds to questions, observe particular traits as evidenced by the applicant's behavior, and delve more into the applicant's background and special attributes.

But this approach can lead to some well-known problems so far as preventing discrimination complaints is concerned. Open-ended decision making allows for discrimination. Our perceptions of others are often not objective, but are affected by the values and customs of our own special subculture and environment. As has been stated in several other parts of this book, and cited by courts, whites making subjective judgments over blacks are likely to let bias interfere with their observations.

Indeed, this susceptibility to discrimination in the interview process seems to be so well understood that any indication of foul play when a protected class member is being interviewed may easily lead to needless problems. In a recent failure-to-rehire case, the rejected black applicant charged the company with discrimination in spite of the fact that the hired white applicant had many more years of job-related experience with the company and greater skills for the position. What prompted the charge was the interviewer's behavior. At one point the black applicant was warned that high absenteeism would not be tolerated; at another point she was told what the normal starting salary for the position would be. Suspicions were raised because the complainant had had an excellent absenteeism record with the company, and the interviewer knew quite well that the applicant would not be starting at the beginning salary since she had previously worked for the company. To higher management it appeared simply as an example of bad interviewing. To the complainant it sounded like discouragement, and represented unfair treatment of a black applicant.

Yet interviewing *is* a valuable hiring tool. In order to lessen the chances that a personal interview will lead to a complaint or violation, the following advice is in order.

Know the Purpose of the Interview

Interviewing does have a legitimate purpose, and one should be able to define that purpose as concretely as possible. Using the application form as a base, the interviewer may gather more meaningful information from the applicant in the following areas: likes and dislikes of past employment; specific nature of jobs held; attitude toward the job being sought; past responsibilities, including supervision; reasons for leaving past employment; detailed information on educational background, including courses taken; special qualifications not reflected on the application form; and other areas. Discussions along these lines may very well assist the employer in determining the relevance of the applicant's abilities to the requirements of a specific job. The interviewer may also be able to provide some answers to the applicant, perhaps clarifying what the job entails or supplying information on salary and benefits.

Stay Away from Intangibles As Much As Possible

Job relatedness should be the rule. Interviewers should not be concerned with such factors as appearance, manner, speech, character, bearing, and several other items which are barely relevant to the question of whether the applicant can do the job well. One should also be wary of the "gut reaction," "overall interview performance," and "general impression" type of evaluation standards. Explanations of hiring decisions based on such considerations are far from plausible. When they refer to an employment action adversely affecting a protected class member, they are seen as a pretext for unlawful discrimination, and perhaps in reality they are.

Record and Structure the Interview

The interviewer should keep a written record of what takes place. This need not be in the form of a running account. There is no need to have a court reporter present! Even some notes will do. The point is that when no record exists, the issue of what took place becomes solely one of credibility. The employer will be better off if there is something detailed and tangible to support the possible rejection of the applicant. In this regard, it is a good idea to utilize a form which lists some of those job-related factors mentioned above under "Know the Purpose of the Interview." Not only would such a form help record important details on the applicant's particular training and work experiences for reference after the interview, it would also provide a structure to the interview process. This makes for greater uniformity and lessens the chances of differential treatment.

Do Not Make Unlawful Inquiries

Questions asked during personal interviews are subject to the same legal limitations as a written application form. Accordingly, questions which may have illegal implications, such as arrest records, garnishments, care of children, etc., should not be asked. When combined with the rejection of a protected class member, such inquiries may easily cause a complaint.

Give the Interview Relative Importance

Entry- and low-level jobs will not require the same type of intensive interviewing as a highly responsible management position. Therefore, gear the importance and nature of the interview accordingly. Again, the guideline should always be what is needed to determine job suitability. In many instances there will be no need to extend the session for an arbitrary length of time. Without any useful purpose, extended interviews will dwell on subjects which are not job-related, such as family background, intellectual aptitude, etc. Again, if the applicant is rejected, this type of unnecessary discussion may become the basis of a complaint.

TESTS

The EEOC's guidelines for testing and selecting employees, which can be found in Appendix 1, have been upheld by two Supreme Court decisions, *Griggs v. Duke Power Company* and *Albemarle Paper Company v. Moody*. It seems, then, that the proper suggestion here should be to adhere to the guidelines to avoid any further difficulties in the area of testing. However, even a casual reading of these guidelines will reveal their great complexity.

So before becoming confused with the many aspects of test validation, the reader would do well to remember that validation need only be demonstrated when it is found that the test has a disproportionate effect on one or more protected groups. Such a discriminatory test then can be used only when:

(a) The test has been validated and evidences a high degree of utility as hereinafter described, and

(b) the person giving or acting upon the results of the particular test can demonstrate that alternative suitable hiring, transfer or promotion procedures are unavailable for his use.[6]

Employers found to have been administering discriminatory tests have consistently been unable to establish their validity as defined by the

---

[6] §1607.3 of Testing and Selecting Employees Guidelines.

guidelines. Indeed, this problem seems to have been in the mind of Justice Blackmun when he disagreed with the court's opinion in *Albemarle*, though he did not dissent from the decision:

> The simple truth is that pre-employment tests, like most attempts to predict the future, will never be completely accurate. We should bear in mind that pre-employment testing, so long as it is fairly related to the job skills or work characteristics desired, possesses the potential of being an effective weapon in protecting equal employment opportunity because it has a unique capacity to measure all applicants objectively on a standardized basis. I fear that a too rigid application of the EEOC Guidelines will leave the employer little choice, save an impossible expensive and complex validation study, but to engage in a subjective quota system of employment selection. This, of course, is far from the intent of Title VII.[7]

What then can the employer do to solve this dilemma? The answer depends somewhat on resources. The big corporation may wish to carry out extensive testing, with the risk of litigation and "an impossibly expensive and complex validation study" of little concern. But the smaller employer cannot be bothered. Does this mean that testing should be eliminated as a determinant in making employee selection? With regard to aptitude tests, this writer says "yes." Tests that supposedly measure general intelligence, mathematical ability, mental ability, verbal ability, personality traits, etc., should not be used. On the other hand, the employer will appear on safer ground when using tests that seem to measure qualifications which are directly job-related: a grammar test for proofreaders, stenography or typing tests for secretaries, an engineering test for engineers. However, it is warned that tests which just *seem* to be valid indicators of job performance may not be able to pass the strict requirements of validation should they be found to have a disproportionate impact on certain minority groups. It is, therefore, recommended that whenever possible testing should either (1) be replaced by considering other qualification factors such as experience and education, or (2) be given low priority as compared with other qualification areas.

PHYSICAL EXAMS

There is a quiet revolution brewing in America, and it has to do with discrimination based on physical handicap.

A common final step in the hiring process is to require the applicant

---

[7] 9 Empl. Prac. Dec. ¶10,230 (1975).

to pass a physical examination. If the company's physician decides that the applicant should not be permitted to work because of certain physical defects or the presence or history of a medical condition, disqualification will normally result. This procedure seems to be standard among many of today's employers. This concern over the physical condition of the applicant is apparently based on one or more of the following: (1) the applicant may not be physically able to perform the required job duties; (2) the applicant may become incapacitated at some time in the future and not be able to do the job; (3) the job duties themselves may cause the applicant's condition to worsen; or (4) the applicant's condition greatly enhances the possibility of his or her receiving a serious work-related injury, thus increasing the employer's insurance liability.

Because of the realization that many handicapped persons are unfairly denied employment despite their ability to do the job, more than 30 states have amended their fair employment laws to prohibit discrimination based on physical handicap. On the federal level, Section 503 of the Rehabilitation Act of 1973, enforced by the Employment Standards Administration of the Department of Labor, prohibits any employer with a federal contract or subcontract of more than $2,500 from discrimination against the handicapped and requires affirmative action for their recruitment and advancement. Section 504 prohibits employment discrimination in any program receiving federal funds. Because these laws are so recent and many cases are resolved without a court decision, very little case law exists defining the parameters of physical handicap discrimination and the circumstances under which it may be warranted.

The Office of Federal Contract Compliance Programs has issued guidelines on the Rehabilitation Act of 1973, as amended, which include the application of the definition of "handicapped individual":

> The Rehabilitation Act of 1973, as amended, defines a handicapped individual for the purposes of the program as any person who has a physical or mental impairment which substantially limits one or more of such person's major life activities, has a record of such impairment, or is regarded as having such an impairment.
>
> "Life Activities" may be considered to include communication, ambulation, selfcare, socialization, education, vocational training, employment, transportation, adapting to housing, etc. For the purpose of Section 503 of the Act, primary attention is given to those life activities that affect employability.
>
> The phrase "substantially limits" means the degree that the impairment affects employability. A handicapped individual who is likely to experience difficulty in securing, retaining, or advancing in employment would be considered substantially limited.

"has a record of such an impairment" means that an individual may be completely recovered from a previous physical or mental impairment. It is included because the attitude of employers, supervisors, and co-workers toward that previous impairment may result in an individual experiencing difficulty in securing, retaining, or advancing in employment. The mentally restored, those who have had heart attacks or cancer often experience such difficulty. Also, this part of the definition would include individuals who may have been erroneously classified and may experience discrimination based on this misclassification. This group may include persons such as those who have been misclassified as mentally retarded or mentally restored.

"is regarded as having such an impairment" refers to those individuals who are perceived as having a handicap, whether an impairment exists or not, but who, because of attitudes or for any other reason, are regarded as handicapped by employers, or supervisors who have an effect on the individual securing, retaining, or advancing in employment.

At this point in time, it is difficult to surmise just how these laws will be interpreted by the state and federal courts. Yet, because of the common legislative intent to end the practice of denying employment opportunities to the handicapped for specious and unconvincing reasons, it appears likely that the courts may apply a narrow "ability to do the job" criterion in determining whether the law has been violated. This means that some of the reasons for disqualification mentioned above, such as incapacitation in the future and added insurance liability, may not be a valid defense against a complaint. Indeed, there is much case law which already applies the doctrine of business necessity in a very strict manner when used as a defense to other bases of discrimination (see Chapter 4).

Of course, we cannot be certain of what the future will bring. Yet a preventive strategy in this area entails that each employer be aware of the applicable state and federal laws and the court decisions as they develop. This means that rejections based on medical factors should be examined closely to see if they meet the standard of job performance. In this regard, the job record of the applicant may be of great significance. Disqualification by medical authorities should *not* be accepted at face value. Doctors should be asked to supply justification for the applicant's present inability to perform the job duties. The Department of Labor estimates that there are presently 7.2 million handicapped persons in America who are able to work, and this figure probably does not include those with heart disease, diabetes, and cancer. There certainly seems to be little doubt that complaints of this type will increase substantially in the future.

I have witnessed many settlements of physical handicap complaints, and in each the employer was unable to justify the applicant's rejection. For example, a young man with an epileptic condition was denied a job delivering mail even though he had a bachelor's degree and had also been working as a laborer for a municipal road department! In two other cases, persons with sight in only one eye were denied the jobs of jeweler and cook in spite of many years' experience in those jobs. In another case, a deaf machinist was denied employment for safety reasons. The company argued that he was likely to be injured in the machine shop during emergency situations. However, investigation revealed that the shop was so noisy that few people would be able to hear the voices of others anyway—few, that is, with the exception of the job applicant, for *he* had the ability to read lips!

One issue may be the meaning of the term "physical handicap" itself. Does it include diabetes, obesity, epilepsy, heart disease, and other physical ailments? Could it possibly mean that a person denied employment because of present participation in a methadone drug treatment program would have basis to file a complaint of handicap discrimination? Of course, some state laws will be more limiting than others. In one case, the Wisconsin State Supreme Court found that asthma was a physical handicap.[8] In another case, filed under the Rhode Island Fair Employment Practices Act, a whiplash injury was not seen as a physical handicap. Although it did result in the wearing of a collar, causing pain and discomfort, it did not meet the Rhode Island requirement of being a serious injury or impairment of more than a temporary nature.[9]

Regarding the Wisconsin case, it is noteworthy that the doctor's testimony did not deter the finding of a violation. Some employers seem to think that it is impossible for administrative agencies to argue with medical determinations which had directed management's behavior involving employees. But the issue is often not only the actual medical determination, but also the nonmedical recommendations that stem from it. For example, the court noted.:

> At the hearing before Examiner Thomas W. Dale of the Department it was revealed that Goodwin's work was terminated on recommendation of its Chief Surgeon. The doctor testified his primary concern and crucial reason for recommending rejection of Goodwin as a laborer in the diesel house was the disclosed history of asthma . . . .

---

[8] *Chicago, Milwaukee, St. Paul and Pacific Railroad Company v. Wisconsin Department of Industry, Labor and Human Relations,* 7 Empl. Prac. Dec. ¶9200 (1974).

[9] *Providence Journal Company v. Mason,* 12 Empl. Prac. Dec. ¶11,080 (R.I. Sup. Ct. 1976).

On review of the record as a whole, there is no evidence that Goodwin was unable to perform the duties of his job as a common laborer efficiently. Goodwin performed without ill effects all of the tasks assigned to him in the diesel house. In fact, there was no medical testimony that, to a reasonable degree of medical certainty, the working conditions were or would be in the future hazardous to his health.[10]

The doctor's testimony—involving concern for Goodwin working in the diesel house because of a history of asthma—was not unwarranted or wrong. But it is for the employer to decide the issue of whether such "concern" can adequately support an adverse employment action such as termination. That action, in the court's view, was unwarranted.

TRAINING

The availability of training may become a hiring issue. This occurs when a protected class member is denied employment because of lack of certain skills or abilities which present employees possess but only through on-the-job training. The argument here is that the applicant is being treated differently, in that others were given training to gain the qualifications necessary for the job. Actually, this type of complaint— the differential application of standards—is quite common. It is also argued that training is given to every new employee; no new employee begins a job without a thorough period of orientation and instruction.

Conversely, orienting a new employee and providing on-the-job training are not always the same. If they were, trainability rather than qualifications would be the only relevant matter to the employer. Still, the possibility of a valid charge of differential treatment is real. It is the present work force which supplies the measure by which comparisons are made. If standards are differentially applied in this area, problems may result. In evaluating the applications of protected class members, the employer should therefore consider the applicants' ability to be trained for the job.

PLACEMENT

Placement refers to what job the successful applicant is given. Placement is a hiring issue because historically women and minorities have been assigned into lower-paying and generally segregated classifications. Such a pattern makes an employer highly liable to both individual and class action complaints.

---

[10] 7 Empl. Prac. Dec. ¶9200 (1974).

The cause of unlawful placement is nothing less than bias. It is sometimes amazing the way an undercurrent of bias can cut across the entire spectrum of employment practices, and this is notably true in the area of placement. An example of this is the typical interview scene, as once portrayed by the EEOC in a television campaign. The company official says to the young woman applicant, "Well, I see no problem. Dean's list in college, majored in business. We think you're qualified. You'll start out, of course, in the typing pool." That type of blatant discrimination would naturally not go unnoticed today, as evidenced by the fact that the EEOC no longer trys to draw complainants to their offices by television advertisements. But unlawful placement still exists, though it is perhaps more subtle than it used to be. It manifests itself in cases in which women and minorities are put in areas such as personnel and accounting rather than sales or marketing, where the chances for advancement are greater. It is seen when a man is hired as a management trainee and a woman with similar qualifications is given the job of clerk or administrative assistant.

In short, management should be aware of the ways in which bias distorts the supposedly objective perspectives of those involved in the employee selection process. Because the hiring process will never be reduced to a mathematical, purely objective equation, employers should be fully conscious of where protected classes are being placed in the work force. Examples of bias will not ordinarily be displayed by neon signs. Interviewers may make eloquent statements about male applicants' interview performances and their "great potential" to the disadvantage of women with similar backgrounds. As has been noted, accepting the existence of bias is the first step in dealing with its effects on employment practices.

THE REJECTION

"The interview went fine, and the interviewer said I seemed qualified. He said he'd get back to me, but he never did." It is the kind of story that has been repeated several times. It is the kind of thing that starts a complaint.

The advice here is simple. First, under no circumstances should anyone involved in the hiring process indicate to the applicant anything which points to whether or not he or she will be selected. This should occur only after a definite decision has been made on who is to be hired.

Second, tell the applicant when he or she will be told of the employer's decision, and then follow through with that promise. If the applicant is told that a letter will be received within two weeks, be sure the applicant receives the letter by that time.

Finally, explain the rejection to the applicant. The reasons given should not be arbitrary or overly nebulous, but as credible as possible. The ability of the employer to give the rejected applicant a decent explanation will, of course, be directly related to the lack of arbitrary and unjustifiable elements in the hiring process as a whole. A credible explanation does not originate from nowhere, but instead reflects the rationality, uniformity, and organization of the hiring process.

8

When Employees
Are Discharged

Quite naturally, complaints relating to discharge are the most common.[1] Indeed, losing one's job is the most adverse thing that can happen to a person in the employment world. A discharge for cause can have damaging and lasting consequences on one's career and life. Logically, then, such a disruption is bound to be contested by the subject employee. And no matter how definite the warning signs, no matter how rational the actions leading up to a discharge, getting fired always seems a little like death—it comes suddenly and with finality. So no matter how gently an employer may try to break the unhappy news, the "thud" which is felt is inevitable. And since the discharged employee often perceives that in-house complaining will be futile, the tendency is great to seek a remedy from an outside source. Enter the EEOC, the Department of Labor, and the state civil rights agencies.

DISCHARGE MEANS FAILURE

Regardless of the cause and who is to blame, firing an employee means failure on the part of the employer. Something definitely went wrong. It might have been in the recruitment process or in judging the employee's qualifications *vis-á-vis* the job's requirements. Or perhaps the failure is to be found in other management areas, such as training, work environment, or performance evaluations. Perhaps the employee was criticized and ignored more often than he or she was given support. Maybe the lines of authority and structure in the organization were

---

[1] Ninth Ann. Rep. EEOC (CCH) 99, at 36 (1976). For the purposes of this chapter, the topic of discharge will include layoffs as well.

disorderly and unclear. Standards may not have been communicated well, or maybe it was a lack of leadership. At any rate, the process of employee selection and ongoing management did not work as planned.

Such failures are real because the employer loses a specifiable amount of time and money: the evaluation of application forms, interviewing, advertising, training programs, and other activities are to some extent wasted. Therefore, discharging workers is not an action to be taken lightly. A high discharge rate is certainly indicative of a poorly managed company. Notwithstanding the fact that discharge is sometimes necessary, it is a sign that business's most pressing activity—paying people for doing a job—was not accomplished. So within the context of the perspective that discharging an employee for cause is a last resort for management, we address the proper means of preventing discrimination complaints in this key area.

THE PERSONNEL DEPARTMENT AND THE DISCHARGE PROCEDURE

As with hiring, the first step is to establish relevant and objective procedures to be followed regarding possible discharge. These policies may deal with reasons for discharge, how a discharge process is initiated, and by whose authority discharges become final. The key element here is one which ensures that all aspects of the discharge process are uniformly applied. Such uniformity necessitates centralized control. If many supervisors and managers throughout the company have the power to fire their subordinates at will, with only a rubber-stamp review by higher management, there will be no chance of achieving uniformity. "But how can I undercut the authority of my supervisors without things getting out of hand?" is the typical response to this advice. The answer, as mentioned elsewhere in this book, is that you are responsible for what the supervisor does and that your direction will better provide lower supervisors with the guidance and training they need in the area of personnel.

Still, in many companies it is the "boss" who wields the absolute power to fire. The personnel department simply lacks the strength to overrule. A typical result of such an arrangement is that policies and procedures are either altered or forgotten. In some organizations this special type of relationship is formalized by the procedures themselves. For example, the personnel manual may contain the following pronouncement: "The personnel department may authorize the discharge of employees apart from the procedures set forth here insofar as such discharge is recommended by the employee's immediate supervisor and is in the best interests of the company." This type of regulation legitimizes the dispersion of the power to discharge, making uniformity difficult if not impossible.

The following memo is illustrative of the problems that may be caused by a weak personnel department.

TO: File
FROM: Personnel Director
SUBJECT: Termination of X

In the early part of the week I was contacted by Mr. Vice President who indicated that he wished to have X transferred or terminated from her position as his secretary. He told me that she had experienced difficulties in handling the telephone contact work with the field staff and that her typing and stenographic skills were not up to the level necessary to accomplish her duties.

I told him that she was in the probationary period, so that if things were not working out we should take steps to remedy the situation. Mr. Vice President told me he had not discussed his feelings about her performance with her; therefore, I told him he should do this before any action could be taken by the personnel department. Later in the week Mr. Vice President talked with X and told her that he did not feel "comfortable" in their working relationship. He did mention to her some of the difficulties she had with telephone contacts; however, he did not discuss other deficiencies in her work. After this discussion he contacted me while X was sitting at his desk and asked me to meet with her to arrange a transfer or termination.

I spent over 1½ hours with X during which time she stated over and over again that she could not understand why Mr. Vice President had been displeased with her work or why he saw fit to have her transferred or terminated. I explained to her that she was still in her probationary period and that since Mr. Vice President felt she did not meet his requirements there was no recourse but for the personnel department to take action. Since there were no other positions in the company to which she could transfer, her employment was terminated. I understand that X has subsequently complained to the president about her treatment. I feel that there was no other course of action that could have been taken since I feel she would have similar types of difficulties in other secretarial positions, assuming one was available.

What role was played by the personnel department in the discharge? The answer is found in one numerical word: zero. At first there was an indication that "we should take steps to remedy the situation." But the only remedy was discharge. When the vice president first discussed the matter with X, he apparently had already made up his mind to fire her because (1) he requested the personnel department to terminate or transfer her while X was still at his desk, and (2) he did not discuss with X the various deficiencies of her work except for "telephone contacts" and his not feeling "comfortable" with her. The personnel department based all its actions on the vice president's recommendation, despite the subjective nature of his judgments and intense disagreement by the secretary. There was no review. Personnel's conclusion, "I feel she would have similar types of difficulties in other secretarial positions," therefore seems unwarranted. And secretary X was left with no adequate justification of her discharge.

This story does not end with secretary X's discharge. Being age 55, she filed a complaint with the Department of Labor under the Age Discrimination in Employment Act and also with a state agency. The state agency found reasonable cause to credit her charge of age discrimination. This finding was based on the following: (1) her 25-year work record as an executive secretary before beginning employment with the company, (2) the fact that she was replaced by a younger woman, (3) the employer's basis for termination was overly subjective and could not be substantiated, and (4) the complainant was terminated while still in the probationary period.

GOVERNMENT INTERROGATORIES: A CHECKLIST

All this seems to signify that the manner of discharge may be just as crucial as its validity in preventing a complaint. Following this, it is not surprising that the interrogatories of a government investigation dwell heavily on the conformity of a discharge to company policies. In fact, the following sample interrogatories implicitly suggest that an employer should not only have a discharge procedure, but also be able to justify its implementation. In this regard, these questions may be used as a helpful checklist to assess the soundness of an employer's discharge practices. How well would you be able to respond to such inquiries after an employee was fired?

- State the specific reason(s) why complainant was discharged.

- State the date and time of discharge.

- Explain in detail each specific act for which the complainant was discharged.

- For each act listed above state the name, address, race, national origin, sex, and phone number of the witness(es) to the act(s) and the date(s) of the act(s).

- Attach hereto any and all documentary evidence concerning complainant's discharge, including statements of all witnesses.

- What explanation did complainant give the respondent for the conduct which gave rise to the discharge?

- Respondent did not accept this explanation because?

- If the complainant in this matter was employed under a collective bargaining agreement, attach a copy of the agreement; list the name, address, and phone number of the local president or bargaining agent; and list the clauses of the contract relied upon to justify the discharge.

- Does the respondent have written rules and regulations which govern employees' duties and conduct? If yes, attach a copy of any such rules and regulations and indicate the provisions relied upon to justify the discharge.

- If no written rules and regulations are established, what are the respondent's policies with respect to the type of conduct involved in the discharge of the complainant?

- Does the respondent utilize written reprimands or warnings? If so, please specify respondent's policy with respect to them.

- Does the respondent utilize oral reprimands or warnings? If so, please state who makes such warnings and specify respondent's policy with respect to them.

- Were any warnings made to the complainant? If so, please state the date, person(s) present, and the circumstances under which such warnings were made and attach copies of any record of such warnings to this interrogatory.

- If one reason for complainant's discharge was absenteeism or tardiness, attach a copy of complainant's attendance and sick day record and specify what respondent's policy is with respect to absenteeism or tardiness.

- State the name, address, phone number, race, national origin, and sex of the person who recommended complainant's discharge. What is his job title? How long has he been in this position? How long has he been employed by respondent?

- State the name, race, national origin, sex, title, and telephone number of the company official who reviews all discharges before they become final.

- Did the person named above review this case? If no, why not? If yes, please attach a copy of the reviewer's report on this case.

These interrogatories certainly scrutinize virtually every phase of a company's actions. A policy vacuum in any area may allow for inconsistency and differential treatment.

REASONS FOR DISCHARGE

There are innumerable reasons which may justify firing an employee. Some employers foolishly try to list and incorporate all possible ones into their operating procedures. There are obvious liabilities to this. For one thing, such a policy is difficult to control simply because of its size. Also, policies which attempt to detail every contingency will not be flexible enough to deal with the daily exigencies of management.

Uniform Application

The first concern of the employer in preventing complaints may not be found in the grounds supporting discharge, but in whether standards have been uniformly applied. As stated in one case, the question is whether "the legal rule was applied to accomplish an illegal purpose."[2] Evidence of differentially applying employment standards to a protected class member will most likely result in a complaint and a violation. Yet, let it be realized that applying standards of discharge uniformly is no easy task.

One typical illustration is found in the following case. A black worker is fired for threatening his supervisor. He is alleged to have said, "Next time you bug me I'm going to slash your throat." In the opinion of management, such an intimidating statement by a subordinate could not be tolerated. However, the worker filed a race complaint with a state civil rights agency. The state requested, among other things, a list of all those discharged or reprimanded during the last year, including their race and the reason for the action. This investigation revealed that a white employee had been suspended a week without pay for engaging in a physical conflict with his boss. In fact, the supervisor had been punched by the subordinate. Now the question which arises is this: "How does threatening a supervisor compare to a physical confrontation?" In the opinion of the state agency, the actual punch was worse than the verbal threat. The result was a finding of racial discrimination, in that the black worker should not have been fired but perhaps suspended. The employer, on the other hand, argued vehemently that a death threat is surely worse than a punch. The case will be settled by litigation in the near future.

Another example of difficulties in uniformly applying a discharge standard can be found in the seemingly simple area of absenteeism. A black woman discharged for excessive absenteeism filed a race discrimination complaint against the company, charging that "white co-workers with similar or worse absenteeism records were not discharged." A state agency investigated the complaint by means of interrogatories. In reply-

---

[2] *Cooper v. Ford Motor Co.*, 5 Empl. Prac. Dec. ¶8036 (1972).

ing, the company stated that their policy on absenteeism is as follows: "Any employee with five or more unexcused absences in a three month period will be discharged." The company also provided the absenteeism records of all its employees, along with what disciplinary action, if any, had been taken against them. Thus it was revealed that both the complainant and a white employee had been absent five days during a three-month period. The black complainant had been terminated; the white employee had received only a warning. The finding of the state agency was therefore predictable: "unlawful differential treatment based on race."

The company, however, protested the finding. In a letter to the state agency, they formally made their objections:

> The finding of discrimination is not warranted. Although it may appear that a prima facie case has been established in that the black complainant was treated differently for similar offenses by a white co-worker, in actuality the differential treatment is justifiable. In the first place, the complainant was absent on four occasions, three times for one day each and once for two days. The white co-worker was absent two times, once for three days and the other for two. Her absences were therefore much less disruptive to the operation of the photo-chemical department than the complainant's. In the second place, absenteeism causes more problems for management in the complainant's section of work, billing, than the white co-worker's section, where she operates a packing machine.

Do you think this defense was successful? On the administrative level it was not, and this case too will have to be decided by a court decision. The employer simply was unable to justify the differential treatment based on a policy which had not previously existed, one that was viewed as an after-the-fact means of avoiding a violation of civil rights law. And perhaps the employer was sincere in its reasoning; perhaps it was trying to exercise sound judgment instead of an overly rigid personnel policy. Looking back, it appears the employer may have been better off had greater consideration been given to rationalizing the decision to fire before it took place. At any rate, it can readily be seen that the uniform application of reasons for discharge may be a nagging and complex problem to resolve.

For the purposes of analysis, we have separated the reasons for discharge into four areas: (1) unlawful, (2) potentially unlawful, (3) performance-related, and (4) non-performance-related.

Unlawful Reasons

Naturally, a discharge based on one of the impermissible categories is clearly unlawful.

Another important consideration is the unlawful disparate effect of discharge or layoff criteria, even when superficially applied in a neutral manner. For instance, in one company the owner was forced to reduce its staff, many of whom were long-term employees, by 20 percent. This was the first time any such reduction had been necessary, and there were no rules whatsoever regarding layoffs. The owner decided the fairest standard would be to let go first those employees who were not the major breadwinners in their families. In this way the economic hardship would be lessened. However, this had the effect of displacing a larger comparative percentage of women in the company than men, an occurrence which was seen as directly linked to the statistical fact that substantially more men than women are major breadwinners. Therefore, the application of this apparently neutral standard would have the effect of unlawful sex discrimination.

Similarly, it would be unlawful to utilize separate lines of seniority by sex in a layoff situation. This would be true regardless of whether such lines were specifically labeled as male and female.

Age complaints often stem from a "reorganization" of a work force, whereby some employees are promoted and retained and others are let go. When a greater percentage of older persons are let go, a *prima facie* case of age discrimination is generally established. The employer then has the burden of justifying the various personnel actions. On the other hand, release based upon a *bona fide* retirement program is not unlawful, so long as it is not a subterfuge for discrimination.

One area of unlawful discharge that is frequently forgotten is reprisal—discharging an employee for complaining about discrimination, filing a complaint, or assisting in an investigation by a government agency. Indeed, discharging a person who is involved in one of these activities will most likely give rise to a complaint, regardless of its merits. Consequently, in such cases employers should be particularly cautious in their actions.

Potentially Unlawful Reasons

Layoff by seniority may have the effect of unlawful discrimination if the minorities and women actually being laid off have been discriminatorily denied jobs in the past with the same employer. The logic here is that had they not been so denied, their present seniority would be greater. The last-hired first-fired rule may also be unlawful when applied by departments if minorities and women have only recently been able to transfer into those departments due to past discrimination. Yet, be sure to realize that (1) layoff by seniority is not by itself unlawful but only under certain circumstances and (2) the case law in this area is still developing. For example, laid-off workers have not been granted fictional seniority for remedial purposes when it was practically impossible for them to have been denied employment earlier since they were children at the time. In order to obtain the remedy of additional seniority and reinstatement, it has been necessary to show, at least to some extent, personal involvement in the prior discrimination.

Just as refusal to hire based on arrests, convictions, and garnishments may have an unlawful disparate effect on certain minorities, so too it may be unlawful to discharge employees on the basis of those factors. The success of a complaint will depend on the ability of the complainant to demonstrate the disparate effect on him or her because of membership in the particular group, and the employer's ability, should this be successful, in justifying the application of the standard in light of the doctrine of business necessity. At the same time, employees cannot be lawfully discharged for lying on an application form if it relates to a standard which has an unlawful effect on the applicant. This would be the case even if the company had a rule that falsification of an application form were grounds for discharge. This may also apply to an applicant who lied about her age or physical condition. If the inquiries lied about were unlawful, the discharge would be difficult to justify.

In one interesting disparate effect case, a black employee was able to demonstrate a *prima facie* violation of Title VII when he was discharged because of a degenerative bone condition which was caused by a sickle cell anemia, a disease that disproportionately affects blacks more than whites.[3]

Reasons Related to Performance

Many, if not most, firings relate to the inadequate performance of the employee in the duties of the particular job. Concomitantly, many, if not most, discharge complaints charge that job performance was equal to or better than nonminority and male employees'. How can such complaints be prevented? One way is that employers must strive for objective criteria by which to evaluate employees. This is not to say that subjective evaluations are never valid or accurate. They may be. But the point to remember is that vague standards breed complaints.

For example, Gardner-Denver Company eventually did win the case against them started by Harrell Alexander, who had charged discrimination based on race in his discharge. But winning came only after a legal battle of five years, including a Supreme Court decision. This does not seem to be an efficient way to fire employees! One court decision takes note of how the case got started:

> The primary difficulty in this dispute is that the company's procedures permitted the plaintiff's employment to be terminated upon the basis

---

[3] *Smith v. Olin Chemical Corporation*, 12 Empl. Prac. Dec. ¶11,084 (1976).

of the subjective evaluation of his performance by a single supervisor. It was Oscar McFarlin who had the sole responsibility for training Harrell Alexander . . . .

There was no company policy setting any numerical standards or other objective criteria to be applied by the foreman to evaluate a trainee's performance in the drills department. Additionally, Mr. McFarlin had no such personal standards and therefore could not communicate any guidelines to the trainees. The unfortunate result is the necessity to decide whether this white foreman was racially motivated in his treatment of this black employee.[4]

Many cases of this type originate with the discharge of probationary employees shortly before their becoming nonprobationary and therefore subject to the terms of a union contract. Under such circumstances, the company is not obligated to provide any explanation to either the employee or the labor union. Accordingly, there is often no explanation at all. The discharge that may result will often stem from the "impressions" of the worker's immediate supervisor. So if a complaint of discrimination is filed, the employer inevitably will be unable to offer an objective justification for its actions. The government then investigates such a case by looking at the comparative success of minority and nonminority trainees in making it through the probationary period. If the failure rate for minorities is much greater, a finding of unlawful discrimination would be made.

Once more we accept the notion that not all job performances will be easily evaluated along objective lines, but the employer should at least aim in that direction. In one case, employees were subjectively evaluated by their supervisors, in spite of the existence of several quantifiable aspects of their responsibilities as collection agents. One Hispanic woman had been given "poor" marks in the area of "collections made" when, in fact, her collections were much greater than her male, non-Hispanic counterparts'. This complaint could have been prevented.

Another area in which the employer may have a tough time justifying a discharge involves the long-term worker. To support the charge of discrimination, the complainant states, "I have been working for the company for over ten years and at no time was I reprimanded for poor work, and during my employment I continually received merit increases in my salary." The irritating questions so often put to the company in these cases are "How did he continually get raises?" or "After all those years, why wasn't she given more of a chance?"

We are not stating that long-term employees should never be fired. Surely there will be times when such action will be recommended.

---

[4] *Alexander v. Gardner-Denver Co.*, 8 Empl. Prac. Dec. ¶9825 (1974).

Employees may have lasted longer than usual for many reasons. Perhaps they were especially friendly with an important management person and job tenure was a form of patronage. Or perhaps past management had been somewhat incompetent and ignored poor performances. But justifying a discharge is always made difficult when the length of employment is great. In the case of older workers who have filed age complaints, justification is even more difficult.

Good preventive medicine in the area of performance-related discharges will be found in a means of evaluation that is both gradual and constructive. After all, the main purpose is not to fire but to assist the employee in improving performance. The emphasis of any form of evaluation program should therefore be positive, keeping in mind that discharges do represent a management failure and are costly. Corrective discipline should not be viewed solely as punishment, but rather as a means of communicating to employees their weaknesses and where their performance is substandard.

By "gradual" it is meant that corrective management actions progress through certain steps, as outlined in a discipline procedure. Carefully following the procedure is extremely important, for, as stated earlier, the manner of discharge may be just as important in causing a complaint as the reasons supporting it. Because such a program is normally carried out at the first level of supervision, there should be a total awareness by supervisors of their responsibilities within the program's structure.

A normal progression of disciplinary actions is as follows. First, the employee receives an oral warning from the supervisor, indicating which areas need to be rectified and stating that further action will be taken should improvement not be forthcoming. Although the supervisor should make a note concerning the warning, there is no need for a written report to be placed in the employee's personnel folder. Second, if the poor behavior continues, the supervisor should have a private conference with the employee to discuss the matter and issue a formal, written warning that future offenses will not be tolerated. The warning, which goes into the employee's personnel folder, should detail the nature of the employee's shortcomings and indicate specific guidelines on future performance. It should also mention the date and nature of the first oral warning. A third step in a discipline procedure, if the poor performance continues, may be to suspend the employee without pay for a period of time such as three days. The notice of suspension should again be detailed, explaining the action with reference to the past warnings. The warning here should be final, for if the employee's behavior continues, the fourth step will result in discharge.

Of course, a procedure only sets the framework for the evaluation and management of employees and the taking of corrective measures. It is people who will make the procedure work properly and effectively, or not at all. Supervisors must be fair and consistent in their judgments, not let violations of policy linger, and take into consideration the manner in which others have been treated for similar violations. Management capability varies in degree from supervisor to supervisor, and periodic training may be needed for those who appear to be unsatisfactory.

Reasons Not Related to Performance

Several possible reasons for discharge may not directly relate to job performance, that is, the quality and quantity of work produced. This does not mean they have no relevance. A worker may get the job done, but behave frequently enough in a disruptive manner to warrant being fired. But because the job may be getting done, discharges relating to these areas will pose special problems of justification. And when personnel actions cannot be well explained, complaints and possibly violations are more likely to occur.

One area for management to be cautious of in evaluating subordinates may be labeled "attitude." This and other related factors are sometimes found in the employee evaluation form under "personal appraisal," as measured by such criteria as attitude toward job, attitude toward coworkers, attitude toward supervisors, eagerness to learn, willingness to work overtime, appearance, willingness to work, cooperation, temperament, judgment and common sense, dependability, etc. These factors are relevant, but how can they be documented? Rating them along a scale from excellent to very poor may not be very convincing to the employee or to a civil rights investigator. Subjective standards have traditionally been used as a pretext for discrimination. As the Fifth Circuit Court of Appeals cited the district court decision in *Martin v. Thompson Tractor Co.*:

> The question that really becomes a very tough one for the court stems from the fact that the words "attitude," "good attitude," or "bad attitude," or "lack of cooperation" can easily be the label to cover and conceal racially motivated prejudices and discriminations, in fact, under some other title that looks acceptable. So the court has to, with great scrutiny, look at what was meant by, and what really undergirded this comment about lack of cooperation and attitude.[5]

Another type of discharge often resulting in a complaint may come under the label of the "the incident" or "insubordination." A subordi-

---

[5] 6 Empl. Prac. Dec. ¶8864 (1973).

nate is fired for refusing the order of a superior or, in some cases, being openly hostile to a management person. In other cases the employee gets highly upset and just walks out. The offense is so serious that a progressive form of discipline is bypassed, and the employee is immediately fired. Management has no other choice. The firing appears to be completely justifiable.

But such "incidents" will often lead to a complaint, the allegation being that race or another prohibited reason was the *causal factor* in the discharge. In other words, the employee was forced to be insubordinate by the unfair treatment of an immediate supervisor. Far from being vindicated by the undisputed act of the employee, the employer is seen as contributing to the incident by its own prodding. This, in turn, causes the investigation to be viewed from a completely different perspective. The conclusion may be "the complainant was forced to do objectionable work outside of her job description and different from the treatment given other employees." Therefore, it is advisable that when such incidents occur, management take a further look into the source of the dispute. In addition, every attempt should be made not to bypass the discharge procedure.

A similar problem of justification is found when an employee is fired due to a "personality clash" with an immediate supervisor or with coworkers. Investigative agencies take quite a skeptical glance at such explanations. If the complainant is a protected class member and those being "clashed" with are not, the suggestion of an action based on bias is very strong. If the complainant's actual job performance is satisfactory as compared with coworkers', the discharge is that much more difficult to explain.

DOCUMENTATION

It seems evident at this point that documenting the reasons for discharge is essential. One reason is that documentation may convincingly demonstrate to the employee that credible evidence exists to support the discharge. This may be enough to prevent the filing of a complaint. More importantly, however, documentation will be needed by the company in defending a complaint of discrimination. The employer does not want the determinations of government agencies to depend on issues of credibility. There is a strong tendency by the agencies to go with the complainant in such circumstances, particularly if some other evidence such as statistics point in that direction. Challenges may of course be made to such findings, but they are costly.

Documentation may come in the form of written warnings pursuant to a discipline procedure, memos written by managers, statements or complaints from unsatisfied customers, production records, quality control records, incident reports, absenteeism records, etc. Yet, let it never be forgotten that such documentation must be credible. For this reason documentation should not come in the form of written reports done after or shortly before the discharge has taken place. They will appear as phony. Accordingly, evaluations and memos that were never seen by the discharged person or that are couched in terms such as "this will confirm our discussion of August 8, at which time you admitted . . ." will also hold little evidentiary weight. In addition, documentation should not be overdone. The extraordinary weight of the complainant's personnel folder will be counterbalanced by the emptiness of others. Filling the files with an inordinate amount of paper may itself be viewed as discrimination.

Of course, the value of documentation is in direct proportion to its being honest and factual. It would be difficult, for example, to argue with production records. On the other hand, general statements that "the work of Mr. X was unsatisfactory" will be contested more easily, as will evidence to support the poor performance of the complainant that is a product of inconsistently applied standards. The utility of documentation is therefore limited by the degree to which it accurately reflects the reality of the complainant's past performance.

In some cases documentation may be a little complex. Employers who release workers due to a cutback in personnel or a reorganization may have to do more than simply give the reason. How many persons were let go? Were any new employees hired? Was there a profit loss to justify the reductions in work force? Why were some persons chosen over others? Documentation in these types of cases will necessitate supplying detailed answers to such inquiries, or the reasons for discharge may be viewed once more as a "smokescreen."

Now there are some employers who may be a little annoyed at what has been stated here. Perhaps the reader will make reference to the "burden of proof" as covered in Chapter 3. I can hear it now: "Making a complaint does not make a case. The complainant must have evidence that a *prima facie* case of discrimination exists before the burden shifts to the employer." That is true. But for practical purposes, the initial burden is to prevent the *prima facie* case from being established. This is the "first line of defense" as outlined in Chapter 4. The employer must be able to appropriately answer the charges with reliable evidence if the complaint is to be dismissed at an early stage. The importance of this will be elucidated in Part III.

THE FINAL INTERVIEW

Another part of the discharge procedure is the final interview. It may be the employer's last attempt to prevent a complaint.

The success of the employer in adequately explaining to the employee the reasons for discharge will naturally be related to the way the rest of the discharge procedure has been carried out. The final explanation should not be a surprise. The areas in which the employee has neglected his or her duties should have been communicated on several occasions, with the aim of possibly remedying the deficiencies. If the reason for discharge is new to the employee, it will probably not be convincing no matter what it is because the employee was not given a chance to correct the mistakes or provide management with an explanation.

Assuming the proper procedure has been followed and there are no surprises, the employer should review the reasons for discharge with the individual. If the termination can be justified, the talk should be a candid one. Try to be pleasant, but at the same time do not pull any punches.

Some employers try to be overly nice at this point, glossing over the real reasons so as not to deflate the pride of the employee. For example, the employer might say: "Look, Gail, I'm sorry but, well, you know, I mean you just didn't fit in well with the staff. There's no need to go into it at this point." The person who hears this sort of gibberish really becomes perplexed. Now she is unable to understand the previous criticisms of her work: "Why was I fired? Maybe there's another answer. What was that he said about 'getting along with the staff'?" The result of this interview might be a complaint such as "I was told that I was fired for not getting along well with the staff, which is entirely male. I charge that I was discharged unlawfully because of my sex, in that my work was satisfactory but the male staff objected to the presence of a woman in the department." Such complaints can be prevented if the employer is honest during the exit interview.

Admittedly, many employers are reluctant to be candid. They feel that whatever is said may be used against them, and so they say nothing at all, at least nothing of much substance. While this view is understandable, the fears seem to be unwarranted. This writer believes that almost any explanation is better than none. The probability of a complaint resulting when no explanation is offered to a discharged person appears far greater. No explanation just raises suspicions and eventually produces a complainant who fervently believes that "something fishy is going on," that the discharge is surely unfair, and that it may be "discrimination."

Another thought is that perhaps the employer who is reluctant to give the discharged employee an honest explanation is in reality unable to do so. Maybe too many intangibles were part of the decision. Maybe there is some doubt as to whether the discharge can be justified. For these employers, the final interview may be another chance for the employer to reconsider any lingering doubts and examine more closely the various factors which brought about the discharge decision.

THE CLAIM FOR UNEMPLOYMENT BENEFITS

When a discharged employee files for unemployment benefits, the employer will have to give some explanation for the termination. The point to be made here is a simple one: be careful. When a discrimination complaint is made, it is a common practice for the employer's explanation on file with the state unemployment benefits office to turn up as evidence for the complainant. In most cases, the discharged person will receive a report of what the claim office was told by the company. If the explanation seems unfair, untrue, or unrelated to previous explanations given to the employee, a complaint may result, with the statement on the claim form to be used as evidence.

For instance, a worker may have been fired for cause, but the employer sees no need to make it more difficult for the employee to receive unemployment benefits. So instead of putting down "fired for poor work" on the form, the employer writes "laid off due to a necessary reduction in the work force." After a complaint of discrimination is filed against the company, the government agency investigating it finds no evidence whatsoever that a reduction in the work force occurred, with the exception of the complainant's dismissal. The false statement will lessen the employer's credibility and may even be viewed as a pretext.

9

Terms and Conditions of Employment

The phrase "terms and conditions of employment" refers to a very broad area of employer-employee relationships and is distinguished from the area of hiring and firing. One lesson to be learned at the start is just how large and inclusive this category may be, for the examples are truly innumerable. A conflict may even relate to desk assignment. After all, the desk may be too far from the window, too close to the door, or too much in line with the air-conditioning unit. (For that matter, it may be too close to the window, too far from the door, or not close enough to the air conditioner!)

In one terms and conditions case it was found that men were allowed to wear rings while working on the assembly line but women were not. In one office men were given individual washroom keys, but the women had to use the one hanging on the wall. One complainant alleged that all male employees (managers) were given long lunch hours, while the all-female clerical staff was limited to just one hour for lunch. In this case, the company argued that it was simply a question of position and had nothing to do with sex. But the complainant responded that sex was the discriminatory basis for the policy since some long-term secretarial persons had a greater salary than many new managers.

These examples may seem quite trivial, but they do illustrate that a terms and conditions complaint may deal with almost anything relating to the circumstances of employment. This point was well articulated in *Rogers v. EEOC*, in which it was stated that Title VII

> . . . provides that it shall be an unlawful employment practice for an employer "to fail or refuse to hire or to discharge any individual, or otherwise to discriminate against any individual with respect to his

compensation, terms, conditions, or privileges of employment, because of such individual's race, color, religion, sex, or national origin."
This language evinces a Congressional intention to define discrimination in the broadest possible terms. Congress chose neither to enumer-
ate specific discriminatory practices, nor to elucidate *in extenso* the pa-
rameter of such nefarious activities. Rather, it pursued the path of
wisdom by being unconstructive, knowing that constant change is the
order of our day and that the seemingly reasonable practices of the
present can easily become the injustices of the morrow. Time was when
employment discrimination tended to be viewed as a series of isolated
and distinguishable events, manifesting itself, for example, in an employer's practices of hiring, firing, and promoting. But today employment discrimination is a far more complex and pervasive phenomenon,
as the nuances and subtleties of discriminatory employment practices
are no longer confined to bread and butter issues. As wages and hours
of employment take subordinate roles in management-labor relationships, the modern employee makes ever-increasing demands in the
nature of intangible fringe benefits. Recognizing the importance of
these benefits, we should neither ignore their need for protection, nor
blind ourselves to their potential misuse.[1]

A second lesson following logically from the first is that employers
will be unable to develop personnel policies to cover all possible sources
of employee discontent. Policies and guidelines will, of course, need to
be established where possible. However, attempting to do so for each
possible condition of employment will, at the very least, make for a
cumbersome and overly rigid means of management.

This point leads to a third: the supervisor once more becomes the key
ingredient in a preventive strategy. As stated in Chapter 6, people who
charge discrimination might complain about the company, but they talk
about their supervisor. Supervising the supervisor will be necessary if
fairness and uniformity in the employment environment are to be maintained. In those areas where formal policies will have less application, the
direction given by branch managers, lead persons, chiefs, forepersons,
directors, and others operating in a supervisory capacity will be of great
consequence.

A fourth lesson is that a terms and conditions charge may hurt an
employer in two ways: Not only may it result in a violation of civil
rights law and accompanying damages, it may also form the substance
of a discharge complaint. For example, a typical charge reads:

> During my employment with X Company, I was not compensated as
> were male coworkers for doing the same work and was treated differ-

---

[1] 4 Empl. Prac. Dec. ¶7597 (1971).

ently in other terms and conditions of employment. I attempted to have my salary raised but instead was discharged. I charge that my discharge was based on my being female.

The assumption here is that the presence of discrimination in one area suggests discrimination in another. Even though this assumption may not be valid, the point remains that discontent over working conditions may stimulate a discharged employee to claim discrimination.

This chapter, therefore, organizes complaint prevention in this area from two perspectives: supervision-related and policy-related issues. Although the differences between the two groups are not always great, the issues discussed in the former tend to be less conducive to the control of a personnel officer or personnel department than the latter. This distinction is made so that management can be alerted to cases in which "supervising the supervisor" may be necessary to ensure that complaints do not get started.

SUPERVISION-RELATED ISSUES

When a company official was asked why the W.T. Grant chain of department stores went bankrupt, he replied, "Bad upper management, bad middle management, and bad lower management." It seems to have been the same old story. So many of an employer's operations are founded in the ability of supervisors to get the job done. Notwithstanding this fact, management is hardly an exact science. Despite a plethora of "how to" management books on the market today, learning "how to" still involves a high degree of intangible and nonquantifiable abilities. People more than policies make up the management process, and the application of many policies is manifested by the supervisory function of several personnel. Realizing this, the following section describes the ways in which supervisory actions may provoke a terms and conditions discrimination complaint and offers some guidelines on preventing their occurrence.

Performance Evaluation

The single most significant determinant in preventing an array of different terms and conditions complaints is the way supervisors evaluate the performances of their subordinates. Obviously, the ratings and judgments of the "boss" will affect many related activities such as promotions, job assignments, merit increases, and other benefits and privileges of employment. Conversely, a judgment that one's work is unsatisfactory may result in transfer, demotion, or even discharge. Performance evaluation is thus a pivotal element in complaint prevention.

Besides averting discrimination complaints, there are several general management procedures that will help in properly examining the abilities and strengths, as well as the shortcomings and weaknesses, of employees. Naturally, the overall objective is the positive one of improving performance, a goal that is surely within the interests of both the company and the employee. Many workers want to know how they are doing and how they can do better. When the observations of management are fair and accurate, high morale and a better working atmosphere are often the result. And by being aware of the special skills and talents of its employees, management will more efficiently be able to assign or transfer personnel, carry out productive training, and provide added incentives by means of promotions and wages to those who have done an outstanding job.

The following suggestions are offered:

1. Supervisors should be as familiar as possible with the work of their subordinates. The absence of a close working relationship with those supervised is likely to result in impressionistic appraisals carrying little weight or validity. Supervisors should therefore make performance evaluations part of an ongoing process of constructive criticism and counsel, and should frequently engage in discussions with employees. These practices very much support subsequent evaluations.

2. Do not let poor performances linger. Criticism of an employee's actions several weeks after their occurrence will have substantially less credibility and will thus cause more complaints than timely evaluations. Evaluations should be made frequently rather than, say, on an annual basis.

3. Supervisors should be sure to look at all aspects of one's job performance rather than just one or two factors. Employees are quick to consider the different way in which coworkers may have been judged when pondering the merits of their own appraisal. A narrow measurement of one worker's abilities will actually lessen management's ability to appraise others by means of several performance variables. The result may be charges of differential treatment.

4. Supervisors must be honest in their appraisals. Sometimes they get too friendly with subordinates, and this develops into favoritism. Such friendships have also been viewed as disproportionately affecting minority employees since they have less familial and social ties with those outside of their

groups. Honesty is also lacking in the supervisor who avoids "making waves" and the human relations problems that are bound to occur when some are rated over others. This reluctance may mean that all subordinates end up with very similar evaluations such as "average" or even "above average," a situation which in fact pleases very few.

5. Supervisory standards should be uniform and not differ with the particular department, office, branch, line, or section within the employer's operational structure. Differences in the application of standards may be found to be related to discrimination regardless of whether the difference is unlawfully motivated. Differing standards may be remedied by uniform job descriptions which spell out the functions and obligations of a given job. Accordingly, worker appraisals should be done by applying standards that are geared to the specific job in question. The universal application of such vague standards as "attitude," "initiative," "ability," and "dependability" not only leave room for a discrimination charge, but also provide little guidance in improving employee performance.

6. Moreover, standards should be relevant. Look at the job first and how it is being performed rather than the person. The following are examples of objective criteria: sales volume, complaints of customers, quality of work, safety, operating within a budget, supervising subordinates, meeting deadlines, writing reports, carrying out training, planning work, complying with company policies, overall productivity, attendance, reducing costs, answering customer complaints, solving problems, staff organization, and accounts handled.

7. Be able to support your observations with facts such as production records, disciplinary reports, attendance records, examples of work quality, statements of others, etc. Making use of objective standards will not be sufficient if observations still rely on general impressions instead of direct factual data and documentation.

8. Make job relatedness the rule. Try not to let personalities and different work habits interfere with a true measurement of what the employee has done with regard to the requirements of the job. Many workers have their own style and particular way of doing things. Look more at the result than the method.

9. Be sure that performance standards are well explained to all employees. Performance appraisal will not be helpful to management and may be disruptive if employees do not understand fully their obligations and how their work is being judged. Ignorance of the standards being applied, moreover, may be used by the employee as a defense of poor performance.

10. Keep a record of performance evaluations, and be sure that the appraised employee has a record also.

Harassment

The term "harassment" encompasses issues of discrimination relating to the intimidation and generally poor treatment of persons for one of the prohibited reasons. One Fifth Circuit Court of Appeals judge defined it as follows:

> [I]t is my belief that employees' psychological as well as economic fringes are statutorily entitled to protection from employer abuse, and that the phrase "terms, conditions, and privileges of employment" in Section 703 is an expansive concept which sweeps within its protective ambit the practice of creating a working environment heavily charged with ethnic or racial discrimination. I do not wish to be interpreted as holding that an employer's mere utterance of an ethnic or racial epithet which engenders offensive feelings in an employee falls within the proscription of Section 703. But by the same token I am simply not willing to hold that a discriminatory atmosphere could under no set of circumstances ever constitute an unlawful employment practice. One can readily envision working environments so heavily polluted with discrimination as to destroy completely the emotional and psychological stability of minority group workers, and I think Section 703 of Title VII was aimed at the eradication of such noxious practices.[2]

Inasmuch as harassment relates to psychological terms and conditions of employment, preventing harassment complaints may entail some careful maneuvering and thought by supervisory personnel. After all, harassment is a matter of perception as much as fact. One person's bad joke may be another's atrocious insult. Thus, the employer must be cognizant of the sensitivities and differing backgrounds of employees. Comments making references to ethnic, racial, and gender characteristics, even when made in jest, may lead to a complaint. What is more, denials that such statements are not demonstrations of evil intent may

---

[2] Ibid.

be met with some skepticism by civil rights authorities. The issue may become a difficultly resolved one of credibility. Furthermore, allowing a "discriminatory atmosphere" to harass protected classes, such as by the comments and actions of coworkers, would be unlawful. For this reason, the argument that an employee "did not get along well with her colleagues" is frequently not a credible defense in discharge cases.

One form of harassment that is increasingly receiving attention has to do with the sexual advances of supervisors to female employees, along with retaliation if the advances are declined. In one case the district court judge did not view such actions as within the scope of Title VII.[3] However, in a recent decision, *Williams v. William B. Saxbe et al.*, the finding was different. The court's explanation was as follows:

> That a rule, regulation, practice, or policy is applied on the basis of gender is alone sufficient for a finding of sex discrimination. *Phillips v. Martin Marietta Corp.*, 400 U.S. 542 (1971); *Sprogis v. United Air Lines, Inc.* In *Martin Marietta*, the Supreme Court, while vacating the decision of the Fifth Circuit, accepted the Fifth Circuit's finding that there was discrimination even though it was not based upon a characteristic peculiar to one gender. The Fifth Circuit had held that a policy which allowed the hiring of men who had pre-school children for certain positions, but not allowing the hiring of women with pre-school children for the same position, was sex discrimination in violation of Title VII. 411 F.2d 1 (1969). The court of appeals rejected the argument that sex discrimination could only be found if the policy depended solely upon gender . . . .

> The requirement of willingness to provide sexual consideration in this case is no different from the "preschool age children" and "no-marriage" rules of *Martin Marietta* and *Sprogis*. As here, none of those rules turned upon a characteristic peculiar to one of the genders. It was and is sufficient to allege a violation of Title VII to claim that the rule creating an artificial barrier to employment has been applied to one gender and not to the other. Therefore, this Court finds that plaintiff has stated a violation of Title VII's prohibitions against "any discrimination based on . . . sex . . . ."[4]

The respondent employer, which ironically was the U.S. Department of Justice, argued that the case

> . . . was not the result of a policy or a regulation of the office, but rather, was an isolated personal incident which should not be the concern of the courts and was not the concern of Congress in enacting Title VII.[5]

---

[3] *Corne v. Bausch and Lomb*, 9 Empl. Prac. Dec. ¶10,093 (1975).
[4] 11 Empl. Prac. Dec. ¶10,840 (1976).
[5] Ibid.

In rejecting this reasoning, the court made some interesting comments on the employer's responsibility for supervisory practices:

> [I]f this was a policy or practice of plaintiff's supervisor, then it was the agency's policy or practice, which is prohibited by Title VII. Secondly, the decision of the Court that plaintiff has stated a cause of action under Title VII will not have the feared result defendants urge. What the statute is concerned with is not interpersonal disputes between employees. Rather, the instant case reveals the statutory prohibition on the alleged discriminatory imposition of a condition of employment by the supervisor of an office of an agency.[6]

The practice of one supervisor becomes the policy of the employer, like it or not. Accordingly, proper supervision is the key variable in preventing this and other types of harassment charges. As a matter of fact, a hearing examiner in the *Saxbe* matter made this very point:

> A review of the proposed termination notice and of Mr. Brinson's testimony concerning the merits of the reasons for complainant's termination shows that such reasons were not serious deficiencies in work performance and/or conduct. It appears that many of the reasons were based on incidents in which good supervision would have been preventative, and that good supervision was not forthcoming because of the situation which Mr. Brinson had created by his attempts at fostering a personal relationship with complainant and the subsequent rejection.[7]

Unlawful harassment by low-level management is often the product of biased attitudes and preconceptions of other groups. Women are referred to as "girls," discouraged from advancement, and degraded by duties outside of their job assignment, such as coffee making. There is a difficulty in viewing minority group employees in the same manner as others. Some supervisors take offense at differences in dress, values, attitudes, and accents. Sensitizing supervisory personnel to the differing cultures of subordinates, as well as to the legal implications of their own biases, will be necessary in resolving these problems.

Discipline

Closely related to a harassment charge are issues involving discriminatory discipline. Unfair and unwarranted warnings, reprimands, and

---

[6] Ibid.
[7] Ibid.

criticisms may form the basis of complaints when they result in demotions, suspensions, discharges, and other adverse actions.

Of course, central to a preventive strategy in this area is the maxim that disciplinary standards should be uniformly applied and performance evaluations properly done. This requires that supervisors involved in evaluating the performance and behavior of subordinates should be consistent and take into consideration the ways others have been treated in the past. Disciplining a protected class member may be hard to justify when it evolves from a sudden application of new requirements to "crack down" on substandard performances. As understandable as the application of new standards may be, it may be seen as a pretext for discriminatory treatment.

Discipline should also be part of a well-known procedure which sets forth objective guidelines, is progressively carried out, and is positive in its approach. If the aim of discipline is eventually to improve poor work, the supervisor must be able to explain satisfactorily to the employee what went wrong and why past performances are less than adequate. The more reluctant management is in following through with needed disciplinary actions, the less justifiable such actions will appear when they are finally carried out. The cry will be, "I've been doing it this way for a long time, so how come it's unsatisfactory now?"

Promotions

Promotions are generally related to performance evaluations, as outlined above.

One of the most often-occuring problems for employers is considering the element of seniority when making promotions. Many complaints state, "I am the most senior person in my department, but I have not been promoted" or "The person promoted had less seniority and background than I did." The criterion of seniority is sometimes written into a promotion policy as part of a union-management contract. Seniority is rarely viewed as an absolute criterion, however, and usually is seen as one of the factors which must be considered when promotions are made. Yet even when seniority is not part of a definite rule, it seems to be one of those universal, unwritten variables that both management and employees feel should rightly be weighed when promotions are made. Evidence for this are the conflicts and complaints which occur when relatively new employees are promoted over those with greater length of service.

In contrast, good management requires that promotions be based on merit. The fact that an employee was able to last in one position for a long time does not mean that he or she can adequately perform other duties. Some employees will show special abilities at an early stage.

Rewarding them and making use of their skill and efficiency is a sound management objective. Many of the problems in government bureaucracies stem from the barely adequate performance of entrenched senior employees, particularly those who function as managers.

Another problem endemic to the area of promotion concerns the need for justification. The fact that good performance in one job may not accurately foretell adequate performance in a higher position makes it somewhat hard to devise credible promotion standards. As noted elsewhere by many writers and thinkers, including Weber, one commonly finds an employee able to gain promotions until his or her level of incompetency is reached; at that level the employee remains. Management then suffers because a whole spectrum of thoroughly incompetent yet highly placed employees exists.

Although the preceding may be an exaggeration, it is true that correctly predicting how an employee will do in a different job is not easy. This point has special merit when the attribute most different from the previous job is increased management responsibilities. A good production worker does not always make a good production supervisor. The required skills are not the same. And to make matters more difficult, when subjective evaluations dealing with initiative and attitude *are* utilized, the effect on protected classes may bring about a finding of unlawful discrimination.[8]

One way to lessen complaints regarding promotions is the establishment of a policy that is formal and is communicated to all employees. The mechanism for promotion should be there for all to see; many complaints get started by unknowing employees. Whenever possible, job vacancies should be posted. In some cases, openings made known by word of mouth have been found to have an unlawful effect on minorities, who tend to be excluded from the procedure. In addition, promotional qualifications should be established and communicated to employees. These qualifications will necessarily be linked to successful job performance in the worker's present position, as well as to other factors especially relevant to the higher position. Finally, employers should avoid the promotion requirement of a certain amount of time spent in lower job categories when the following two factors are present: (1) performance in the other positions is not essential, and (2) there are no or relatively few minorities and women in the other positions. Under such circumstances these requirements for promotion may be found to be unlawful.

---

[8] See for example, *Rowe v. General Motors*, 4 Empl. Prac. Dec. ¶7689 (1972).

Training

Training and promotion may be closely related since special training programs will provide the means of obtaining the qualifications needed for advancement.

Training is the most important means of making up for past under-utilization of minorities and women. People, including managers, tend to categorize others and assign them to certain static levels of ability. But training implies change. It assumes the existence of "potential" among those who come to work and find the motivation to achieve. We sometimes become overly preoccupied with the credentials of one's past, and perhaps we can and should focus equally on the possibilities for the future.

Training should definitely be carried out with a degree of consistency. There should be a check on supervisors to see that training sessions are periodic and that all applicable employees are involved. Many discharge complaints allege that equal training was not afforded to the complainant and that this discrimination explains his or her poor performance. When such an allegation is upheld, it negates the validity of the discharge. Likewise, discrimination in providing training may form the basis of a failure-to-promote charge. Care should therefore be taken in seeing that employees are evenly and without exception instructed in the various methods and requirements of their jobs. Also, be sure that only supervisors carry out training. When lower-echelon personnel participate in instructing new employees who eventually gain promotion over them, an obvious complaint is possible.

Job Assignment

Many complaints are caused by the employee's dissatisfaction with the kinds of obligations and duties within a particular job classification. In many situations, one job title may refer to several different combinations of activities as a result of the need for flexibility in the employer's operations. For example, a mechanic may be confined to working on radiators, shock absorbers, and mufflers because of experience or expertise in these kinds of repairs. One secretary may be assigned substantial amounts of dictation while another will have almost none. A salesperson may occasionally have to do some clerical work, answer phones, or place advertisements in local newspapers. Surely there are few job descriptions so tightly defined that disparities within the same job title will not exist.

A charge that the job assignment is unpleasant, unfair, and not as good those given to coworkers is difficult to prevent, mainly because it is often impossible to predict the likes and dislikes of subordinates. Yet such a dispute should not evolve into a formal discrimination complaint if there is adequate communication between workers and their supervisors. Proper performance evaluation should reveal where the employee may be best placed, and the employee's preferences and special abilities or skills.

Perhaps the most typical complaint in this area alleges that the duties of the job do not match up with the job title. One notably finds such conflicts in the area of clerical personnel who allegedly assume many of the functions and responsibilities of lower management or other staff positions. Managers who delegate much of their work to secretaries, including some decision making, may find the employee threatening a discrimination charge unless a promotion and concomitant salary change is forthcoming. This problem will be discussed further with regard to the issue of wages. At this point, supervisors should be aware of the problems caused when job duties and job titles are not well aligned. In a legal sense it is the duties that matter, regardless of what name the job is given.

One of the more certain ways of getting charged with sex discrimination is to give a woman a management position without its accompanying responsibility and authority. In some cases this occurs because of the desire to have female representation in management, but purely for the sake of appearances; in others it stems from simple bias against women managers.

Of course, preventing job assignment complaints will be greatly assisted by a personnel policy which describes in detail the functions and obligations of each position. As stated previously, job descriptions are a must not only from the perspective of dealing with discrimination, but also from the viewpoint of good management. They definitely assist in communicating to employees what is expected of them and facilitate management's ability to justifiably evaluate job performance.

Job descriptions are also essential in setting policy on wages. In one actual case, a federally funded county agency employed 15 persons in management positions, *all* with different job titles and salaries. The lowest-paid manager was a woman who charged sex discrimination in the compensation of her employment. Interrogatories served upon the employer requiring a listing of all management positions, along with their functions and salaries, was met with great perplexity because neither a salary guideline nor an examination of job assignments had ever been formally undertaken. To make matters worse, two more discrimination complaints relating to salary were filed during the investigation. One alleged race discrimination and the other creed! Unable to explain the differing salaries of such jobs as director, executive director, program director, administrator, program administrator, budget administrator, program manager, director of personnel administration, etc., the employer could not even determine the legal merits of the charges.

Indeed, conflicts over job assignment have an obvious interrelationship with other terms and conditions of employment. An employee may be insubordinate, and thus disciplined, because of unhappiness over the nature of work assigned. As noted earlier, obligations which do not seem to go along with the job title may result in the demand for a promotion and/or salary change. Some disgruntled workers may charge harassment. The complaint-causing potential of a job assignment conflict is therefore considerable and not to be underestimated. Supervisors should attempt to resolve such conflicts before they expand, adhering as consistently as possible to policy guidelines.

Reprisal

Section 704(a) of Title VII prohibits discrimination by an employer against any individual

. . . because he has opposed any practice made an unlawful practice
by this title, or because he has made a charge, testified, assisted, or
participated in any manner in an investigation, proceeding, or hearing
under this title.

Most state laws prohibiting employment discrimination contain a similar antireprisal clause.

The biggest cause of a complaint relating to an alleged reprisal action by the employer is ignorance of the fact that reprisal actions are unlawful. Not knowing about this section of civil rights laws results in some managers' admitting that reprisal actions such as harassment, demotion, suspension, or discharge are being undertaken because the employee has filed a complaint or assisted in an investigation. In at least one case, I have observed civil rights investigators listening in to a phone conversation between an employer and a discharged worker in which the admission was made. In other cases, unexplained and unjustifiable actions are taken against the employee, producing a complaint and probably a violation.

Some agencies have interpreted the phrase "because he has opposed any practice made an unlawful practice by this title" as prohibiting reprisals against an employee who complains about discrimination, whether in regard to himself or others. The complaint need not be formal or, for that matter, meritorious.[9] This raises the question, "What should an employer do if an employee's complaints truly become disruptive to the employer's operations?" The answer rests in the manner with which the complaint is handled. It should not be offhandedly rejected. Instead, the employer should attempt to investigate objectively and with some degree of thoroughness the charges being made. Once an investigation is completed, a written response should be provided to the complaining party with an indication of what actions will or will not be taken. If the employee's subsequent actions are actually disruptive, the employer will be on firmer ground in seeking to correct it. However, discussing discrimination charges with coworkers may not be seen as sufficiently disruptive to preclude a reprisal violation.[10]

In one case, an employer was held liable for monetary damages for violating the antireprisal section of Title VII because it had mentioned a past employee's EEOC charge in a letter of reference to another employer. The court found that the practice of obtaining letters of reference "is so common that such a letter might well be a 'privilege of employment.' " It had an obvious adverse affect on the complainant's chances of getting another job, and mentioning the civil rights complaint could not be justified by business necessity.[11]

Adverse Actions Which Are Unlawfully Related

Some complaints occur due to an adverse action that is seen as related to one's ethnic, racial, religious, or sexual identity. Although the employer may not have been directly motivated by unlawful considerations, a relationship is drawn between the basis of the action and the characteristics, behavior, and attitudes indicative of a particular group. The following are illustrative of race-related characteristics: an Afro hairstyle, the wearing of a dashiki, membership in a civil rights organization, interracial dating, and racially derogatory remarks. Accordingly, prohibiting employees from speaking a foreign language while at work may be construed as national origin discrimination. Reprimanding a female employee for wearing a "women's lib" button may be seen as sex discrimination.

---

[9] See for example, *Hyland v. Kenner Products Co.*, 11 Empl. Prac. Dec. ¶10,926 (1976); also note, *Rutherford v. American Bank of Commerce*, 11 Empl. Prac. Dec. ¶10,829 (1976), "The protection of [the reprisal] section has been interpreted by the Commission not to depend upon the actual existence of the unlawful employment practice so long as the individual acted on the good faith belief that she was opposing an unlawful practice."

[10] *EEOC v. Kallir, Phillips, Ross, Inc.*, 10 Empl. Prac. Dec. ¶10,366 (1975).

[11] *Rutherford v. American Bank of Commerce*, 11 Empl. Prac. Dec. ¶10,829 (1976).

The EEOC generally refers to discrimination which may be associated with a particular characteristic as "race-related," with the understanding that it may also be "color-, religion-, sex-, or national origin-related" as well. The commission suggests that a respondent's adverse actions may be unlawfully race-related if the following three conditions are met: (1) the employee's behavior is in fact "race-related," (2) the employer knew, or should have known, that the behavior was "race-related," and (3) the employer's adverse treatment was not justified by legitimate business concerns.[12]

The following examples will serve to enlighten the employer as to the kinds of "terms and conditions" complaints that stem from unlawfully related characteristics. The examples are cited in the EEOC's Compliance Manual, which is used as a guide by its investigative field staff. The citation "CD" refers to an administrative decision by the EEOC which is not binding on the charged employer.

RELIGION-RELATED DRESS

Complainant, a nurse, contended that her "religion" required that her hair be covered at all times, and the Commission concluded that her belief concerning keeping her hair covered was "religious" within the meaning of Title VII. Complainant previously worked in respondent's Nursery, where she wore a close-fitting scarf under her scrub cap. Respondent then transferred Complainant to another part of its hospital, informing her that she would now have to wear a nurse's cap and that she could not wear a scarf underneath the cap. Rather than conform to this requirement, Complainant resigned. Held: cause/ religion/discharge—Respondent's seemingly neutral policy regarding the wearing of nurse's caps had a foreseeable adverse impact upon Complainant "because of her religion." The evidence showed the nurse's cap was primarily symbolic, and that it was no more sanitary than the simple white scarf Complainant desired to wear. Since the discriminatory impact of Respondent's policy was not shown to be justified, Complainant's constructive discharge pursuant to this policy violated Title VII. CD 71, at 799, CCH ¶6180.[13]

USE OF FAMILIAR LANGUAGE

Respondent refused to permit its employees to speak Spanish during either working or non-working time. Such a policy has a significant adverse effect upon the terms and conditions of employment of Respondent's Spanish-surnamed American employees. The policy was

---

[12] EEOC Compl. Man. (CCH) §133.5.
[13] EEOC Compl. Man. (CCH) §475.2(a).

not shown to be justified by substantial business considerations. Held: cause. CD 71, at 446, CCH ¶6173.[14]

REACTION TO RACIAL EPITHET

Negro Complainant, believing she had been called a racial epithet by her Caucasian co-worker, approached the co-worker while carrying a knife which she used in the course of her work. Held: "When an employer is determining the appropriate discipline for participants in an incident such as the one under consideration, the employer's refusal to take into account the unusually provocative nature of racial insults constitutes discrimination because of race within the meaning of Section 703(a) of Title VII." CD 71 (1952).[15]

CUSTOMER PREJUDICE

In general, the prejudices of Respondent's customers or employees against a given race-related activity should not be considered a "legitimate, non-racial business consideration." However, where the race-related activity is so unreasonable or outlandish as to be deeply offensive to others, then Respondent's business needs may be held to outweigh the interests of Title VII which are served by protecting Complainant's "racial" activity. Thus if Complainant is publicly known to be a "Black Panther," or if he wears a relatively inconspicuous symbol of his Panther party membership, Title VII should forbid his employer to discriminate against him for his activities. But if he were to arrive at work wearing a panther mask, or with a tame panther walking at his side, Respondent should be held to be justified in taking appropriate action. Similarly, it is unlikely that Title VII would be construed to forbid the discipline of a female employee who arrived at work "topless" as an expression of sexual pride.[16]

POLICY-RELATED ISSUES

Some issues regarding terms and conditions of employment are especially conducive to management by policy implementation controlled and directed by a central authority such as a personnel department or office. They are not so subject to the peculiar differences and styles of the supervisory staff.

Wages

One big area of possible conflict concerns compensation for employment. Differences in compensation for substantially similar jobs related to one of the impermissible basis of discrimination would of course be

---

[14] EEOC Compl. Man. (CCH) §466.3(a).
[15] EEOC Compl. Man., §133.6(d).
[16] EEOC Compl. Man. (CCH) §133.5(c).

unlawful. The Equal Pay Act of 1963 specifically prohibits wage discrimination based on sex, since women have historically been underpaid while doing the same job as male employees. The Equal Pay Act was amended in 1972 to extend coverage to include executive, administrative, and professional employees and outside salespersons. Regulations which explain the provisions of the Equal Pay Act can be found in Appendix 3.

The results of equal pay investigations by the Wage and Hour Division of the U.S. Department of Labor may be very costly to an employer because such complaints are almost always viewed on a class basis. The amount of wages found owing between 1964 and the beginning of 1973 amounted to $55 million for 129,000 employees. What then can an employer do to prevent such complaints, and possibly violations, from occurring? The following guidance is offered.

First, be sure that job titles sensibly relate to job duties. Although the job title has no legal bearing in determining the existence of an equal pay violation, the wrong title may very easily provide the impetus to a time-consuming and expensive court battle, one that might very well have been prevented. A highly illustrative example of this point is found in a recent case, *Hyland v. Kenner Products Co.*[17]

Kenner Products Company is a manufacturer of toys. The complainant, Marilyn J. S. Hyland, was initially hired to test toys still in the development stage by "observing the conduct of children during play sessions." When recruiting applicants the position was described by Kenner as "child-tester," requiring "a college degree as well as some experience with children." The complainant met those requirements. However, on her first day of employment she was advised that her title would be director of market research. It was reported in Kenner's affirmative action plan that plaintiff was hired as "management and official." It was emphasized that Kenner had a female director. Her position was characterized as an executive position, and her responsibility was to get the job done, regardless of the number of hours it took. She was also to report directly to top officials of Kenner, as well as the research department of the parent company, General Mills.

The characterization of the complainant's job as director of market research, one which was originally labeled "child-tester," seems to have been the company's key mistake, and was indicative of a loose policy on job titles in general. As subsequent testimony revealed:

> The job content of directors at Kenner varies greatly. The title of director is not indicative of the importance of the position. Directors often report to other directors, or to managers, and job titles often change without a change in job content.

---

[17] 11 Empl. Prac. Dec. ¶10,926 (1976) (also for the excerpts that follow).

This lack of clarity in job titles apparently gave rise to the complainant's perception of discrimination:

> After several months at Kenner, plaintiff began to feel some dissatisfaction as to the company's treatment of her specifically and as to its treatment of females generally. She was openly dissatisfied with her salary, which was increased to $9,600 in June of 1973. Also, it was her opinion that she was not receiving many of the additional privileges and courtesies which accompanied "director" status. For example, her name was not included in the phone directory along with other Kenner "executives"; she was not given a "budget"; she had no assistants; she was not promptly provided a parking space; and she did not receive a push-button telephone or new furniture.

Consequently, Ms. Hyland filed sex discrimination charges with the Ohio Civil Rights Commission and the EEOC. In the meantime, the company hired a man with a marketing background to become director of market research. His title was then changed to director of consumer research, and the complainant became a child play-test analyst. This action led, in turn, to the complainant charging that she had been demoted! Finally, after complaining bitterly of her present situation, the complainant was terminated from her position, allegedly for insubordination. This led to another charge of retaliation for filing a complaint!

The court's decision was as follows. First, the equal pay complaint was dismissed:

> [P]laintiff has not shown that she was required to perform equal work or that her job required equal skill, effort, and responsibility.

As to the demotion:

> [P]laintiff alleges that the hiring of Robert Steiner as Director of Consumer Research and her 'demotion' to Child Play-test Analyst amounted to sex discrimination. We disagree. It is clear that Steiner was more qualified than plaintiff for the position of Director of Consumer Research. He had an MBA in Marketing and four years experience in a consumer industry. Therefore, defendant's decision to place the plaintiff under the supervision of Steiner was by no means discriminatory. Also, plaintiff's claim that she was demoted is not supported by the evidence. There is nothing in the record to indicate that plaintiff received a cut in pay (in fact, she got a raise) or that her duties changed in any way, at least prior to July, 1974. *The more apt description is that her job title was changed to more accurately reflect her position.* [*Emphasis added.*]

However, the reprisal charge was upheld by the district court and more than fifty thousand dollars was awarded to the complainant for loss of pay and attorney's fees![18] Would this complaint have occurred had the original job title given to the complainant, and to others in the company, been more in line with actual duties?

Another preventive step is to review salaries and job duties and take action where necessary, such as reassigning people, reclassifying jobs, or making salary adjustments. But be sure not to make corrections by lowering salaries. This would be a violation of the Equal Pay Act and a poor practice generally. Recalcitrant unions may pose a problem here, but remember it is an unfair labor practice for a union to impose an unlawful contractual provision on an employer.

Also, be sure that salary policies are well articulated and well structured. Setting salary ranges and letting various management personnel, or even one company official, make general judgments as to what the salary should be will not do. The better way is to incorporate objective criteria into salary policies so that the method of determination is a reliable one, that is, one which will tend to be applied in the same manner no matter who does the applying. To do otherwise is to increase the risk of a complaint and force the employer to search for after-the-fact salary explanations.

For example, the Equal Pay Act prohibits sex discrimination in salary assignment when the jobs in question "meet the statutory tests of equal skill, effort, and responsibility, and similar working conditions," except that

> . . . where it can be established that a differential in pay is the result of a wage payment made pursuant to a seniority system, a merit system, a system measuring earnings by quantity or quality of production, or that the differential is based on any other factor other than sex, the differential is expressly excluded from the statutory prohibition of wage discrimination based on sex.[19]

As stated in the Interpretive Bulletin of the Equal Pay Act, if the employer "relies on the excepting language to exempt a differential in pay from the operation of the equal pay provisions, he will be expected to show the necessary facts."[20] Moreover, "formal or written systems or plans" would better demonstrate that the exceptions are justified. Unwritten or informal policies may be satisfactory, but only

---

[18] 13 Empl. Prac. Dec. ¶11,427 (1976).
[19] Equal Pay for Equal Work, Interpretive Bulletin, §800.140.
[20] §800.141(a).

. . . if it can be demonstrated that the standards or criteria applied under it are applied pursuant to an established plan *the essential terms and conditions of which have been communicated to the affected employees.*[21] [*Emphasis added.*]

Uncommunicated policies are suggestive of contrived explanations.

One common pitfall of an unstructured or nonexistent salary policy is revealed when employers attempt to explain a salary difference by means of the greater experience of the higher-paid employee. Perhaps a general statement was communicated to employees, such as "wages will take into consideration the experience of the wage earner." However, the following section of the equal pay regulations is too often forgotten: "Possession of a skill not needed to meet requirements of the job cannot be considered in making a determination regarding equality of skill."[22] Accordingly, it should be specified that only *job-related* experience is to be considered when that factor is used in making wage assignments. Similarly, the success of explaining a salary difference on merit considerations will directly relate to the structure of the performance evaluation program.

Finally, do not assign starting salaries based on the most recent wage of the applicant or the "what I can get her for" standard. Both methods have a disproportionate effect on minorities and women, who generally make less than others.

Fringe Benefits

Fringe benefits refer to such items as vacations, insurance coverage, pensions, profit-sharing plans, bonuses, holidays, and disability leaves. Most of the cases in this area have dealt with sex discrimination and thus are covered by the sections of the EEOC's sex discrimination guidelines entitled Fringe Benefits and Employment Policies Relating to Pregnancy and Childbirth. Although the entire guidelines can be found in Appendix 1, these sections deserve to be quoted here:

- Where an employer conditions benefits available to employees and their spouses and families on whether the employee is the "head of the household" or "principal wage earner" in the family unit, the benefits tend to be available only to male employees and their families. Due to the fact that such conditioning discriminatorily affects the rights of women employees, and the "head of household" or "principal wage earner"

---

[21] §800.144.
[22] §800.125.

status bears no relationship to job performance, benefits which are so conditioned will be found a *prima facie* violation of the prohibitions against sex discrimination contained in the Act.

• It shall be unlawful employment practice for an employer to make available benefits for the wives and families of male employees where the same benefits are not made available for the husbands and families of female employees; or to make available benefits for the wives of male employees which are not made available for female employees; or to make available benefits to the husbands of female employees which are not made available for male employees. An example of such an unlawful employment practice is a situation in which wives of male employees receive maternity benefits while female employees receive no such benefits.

• It shall not be a defense under Title VII to a charge of sex discrimination in benefits that the cost of such benefits is greater with respect to one sex than the other.

• It shall be an unlawful employment practice for an employer to have a pension or retirement plan which establishes different optional or compulsory retirement ages based on sex, or which differentiates in benefits on a basis of sex. A statement of the General Counsel of September 13, 1968, providing for a phasing out of differentials with regard to optional retirement age for certain incumbent employees is hereby withdrawn.

• A written or unwritten employment policy or practice which excludes from employment applicants or employees because of pregnancy is in *prima facie* violation of Title VII.

• Where the termination of an employee who is temporarily disabled is caused by an employment policy under which insufficient or no leave is available, such a termination violates the Act if it has a disparate impact on employees of one sex and is not justified by business necessity.[23]

However, in an important decision the Supreme Court struck down the following sections (italicized) of the EEOC guidelines and found them to be *not* violative of Title VII:

Disabilities caused or contributed to by pregnancy, miscarriage, abortion, childbirth, and recovery therefrom are, for all job-related purposes, tempo-

---

[23] §1604.9 and §1604.10.

rary disabilities and should be treated as such under any health or temporary
disability insurance or sick leave plan available in connection with employ-
ment. Written and unwritten employment policies and practices involving matters such as the commencement and duration of leave, the
availability of extensions, the accrual of seniority and other *benefits* and
privileges, reinstatement, and payment under any health or temporary disability insurance or sick leave plan, formal or informal, *shall be*
applied to disability due to pregnancy or childbirth on the same terms and
conditions as they are applied to other temporary disabilities.[24] *[Emphasis*
added.]

The ruling in the *General Electric v. Gilbert* case was a major setback for
civil rights authorities and the women's movement for it rejected the
opinions of all six courts of appeals which had ruled on the issue.[25]
Because of its possible effects on other pregnancy-related sex discrimination areas, it seems worthwhile to look at the reasons presented by the
majority opinion in this six-to-three decision.

Of major importance is the Court's consideration of discrimination
cases pursuant to the equal protection clause of the Fourteenth Amendment as "a useful starting point in interpreting" Title VII. The majority
of the appellate courts had drawn a distinction between the "invidious"
discrimination standard of those cases and Title VII decisions, which
take the position that "intent" need not be shown in order to make a
case, and chose not to follow the Supreme Court's equal protection
decision in *Geduldig v. Aiello*. However, the Court cited *Aiello* as being
controlling, a decision which did not find California's exclusion of pregnancy from its disability insurance system to be discriminatory. The
Court stated that the "underinclusiveness" of risks covered by the program did not amount to gender-based discrimination, nor was it a pretext, because:

> There is no evidence in the record that the selection of the risks insured
> by the program worked to discriminate against any definable group or
> class in terms of the aggregate risk protection derived by that group or
> class from the program. There is no risk from which men are protected
> and women are not. Likewise, there is no risk from which women are
> protected and men are not.[26]

---

[24] *General Electric v. Gilbert*, 12 Empl. Prac. Dec. ¶11,240 (1976).
[25] *Communication Workers of America v. A.T.&T. Co.*, 9 Empl. Prac. Dec. ¶10,035 (1975);
Wetzel v. Liberty Mutual Insurance Co., 9 Empl. Prac. Dec. ¶9942 (1975); *Gilbert v. General*
Electric, ibid; *Tyler v. Vickery*, 10 Empl. Prac. Dec. ¶10,388 (1975); *Satty v. Nashville Gas*
Co., 10 Empl. Prac. Dec. ¶10,359 (1975); and *Hutchinson v. Lake Oswego School Dist.*, 10
Empl. Prac. Dec. ¶10,325 (1975).
[26] *General Electric v. Gilbert*, 12 Empl. Prac. Dec. ¶11,240 (1976).

But in its opinion the Court went beyond this issue as to the proper standard of proof and stated that even assuming it were not necessary to prove intent Gilbert had not made out a case of disparate effect. In support of this the Court once more stressed that the issue was one of "underinclusiveness" and that the "aggregate" risk protection for men and women was the same. Pregnancy-related disabilities were seen as "an *additional* risk, unique to women, and the failure to compensate them for this risk does not destroy the presumed parity of the benefits, accruing to men and women alike, which results from the facially evenhanded inclusion of risks."[27] The Court added that to rule otherwise would mean that an employer with no disability benefits program at all, affecting women still more, would not violate Title VII, while an employer with a program excluding pregnancy would be in violation.

Finally, the Court attempted to justify its departure from the EEOC's sex discrimination guidelines by noting that it conflicted with earlier pronouncements, was contrary to the unchanging guidelines of the Wage and Hour Administration interpreting the Equal Pay Act,[28] and seemed to oppose the intent of Congress.

The *General Electric v. Gilbert* decision is certainly precedent setting in its treatment of pregnancy-related disabilities in an employer's fringe benefits program. And the Court's subsequent vacating and remanding the Ninth Circuit's decision in *Hutchinson v. Lake Oswego School District*, which has found the exclusion of pregnancy-related disabilities from a sick leave program to be unlawful, means that such inclusions will no longer be seen as a violation of Title VII. However, it deserves mention that state civil rights enforcement agencies, subject to their own state courts, may take an opposite view in the processing of complaints. In a case decided after *Gilbert*, the New York State Court of Appeals, the state's highest court, ruled that the exclusion of such benefits violated state law. The federal court's ruling was seen as instructive but not controlling on the state level. Although in New York the issue was somewhat complicated by the fact that the state's disability benefits law specifically excludes benefits relating to pregnancy, other states can be expected to take their own view on the matter.

Many employers are confused about maternity leave. Is it compulsory to allow employees to take a maternity leave of absence? If leaves of absence are granted for other reasons, the answer is "yes." Must an employer rehire a woman who is returning from maternity leave? Yes, unless the employer can show that the denial was based on "business necessity" or "any appropriate 'objective criteria.' "[29] This burden will

---

[27] Ibid.
[28] §800.116(d).
[29] *St. John v. G.W. Murphy Industries, Inc.*, 11 Empl. Prac. Dec. ¶10,651 (1976).

likely be on the employer. As stated in the guidelines above, a "practice which excludes from employment applicants or employees because of pregnancy is in *prima facie* violation of Title VII." And any investigation into such a complaint will examine how others have been treated after a leave of absence. The landmark case in this regard is *Cleveland Board of Education v. LaFleur* in which the Supreme Court found that it was a violation of the due process clause of the Fourteenth Amendment to impose mandatory and arbitrary maternity leave and return to work conditions on women employees.[30]

Another benefit that has frequently been found to be unlawfully applied is that of retirement plans. Pension programs that favor one sex over another, usually to the benefit of women, have been ruled a violation of Title VII.[31]

Seniority

Policies on seniority may be both written and unwritten. The former are normally part of a union-management contract, the provisions of which may stipulate the use of seniority in determining a multitude of employment conditions such as promotion, layoff, transfer, job assignment, training, scheduling, wages, recall rights, overtime, and vacation time. In addition, several employers look at the length of service in an informal way when making decisions regarding many of these practices.

There are two main circumstances under which employers will be concerned about seniority provisions and may find it necessary to make alterations. The first is where the rule of departmental seniority is coupled with a clustering of minorities and/or women into the lower-paying, less desirable departments. In such a situation, it may be found that the department seniority standard has a disparate and unlawful effect on those affected groups. The obvious cure to this problem is the elimination of department seniority.

Second, the use of seniority in selecting employees for promotion and training, and especially layoff and recall rights, may be unlawful if the less senior individuals are made up of women and/or minorities who can show they were personally denied employment unlawfully by the same employer in the past. Such past discrimination would account for these groups having less seniority.

The remedy of this type of case appears simply to be an awarding of certain amounts of seniority to those discriminated persons who should

---

[30] 7 Empl. Prac. Dec. ¶9072 (1974).

[31] See *Fitzpatrick v. Bitzer*, 10 Empl. Prac. Dec. ¶10,270 (1975); *Chastang v. Flynn and Emrich Co.*, 12 Empl. Prac. Dec. ¶11,003 (4th Cir. 1976).

be compensated. But this is far from simple. Essentially, the conflicts that arise from such actions, which are to the obvious detriment of innocent employees, seem to make resolution by a court decision almost inevitable. If nonminorities appear to lose out by the employer's attempts to remedy past discrimination, they may file a complaint of reverse discrimination. On the other hand, affected minority and female workers may file suit if their seniority status is not changed.

This writer has had the unfortunate experience of being employed under just such circumstances. For several months when it appeared that layoffs might occur, there were numerous heated discussions as to which employees were to be retained. Since no union contract was applicable to the employer, management was considering making the selections so that recently hired female and Hispanic employees would maintain a fair representation in the work force. Indeed, a new section was added to the New Jersey *Civil Service Personnel Manual* for just such a situation:

> When a layoff situation of provisional, temporary, or unclassified employees occurs, recognition will be given to the department's affirmative action plan. In these situations where seniority is not provided for, layoffs for the aforementioned types of employees will be at least in proportion to the complement of minorities and females in the department as a minimum leading to the proportion of minorities and females in the relevant labor area.[32]

The layoffs never occurred, thankfully. But the latent conflicts that developed over the possibility that seniority would be bypassed for race and sex considerations is worth mentioning. Although seniority was in fact not a formal rule, for many it represented the fairest standard to be followed when an employment action such as layoff was being considered. At this stage, then, it seems unlikely that present employers facing these same problems will be able to take voluntary steps to prevent a complaint from one side or the other.

---

[32] State of New Jersey, *Civil Service Personnel Manual*, subpt. 21-1.101 (June 13, 1975).

III

RESOLVING
COMPLAINTS

10

How Agencies
Handle Complaints

The key characteristic distinguishing the enforcement of laws prohibiting job discrimination from most other civil statutes is their administration by government agencies. The importance of this difference is not to be underestimated, for the matter of enforcement is often misunderstood or neglected when laws are being discussed. How a law is enforced is central to the law's meaning; certainly, the absence of enforcement makes the law irrelevant.

Complaints made pursuant to Title VII, the Age Discrimination in Employment Act, and the Rehabilitation Act must first be processed through their respective agencies—the EEOC, Wage and Hour Division of the Department of Labor, and the OFCC—before court actions can begin. This requirement is referred to as the "exhaustion of administrative remedies." However, federal agencies may most likely be bypassed when complaints are lodged pursuant to the Equal Pay Act, the Civil Rights Act of 1866, or on constitutional grounds. The exhaustion of administrative remedies requirement will also vary when actions are based on state statutes.

The use of government agencies to handle complaints is certainly a great advantage for the complaining party. It is quite easy to initiate a complaint, and, in varying degrees, the complainant will be making use of the resources and legal representation of a specialized group of professionals without charge. The average person seeking restitution for damages caused by the violation of a civil law, such as in the case of someone driving onto your lawn, refusing to pay rent, or not living up to the terms of a contract, must contact a lawyer and spend money to file suit.

Thus, knowing how to resolve complaints entails an understanding of just how these government agencies work. To this end, Chapter 10 goes beyond a recitation of the procedural rules of each applicable agency and focuses more on key characteristics common to all of them. The procedures of the EEOC are fairly typical of the way administrative agencies, particularly the federal ones, work. By dispelling some of the commonly held misconceptions regarding civil rights law enforcement, a foundation may be provided for rational and efficient decision making on the part of employers involved in complaint resolution.

THE NATURE OF COMPLAINTS

A complaint is nothing more than an allegation that an unlawful act has occurred. It is rarely the product of even a preliminary investigation and originates mainly from the statements of the complaining party.

Who Can File

According to Title VII, a charge of discrimination may be made by any "person aggrieved" by an unlawful employment practice, persons acting on behalf of those aggrieved, or a member of the EEOC. The "person aggrieved" requirement has been loosely defined to include those other than individuals, employees, or applicants so long as there is "some ill effect as a result of an unlawful employment practice."[1] In *Mixson v. Southern Bell*, the district court upheld the right of a deceased employee's spouse to state a claim since she was affected by the alleged discriminatory pension program of her late husband.[2] And the Third Circuit has upheld the right of a past employee to file a terms and conditions complaint.[3] The right of a labor union to file a complaint has also been upheld, the court noting that:

> [R]ecent court decisions have recognized the standing of group plaintiffs as a "person aggrieved" where the group, *qua* group, has an interest in the outcome of the administrative agency's determination although it might, incidentally, represent broader community interests as well.[4]

Furthermore, the EEOC has taken the position that an employer may sometimes be a "person aggrieved," such as when the complaint relates

---

[1] EEOC Compl. Man. (CCH) §201.5.

[2] 4 Empl. Prac. Dec. ¶7606 (1971).

[3] *Hackett v. McGuire Brothers, Inc.*, 3 Empl. Prac. Dec. ¶8276 (1971).

[4] *International Chemical Workers Union v. Planters Manufacturing Company*, 1 Empl. Prac. Dec. ¶9751 (1966).

to "violations by a union, employment agency or employer association, with which the employer deals on matters affecting the terms and conditions of the latter's employees."[5]

Contents of a Complaint

The EEOC's procedural rules require that a charge contain "a clear and concise statement of the facts, including pertinent dates, constituting the alleged unlawful employment practice."[6] A sample EEOC charge form can be found in Figure 3.

But, as stated previously, a complaint is only an allegation. Section 706(b) of Title VII speaks of a charge filed by a person *"claiming* to be aggrieved." The complaint does *not* have to "state sufficient facts to make out a *prima facie* case," nor is there any provision in Title VII "authorizing a general inquiry into the sufficiency of the evidence supporting a charge."[7]

> A charge of discrimination is *not* filed as a preliminary to a lawsuit. On the contrary, the purpose of a charge of discrimination is to trigger the investigatory and conciliatory procedures of the EEOC.[8]

This liberal attitude on what the charging party must provide is based on the assumption that "the Civil Rights Act is designed to protect those who are least able to protect themselves."[9] As summarized by the Fifth Circuit:

> Mindful of the "remedial and humanitarian underpinning" of Title VII, and in the belief that the Civil Rights Act of 1964 was designed "to protect the many who are unlettered and unschooled in the nuances of literary draftsmanship" and that "it would falsify the Act's hopes and ambitions to require verbal precision and finesse from those to be protected . . . ," this Court has held that "all that is required of a charge is that it give sufficient information to enable the EEOC to see what the grievance is all about."[10]

The ease with which complaints may be filed must be firmly realized by the employer. It is one of the factors which stimulated the writing of this book. The validity of a complaint is first seen within the context of

---

[5] EEOC Compl. Man. (CCH) §201.5(b).
[6] C.F.R. 29, §1601.11(a)(3).
[7] *Graniteville Co., Sibley Division v. EEOC,* 3 Empl. Prac. Dec. ¶8109 (4th Cir. 1971).
[8] *Sanchez v. Standard Brands, Inc.,* 2 Empl. Prac. Dec. ¶10,252 (5th Cir. 1970).
[9] *Sciaraffa v. Oxford Paper Company,* 2 Empl. Prac. Dec. ¶10,167 (1970).
[10] *Parliament House Motor Hotel v. EEOC,* 3 Empl. Prac. Dec. ¶8277 (1971).

jurisdiction, which is distinct from the issue of the complaint's merit. The latter question is to be answered by the agency's investigatory activities and not by its initial "impressions" of the evidence provided by the charging party.

Moreover, it is the charge that ultimately guides the investigation rather than the facts alleged in the complaint; accordingly, the charge should be given as much consideration by the employer as the statement of facts. For example, a woman may charge sex discrimination, alleging that a male coworker had a greater salary but his job required equal skill, effort, and responsibility under similar working conditions. An investigation may reveal that the statement of facts is incorrect—the male coworker had greater seniority, which justified the higher salary. However, it may have been found, by means of a thorough examination of other employees, that the complainant *was* being underpaid when her salary was compared with those of other male coworkers. Although the statement of facts had been incorrect, the charge still had merit.

Amendments

Complaints may also be easily amended. As stated in the EEOC's *Procedural Regulations:*

> A charge may be amended to cure technical defects or omissions, including failure to swear to the charge, or to clarify and amplify allegations made therein, and such amendments alleging additional acts which constitute unlawful employment practices directly relating to or growing out of the subject matter of the original charge will relate back to the original filing date.[11]

This ability to amend a complaint once more gives the complainant a considerable advantage since a correctable defect may even include checking off the wrong basis of discrimination on the charge form. In *Sanchez v. Standard Brands, Inc.* the Fifth Circuit gave three reasons for supporting this position:

> First, the charging party may have precise knowledge of the facts concerning the "unfair thing" done to him, yet not be fully aware of the employer's *motivation* for perpetuating the "unfair thing." Secondly, the charging party may be so unlettered and inarticulate that he does not fully comprehend the distinction between an act motivated by "sex discrimination" and an identical act motivated by "national origin discrimination." Finally, the charging party may simply be unschooled and unsophisticated in the use of forms.[12]

---

[11] C.F.R. 29, §1601.11(5)(b).
[12] 2 Empl. Prac. Dec. ¶10,252 (1970).

In spite of the court's justification, amending a complaint may have the effect of manufacturing a violation. For example, the investigation of a race discrimination charge may uncover evidence of differential treatment based on sex, or perhaps age, national origin, or marital status (such as pursuant to an all-inclusive state law). When this occurs, it is the agency, not the complainant, that initiates and formulates an amended charge to match the evidence obtained. Granted, a person may "not be fully aware of the employer's motivation for perpetuating the 'unfair thing,' " but that motivation, rather than simply unfairness, was the sole reason for enacting civil rights laws in the first place. At any rate, this ability of agencies to "reframe charges and to use available materials and information to articulate lay complainants' charges"[13] greatly favors complainants.

Class Actions

This book concerns the prevention and resolution of individual complaints of employment discrimination. For our purposes, class actions have not been discussed in detail. But it does deserve mention that these types of complaints, which may be highly damaging, can easily develop from individual ones. As stated in a much-cited court decision:

> Racial discrimination is by definition class discrimination, and to require a multiplicity of separate, identical charges before the EEOC, filed against the same employer, as a prerequisite to relief through resort to the court would tend to frustrate our system of justice and order.[14]

The general requirements for an action to be brought on a class basis are set forth in Rule 23(a) of the *Federal Rules of Civil Procedure:*

> (a) Prerequisites to a Class Action. One or more members of a class may sue or be sued as representative parties on behalf of all only if (1) the class is so numerous that joinder of all members is impracticable, (2) there are questions of law or fact common to the class, (3) the claims or defenses of the representative parties are typical of the claims or defenses of the class, and (4) the representative parties will fairly and adequately protect the interests of the class.

Because the ability of unnamed class members to obtain back pay awards was recently affirmed by the Supreme Court,[15] the employer

---

[13] *Blue Bell Boots, Inc. v. EEOC,* 2 Empl. Prac. Dec. ¶10,115 (1969).
[14] *Oatis v. Crown Zellerbach Corporation,* 1 Empl. Prac. Dec. ¶9894 (1968).
[15] *Albemarle Paper Co. v. Moody,* 9 Empl. Prac. Dec. ¶10,230 (1975).

should be familiar with the ways in which these requirements have been generally interpreted.

The question of numerosity is a rather simple one. As a point of reference, some decisions have indicated that classes of six,[16] ten,[17] and eleven[18] persons were not large enough to sustain a class action.

The requirement of "questions of law or fact common to the class" has been generally used to determine not only the existence of a class but also its size. In determining its existence, the federal courts have viewed the issue in two ways, one quite liberal and the other more limiting. The former view, which is espoused by the Fifth Circuit and the EEOC, and which has been adopted elsewhere, states that since an allegation relates to discriminatory employment practices, this alone is sufficient to establish a class action. As recently noted in a decision by the District Court for the Northern District of California:

> In Title VII cases, the alleged existence of common discriminatory employment practices affecting all members of the class satisfies the common question requirement. Although the alleged discriminatory practices may affect various class members differently, Title VII suits are aimed at the common underlying discriminatory employment system and not merely at the system's particular manifestations.[19]

Thus, in this case the sex discrimination complaint construed the size of the class to include "all past, present, and future women employees and applicants for employment"[20] with the defendant employer. This all-encompassing approach to class actions was explained in an early Title VII case as follows:

> [A]lthough the actual effects of a discriminatory policy may thus vary throughout the class, the existence of the discriminatory policy threatens the entire class. And whether the Damoclean threat of a racially discriminatory policy hangs over the racial class is a question of fact common to all the members of the class.[21]

The less liberal view narrows the class based on the specific type of discriminatory practices alleged, such as failure to hire, failure to pro-

---

[16] *Hill v. American Airlines, Inc.*, 6 Empl. Prac. Dec. ¶8703 (5th Cir. 1973).

[17] *Chavez v. Rust Tractor Company*, 2 Empl. Prac. Dec. ¶10,171 (1969).

[18] *Tolbert v. Western Electric Co.*, 56 F.R.D. 108 (N.D. Ga. 1972).

[19] *Waters v. Heublein, Inc.*, 11 Empl. Prac. Dec. ¶10,620 (1975). See also *Johnson v. Georgia Highway Express, Inc.*, 2 Empl. Prac. Dec. ¶10,119 (5th Cir. 1969); *Mosley v. General Motors Corp.*, 7 Empl. Prac. Dec. ¶9408 (8th Cir. 1974); and *Bowe v. Colgate-Palmolive Co.*, 2 Empl. Prac. Dec. ¶10,090 (7th Cir. 1969).

[20] *Waters v. Heublein, Inc.*, 11 Empl. Prac. Dec. ¶10,620 (1975).

[21] *Hall v. Werthan Bag Corp.*, 1 Empl. Prac. Dec. ¶9732 (1966).

mote, discharge, etc., or the specific department or area where the discrimination is occurring. Furthermore, a class action may be disallowed altogether where there is no indication that the employer acted in a generally discriminatory manner, and the alleged act of discrimination was an isolated one.

The third requirement under Rule 23(a) refers to the proper representative of the class. Logically, when a class is liberally defined, it will be relatively easy to gain representation of the class. This is in line with the EEOC position:

> [E]ven where a charging party is not directly aggrieved by alleged unlawful practices, he nevertheless may have standing to protest those practices where he is a member of the same "class," i.e., the same race, sex, national origin, etc., as those who are directly aggrieved, provided charging party does claim to be directly aggrieved by some other unlawful employment practices.[22]

Accordingly, in *Parham v. Southwestern Bell Telephone,* a black applicant who was not rejected for employment for discriminatory reasons was not prevented from representing the class of black employees and applicants.[23] And other cases have held that a discharged employee could represent a class of present workers.[24] On the other hand, class actions have been denied when the charging party was not seen as representative. For example, in *Chavez v. Rust Tractor Company* a discharged Hispanic individual could not represent Hispanic individuals who were discriminatorily denied employment because he had personally never been refused employment and therefore was not a member of the class.[25]

The fourth Rule 23(a) requirement more stringently applies the representation criteria with fair and adequate protection of class interests. Decisions from two circuit courts suggest that when the charging party's particular claim has been found to be without merit[26] or moot because he no longer seeks reinstatement,[27] he no longer has standing as a class representative. This is in contrast to the EEOC's view, as held by the Eighth Circuit's decision in *Parham v. Southwestern Bell Telephone* cited above.

Finally, in regard to class actions it deserves mention that once a class action is certified by the courts, it acquires a "legal status separate from the interest asserted by the named representative"[28] and cannot be dis-

---

[22] EEOC Compl. Man., §203.4.
[23] 3 Empl. Prac. Dec. ¶8021 (8th Cir. 1970).
[24] Such as *Johnson v. Georgia Highway Express, Inc.,* 2 Empl. Prac. Dec. ¶10,119 (1969).
[25] 2 Empl. Prac. Dec. ¶10,171 (1969).
[26] *Huff v. N.D. Cass Company of Alabama,* 4 Empl. Prac. Dec. ¶7757 (5th Cir. 1972).
[27] *Heard v. Mueller Co.,* 4 Empl. Prac. Dec. ¶7904 (6th Cir. 1972).
[28] *Franks v. Bowman Transportation Co.,* 11 Empl. Prac. Dec. ¶10,777 (U.S. 1976).

missed because the representative's case is settled or *subsequently* dismissed and the representative no longer has a personal stake in the case.

Time Limitations

A common trait of complaints is a time limitation within which they must be filed. Regarding Title VII, this statute of limitations is as follows:

> A charge under this section shall be filed within one hundred and eighty days after the alleged unlawful employment practice occurred . . . except that in a case of an unlawful employment practice with respect to which the person aggrieved has initially instituted proceedings with a State or local agency with authority to grant or seek relief from such practice or to institute criminal proceedings with respect thereto upon receiving notice thereof, such charge shall be filed by or on behalf of the person aggrieved within three hundred days after the alleged unlawful employment practice occurred, or within thirty days after receiving notice that the State or local agency has terminated the proceedings under the State or local law.[29]

Many state agencies which have a working relationship with the EEOC have the complainant make out an EEOC charge form at the same time that the state complaint is being made.

The statute of limitations under the Age Discrimination in Employment Act is also 180 days after the alleged act with an extension to 300 days if a comparable state authority to seek relief exists. Regarding the Equal Pay Act, which is actually Section 6 of the Fair Labor Standards Act of 1938, as amended, the limitation for filing a complaint is two years. This may be extended to three years in the case of willful violations, which are rather difficult to prove. And if a complaint is filed under the Rehabilitation Act of 1973, it must be made to the director of the Office of Federal Contract Compliance Programs within 180 days.

Under various circumstances an act of discrimination may be viewed as continuing, thereby extending the limitation period. In cases dealing with a failure to promote, the act may in effect take place over a long period of time if the reason for the person's rejection, such as an unlawful educational requirement, will continue to hinder the complainant's promotion to a similar position.[30] Likewise, transfer complaints may also be seen as continuing.[31] And while layoffs are seemingly not subject to the principle of continuing violations, the failure to recall may be,

---

[29] §706(e).
[30] *Mack v. General Electric Co.*, 3 Empl. Prac. Dec. ¶8272 (1971).
[31] *Belt v. Johnson Motor Lines*, 4 Empl. Prac. Dec. ¶7751 (5th Cir. 1972).

under certain circumstances, as outlined in the case of *Cox v. United States Gypsum:*

> (1) A layoff, as distinguished from discharge or quitting, suggests a possibility of re-employment. (2) A layman's claim of "continuing" discrimination, after a discriminatory layoff, readily suggests that he claims there has been subsequent recall or new hiring which discriminates against him. (3) The record shows that the company had bound itself, by its collective bargaining agreement, to consider seniority in making a recall, and the agreement provides that an employee does not lose seniority by reason of layoff until one year has expired. (4) The commission chose to accept these charges as timely. (5) The Company received notices of other charges of similar current discrimination at or about the same time.[32]

In addition, there have been cases where discrimination relating to a pension plan[33] and even a refusal to hire that involved a "discriminatory system rather than one isolated instance"[34] were seen as continuing in nature.

And in an important precedent-setting case, *Culpepper v. Reynolds Metals Company*, the Fifth Circuit Court of Appeals ruled that the statute of limitations is tolled "once an employee invokes his contractual grievance remedies in a constructive effort to seek a 'private settlement of his complaint.' "[35] However, the *Culpepper* rule was found invalid by the Supreme Court in *Electrical Workers Local 790 v. Robbins & Myers, Inc.*, a discharge case; the ruling was that:

> The existence and utilization of grievance procedures does not toll the running of the limitations period that would otherwise begin on the date of the firing, Title VII remedies being independent of other pre-existing remedies available to an aggrieved employee. *Alexander v. Gardner-Denver Co.*, 415 U.S. 36; *Johnson v. Railway Express Agency*, 421 U.S. 454.[36]

Deferrals

The deferral of EEOC complaints to state and local fair employment agencies is provided for in Sections 706(c) and 706(b) of Title VII:

> (c) In the case of an alleged unlawful employment practice occurring in a State, or political subdivision of a State, which has a State or local law

---

[32] 2 Empl. Prac. Dec. ¶9988 (7th Cir. 1969).
[33] *Mixson v. Southern Bell Telephone and Telegraph Co.*, 4 Empl. Prac. Dec. ¶7606 (1971).
[34] *Watson v. Limbach Corp.*, 4 Empl. Prac. Dec. ¶7648 (1971).
[35] 2 Empl. Prac. Dec. ¶10,138 (1970).
[36] 12 Empl. Prac. Dec. ¶11,256 (1976).

prohibiting the unlawful employment practice alleged and establishing
or authorizing a State or local authority to grant or seek relief from such
practice or to institute criminal proceedings with respect thereto upon
receiving notice thereof, no charge may be filed under subsection (a) by
the person aggrieved before the expiration of sixty days after proceedings have been commenced under the State or local law, unless such
proceedings have been earlier terminated, provided that such sixty-
day period shall be extended to one hundred and twenty days during
the first year after the effective date of such State or local law.

In determining whether reasonable cause exists, the Commission shall
accord substantial weight to final findings and orders made by State or
local law pursuant to the requirements of subsections (c) and (d).

A list of these so-called 706 agencies can be found in Appendix 4. In
addition, Section 709(b) authorizes the EEOC to:

. . . engage in and contribute to the cost of research and other projects
of mutual interest undertaken by such agencies, and utilize the services
of such agencies and their employees, and, notwithstanding any other
provision of law, pay by advance or reimbursement such agencies and
their employees for services rendered to assist the Commission in carrying out this title.

The deferral of EEOC charges to state and local agencies is an important aspect of civil rights law enforcement. As indicated, these agencies
are compensated for their work, and their progress is monitored by the
EEOC. Although the period of deferral is 60 days, in actuality the deferral agencies may have the complaint for a much longer period due to
backlogs in both agencies.

Deferral means that in many, if not most, cases a complainant will
have two chances of getting his or her case resolved and obtaining some
sort of compensatory relief. If the deferral agency finds reasonable cause
to credit the complainant's allegations and is unsuccessful at obtaining
relief, the EEOC will most likely give "substantial weight" to those
findings and also attempt settlement through the conciliation process.
And even when the deferral agency does not make such a finding, the
EEOC may come to an opposite conclusion as to the case's merits. The
deferral procedure gives the complainant two avenues of legal action
that would not normally be available. On the one hand, a person making out a charge with the EEOC may be able to make use of the administrative hearings and legal representation frequently provided to complainants on the state level. On the other hand, persons filing with the
state will, as part of most contractual agreements with 706 agencies,
have the complainant make out an EEOC charge form as well. This will

give the complainant the subsequent option of taking the case to federal court should both the state and EEOC be unable to obtain a satisfactory settlement of the case.

Relationship of Complaints to Other Avenues of Relief

Several employers are disturbed that complainants failed to use the grievance procedures available to them before proceeding to file a Title VII complaint; conversely, employers become equally upset when persons continue a grievance by way of Title VII after having used the other means of obtaining remedies, such as a grievance/arbitration decision. However, both occurrences are generally appropriate. There is no need to exhaust grievance machinery before making a charge with the EEOC; nor can the fact that other such remedial attempts have been made preclude the complainant's right to continue under Title VII. This is true even when the complainant had received a partial settlement pursuant to the efforts of a state agency.[37]

The landmark case in this area is *Alexander v. Gardner-Denver Co.*, decided by the Supreme Court in 1974:

> There is no suggestion in the statutory scheme that a prior arbitral decision either forecloses an individual's right to sue or divests federal courts of jurisdiction . . . .

> Moreover, the legislative history of Title VII manifests a congressional intent to allow an individual to pursue independently his rights under both Title VII and other applicable state and federal statutes. The clear inference is that Title VII was designed to supplement, rather than supplant, existing laws and institutions relating to employment discrimination. In sum, Title VII's purpose and procedures strongly suggest that an individual does not forfeit his private cause of action if he first pursues his grievance to final arbitration under the nondiscrimination clause of a collective-bargaining agreement.[38]

INVESTIGATIONS

Most civil rights laws contain a provision which authorizes the obtaining of information by way of documents, as well as testimony, to investigate complaints. It is a common investigatory technique to threaten the use of such authority to compel the production of evidence. Challenges to the scope and authority of such actions by the government may

---

[37] *Voutsis v. Union Carbide Corporation*, 4 Empl. Prac. Dec. ¶7592 (2d Cir. 1972); *Cooper v. Phillip Morris, Inc.*, 4 Empl. Prac. Dec. ¶7888 (6th Cir. 1972).

[38] 7 Empl. Prac. Dec. ¶9148 (1974).

require legal counsel, and to that extent no advice is offered here. However, in many situations employers themselves will be able to contest, and possibly limit, the scope of an investigation.

Scope

Because of the generally accepted notion concerning the "class" nature of discrimination, the information sought may be far-ranging and spread across a broad spectrum of employment activities. Minimally, however, there will be an attempt to obtain comparison evidence so as to determine whether the complainant was treated differently from those outside of his or her class. For example, if it has been indicated that an employee was fired for excessive absenteeism, the investigation will logically seek records relating to all other employees' rates of absences. If the complainant was allegedly not hired because of a lack of experience or other factor, the investigator will want to review all accepted applicants for the same job. Another element of proof which shapes the search for evidence is statistics. Thus, the investigation will require the last EEO-1 form submitted by the employer (see page 58) or the divulging of similar information. The breadth of information typically requested in a discharge complaint by means of a standard government interrogatory can be found in Chapter 8.

The employer has two main legal defenses to the amount and nature of information sought. The first argues that such information is not relevant to the charge being investigated. The issue of relevance was succinctly stated in *EEOC v. University of New Mexico*, citing a Supreme Court decision:

> The law governing the limits on the administrative power of investigation has evolved from the earlier judicial condemnation of fishing expeditions to that of enforcement of the subpoena power "if the inquiry is within the authority of the agency, the demand is not too indefinite and the information sought is reasonably relevant." *United States v. Morton Salt Co.*, 338 U.S. 632, 652, 70 S.Ct. 357, 369, 94 L.Ed. 401 (1950). . . .[39]

Employers may achieve some success in making the "fishing expedition" argument, although it will certainly depend upon the inclinations of the agency being contested as well as the actual charges. Court decisions also will vary. In the *University of New Mexico* case just noted, information concerning the university's employment practices was seen

---

[39] 11 Empl. Prac. Dec. ¶10,935 (1976).

as relevant to a charge of retaliation and discriminatory references. In another decision, however, a demand for information was denied because it "reached back in time nearly eight years" and "demanded evidence going to forms of discrimination not even charged or alleged."[40]

A second defense to the scope of information sought claims that it is unduly burdensome on the employer. Yet the success of this argument is directly related to the validity of the first. As stated in the *University of New Mexico* decision:

> The Court holds that, assuming it to be true that compliance with the subpoena would be burdensome, burdensomeness alone is not a sufficient basis for refusal to enforce a subpoena. 42 U.S.C. 2000(e)-8(a) provides that the Commission shall have access to all information that relates to unlawful employment practices and is relevant to the charge under investigation. It places no limitations on the Commission's access to materials on the basis of the burden to the company. As the court stated in *H. Kessler & Co. v. EEOC:* "If the information on records sought is relevant or material to the charge under investigation and the EEOC proceeds as authorized by the statute, then any inconvenience or difficulty (which is actually inherent in any compulsory process proceeding) must be considered as a 'part of the social burden of living under government.' "[41]

Interviewing Witnesses

The evidence obtained by witnesses' statements frequently plays an important part in an agency's investigation. Their observations may act to contradict or otherwise discredit other evidence put forth by the company, such as written policies, statements by management, and even documentary evidence. For example, substantial testimony by coworkers may serve to neutralize or invalidate the complainant's written performance evaluations.

EEOC investigators will attempt to speak to company officials separately, suggesting that "each has a particular area of expertise." Actually the suggestion is aimed at preventing "one person from being influenced by the comments of others."[42] The EEOC Compliance Manual

---

[40] *General Insurance Co. of America v. EEOC*, 7 Empl. Prac. Dec. ¶9086 (9th Cir. 1974).

[41] 11 Empl. Prac. Dec. ¶10,935 (1976), *citing* 4 Empl. Prac. Dec. ¶7537 (1971), *aff'd* 5th Cir. Other cases coming to the same conclusion are *New Orleans Public Service, Inc. v. Brown*, 9 Empl. Prac. Dec. ¶9928 (5th Cir. 1975); *Sheet Metal Workers, Local 104 v. EEOC*, 3 F.E.P. Cas. 218 (9th Cir. 1971); and *Circle K Corp., Inc. v. EEOC*, 8 F.E.P. Cas. 758 (10th Cir. 1972).

[42] EEOC Compl. Man., §23.2(c)(2).

instructs the investigator to honor a respondent's insistence on having an attorney present during these interviews. However, it also notes that

> . . . hourly paid employees, on the other hand, are not part of management; if Respondent remains adamant in their request for an attorney, make arrangements to talk with these persons at another time, away from Respondent's premises, if possible.[43]

Similarly, the manual advises that if the employer "insists on having a representative present during an on-the-job interview," the witness may be understandably uncooperative, thus requiring "a simple rescheduling of the time of the interview and/or a change of location."[44] When this is not possible, the testimony of employees with company officials present will apparently be given less weight.

In order to make use of witnesses' statements, notably those in support of the complainant, investigators will normally try to have those questioned sign an affidavit or, at least, a written statement as to what was said. When this is not possible, notes taken during the interview or recollections made shortly afterward will be used as evidence. Regarding the latter, questions of credibility as to what statements were in fact made may arise.

Use of Subpoenas and Interrogatories

Two legal instruments of investigation are the subpoena and interrogatory. The former compels a person to give testimony under oath or produce documents or other evidence. The latter refers to questions which must be answered in writing and under oath.

The New Jersey Division on Civil Rights was one of the first state fair employment agencies to implement wide and consistent use of the interrogatory, a practice which is now common in many other states. Standard interrogatories exist for various types of cases, such as discharge, refusal to hire, failure to promote, etc., and are therefore easily served on employers when the applicable complaint is filed with the agency. While this approach results in greater efficiency on the part of the government, it effectively shifts the burden of the investigation to the one being investigated! Indeed, answering government interrogatories may entail the spending of long hours by company personnel. With this in mind, attempts are made to settle a case when the interrogatories are served.

As noted previously, the "overly burdensome" argument is only effective when the information sought is not relevant to the charge. Defen-

---

[43] §23.2(c)(3).
[44] §23.3(b) and §23.3(c).

dant companies may rightly object that the questions should be tailored to the particular case. On the other hand, employers who are vague in their responses or plainly uncooperative in answering the interrogatory may be met, in New Jersey, with the *interrogatory default procedure rule*. Under this procedure, questions not answered are "taken as established for the purposes of the case in accordance with the claim of the complainant," and a public hearing is held with the defendant employer unable to offer proofs. Based on the hearing examiner's recommendation, the director of the agency issues an order providing "appropriate relief."[45] Of course, each state will vary in its ability to enforce its investigatory authority. The New Jersey method of enforcing the power to issue interrogatories is especially effective because it is done administratively and by means of threatening a default of the employer's ability to defend the merits of a case.

The use of subpoena power is less frequent than interrogatories. Enforcing a subpoena, as with any type of administrative authority, requires use of the courts. As mentioned in one case:

> But enforcement against a really intransigent party can be costly and time consuming, particularly in administrative proceedings where the enforcement process is of necessity collateral to the main case.[46]

Considering the number of cases investigated, subpoenas are rarely used by the EEOC.

Statistical Evidence

Many investigations will seek statistical data on the number and location of women and minorities in the work force; comparative rates of hire, promotion, discharge, etc., between minorities and non-minorities; and other such information. The use of statistics as an element of proof is covered in detail in Chapter 3. Thus, the employer should not be surprised when this type of evidence is sought. This evidence may be obtained by means of interrogatories or a review of personnel records. Moreover, employers who file the EEO-1 report may find this information to be on file with the EEOC and the 706 agencies.

Documentary Evidence

This may take many forms, such as personnel records, pay records, standard operating procedures, employment applications, interoffice

---

[45] A New Jersey appellate court upheld the default procedure in *General Motors Corp. v. Blair*, 8 Empl. Prac. Dec. ¶9654 (1974).

[46] Ibid.

memos, seniority lists, labor contracts, job descriptions, job advertisements, discharge notices, grievances, absenteeism records, and layoff notices.

Confidentiality

EEOC's *Procedural Rules* contain a section dealing with the confidentiality of investigations:

> Neither a charge, nor information obtained pursuant to Section 709(a) of Title VII, nor information obtained from records required to be kept or reports required to be filed pursuant to Sections 709(c) and (d) of said Title, shall be made matters of public information by the Commission prior to the institution of any proceedings under this Title involving such charge or information. This provision does not apply to such earlier disclosures to the charging party, the respondent, witnesses, and representatives of interested Federal, State and local agencies as may be appropriate or necessary to the carrying out of the Commission's functions under the Title, nor to the publication of data derived from such information in a form which does not reveal the identity of the charging party, respondent, or person supplying the information.[47]

State fair employment statutes, however, may not be bound by confidentiality requirements.

ADMINISTRATIVE DETERMINATIONS

Agency determinations regarding the merits of a complaint are *not* equivalent to the kinds of judgments that come after an administrative or court hearing. Pertaining to the EEOC, the employer will receive a Letter of Determination explaining in a page or two how "there is not reasonable cause to credit Charging Party's allegation" or how "there is reasonable cause to believe the charge is true." State and local agencies will also state and explain whether reasonable or "probable cause" has been found. The legal weight of these findings is similar to that of indictments. They do not empower the administrative agency to award damages or order that certain actions be taken. Reasonable cause determinations both allow for an attempt to settle the case to the satisfaction of all parties and increase the likelihood of the case's proceeding to a more formal decision. Administrative findings without a public hearing are subject to judicial review. Employers who reject determinations not in their favor will have the opportunity to defend themselves in a com-

---

[47] §1601.20.

pletely new trial. As stated in a decision which upheld the EEOC's procedural regulations:

> The administrative actions of the commission do not in themselves enforce any rights or impose any obligations. This can be done only by a voluntary conciliation agreement or by a court after a trial *de novo*.[48]

Administrative determinations coming after a full hearing may also be appealed, though not normally in the form of a whole new trial.

A Note on Objectivity

The need for a legal, objective approach to the study of unlawful discrimination was the first topic covered in this book. The need for objectivity applies equally to those who investigate complaints, for this is an area which is notably subject to one's predispositions and values. The EEOC's Compliance Manual contains a suggestion for investigators that deserves mention in this regard:

> It should be kept in mind that Respondent's failure to "justify" an adverse employment action against a minority group person does not constitute proof of discrimination.[49]

Indeed it does not. But investigators who are unfairly predisposed to the motivations of employers may see an absence of justification as proof of discrimination. Possible investigator bias is not to be taken lightly. Although their recommendations are assuredly subject to the review and guidance of government supervisors, the enforcement agency depends on their reviewing all relevant evidence fairly and rationally. The fact remains, unfortunately, that it *is* relatively easy for one to ignore evidence from one quarter while emphasizing that from another.

Adverse Inference Rule

This rule states the following:

> Whenever a Respondent has a record or other evidence within its control and fails or refuses to produce it, the Commission may infer that the evidence goes against the Respondent.[50]

---

[48] *EEOC v. Raymond Metal Products Co.*, 11 Empl. Prac. Dec. ¶10,629 (4th Cir. 1976).
[49] §121.3(b).
[50] EEOC Compl. Man., §161.1.

In a sense, this is a mild form of the default procedure mentioned above and is one technique for getting information. As suggested to the investigator in the EEOC Compliance Manual:

> In any case, whether the investigator anticipates using the rule eventually or not, a Respondent that hesitates to produce evidence should be told that the Commission may draw an adverse inference from its failure to produce the requested evidence. Besides putting the Respondent on notice that the rule might be used against it, such a statement could motivate the Respondent to produce the requested evidence.[51]

The Manual also lists conditions that must be met before using the adverse inference rule. They are:

> (1) that the evidence requested is relevant; (2) that the Respondent was asked for the evidence, with ample time to produce it and with notice that failure to produce it would result in an adverse inference; and (3) that Respondent produced neither the evidence nor an acceptable explanation as to why the evidence was not produced.[52]

Issues of Credibility

There will be cases in which statements made by witnesses directly contradict each other and will not be resolved by other forms of evidence such as statistics or personnel records. Judges resolve such conflicts by looking at the credibility of the witnesses by analyzing their demeanor, the nature of their observations, and their interests in the outcome of the case. Government field representatives, however, are not judges. In such situations, how are issues of credibility decided?

Neither of the options available to the field representative are beneficial to the charged employer. As just noted, if the investigator is predisposed one way or the other in the case, he or she may wish to accept one statement and ignore another. While this is hardly a reliable means of investigation, it does occur. The other alternative is to give the benefit of the doubt to the complainant and recommend reasonable cause with the indication that issues of credibility can only be adequately resolved by a formal hearing. All this makes for one key suggestion: be sure that employment decisions can be documented. It is the best way of preventing issues of credibility from controlling the government's decision on the merits of a complaint.

---

[51] Ibid.
[52] §161.2.

SETTLEMENTS

When fair employment agencies make reasonable cause determinations, they are usually empowered, in fact required, to attempt a settlement of the case without further legal action. In Title VII this requirement is found at Section 706(b):

> If the Commission determines after much investigation that there is reasonable cause to believe that the charge is true, the Commission shall endeavor to eliminate any such alleged unlawful employment practice by informal methods of conference, conciliation, and persuasion.

Trying to settle complaints without further action is a standard practice of all government agencies administering civil laws. To do otherwise would require great expenditure of resources and result in an immense backlog in the courts.

Pre-Determination Settlement

Settlements may be made before the agency has taken a position on a complaint's merits. This is stated in the EEOC's *Procedural Rules* and is a common practice:

> At any time subsequent to a preliminary investigation and prior to the issuance of a determination as to reasonable cause, the District Directors, or other designated officers, may engage in settlement discussion. The District Directors, or other designated officers, may make and approve settlements, on behalf of the Commission, in those cases where such authority has been delegated to them by the Commission.[53]

Such settlements may be within the interests of both the government and the employer. In reference to the former, it may substantially lessen the amount of hours the agency needs to spend on a case. Regarding the employer, early settlement may be particularly beneficial because drawn-out investigations, which are far from uncommon, could result in large expenditures of time and money. This is especially true when the damages of a case are of a continuing nature, such as in a refusal-to-hire or discharge complaint where the complainant remains unemployed for long periods.

---

[53] §1601.19(a).

EEOC Conciliation Strategy

When a reasonable cause determination is made, the EEOC attempts to settle the case by means of a written agreement acceptable to all parties.

> Nothing said or done during and as a part of such informal endeavors may be made public by the Commission, its officers or employees, or used as evidence in a subsequent proceeding without the written consent of the persons concerned.[54]

The EEOC's strategy at conciliation conferences can be found in its Compliance Manual:

> The conciliator, after describing the Commission's procedures from receipt of the charge through the investigation and reasonable cause determination, should explain the following:
>
> (a) that the Commission is seeking a written agreement which remedies the violation and provides appropriate relief for charging party and other similarly situated person;
>
> (b) the agreement will contain a waiver of the charging party's right-to-sue where the charging party is a signatory;
>
> (c) that if an agreement acceptable to the Commission is obtained, the matter will not be referred to the Attorney General or the OFCC;
>
> (d) that no admission of the violation is necessary in order to make a settlement and none is presumed;
>
> (e) that conciliation efforts are confidential under the Commission's procedural regulations and under the statute; and
>
> (f) that it is advantageous for Respondent to settle through conciliation thus avoiding a lawsuit, adverse publicity and extra expense accompanying such action.[55]

IF CONCILIATION FAILS

How is the law enforced when the case cannot be settled? Under Title VII, either the EEOC or the charging party or both can take the case to federal court. The charging party can proceed to federal court whether or not the EEOC had made a reasonable cause determination, as long as the complaint is filed in court no more than 90 days after receiving a right-to-sue letter. Compared to the number of unsuccessful conciliations, the chance that the EEOC will take a complainant's case to court is

---

[54] Title VII, §706(b).
[55] §64.1.

quite slim. Complainants pursuant to the Age Discrimination in Employment Act and the Equal Pay Act may also seek redress in federal court unless the government files in their behalf.

Enforcement pursuant to state agencies is noticeably different. Many will represent the charging party at an administrative hearing and issue orders when the hearing officer's recommendations are in their favor. These orders, which may award damages, as can any other court decision, are subject to judicial review, but here too the complainant may have free legal representation.

11

Handling Investigations and Resolving Complaints

The manner in which an employer reacts to the investigation of a complaint and participates in settlement discussions will have an effect on their outcome. And although government representatives will mention nothing of this in their training seminars and workshops for employers, the fact remains that employers unknowingly commit many errors in this often-forgotten area, sometimes causing irreparable harm. This chapter offers some suggestions for avoiding such mistakes and dealing with administrative agencies in a way that will promote the employer's best interests.

RECEIVING THE COMPLAINT

Because of the 1972 amendments to Title VII, employers should receive notices of charges against them within 10 days of their being filed. This is a welcome change from the past when the EEOC was known to hold complaints for a long time, a practice which may have the effect of greatly extending damages when they are continuing. The time limitation on serving complaints will vary from state to state, and there may be no limitation at all. At any rate, employers should not let the investigation and processing of complaints drag on once they are received. Every effort should be made to have the complaint promptly looked into by the investigating agency, especially in failure-to-hire, failure-to-promote, discharge, and equal pay cases. The back pay liability may run for a long period, due to the general backlog in the government. The longer a complaint is pending, the greater the probability that damages will be high, and the greater the chance that a little case will turn into a major one.

Management frequently makes the mistake of overreacting at this point. The automatic reflex of "we're not guilty of discrimination" surfaces, along with the attitude of "let's call the lawyer and fight it all the way." Those who have dutifully read this book will know that such emotional reactions may severely limit the ability to deal effectively with the complaint. Furthermore, this book is aimed at enabling the employer to handle complaints properly without the burden of legal expenses.

REVIEWING THE COMPLAINT'S MERITS

The first step is to determine the relative merit of the complaint by objectively viewing it within the context of how unlawful discrimination is proved, as covered in Chapter 3. When doing this, emphasis should be given to determining the merits of the charge, such as "discharge because of race," and the analysis should not be limited to the statement of facts supporting the allegation. The accuracy of these facts is important, but a charge may be upheld even when they are incorrect.

Doing an *objective* analysis represents the real challenge to successful complaint resolution. Many employers fail here because they begin with the premise that no discrimination occurred and then proceed to gather evidence in support of this position. This is not objectivity. Instead, there should be an overall appraisal of the evidence from both the complainant and respondent, and a realization that the evidence will most likely be circumstantial in nature. Are there any indications of evil intent, differential treatment, or disparate effect? Will relevant statistics be an asset or liability to the complainant? Are there issues of credibility? An expeditious, yet accurate, investigation must be made by the employer so as to approximate the probability of the complaint's prevailing and the concomitant viability of a defense.

CLASS RAMIFICATIONS

The employer must weigh the likelihood of the complaint's becoming a class action. Does the allegation refer to an isolated incident or a pattern and practice of company-wide discrimination? Does it refer to a policy or practice which may be applicable to several other employees or job applicants? Great effort should be made to resolve such complaints at an early stage. The class aspects of the case may be limited or eliminated by settling the individual charge well before the litigation phase. Immediate corrective action can be called for, which will quickly change the unlawful practice to the satisfaction of other potential complainants.

STOPPING CONTINUING DAMAGES

As noted above, in certain instances complainants will continue to build up a potential back pay liability during the course of their case. If the complainant does win out, particularly in times of high unemployment, the monetary damages will be overly large. This danger is amplified not only by the backlog of pending cases, but also the fact that the doctrine of laches, or negligent delay, has not been found applicable to government agencies. But there is one way to stop such liability from continuing during the time in which a complaint is being handled: an unconditional offer of employment to the complainant. "Unconditional" means that it will be under the same terms and conditions as with other employees and that the complainant is not required to drop the complaint. No matter how the complainant responds, the back pay liability will have ended at that point. If it is accepted the complainant obviously will no longer be unemployed. On the other hand, rejection of the offer will signify a failure in the duty to mitigate damages. As discussed in Chapter 5, back pay awards are deducted by "amounts earnable with reasonable diligence."

Some will not wish to end continuing damages in this way. The reinstatement of a formerly discharged employee may have a disturbing effect on personnel relations and be a sign of employer weakness. Or it may be difficult, if not impossible, to provide the complainant with a job. Perhaps he or she is substantially less qualified than others presently in the work force. Still, in many cases an unconditional offer will be a good way to lessen what the employer stands to lose by a complaint. A good many complainants will likely turn down such an offer. Although they may have stated their intent to return to work, or be instated in the job for which they had applied, they are hesitant about working where they feel they may not be well liked.

GETTING THE DEFENSE ORGANIZED

Employers who take the position that the complaint is lacking in merit should organize the evidentiary material supporting a defense. Persons having information on the alleged discriminatory acts should be contacted, personnel records and other pertinent data should be collected, and the general defensive posture should be constructed. The ability to make a credible defense will depend on several factors, as detailed in Chapter 4. What are the facts? Can they be documented? Are there legal limitations in the defense? Can the establishment of a *prima facie* case be negated? Emphasis should be on documentary evidence, such as interoffice memos, performance evaluations, and comparative rates of absenteeism, rather than after-the-fact statements of supervisory personnel. Do not waste time on arguments having little legal weight, such as protestations of good intent, client preference, etc.

In some instances investigators may personally surprise the employer with a demand for information, interviews with employees, and a tour of the facilities. If the employer has not at that point organized a defense and consulted with other management personnel, it is advisable to postpone the visit. Indicate to the investigator that the investigation should be scheduled for another, more convenient time. If the investigator is insistent on doing the investigation now, the employer should state its desire to be represented by legal counsel first, and should state that it intends to cooperate fully with the investigation at a later date.

DEALING WITH THE INVESTIGATOR

In the previous chapter it was mentioned that the issue of discrimination is notably subject to one's predispositions and values, and that enforcement agencies depend on their investigators' reviewing all relevant evidence fairly and rationally. With this in mind, as well as the fact that government field representatives are human, employers should be careful not to intimidate, insult, or otherwise antagonize them. While this advice may appear simple or inappropriate, unquestionably the attitude of the investigator may affect his or her recommendations on the merits of a complaint. The proofs are such that many cases are difficult to decide and can easily go either way. Thus, the stance taken by company officials meeting with investigators should be professional in nature, and the officials should understand the investigator's critical role.

PREVENTING REASONABLE CAUSE

A frequent mistake is to sit back and wait for an agency's determination on the merits of a complaint. Instead, defendants should aim at preventing the unfavorable determination from being made. Better to defend a case now than later on. For one thing, agency findings are difficult to reverse. Regarding the EEOC, its procedural rules state that the "determination is final when issued; therefore, requests for consideration will not be granted."[1] Changing a finding implies that the agency made an error, and there is a natural bureaucratic reluctance to make such a reversal. More significantly, an unfavorable finding will more likely motivate the complainant to continue litigation of the case if it is not settled. On the state level, a finding of reasonable cause will bring on

---

[1] §1601.19(b).

attempts by the agency to settle the case. If those attempts fail, a public hearing may result. Even when we assume that the employer will prevail in its defense, the cost of formal litigation may be greater than the original damages.

COMMUNICATING WITH THE AGENCY

Stating the defensive position to the investigator may be insufficient. Oral presentations are lacking in effect and may easily be ignored. Many employers put together a suitable argument to a complaint but fail to present it properly to government authorities. Therefore, it will often be necessary to state the company's position to the agency in writing. A written response cannot be ignored, and may readily be reviewed and better understood by the agency. Because some investigators may neglect to consider or to comprehend the defendant's side of the case, it is suggested that copies of all communications to the investigator go to the head of the agency. This provides some assurance that the employer's viewpoints will be adequately reviewed and evaluated.

CONSIDERING SETTLEMENT

Cases are generally resolved in three ways: (1) the agency closes the case for lack of a finding of reasonable cause or some other reason; (2) the case proceeds to a formal court hearing and a decision is rendered; and (3) the case is settled. Settlement means an agreement of some sort between the parties, usually providing compensation or a job, or both, to the charging party.

Resolving a case by settlement is a very common practice in legal disputes. Civil rights authorities are required to seek amicable settlements prior to any further legal action by the complaining party. One wonders what our legal system would be like if every controversy were resolved by the rendering of a judgment. The delay in court proceedings would probably be tremendous.

Many variables are involved in a settlement decision. Let us look at four of the more important considerations.

The Factor of Money

Much of what the employer stands to lose is money, whether in the form of back pay, attorney's fees, or time. When calculating back pay, the employer should refer to the guidelines presented in Chapter 5. By indicating to government representatives its interest in settling the case, a respondent can find out how the agency computes the amount they feel is owed to the complainant and obtain information relative to the reduction of the amount, such as interim earnings, efforts at seeking employment elsewhere, the unreasonable refusal of other jobs, etc. Calculating the amount is far from an exact science, and it can be expected that investigating agencies will be liberal in applying the standard of "making the complainant whole." Consequently, the employer should obtain as much meaningful data as possible which might have a bearing on lessening the damages, either from the agency or by its own inquiries.

Of course, the key aspect of damages is whether they are continuing. If so, there must be an estimate of future damages. When the final resolution in a case will be long in coming, continuing damages plainly increase the pressure to settle. On the other hand, if the amount is static, as when the discriminatory act refers to a week's suspension without pay, the need to settle quickly is certainly less.

As noted above, the cost of formal litigation may be greater than the original damages. The employer must therefore determine what the cost of litigation is and whether it is better to continue or to settle now. However, the boundaries of such a decision will not always be clear. The key question is whether the complainant will take the case to a public hearing or court proceeding. In Title VII cases, the complainant may not be willing to spend the funds necessary for legal representation. Some lawyers will take such cases on a contingency basis since attorney's fees will be awarded to prevailing parties pursuant to Title VII. Others will not. It may also be difficult to predict whether state agencies will actually take cases in which conciliation failed to an administrative hearing. Generally, there will be a further review of the case's merits by the agency's legal staff before a hearing is scheduled. In summary, the employer will have to balance the cost of an immediate monetary settlement with the risk of expending more money, or none, later on.

Effect of a Settlement on Operations

Another major worry for employers is the effect of a settlement on its operations, particularly when it involves the reinstatement of a discharged worker. Not only may the employer "lose face" in such circumstances and perhaps suffer because of the effect of the settlement on management's authority, the reinstated employee may indicate to coworkers that the employer is vulnerable to other discrimination complaints. Coworkers may therefore be more inclined to carry their grievances into the legal arena rather than attempt resolution internally. In like manner, employers are often concerned that public knowledge of a settlement will bring more complaints.

Determining the effect will not be easy. Part of the problem is resolved by the fact that settlement agreements are confidential when made with the EEOC, although this may not be true if the settlement is with a state agency. Confidentiality may not ensure that a settlement will not, by word of mouth, become common knowledge, however.

In some situations employer anxieties are unwarranted. For example, the case may have to do with a policy which is not continuing in effect and is beyond the statute of limitations on others' filing a complaint. Or the complaint may have been an isolated incident. Even if news of the settlement does stimulate others to file a complaint, it must be emphasized that not every grievance meets the jurisdictional requirements of civil rights law. And the fact that a complaint is filed says nothing about its merits. Furthermore, many people are not particularly disposed to bring legal actions against employers, particularly their own.

In some instances a settlement will actually have a positive effect on the thoughts and actions of the employer's work force, promoting an improvement in morale. This occurs when the corrective actions of the settlement remedy what has been an unfair, or clearly unlawful, situation and thereby gain the respect of workers.

Considering Principles

All along we have viewed discrimination as a legal concept and insisted that dealing with it requires that one view it from this perspective. Nevertheless, principle becomes a factor when employers sincerely feel that the acts alleged to be discriminatory were not, in fact, unlawfully motivated. No one likes to be accused of discrimination, and the desire to have one's reputation vindicated may be a block to settlement talks. It is true that evidence of evil intent need not be demonstrated to prove unlawful discrimination, and the employer must remember this when the proof being applied is disparate effect. But the underlying assumption in the differential treatment proof, as well as the use of circumstantial evidence in these cases, definitely suggests the presence of an unlawful motive. It is this assumption which irritates many company officials charged with discrimination.

No solutions to the problem of principle are offered here. The legal proofs of discrimination have evolved as part of a national commitment to end discriminatory practices against certain persecuted groups, and it is realized that unlawful discrimination by its very nature will be covert. This, in turn, has resulted in the use of circumstantial evidence and the assumption that differentially treating a protected class member results from that person's class identity. The application of the evidence will not always seem fair. The problem of principles must be viewed within this framework. It is a matter of relative worth. The employer who cannot live with a settlement that seems unfair may have to decide if those feelings are outweighed by the possible costs of further litigation.

The Key Factor: The Merits of the Complaint

Last, but certainly not least, consideration must be given to the merits of the complaint and the probability of its success. This projection must be in terms of the proofs, as presented in Chapter 3. If the employer will probably lose the case, there will be little reason not to settle unless it is unlikely that the case will ever proceed to court. In cases where the damages are static, it may be better to wait and see if this occurs. On the other hand, if damages are continuing, an evaluation of the complaint's merits will be that much more crucial.

APPROACHES TO SETTLEMENT

Settlement is always an option and may be initiated even upon receipt of a complaint. Since the passage of time may increase the amount of monetary liability, it is advisable that the decision on whether to settle be made as soon as possible.

The Pre-Determination Settlement, as provided for in the EEOC's regulations, is the employer's best means of complaint resolution. The 10-day rule on serving complaints enables the employer to consider settlement when the liability is low, and to enhance its negotiating position because a determination on the merits of the case has yet to have been made. In addition, the complainant will be in an awkward position if a full settlement offer is refused.

At a conciliation conference the complainant will normally not take part, although his or her consent will be sought. What if the complainant is highly unreasonable and demands every penny of a full back pay settlement, or perhaps even more than the damages requested? In varying degrees agencies will attempt to persuade the charging party to be more reasonable. In the case of state agencies, they may refuse to proceed further with the complaint. Of course, pursuant to Title VII and other laws, the complainant may continue litigation alone.

At the conference the agency's attitude toward the case may be influenced by the defendant's comments on its merits, even though it is professed that this is not so. Yet employers should not go "overboard" in getting their defensive posture across and should try to remain calm and not overly argumentative. In this way one can be more assured that the government's representatives are listening to what the employer is saying and are not "tuned out" or "turned off" by the emotional level of the discussions. Be sure that the position put forth has evidentiary value. Conciliators are quite accustomed to hearing, and ignoring, meaningless arguments from employers. Factual issues should be presented as much as possible with the realization that issues of credibility will not be decided at the conference.

After discussing the merits of the case, the employer should state its interest in resolving the matter and turn to the amount of monetary damages and other remedial actions proposed by the agency as settlement. Not only should the employer inquire as to how the damages were computed, but it should seek further information on the length of the back pay period, the complainant's interim earnings, the standards used in computations, etc. If the agency does not justify the amount requested, the employer should indicate that such justification will be necessary before a settlement can be considered. The employer has every right to make this demand. What is more, if the employer has evidence that either the calculations or other data are incorrect, this information should be presented.

Basing its offer on these discussions, the employer should make a counteroffer. The amount should be less than what the employer sees as its limit, and should be explained in terms of the employer's own computation of damages and any questionable aspects of the case's merits. Of course, the employer will have to decide on what combination of remedial actions is acceptable. If the complainant's eventual reply is negative, indicate a willingness to continue settlement talks but insist now on a counteroffer from the complainant. This should be done in writing. Requiring a counteroffer is important. Do not get into the position of continually raising the offer, as in an auction, until the complainant accepts.

In its negotiations the agency may indicate that it is flexible on the language of an agreement, as a trade-off for other provisions such as back pay and reinstatement. This may be a ploy, for the language of the agreement is hardly important. These settlements normally contain a disclaimer clause, such as "this is not an admission by the respondent of any violation of the law." It's fine to have such a provision; in fact, it is standard. Therefore, the acceptance by the government of such a clause should not be used by them to keep the monetary damages high. There have been several multimillion dollar settlements which contained a disclaimer clause. Any implication of guilt in the agreement will be in the mind of the beholder and have little, if anything, to do with the language of its terms. However, one provision that should be included is an agreement by the complainant not to take any further legal action relating to the complaint against the employer. Such a release, in one form or another, should be part of any settlement.

Title VII and the EEOC Guidelines

Title VII of the Civil Rights Act of 1964, and its guidelines as issued by the Equal Employment Opportunity Commission, represent the most comprehensive federal statute prohibiting employment discrimination.

Title VII is that section of the Civil Rights Act of 1964 which prohibits job discrimination and was amended, as shown by italics, in 1972.

CIVIL RIGHTS ACT OF 1964 AS AMENDED

AN ACT To enforce the constitutional right to vote, to confer jurisdiction upon the district courts of the United States to provide injunctive relief against discrimination in public accommodations, to authorize the Attorney General to institute suits to protect constitutional rights in public facilities and public education, to extend the Commission on Civil Rights, to prevent discrimination in federally assisted programs, to establish a Commission on Equal Employment Opportunity, and for other purposes.

Be it enacted by the Senate and House of Representatives of the United States of America in Congress assembled, That this Act may be cited as the "Civil Rights Act of 1964".

* * *

Title VII—Equal Employment Opportunity[1]

DEFINITIONS

Sec. 701. For the purposes of this title—

(a) The term "person" includes one or more individuals, *governments, governmental agencies, political subdivisions,* labor unions, partnerships, associations, corporations, legal representatives, mutual companies, joint-stock companies, trusts, unincorporated organizations, trustees, trustees in bankruptcy, or receivers.

---

[1] Includes 1972 amendments made by P.L. 92-261 printed in italic.

(b) The term "employer" means a person engaged in an industry affecting commerce who has *fifteen* or more employees for each working day in each of twenty or more calendar weeks in the current or preceding calendar year, and any agent of such a person, but such term does not include (1) the United States, a corporation wholly owned by the Government of the United States, an Indian tribe, or *any department or agency of the District of Columbia subject by statute to procedures of the competitive service (as defined in section 2102 of title 5 of the United States Code), or* (2) a bona fide private membership club (other than a labor organization) which is exempt from taxation under section 501(c) of the Internal Revenue Code of 1954, *except that during the first year after the date of enactment of the Equal Employment Opportunity Act of 1972,* persons having fewer than *twenty-five* employees (and their agents) shall not be considered *employers*.

(c) The term "employment agency" means any person regularly undertaking with or without compensation to procure employees for an employer or to procure for employees opportunities to work for an employer and includes an agent of such a person.

(d) The term "labor organization" means a labor organization engaged in an industry affecting commerce, and any agent of such an organization, and includes any organization of any kind, any agency, or employee representation committee, group, association, or plan so engaged in which employees participate and which exists for the purpose, in whole or in part, of dealing with employers concerning grievances, labor disputes, wages, rates of pay, hours, or other terms or conditions of employment, and any conference, general committee, joint or system board, or joint council so engaged which is subordinate to a national or international labor organization.

(e) A labor organization shall be deemed to be engaged in an industry affecting commerce if (1) it maintains or operates a hiring hall or hiring office which procures employees for an employer or procures for employees opportunities to work for an employer, or (2) the number of its members (or, where it is a labor organization composed of other labor organizations or their representatives, if the aggregate number of the members of such other labor organization) is (*A*) *twenty-five* or more during the first year after the *date of enactment of the Equal Employment Opportunity Act of 1972, or* (*B*) *fifteen* or more thereafter, and such labor organization—

(1) is the certified representative of employees under the provisions of the National Labor Relations Act, as amended, or the Railway Labor Act, as amended;

(2) although not certified, is a national or international labor organization or a local labor organization recognized or acting as the representative of employees of an employer or employers engaged in an industry affecting commerce; or

(3) has chartered a local labor organization or subsidiary body which is representing or actively seeking to represent employees of employers within the meaning of paragraph (1) or (2); or

(4) has been chartered by a labor organization representing or actively seeking to represent employees within the meaning of paragraph (1) or (2) as the local or subordinate body through which such employees may enjoy membership or become affiliated with such labor organization; or

(5) is a conference, general committee, joint or system board, or joint council subordinate to a national or international labor organization, which includes a labor organization engaged in an industry affecting commerce within the meaning of any of the preceding paragraphs of this subsection.

(f) The term "employee" means an individual employed by an employer, *except that the term 'employee' shall not include any person elected to public office in any State or political subdivision of any State by the qualified voters thereof, or any person chosen by such officer to be on such officer's personal staff, or an appointee on the policymaking level or an immediate adviser with respect to the exercise of the constitutional or legal powers of the office. The exemption set forth in the preceding sentence shall not include employees subject to the civil service laws of a State government, governmental agency or political subdivision.*

(g) The term "commerce" means trade, traffic, commerce, transportation, transmission, or communication among the several States; or between a State and any place outside thereof; or within the District of Columbia, or a possession of the United States; or between points in the same State but through a point outside thereof.

(h) The term "industry affecting commerce" means any activity, business, or industry in commerce or in which a labor dispute would hinder or obstruct commerce or the free flow of commerce and includes any activity or industry "affecting commerce" within the meaning of the Labor-Management Reporting and Disclosure Act of 1959, *and further includes any governmental industry, business, or activity.*

(i) The term "State" includes a State of the United States, the District of Columbia, Puerto Rico, the Virgin Islands, American Samoa, Guam, Wake Island, the Canal Zone, and Outer Continental Shelf lands defined in the Outer Continental Shelf Lands Act.

(j) *The term "religion" includes all aspects of religious observance and practice, as well as belief, unless an employer demonstrates that he is unable to reasonably accommodate to an employee's or prospective employee's, religious observance or practice without undue hardship on the conduct of the employer's business.*

EXEMPTION

Sec. 702. This title shall not apply to an employer with respect to the employment of aliens outside any State, or to a religious corporation, association, *educational institution,* or society with respect to the employment of individuals of a particular religion to perform work connected with the carrying on by such corporation, association, *educational institution,* or society of its *activities.*

DISCRIMINATION BECAUSE OF RACE, COLOR, RELIGION, SEX, OR NATIONAL ORIGIN

Sec. 703. (a) It shall be an unlawful employment practice for an employer—

(1) to fail or refuse to hire or to discharge any individual or otherwise to discriminate against any individual with respect to his compensation, terms, conditions, or privileges of employment, because of such individual's race, color, religion, sex, or national origin; or

(2) to limit, segregate, or classify his employees *or applicants for employment* in any way which would deprive or tend to deprive any individual of employment opportunities or otherwise adversely affect his status as an employee, because of such individual's race, color, religion, sex, or national origin.

(b) It shall be an unlawful employment practice for an employment agency to fail or refuse to refer for employment, or otherwise to discriminate against, any individual because of his race, color, religion, sex, or national origin, or to classify or refer for employment any individual on the basis of his race, color, religion, sex, or national origin.

(c) It shall be an unlawful employment practice for a labor organization—

(1) to exclude or to expel from its membership, or otherwise to discriminate against, any individual because of his race, color, religion, sex, or national origin;

(2) to limit, segregate, or classify its membership, *or applicants for membership* or to classify or fail or refuse to refer for employment any individual, in any way which would deprive or tend to deprive any individual of employment opportunities, or would limit such employment opportunities or otherwise adversely affect his status as an employee or as an applicant for employment, because of such individual's race, color, religion, sex, or national origin; or

(3) to cause or attempt to cause an employer to discriminate against an individual in violation of this section.

(d) It shall be an unlawful employment practice for any employer, labor organization, or joint labor-management committee controlling apprenticeship or other training or retraining, including on-the-job training programs to discriminate against any individual because of his race, color, religion, sex, or national origin in admission to, or employment in, any program established to provide apprenticeship or other training.

(e) Notwithstanding any other provision of this title, (1) it shall not be an unlawful employment practice for an employer to hire and employ employees, for an employment agency to classify, or refer for employment any individual, for a labor organization to classify its membership or to classify or refer for employment any individual, or for an employer, labor organization, or joint labor-management committee controlling apprenticeship or other training or retraining programs to admit or employ any individual in any such program, on the basis of his religion, sex, or national origin in those certain instances where religion, sex, or national origin is a bona fide occupational qualification reasonably necessary to the normal operation of that particular business or enterprise, and (2) it shall not be an unlawful employment practice for a school, college, university, or other educational institution or institution of learning to hire and employ employees of a particular religion if such school, college, university, or other educational institution or institution of learning is, in whole or in substantial part, owned, supported, controlled, or managed by a particular religion or by a particular religious corporation, association, or society, or if the curriculum of such school, college, university, or other educational institution or institution of learning is directed toward the propagation of a particular religion.

(f) As used in this title, the phrase "unlawful employment practice" shall not be deemed to include any action or measure taken by an employer, labor organization, joint labor-management committee, or employment agency with respect to an individual who is a member of the Communist Party of the United States or of any other organization required to register as a Communist-action or Communist-front organization by final order of the Subversive Activities Control Board pursuant to the Subversive Activities Control Act of 1950.

(g) Notwithstanding any other provision of this title, it shall not be an unlawful employment practice for an employer to fail or refuse to hire and employ any individual for any position, for an employer to discharge any individual from any position, or for an employment agency to fail or refuse to refer any individual for employment in any position, or for a labor organization to fail or refuse to refer any individual for employment in any position, if—

(1) the occupancy of such position, or access to the premises in or upon which any part of the duties of such position is performed or is to be performed, is subject to any requirement imposed in the interest of the national security of the United States under any security program in effect pursuant to or administered under any statute of the United States or any Executive order of the President; and

(2) such individual has not fulfilled or has ceased to fulfill that requirement.

(h) Notwithstanding any other provision of this title, it shall not be an unlawful employment practice for an employer to apply different standards of compensation, or different terms, conditions, or privileges of employment pursuant to a bona fide seniority or merit system, or a system which measures earnings by quantity or quality of production or to employees who work in different locations, provided that such differences are not the result of an intention to discriminate because of race, color, religion, sex, or national origin, nor shall it be an unlawful employment practice for an employer to give and to act upon the results of any professionally developed ability test provided that such test, its administration or action upon the results is not designed, intended or used to discriminate because of race, color, religion, sex or national origin. It shall not be an unlawful employment practice under this title for any employer to differentiate upon the basis of sex in determining the amount of the wages or compensation paid or to be paid to employees of such employer if such differentiation is authorized by the provisions of section 6(d) of the Fair Labor Standards Act of 1938, as amended (29 U.S.C. 206(d)).

(i) Nothing contained in this title shall apply to any business or enterprise on or near an Indian reservation with respect to any publicly announced employment practice of such business or enterprise under which a preferential treatment is given to any individual because he is an Indian living on or near a reservation.

(j) Nothing contained in this title shall be interpreted to require any employer, employment agency, labor organization, or joint labor-management committee subject to this title to grant preferential treatment to any individual or to any group because of the race, color, religion, sex, or national origin of such individual or group on account of an imbalance which may exist with respect to the total number or percentage of persons of any race, color, religion, sex, or national origin employed by any employer, referred or classified for employment by any employment agency or labor organization, admitted to membership or classified by any labor organization, or admitted to, or employed in, any apprenticeship or other training program, in comparison with the total number or percentage of persons of such race, color, religion, sex, or national origin in any community, State, section, or other area, or in the available work force in any community, State, section, or other area.

OTHER UNLAWFUL EMPLOYMENT PRACTICES

Sec. 704. (a) It shall be an unlawful employment practice for an employer to discriminate against any of his employees or applicants for employment, for an employment agency, *or joint labor-management committee controlling apprenticeship or other training or retraining, including on-the-job training programs,* to discriminate against any individual, or for a labor organization to discriminate against any member thereof or applicant for membership, because he has opposed any practice made an unlawful employment practice by this title, or because he has made a charge, testified, assisted, or participated in any manner in an investigation, proceeding, or hearing under this title.

(b) It shall be an unlawful employment practice for an employer, labor organization, employment *agency, or joint labor-management committee controlling apprenticeship or other training or retraining, including on-the-job training programs,* to print or publish or cause to be printed or published any notice or advertisement relating to employment by such an employer or membership in or any classification or referral for employment by such a labor organization, or relating to any classification or referral for employment by such an employment *agency, or relating to admission to, or employment in, any program established to provide apprenticeship or other training by such a joint labor-management committee* indicating any preference, limitation, specification, or discrimination, based on race, color, religion, sex, or national origin, except that such a notice or advertisement may indicate a preference, limitation, specification, or discrimination based on religion, sex, or national origin when religion, sex, or national origin is a bona fide occupational qualification for employment.

EQUAL EMPLOYMENT OPPORTUNITY COMMISSION

Sec. 705. (a) There is hereby created a Commission to be known as the Equal Employment Opportunity Commission, which shall be composed of five members, not more than three of whom shall be members of the same political party. *Members of the Commission* shall be appointed by the President by and with the advice and consent of the *Senate* for a term of five *years. Any individual chosen to fill a vacancy shall be appointed only for the unexpired term of the member whom he shall succeed, and all members of the Commission shall continue to serve until their successors are appointed and qualified, except that no such member of the Commission shall continue to serve (1) for more than sixty days when the Congress is in session unless a nomination to fill such vacancy shall have been submitted to the Senate, or (2) after the adjournment sine die of the session of the Senate in which such nomination was submitted.* The President shall designate one member to serve as Chairman of the Commission, and one member to serve as Vice Chairman. The Chairman shall be responsible on behalf of the Commission for the administrative operations of the Commission, and *except as provided in subsection (b),* shall appoint, in accordance with the *provisions of title 5, United States Code, governing appointments in the competitive service, such officers, agents, attorneys, hearing examiners, and employees as he deems necessary to assist it in the performance of its functions and to fix their compensation in accordance with the provisions of chapter 51 and subchapter III of chapter 53 of title 5, United States Code, relating to classification and General Schedule pay rates: Provided, That assignment, removal, and compensation of hearing examiners shall be in accordance with sections 3105, 3344, 5362, and 7521 of title 5, United States Code.*

(b)(1) There shall be a General Counsel of the Commission appointed by the President, by and with the advice and consent of the Senate, for a term of four years. The General Counsel shall have responsibility for the conduct of litigation as provided in sections 706 and 707 of this title. The General Counsel shall have such other duties as the Commission may prescribe or as may be provided by law and shall concur with the Chairman of the Commission on the appointment and supervision of regional attorneys. The General Counsel of the Commission on the effective date of this Act shall continue in such position and perform the functions specified in this subsection until a successor is appointed and qualified.

(2) Attorneys appointed under this section may, at the direction of the Commission, appear for and represent the Commission in any case in court, provided that the Attorney General shall conduct all litigation to which the Commission is a party in the Supreme Court pursuant to this title.

(c) A vacancy in the Commission shall not impair the right of the remaining members to exercise all the powers of the Commission and three members thereof shall constitute a quorum.

(d) The Commission shall have an official seal which shall be judicially noticed.

(e) The Commission shall at the close of each fiscal year report to the Congress and to the President concerning the action it has taken; the names, salaries, and duties of all individuals in its employ and the moneys it has disbursed; and shall make such further reports on the case of and means of eliminating discrimination and such recommendations for further legislation as may appear desirable.

(f) The principal office of the Commission shall be in or near the District of Columbia, but it may meet or exercise any or all its powers at any other place. The Commission may establish such regional or State offices as it deems necessary to accomplish the purpose of this title.

(g) The Commission shall have power—

(1) to cooperate with and, with their consent, utilize regional, State, local, and other agencies, both public and private, and individuals;

(2) to pay to witnesses whose depositions are taken or who are summoned before the Commission or any of its agents the same witness and mileage fees as are paid to witnesses in the courts of the United States;

(3) to furnish to persons subject to this title such technical assistance as they may request to further their compliance with this title or an order issued thereunder;

(4) upon the request of (i) any employer, whose employees or some of them, or (ii) any labor organization, whose members or some of them, refuse or threaten to refuse to cooperate in effectuating the provisions of this title, to assist in such effectuation by conciliation or such other remedial action as is provided by this title;

(5) to make such technical studies as are appropriate to effectuate the purposes and policies of this title and to make the results of such studies available to the public;

(6) to *intervene* in a civil action brought *under section 706* by an aggrieved party *against a respondent other than a government, governmental agency, or political subdivision.*

(*h*) The Commission shall, in any of its educational or promotional activities, cooperate with other departments and agencies in the performance of such educational and promotional activities.

(*i*) All officers, agents, attorneys, and employees of the Commission shall be subject to the provisions of section 9 of the Act of August 2, 1939, as amended (the Hatch Act), notwithstanding any exemption contained in such section.

PREVENTION OF UNLAWFUL EMPLOYMENT PRACTICES

Sec. 706. (*a*) *The Commission is empowered, as hereinafter provided, to prevent any person from engaging in any unlawful employment practice as set forth in section 703 or 704 of this title.*

(*b*) Whenever *a charge is filed by or on behalf of a* person claiming to be aggrieved, or by a member of the Commission, *alleging* that an employer, employment agency, labor *organization, or joint labor-management committee controlling apprenticeship or other training or retraining, including on-the-job training programs,* has engaged in an unlawful employment practice, the Commission shall *serve a notice of the charge (including the date, place and circumstances of the alleged unlawful employment practice) on* such employer, employment agency, labor *organization, or joint labor-management committee* (hereinafter referred to as the "respondent") *within ten days, and shall make an investigation thereof. Charges shall be in writing under oath or affirmation and shall contain such information and be in such form as the Commission requires. Charges* shall not be made public by the Commission. If the Commission *determines* after such investigation that there is *not* reasonable cause to believe that the charge is true, *it shall dismiss the charge and promptly notify the person claiming to be aggrieved and the respondent of its action. In determining whether reasonable cause exists, the Commission shall accord substantial weight to final findings and orders made by State or local authorities in proceedings commenced under State or local law pursuant to the requirements of subsections (c) and (d). If the Commission determines after such investigation that there is reasonable cause to believe that the charge is true,* the Commission shall endeavor to eliminate any such alleged unlawful employment practice by informal methods of conference, conciliation, and persuasion. Nothing said or done during and as a part of such *informal* endeavors may be made public by the *Commission, its officers or employees, or used as evidence in a subsequent proceeding* without the written consent of the *persons concerned.* Any *person* who *makes* public information in violation of this subsection shall be fined not more than $1,000 or imprisoned *for* not more than one *year, or both. The Commission shall make its determination on reasonable cause as promptly as possible and, so far as practicable, not later than one hundred and twenty days from the filing of the charge or, where applicable under subsection (c) or (d) from the date upon which the Commission is authorized to take action with respect to the charge.*

(*c*) In the case of an alleged unlawful employment practice occurring in a State, or political subdivision of a State, which has a State or local law prohibiting the unlawful employment practice alleged and establishing or authorizing a State or local authority to grant or seek relief from such practice or to institute criminal proceedings with respect thereto upon receiving notice thereof, no charge may be filed under subsection (a) by the person aggrieved before the expiration of sixty days after proceedings have been commenced under the State or local law, unless such proceedings have been earlier terminated, provided that such sixty-day period shall be extended to one hundred and twenty days during the first year after the effective date of such State or local law. If any requirement for the commencement of such proceedings is imposed by a State or local authority other than a requirement of the filing of a written and signed statement of the facts upon which the proceeding is based, the proceeding shall be deemed to have been commenced for the purposes of this subsection at the time such statement is sent by registered mail to the appropriate State or local authority.

(d) In the case of any charge filed by a member of the Commission alleging an unlawful employment practice occurring in a State or political subdivision of a State which has a State or local law prohibiting the practice alleged and establishing or authorizing a State or local authority to grant or seek relief from such practice or to institute criminal proceedings with respect thereto upon receiving notice thereof, the Commission shall, before taking any action with respect to such charge, notify the appropriate State or local officials and, upon request, afford them a reasonable time, but not less than sixty days (provided that such sixty-day period shall be extended to one hundred and twenty days during the first year after the effective *date* of such State or local law), unless a shorter period is requested, to act under such State or local law to remedy the practice alleged.

(e) A charge under *this section* shall be filed within *one hundred and eighty* days after the alleged unlawful employment practice *occurred and notice of the charge (including the date, place and circumstances of the alleged unlawful employment practice) shall be served upon the person against whom such charge is made within ten days thereafter,* except that in *a case of an* unlawful employment practice with respect to which the person aggrieved his *initially instituted proceedings with a State or local agency with authority to grant or seek relief from such practice or to institute criminal proceedings with respect thereto upon receiving notice thereof,* such charge shall be filed by *or on behalf of* the person aggrieved within *three hundred* days after the alleged unlawful employment practice occurred, or within thirty days after receiving notice that the State or local agency has terminated the proceedings under the State or local law, whichever is earlier, and a copy of such charge shall be filed by the Commission with the State or local agency.

(f)(1) If within thirty days after a charge is filed with the Commission or within thirty days after expiration of any period of reference under subsection (c) or (d), the Commission has been unable to *secure from the respondent a conciliation agreement acceptable to the Commission,* the Commission *may bring a civil action against any respondent not a government, governmental agency, or political subdivision named in the charge. In the case of a respondent which is a government, governmental agency, or political subdivision, if the Commission has been unable to secure from the respondent a conciliation agreement acceptable to the Commission, the Commission shall take no further action and shall refer the case to the Attorney General who may bring a civil action against such respondent in the appropriate United States district court. The person or persons aggrieved shall have the right to intervene in a civil action brought by the Commission or the Attorney General in a case involving a government, governmental agency, or political subdivision. If a charge filed with the Commission pursuant to subsection (b) is dismissed by the Commission, or if within one hundred and eighty days from the filing of such charge or the expiration of any period of reference under subsection (c) or (d), whichever is later, the Commission has not filed a civil action under this section or the Attorney General has notified a civil action in a case involving a government, governmental agency, or political subdivision, or the Commission has not entered into a conciliation agreement to which the person aggrieved is a party, the Commission, or the Attorney General in a case involving a government, governmental agency, or political subdivision, shall so notify the person aggrieved and within ninety days after the giving of such notice a civil action may* be brought against the respondent named in the charge (A) by the person claiming to be aggrieved, or (B) if such charge was filed by a member of the Commission, by any person whom the charge alleges was aggrieved by the alleged unlawful employment practice. Upon application by the complainant and in such circumstances as the court may deem just, the court may appoint an attorney for such complainant and may authorize the commencement of the action without the payment of fees, costs, or security. Upon timely application, the court may, in its discretion, permit the *Commission,* or the Attorney General in a case involving a government, governmental agency, or political subdivision, to intervene in such civil action *upon certification* that the case is of general public importance. Upon request, the court may, in its discretion, stay further proceedings for not more than sixty days pending the termination of State or local proceedings described in subsections *(c) or (d) of this section or further* efforts of the Commission to obtain voluntary compliance.

(2) *Whenever a charge is filed with the Commission and the Commission concludes on the basis of a preliminary investigation that prompt judicial action is necessary to carry out the purposes of this Act, the Commission, or the Attorney General in a case involving a government, governmental agency, or political subdivision, may bring an action for appropriate temporary or preliminary relief pending final disposition of such charge. Any temporary restraining order or other order granting preliminary or temporary relief shall be issued in accordance with rule 65 of the Federal Rules of Civil Procedure. It shall be the duty of a court having jurisdiction over proceedings under this section to assign cases for hearing at the earliest practicable date and to cause such cases to be in every way expedited.*

(3) *Each United States district court and each United States court of a place subject to the jurisdiction of the United States shall have jurisdiction of actions brought under this title. Such an action may be brought in any judicial district in the State in which the unlawful employment practice is alleged to have been committed, in the judicial district in which the employment records relevant to such practice are maintained and administered, or in the judicial district in which the aggrieved person would have worked but for the alleged unlawful employment practice, but if the respondent is not found within any such district, such an action may be brought within the judicial district in which the respondent has his principal office. For purposes of sections 1404 and 1406 of title 28 of the United States Code, the judicial district in which the respondent has his principal office shall in all cases be considered a district in which the action might have been brought.*

(4) *It shall be the duty of the chief judge of the district (or in his absence, the acting chief judge) in which the case is pending immediately to designate a judge in such district to hear and determine the case. In the event that no judge in the district is available to hear and determine the case, the chief judge of the district, or the acting chief judge, as the case may be, shall certify this fact to the chief judge of the circuit (or in his absence, the acting chief judge) who shall then designate a district or circuit judge of the circuit to hear and determine the case.*

(5) *It shall be the duty of the judge designated pursuant to this subsection to assign the case for hearing at the earliest practicable date and to cause the case to be in every way expedited. If such judge has not scheduled the case for trial within one hundred and twenty days after issue has been joined, that judge may appoint a master pursuant to rule 53 of the Federal Rules of Civil Procedure.*

(g) *If the court finds that the respondent has intentionally engaged in or is intentionally engaging in an unlawful employment practice charged in the complaint, the court may enjoin the respondent from engaging in such unlawful employment practice, and order such affirmative action as may be appropriate, which may include, but is not limited to, reinstatement or hiring of employees, with or without back pay (payable by the employer, employment agency, or labor organization, as the case may be, responsible for the unlawful employment practice), or any other equitable relief as the court deems appropriate. Back pay liability shall not accrue from a date more than two years prior to the filing of a charge with the Commission. Interim earnings or amounts earnable with reasonable diligence by the person or persons discriminated against shall operate to reduce the back pay otherwise allowable. No order of the court shall require the admission or reinstatement of an individual as a member of a union, or the hiring, reinstatement, or promotion of an individual as an employee, or the payment to him of any back pay, if such individual was refused admission, suspended, or expelled, or was refused employment or ad-*

vancement or was suspended or discharged for any reason other than discrimination on account of race, color, religion, sex, or national origin or in violation of section 704(a).

(h) The provisions of the Act entitled "An Act to amend the Judicial Code and to define and limit the jurisdiction of courts sitting in equity, and for other purposes," approved March 23, 1932 (29 U.S.C. 101–115), shall not apply with respect to civil actions brought under this section.

(i) In any case in which an employer, employment agency, or labor organization fails to comply with an order of a court issued in a civil action brought under *this section,* the Commission may commence proceedings to compel compliance with such order.

(j) Any civil action brought under *this section* and any proceedings brought under subsection (i) shall be subject to appeal as provided in sections 1291 and 1292, title 28, United States Code.

(k) In any action or proceeding under this title the court, in its discretion, may allow the prevailing party, other than the Commission or the United States, a reasonable attorney's fee as part of the costs, and the Commission and the United States shall be liable for costs the same as a private person.

Sec. 707. (a) Whenever the Attorney General has reasonable cause to believe that any person or group of persons is engaged in a pattern or practice of resistance to the full enjoyment of any of the rights secured by this title, and that the pattern or practice is of such a nature and is intended to deny the full exercise of the rights herein described, the Attorney General may bring a civil action in the appropriate district court of the United States by filing with it a complaint (1) signed by him (or in his absence the Acting Attorney General), (2) setting forth facts pertaining to such pattern or practice, and (3) requesting such relief, including an application for a permanent or temporary injunction, restraining order or other order against the person or persons responsible for such pattern or practice, as he deems necessary to insure the full enjoyment of the rights herein described.

(b) The district courts of the United States shall have and shall exercise jurisdiction of proceedings instituted pursuant to this section, and in any such proceeding the Attorney General may file with the clerk of such court a request that a court of three judges be convened to hear and determine the case. Such request by the Attorney General shall be accompanied by a certificate that, in his opinion, the case is of general public importance. A copy of the certificate and request for a three-judge court shall be immediately furnished by such clerk to the chief judge of the circuit (or in his absence, the presiding circuit judge of the circuit) in which the case is pending. Upon receipt of such request it shall be the duty of the chief judge of the circuit or the presiding circuit judge, as the case may be, to designate immediately three judges in such circuit, of whom at least one shall be a circuit judge and another of whom shall be a district judge of the court in which the proceeding was instituted, to hear and determine such case, and it shall be the duty of the judges so designated to assign the case for hearing at the earliest practicable date, to participate in the hearing and determination thereof, and to cause the case to be in every way expedited. An appeal from the final judgment of such court will lie to the Supreme Court.

In the event the Attorney General fails to file such a request in any such proceeding, it shall be the duty of the chief judge of the district (or in his absence, the acting chief judge) in which the case is pending immediately to designate a judge in such district to hear and determine the case. In the event that no judge in the district is available to hear and determine the case, the chief judge of the district, or the acting chief judge, as the case may be, shall certify this fact to the chief judge of the circuit (or in his absence, the acting chief judge) who shall then designate a district or circuit judge of the circuit to hear and determine the case.

It shall be the duty of the judge designated pursuant to this section to assign the case for hearing at the earliest practicable date and to cause the case to be in every way expedited.

(c) *Effective two years after the date of enactment of the Equal Employment Opportunity Act of 1972, the functions of the Attorney General under this section shall be transferred to the Commission, together with such personnel, property, records, and unexpended balances of appropriations, allocations, and other funds employed, used, held, available, or to be made available in connection with such functions unless the President submits, and neither House of Congress vetoes, a reorganization plan pursuant to chapter 9, of title 5, United States Code, inconsistent with the provisions of this subsection. The Commission shall carry out such functions in accordance with subsections (d) and (e) of this section.*

(d) *Upon the transfer of functions provided for in subsection (c) of this section, in all suits commenced pursuant to this section prior to the date of such transfer, proceedings shall continue without abatement, all court orders and decrees shall remain in effect, and the Commission shall be substituted as a party for the United States of America, the Attorney General, or the Acting Attorney General, as appropriate.*

(e) *Subsequent to the date of enactment of the Equal Employment Opportunity Act of 1972, the Commission shall have authority to investigate and act on a charge of a pattern or practice of discrimination, whether filed by or on behalf of a person claiming to be aggrieved or by a member of the Commission. All such actions shall be conducted in accordance with the procedures set forth in section 706 of this Act.*

EFFECT ON STATE LAWS

Sec. 708. Nothing in this title shall be deemed to exempt or relieve any person from any liability, duty, penalty, or punishment provided by any present or future law of any State or political subdivision of a State, other than any such law which purports to require or permit the doing of any act which would be an unlawful employment practice under this title.

INVESTIGATIONS, INSPECTIONS, RECORDS, STATE AGENCIES

Sec. 709. (a) In connection with any investigation of a charge filed under section 706, the Commission or its designated representative shall at all reasonable times have access to, for the purposes of examination, and the right to copy any evidence of any person being investigated or proceeded against that relates to unlawful employment practices covered by this title and is relevant to the charge under investigation.

(b) The Commission may cooperate with State and local agencies charged with the administration of State fair employment practices laws and, with the consent of such agencies, may, for the purpose of carrying out its functions and duties under this title and within the limitation of funds appropriated specifically for such purpose, *engage in and contribute to the cost of research and other projects of mutual interest undertaken by such agencies, and* utilize the services of such agencies and their employees, and, notwithstanding any other provision of law, *pay by advance or reimbursement* such agencies and their employees for services rendered to assist the Commission in carrying out this title. In furtherance of such cooperative efforts, the Commission may enter into written agreements with such State or local agencies and such agreements may include provisions under which the Commission shall refrain from processing a charge in any cases or class of cases specified in such agreements or under which the Commission shall relieve any person or class of persons in such State or locality from requirements imposed under this section. The Commission shall rescind any such agreement whenever it determines that the agreement no longer serves the interest of effective enforcement of this title.

(c) *Every* employer, employment agency, and labor organization subject to this title shall (1) make and keep such records relevant to the determinations of whether unlawful employment practices have been or are being committed, (2) preserve such records for such periods, and (3) make such reports therefrom, as the Commission shall prescribe by regulation or order, after public hearing, as reasonable, necessary, or appropriate for the enforcement of this title or the regulations or orders thereunder. The Commission shall, by regulation, require each employer, labor organization, and joint labor-management committee subject to this title which controls an apprenticeship or other training program to maintain such records as are reasonably necessary to carry out the purpose of this title, including, but not limited to, a list of applicants who wish to participate in such program, including the chronological order in which applications were received, and *to* furnish to the Commission upon request, a detailed description of the manner in which persons are selected to participate in the apprenticeship or other training program. Any employer, employment agency, labor organization, or joint labor-management committee which believes that the application to it of any regulation or order issued under this section would result in undue hardship may apply to the Commission for an exemption from the application of such regulation or order, *and, if such application for an exemption is denied,* bring a civil action in the United States district court for the district where such records are kept. If the Commission or the court, as the case may be, finds that the application of the regulation or order to the employer, employment agency, or labor organization in question would impose an undue hardship, the Commission or the court, as the case may be, may grant appropriate relief. *If any person required to comply with the provisions of this subsection fails or refuses to do so, the United States district court for the district in which such person is found, resides, or transacts business, shall, upon application of the Commission, or the Attorney General in a case involving a government, governmental agency or political subdivision, have jurisdiction to issue to such person an order requiring him to comply.*

(d) In prescribing requirements pursuant to subsection (c) of this section, the Commission shall consult with other interested State and Federal agencies and shall endeavor to coordinate its requirements with those adopted by such agencies. The Commission shall furnish upon request and without cost to any State or local agency, charged with the administration of a fair employment practice law information obtained pursuant to subsection (c) of this section from any employer, employment agency, labor organization, or joint labor-management committee subject to the jurisdiction of such agency. Such information shall be furnished on condition that it not be made public by the recipient agency prior to the institution of a proceeding under State or local law involving such information. If this condition is violated by a recipient agency, the Commission may decline to honor subsequent requests pursuant to this subsection.

(e) It shall be unlawful for any officer or employee of the Commission to make public in any manner whatever any information obtained by the Commission pursuant to its authority under this section prior to the institution of any proceeding under this title involving such information. Any officer or employee of the Commission who shall make public in any manner whatever any information in violation of this subsection shall be guilty of a misdemeanor and upon conviction thereof, shall be fined not more than $1,000, or imprisoned not more than one year.

INVESTIGATORY POWERS

Sec. 710. For the purpose of all hearings and investigations conducted by the Commission or its duly authorized agents or agencies, section 11 of the National Labor Relations Act (49 Stat. 455; 29 U.S.C. 161) shall apply.

NOTICES TO BE POSTED

Sec. 711. (a) Every employer, employment agency, and labor organization, as the case may be, shall post and keep posted in conspicuous places upon its premises where notices to employees, applicants for employment, and members are customarily posted a notice to be prepared or approved by the Commission setting forth excerpts from, or summaries of, the pertinent provisions of this title and information pertinent to the filing of a complaint.

(b) A willful violation of this section shall be punishable by a fine of not more than $100 for each separate offense.

VETERANS' PREFERENCE

Sec. 712. Nothing contained in this title shall be construed to repeal or modify any Federal, State, territorial, or local law creating special rights or preference for veterans.

RULES AND REGULATIONS

Sec. 713. (a) The Commission shall have authority from time to time to issue, amend, or rescind suitable procedural regulations to carry out the provisions of this title. Regulations issued under the section shall be in conformity with the standards and limitations of the Administrative Procedure Act.

(b) In any action or proceeding based on any alleged unlawful employment practice, no person shall be subject to any liability or punishment for or on account of (1) the commission by such person of an unlawful employment practice if he pleads and proves that the act or omission complained of was in good faith, in conformity with, and in reliance on any written interpretation or opinion of the Commission, or (2) the failure of such person to publish and file any information required by any provision of this title if he pleads and proves that he failed to publish and file such information in good faith, in conformity with the instructions of the Commission issued under this title regarding the filing of such information. Such a defense, if established, shall be a bar to the action or proceeding, notwithstanding that (A) after such act or omission, such interpretation or opinion is modified or rescinded or is determined by judicial authority to be invalid or of no legal effect, or (B) after publishing or filing the description and annual reports, such publication or filing is determined by judicial authority not to be in conformity with the requirements of this title.

FORCIBLY RESISTING THE COMMISSION OR ITS REPRESENTATIVES

Sec. 714. The provisions of *sections 111 and 1114* title 18, United States Code, shall apply to officers, agents, and employees of the Commission in the performance of their official duties. *Notwithstanding the provisions of sections 111 and 1114 of title 18, United States Code, whoever in violation of the provisions of section 1114 of such title kills a person while engaged in or an account of the performance of his official functions under this Act shall be punished by imprisonment for any term of years or for life.*

EQUAL EMPLOYMENT OPPORTUNITY COORDINATING COUNCIL

Sec. 715. There shall be established an Equal Employment Opportunity Coordinating Council (hereinafter referred to in this section as the Council) composed of the Secretary of Labor, the Chairman of the Equal Employment Opportunity Commission, the Attorney General, the Chairman of the United States Civil Service Commission, and the Chairman of the United States Civil Rights Commission, or their respective delegates. The Council shall have the responsibility for developing and implementing agreements, policies and practices designed to maximize effort, promote efficiency, and eliminate conflict, competition, duplication and inconsistency among the operations, functions and jurisdictions of the various departments, agencies and branches of the Federal government responsible for the implementation and enforcement of equal employment opportunity legislation, orders, and policies. On or before July 1 of each year, the Council shall transmit to the President and to the Congress a report of its activities, together with such recommendations for legislative or administrative changes as it concludes are desirable to further promote the purposes of this section.

EFFECTIVE DATE

Sec. 716. (a) This title shall become effective one year after the date of its enactment.

(b) Notwithstanding subsection (a), sections of this title other than sections 703, 704, 706, and 707 shall become effective immediately.

(c) The President shall, as soon as feasible after the enactment of this title, convene one or more conferences for the purpose of enabling the leaders of groups whose members will be affected by this title to become familiar with the rights afforded and obligations imposed by its provisions, and for the purpose of making plans which will result in the fair and effective administration of this title when all of its provisions become effective. The President shall invite the participation in such conference or conferences of (1) the members of the President's Committee on Equal Employment Opportunity, (2) the members of the Commission on Civil Rights, (3) representatives of State and local agencies engaged in furthering equal employment opportunity, (4) representatives of private agencies engaged in furthering equal employment opportunity, and (5) representatives of employers, labor organizations, and employment agencies who will be subject to this title.

NONDISCRIMINATION IN FEDERAL GOVERNMENT EMPLOYMENT

Sec. 717. (a) All personnel actions affecting employees or applicants for employment (except with regard to aliens employed outside the limits of the United States) in military departments as defined in section 102 of title 5, United States Code, in executive agencies (other than the General Accounting Office) as defined in section 105 of title 5, United States Code (including employees and applicants for employment who are paid from nonappropriated funds), in the United States Postal Service and the Postal Rate Commission, in those units of the Government of the District of Columbia having positions in the competitive service, and in those units of the legislative and judicial branches of the Federal Government having positions in the competitive service, and in the Library of Congress shall be made free from any discrimination based on race, color, religion, sex, or national origin.

(b) Except as otherwise provided in this subsection, the Civil Service Commission shall have authority to enforce the provisions of subsection (a) through appropriate remedies, including reinstatement or hiring of employees with or without back pay, as will effectuate the policies of this section, and shall issue such rules, regulations, orders, and instructions as it deems necessary and appropriate to carry out its responsibilities under this section. The Civil Service Commission shall—

(1) be responsible for the annual review and approval of a national and regional equal employment opportunity plan which each department and agency and each appropriate unit referred to in subsection (a) of this section shall submit in order to maintain an affirmative program of equal employment opportunity for all such employees and applicants for employment;

(2) be responsible for the review and evaluation of the operation of all agency equal employment opportunity programs, periodically obtaining and publishing (on at least a semiannual basis) progress reports from each such department, agency, or unit; and

(3) consult with and solicit the recommendations of interested individuals, groups, and organizations relating to equal employment opportunity.

The head of each such department, agency, or unit shall comply with such rules, regulations, orders, and instructions which shall include a provision that an employee or applicant for employment shall be notified of any final action taken on any complaint of discrimination filed by him thereunder. The plan submitted by each department, agency, and unit shall include, but not be limited to—

(1) *provision for the establishment of training and education programs designed to provide a maximum opportunity for employees to advance so as to perform at their highest potential; and*

(2) *a description of the qualifications in terms of training and experience relating to equal employment opportunity for the principal and operating officials of each such department, agency, or unit responsible for carrying out the equal employment opportunity program and of the allocation of personnel and resources proposed by such department, agency, or unit to carry out its equal employment opportunity program.*

With respect to employment in the Library of Congress, authorities granted in this subsection to the Civil Service Commission shall be exercised by the Librarian of Congress.

(c) *Within thirty days of receipt of notice of final action taken by a department, agency, or unit referred to in subsection 717(a), or by the Civil Service Commission upon an appeal from a decision or order of such department, agency, or unit on a complaint of discrimination based on race, color, religion, sex, or national origin, brought pursuant to subsection (a) of this section, Executive Order 11478 or any succeeding Executive orders, or after one hundred and eighty days from the filing of the initial charge with the department, agency, or unit or with the Civil Service Commission on appeal from a decision or order of such department, agency, or unit until such time as final action may be taken by a department, agency, or unit, an employee or applicant for employment, if aggrieved by the final disposition of his complaint, or by the failure to take final action on his complaint, may file a civil action as provided in section 706, in which civil action the head of the department, agency, or unit, as appropriate, shall be the defendant.*

(d) *The provisions of section 706(f) through (k), as applicable, shall govern civil actions brought hereunder.*

(e) *Nothing contained in this Act shall relieve any Government agency or official of its or his primary responsibility to assure nondiscrimination in employment as required by the Constitution and statutes or of its or his responsibilities under Executive Order 11478 relating to equal employment opportunity in the Federal Government.*

SPECIAL PROVISIONS WITH RESPECT TO DENIAL, TERMINATION, AND SUSPENSION OF GOVERNMENT CONTRACTS

Sec. 718. No Government contract, or portion thereof, with any employer, shall be denied, withheld, terminated, or suspended, by any agency or officer of the United States under any equal employment opportunity law or order, where such employer has an affirmative action plan which has previously been accepted by the Government for the same facility within the past twelve months without first according such employer full hearing and adjudication under the provisions of title 5, United States Code, section 554, and the following pertinent sections: Provided, That if such employer has deviated substantially from such previously agreed to affirmative action plan, this section shall not apply: Provided further, That for the purposes of this section an affirmative action plan shall be deemed to have been accepted by the Government at the time the appropriate compliance agency has accepted such plan unless within forty-five days thereafter the Office of Federal Contract Compliance has disapproved such plan.

Provisions of Equal Employment Opportunity Act of 1972 Which Relate to but do not Amend the Civil Rights Act of 1964

Sec. 9. (a) Section 5314 of title 5 of the United States Code is amended by adding at the end thereof the following new clause:

"(58) *Chairman, Equal Employment Opportunity Commission.*"

(b) *Clause (72) of section 5315 of such title is amended to read as follows:*

"(72) *Members, Equal Employment Opportunity Commission(4).*"

(c) *Clause (111) of section 5316 of such title is repealed.*

(d) *Section 5316 of such title is amended by adding at the end thereof the following new clause:*

"(131) *General Counsel of the Equal Employment Opportunity Commission.*"

Sec. 12. *Section 5108(c) of title 5, United States Code, is amended by—*

(1) *striking out the word "and" at the end of paragraph (9);*

(2) *striking out the period at the end of paragraph (10) and inserting in lieu thereof a semicolon and the word "and"; and*

(3) *by adding immediately after paragraph (10) the last time it appears therein in the following new paragraph:*

"(11) *the Chairman of the Equal Employment Opportunity Commission, subject to the standards and procedures prescribed by this chapter, may place an additional ten positions in the Equal Employment Opportunity Commission in GS–16, GS–17, and GS–18 for the purposes of carrying out title VII of the Civil Rights Act of 1964.*"

Sec. 14. *The amendments made by this Act to section 706 of the Civil Rights Act of 1964 shall be applicable with respect to charges pending with the Commission on the date of enactment of this Act and all charges filed thereafter.*

GUIDELINES ON DISCRIMINATION BECAUSE OF SEX

These guidelines spell out the EEOC's policies in several key areas of sex discrimination. (Note: see Chapter 9 for the modification of Section 1604.10 by the Supreme Court in *General Electric v. Gilbert.*)

By virtue of the authority vested in it by section 713(b) of Title VII of the Civil Rights Act of 1964, 42 U.S.C., section 2000e-12, 78 Stat. 265, the Equal Employment Opportunity Commission hereby revises Title 29, Chapter XIV, §1604 of the Code of Federal Regulations.

These Guidelines on Discrimination Because of Sex supersede and enlarge upon the Guidelines on Discrimination Because of Sex, issued by the Equal Employment Opportunity Commission on December 2, 1965, and all amendments thereto. Because the material herein is interpretive in nature, the provisions of the Administrative Procedure Act (5 U.S.C. 553) requiring notice of proposed rule making, opportunity for public participation, and delay in effective date are inapplicable. The Guidelines shall be applicable to charges and cases presently pending or hereafter filed with the Commission.

Sec. 1604.1 General principles.

(a) References to "employer" or "employers" in Part 1604 state principles that are applicable not only to employers, but also to labor organizations and to employment agencies insofar as their action or inaction may adversely affect employment opportunities.

(b) To the extent that the views expressed in prior Commission pronouncements are inconsistent with the views expressed herein, such prior views are hereby overruled.

(c) The Commission will continue to consider particular problems relating to sex discrimination on a case-by-case basis.

Sec. 1604.2 Sex as a bona fide occupational qualification.

(a) The Commission believes that the bona fide occupational qualification exception as to sex should be interpreted narrowly. Labels—"Men's jobs" and "Women's jobs"—tend to deny employment opportunities unnecessarily to one sex or the other.

(1) The Commission will find that the following situations do not warrant the application of the bona fide occupational qualification exception:

(i) The refusal to hire a woman because of her sex based on assumptions of the comparative employment characteristics of women in general. For example, the assumption that the turnover rate among women is higher than among men.

(ii) The refusal to hire an individual based on stereotyped characterizations of the sexes. Such stereotypes include, for example, that men are less capable of assembling intricate equipment; that women are less capable of aggressive salesmanship. The principle of non-discrimination requires that individuals be considered on the basis of individual capacities and not on the basis of any characteristics generally attributed to the group.

(iii) The refusal to hire an individual because of the preferences of coworkers, the employer, clients or customers except as covered specifically in subparagraph (2) of this paragraph.

(2) Where it is necessary for the purpose of authenticity or genuineness, the Commission will consider sex to be a bona fide occupational qualification, e.g., an actor or actress.

(b) Effect of sex-oriented state employment legislation.

(1) Many States have enacted laws or promulgated administrative regulations with respect to the employment of females. Among these laws are those which prohibit or limit the employment of females, e.g., the employment of females in certain occupations, in jobs requiring the lifting or carrying of weights exceeding certain prescribed limits, during certain hours of the night, for more than a specified number of hours per day or per week, and for certain periods of time before and after childbirth. The Commission has found that such laws and regulations do not take into account the capacities, preferences, and abilities of individual females and, therefore, discriminate on the basis of sex. The Commission has concluded that such laws and regulations conflict with and are superseded by Title VII of the Civil Rights Act of 1964. Accordingly, such laws will not be considered a defense to an otherwise established unlawful employment practice or as a basis for the application of the bona fide occupational qualification exception.

(2) The Commission has concluded that state laws and regulations which discriminate on the basis of sex with regard to the employment of minors are in conflict with and are superseded by Title VII to the extent that such laws are more restrictive for one sex. Accordingly, restrictions on the employment of minors of one sex over and above those imposed on minors of the other sex will not be considered a defense to an otherwise established unlawful employment practice or as a basis for the application of the bona fide occupational qualification exception.

(3) A number of states require that minimum wage and premium pay for overtime be provided for female employees. An employer will be deemed to have engaged in an unlawful employment practice if:

(i) It refuses to hire or otherwise adversely affects the employment opportunities of female applicants or employees in order to avoid the payment of minimum wages or overtime pay required by state law; or

(ii) It does not provide the same benefits for male employees.

(4) As to other kinds of sex-oriented state employment laws, such as those requiring special rest and meal periods or physical facilities for women, provision of these benefits to one sex only will be a violation of Title VII. An employer will be deemed to have engaged in an unlawful employment practice if:

(i) It refuses to hire or otherwise adversely affects the employment opportunities of female applicants or employees in order to avoid the provision of such benefits; or

(ii) It does not provide the same benefits for male employees. If the employer can prove that business necessity precludes providing these benefits to both men and women, then the state law is in conflict with and superseded by Title VII as to this employer. In this situation, the employer shall not provide such benefits to members of either sex.

(5) Some states require that separate restrooms be provided for employees of each sex. An employer will be deemed to have engaged in an unlawful employment practice if it refuses to hire or otherwise adversely affects the employment opportunities of applicants or employees in order to avoid the provision of such restrooms for persons of that sex.

Sec. 1604.3   Separate lines of progression and seniority systems.

(a) It is an unlawful employment practice to classify a job as "male" or "female" or to maintain separate lines of progression or separate seniority lists based on sex where this would adversely affect any employee unless sex is a bona fide occupational qualification for that job. Accordingly, employment practices are unlawful which arbitrarily classify jobs so that:

(1) A female is prohibited from applying for a job labeled "male," or for a job in a "male" line of progression and vice versa.

(2) A male scheduled for layoff is prohibited from displacing a less senior female on a "female" seniority list; and vice versa.

(b) A seniority system or line of progression which distinguishes between "light" and "heavy" jobs constitutes an unlawful employment practice if it operates as a disguised form of classification by sex, or creates unreasonable obstacles to the advancement by members of either sex into jobs which members of that sex would reasonably be expected to perform.

Sec. 1604.4   Discrimination against married women.

(a) The Commission has determined that an employer's rule which forbids or restricts the employment of married women and which is not applicable to married men is a discrimination based on sex prohibited by Title VII of the Civil Rights Act. It does not seem to us relevant that the rule is not directed against all females, but only against married females, for so long as sex is a factor in the application of the rule, such application involves a discrimination based on sex.

(b) It may be that under certain circumstances, such a rule could be justified within the meaning of Section 703(e)(1) of Title VII. We express no opinion on this question at this time except to point out that sex as a bona fide occupational qualification must be justified in terms of the peculiar requirements of the particular job and not on the basis of a general principle such as the desirability of spreading work.

Sec. 1604.5   Job opportunities advertising.

It is a violation of Title VII for a help-wanted advertisement to indicate a preference, limitation, specification, or discrimination based on sex unless sex is a bona fide occupational qualification for the particular job involved. The placement of an advertisement in columns classified by publishers on the basis of sex, such as columns headed "Male" or "female," will be considered an expression of a preference, limitation, specification, or discrimination based on sex.

Sec. 1604.6   Employment agencies.

(a) Section 703(b) of the Civil Rights Act specifically states that it shall be unlawful for an employment agency to discriminate against any individual because of sex. The Commission has determined that private employment agencies which deal exclusively with one sex are engaged in an unlawful employment practice, except to the extent that such agencies limit their services to furnishing employees for particular jobs for which sex is a bona fide occupational qualification.

(b) An employment agency that receives a job order containing an unlawful sex specification will share responsibility with the employer placing the job order if the agency fills the order knowing that the sex specification is not based upon a bona fide occupational qualification. However, an employment agency will not be deemed to be in violation of the law, regardless of the determination as to the employer, if the agency does not have reason to believe that the employer's claim of bona fide occupations qualification is without substance and the agency makes and maintains a written record available to the Commission of each such job order. Such record shall include the name of the employer, the description of the job and the basis for the employer's claim of bona fide occupational qualification.

(c) It is the responsibility of employment agencies to keep informed of opinions and decisions of the Commission on sex discrimination.

Sec. 1604.7   Pre-employment inquiries as to sex.

A pre-employment inquiry may ask "Male _____, Female _____"; or "Mr. Mrs. Miss," provided that the inquiry is made in good faith for a non-discriminatory purpose. Any pre-employment inquiry in connection with prospective employment which expresses directly or indirectly any limitation, specification or discrimination as to sex shall be unlawful unless based upon a bona fide occupational qualification.

Sec. 1604.8   Relationship of Title VII to the Equal Pay Act.

(a) The employee coverage of the prohibitions against discrimination based on sex contained in Title VII is co-extensive with that of the other prohibitions contained in Title VII and is not limited by Section 703(h) to those employees covered by the Fair Labor Standards Act.

(b) By virtue of Section 703(h), a defense based on the Equal Pay Act may be raised in a proceeding under Title VII.

(c) Where such a defense is raised the Commission will give appropriate consideration to the interpretations of the Administrator, Wage and Hour Division, Department of Labor, but will not be bound thereby.

Sec. 1604.9   Fringe benefits.

(a) "Fringe benefits," as used herein, includes medical, hospital, accident, life insurance and retirement benefits; profit-sharing and bonus plans; leave; and other terms, conditions, and privileges of employment.

(b) It shall be an unlawful employment practice for an employer to discriminate between men and women with regard to fringe benefits.

(c) Where an employer conditions benefits available to employees and their spouses and families on whether the employee is the "head of the household" or "principal wage earner" in the family unit, the benefits tend to be available only to male employees and their families. Due to the fact that such conditioning discriminatorily affects the rights of women employees, and that "head of household" or "principal wage earner" status bears no relationship to job performance, benefits which are so conditioned will be found a *prima facie* violation of the prohibitions against sex discrimination contained in the Act.

(d) It shall be an unlawful employment practice for an employer to make available benefits for the wives and families of male employees where the same benefits are not made available for the husbands and families of female employees; or to make available benefits for the wives of male employees which are not made available for female employees; or to make available benefits to the husbands of female employees which are not made available for male employees. An example of such an unlawful employment practice is a situation in which wives of male employees receive maternity benefits while female employees receive no such benefits.

(e) It shall not be a defense under Title VII to a charge of sex discrimination in benefits that the cost of such benefits is greater with respect to one sex than the other.

(f) It shall be an unlawful employment practice for an employer to have a pension or retirement plan which establishes different optional or compulsory retirement ages based on sex, or which differentiates in benefits on the basis of sex. A statement of the General Counsel of September 13, 1968, providing for a phasing out of differentials with regard to optional retirement age for certain incumbent employees is hereby withdrawn.

Sec. 1604.10   Employment policies relating to pregnancy and childbirth.

(a) A written or unwritten employment policy or practice which excludes from employment applicants or employees because of pregnancy is in *prima facie* violation of Title VII.

(b) Disabilities caused or contributed to by pregnancy, miscarriage, abortion, childbirth, and recovery therefrom are, for all job-related purposes, temporary disabilities and should be treated as such under any health or temporary disability insurance or sick leave plan available in connection with employment. Written and unwritten employment policies and practices involving matters such as the commencment and duration of leave, the availability of extensions, the accrual of seniority and other benefits and privileges, reinstatement, and payment under any health or temporary disability insurance or sick leave plan, formal or informal, shall be applied to disability due to pregnancy or childbirth on the same terms and conditions as they are applied to other temporary disabilities.

(c) Where the termination of an employee who is temporarily disabled is caused by an employment policy under which insufficient or no leave is available, such a termination violates the Act if it has a disparate impact on employees of one sex and is not justified by business necessity.

GUIDELINES ON DISCRIMINATION BECAUSE OF NATIONAL ORIGIN

In 1970 the EEOC issued guidelines on practices relating to national origin discrimination.

By virtue of the authority vested in it by section 713(b) of the Act, 42 U.S.C., section 2000e-12(b), the Commission hereby issues Title 29, Chapter XIV, §1601.1 in the Code of the Federal Regulations.

Because the provisions of the Administrative Procedure Act (5 U.S.C. 1003) requiring notice of proposed rule making, opportunity for public participation, and delay in effective date, are inapplicable to these interpretive rules, the guideline shall become effective immediately and shall be applicable with respect to charges presently before or hereafter filed with the Commission.

Sec. 1606.1   Guidelines on discrimination because of national origin.

(a) The Commission is aware of the widespread practices of discrimination on the basis of national origin, and intends to apply the full force of the law to eliminate such discrimination. The bona fide occupational qualification exception as it pertains to national origin cases shall be strictly construed.

(b) Title VII is intended to eliminate covert as well as overt practices of discrimination and the Commission will, therefore, examine with particular concern cases where persons within the jurisdiction of the Commission have been denied equal employment opportunity for reasons which are grounded in national origin considerations. Examples of cases of this character which have come to the attention of the Commission include: The use of tests in the English language where the individual tested came from circumstances where English was not that person's language or mother tongue, and where English language skill is not a requirement of the work to be performed; denial of equal opportunity to persons married to or associated with persons of a specific national origin; denial of equal opportunity because of membership in lawful organizations identified with or seeking to promote the interests of national groups; denial of equal opportunity because of attendance at schools or churches commonly utilized by persons of a given national origin; denial of equal opportunity because their name or that of their spouse reflects a certain national origin, and denial of equal opportunity to persons who as a class of persons tend to fall outside national norms for height and weight where such height and weight specifications are not necessary for the performance of the work involved.

(c) Title VII of the Civil Rights Act of 1964 protects all individuals, both citizen and noncitizens, domiciled or residing in the United States, against discrimination on the basis of race, color, religion, sex, or national origin.

(d) Because discrimination on the basis of citizenship has the effect of discriminating on the basis of national origin, a lawfully immigrated alien who is domiciled or residing in this country may not be discriminated against on the basis of his citizenship, except that it is not an unlawful employment practice for an employee, pursuant to section 703(g), to refuse to employ any person who does not fulfill the requirements imposed in the interests of national security pursuant to any statute of the United States or any Executive order of the President respecting the particular position or the particular premises in question.

(e) In addition, some States have enacted laws prohibiting the employment of noncitizens. For the reasons stated above such laws are in conflict with and are, therefore, superseded by Title VII of the Civil Rights Act of 1964.

GUIDELINES ON EMPLOYEE SELECTION PROCEDURES

The EEOC's Guidelines on Employee Selection Procedures were issued in 1970 and set forth standards on discriminatory testing.

TITLE 29—LABOR

Chapter XIV—Equal Employment Opportunity Commission

PART 1607—GUIDELINES ON EMPLOYEE SELECTION PROCEDURES

By virtue of the authority vested in it by section 713 of title VII of the Civil Rights Act of 1964, 42 U.S.C., section 2000e-12, 78 Stat. 265, the Equal Employment Opportunity Commission hereby issues Title 29, Chapter XIV, §1607 of the Code of Federal Regulations.

These Guidelines on Employee Selection Procedures supersede and enlarge upon the Guidelines on Employment Testing Procedures, issued by the Equal Employment Opportunity Commission on August 24, 1966. Because the material herein is interpretive in nature, the provisions of the Administrative Procedure Act (5 U.S.C. 553) requiring notice of proposed rule making, opportunity for public participation, and delay in effective date are inapplicable. The Guidelines shall be applicable to charges and cases presently pending or hereafter filed with the Commission.

Sec. 1607.1 Statement of purpose.

(a) The guidelines in this part are based on the belief that properly validated and standardized employee selection procedures can significantly contribute to the implementation of nondiscriminatory personnel policies, as required by title VII. It is also recognized that professionally developed tests, when used in conjunction with other tools of personnel assessment and complemented by sound programs of job design, may significantly aid in the development and maintenance of an efficient work force and, indeed, aid in the utilization and conservation of human resources generally.

(b) An examination of charges of discrimination filed with the Commission and an evaluation of the results of the Commission's compliance activities has revealed a decided increase in total test usage and a marked increase in doubtful testing practices which, based on our experience, tend to have discriminatory effects. In many cases, persons have come to rely almost exclusively on tests as the basis for making the decision to hire, transfer, promote, grant membership, train, refer or retain, with the result that candidates are selected or rejected on the basis of a single test score. Where tests are so used, minority candidates frequently experience disproportionately high rates of rejection by failing to attain score levels that have been established as minimum standards for qualification.

It has also become clear that in many instances persons are using tests as the basis for employment decisions without evidence that they are valid predictors of employee job performance. Where evidence in support of presumed relationships between test performance and job behavior is lacking, the possibility of discrimination in the application of test results must be recognized. A test lacking demonstrated validity (i.e., having no known significant relationship to job behavior) and yielding lower scores for classes protected by title VII may result in the rejection of many who have necessary qualifications for successful work performance.

(c) The guidelines in this part are designed to serve as a workable set of standards for employers, unions and employment agencies in determining whether their selection procedures conform with the obligations contained in title VII of the Civil Rights Act of 1964. Section 703 of title VII places an affirmative obligation upon employers, labor unions, and employment agencies, as defined in section 701 of the Act, not to discriminate because of race, color, religion, sex, or national origin. Subsection (h) of section 703 allows such persons "to give and to act upon the results of any professionally developed ability test provided that such test, its administration or action upon the results is not designed, intended or used to discriminate because of race, color, religion, sex or national origin."

Sec. 1607.2 "Test" defined.

For the purpose of the guidelines in this part, the term "test" is defined as any paper-and-pencil or performance measure used as a basis for any employment decision. The guidelines in this part apply, for example, to ability tests which are designed to measure eligibility for hire, transfer, promotion, membership, training, referral or retention. This definition includes, but is not restricted to, measures of general intelligence, mental ability and learning ability; specific intellectual abilities; mechanical, clerical and other aptitudes; dexterity and coordination; knowledge and proficiency; occupational and other interests; and attitudes, personality or temperament. The term "test" includes all formal, scored, quantified or standardized techniques of assessing job suitability including, in addition to the above, specific qualifying or disqualifying personal history or background requirements, specific educational or work history requirements, scored interviews, biographical information blanks, interviewers' rating scales, scored application forms, etc.

Sec. 1607.3 Discrimination defined.

The use of any test which adversely affects hiring, promotion, transfer or any other employment or membership opportunity of classes protected by title VII constitutes discrimination unless: (a) the test has been validated and evidences a high degree of utility as hereinafter described, and (b) the person giving or acting upon the results of the particular test can demonstrate that alternative suitable hiring, transfer or promotion procedures are unavailable for his use.

Sec. 1607.4   Evidence of validity.

(a) Each person using tests to select from among candidates for a position or for membership shall have available for inspection evidence that the tests are being used in a manner which does not violate §1607.3. Such evidence shall be examined for indications of possible discrimination, such as instances of higher rejection rates for minority candidates than nonminority candidates. Furthermore, where technically feasible, a test should be validated for each minority group with which it is used; that is, any differential rejection rates that may exist, based on a test, must be relevant to performance on the jobs in question.

(b) The term "technically feasible" as used in these guidelines means having or obtaining a sufficient number of minority individuals to achieve findings of statistical and practical significance, the opportunity to obtain unbiased job performance criteria, etc. It is the responsibility of the person claiming absence of technical feasibility to positively demonstrate evidence of this absence.

(c) Evidence of a test's validity should consist of empirical data demonstrating that the test is predictive of or significantly correlated with important elements of work behavior which comprise or are relevant to the job or jobs for which candidates are being evaluated.

(1) If job progression structures and seniority provisions are so established that new employees will probably, within a reasonable period of time and in a great majority of cases, progress to a higher level, it may be considered that candidates are being evaluated for jobs at that higher level. However, where job progression is not so nearly automatic, or the time span is such that higher level jobs or employees' potential may be expected to change in significant ways, it shall be considered that candidates are being evaluated for a job at or near the entry level. This point is made to underscore the principle that attainment of or performance at a higher level job is a relevant criterion in validating employment tests only when there is a high probability that persons employed will in fact attain that higher level job within a reasonable period of time.

(2) Where a test is to be used in different units of a multiunit organization and no significant differences exist between units, jobs, and applicant populations, evidence obtained in one unit may suffice for the others. Similarly, where the validation process requires the collection of data throughout a multiunit organization, evidence of validity specific to each unit may not be required. There may also be instances where evidence of validity is appropriately obtained from more than one company in the same industry. Both in this instance and in the use of data collected throughout a multiunit organization, evidence of validity specific to each unit may not be required: *Provided,* That no significant differences exist between units, jobs, and applicant populations.

Sec. 1607.5   Minimum standards for validation.

(a) For the purpose of satisfying the requirements of this part, empirical evidence in support of a test's validity must be based on studies employing generally accepted procedures for determining criterion-related validity, such as those described in "Standards for Educational and Psychological Tests and Manuals" published by American Psychological Association, 1200 17th Street NW., Washington, D.C. 20036. Evidence of content or construct validity, as defined in that publication, may also be appropriate where criterion-related validity is not feasible. However, evidence for content or construct validity should be accompanied by sufficient information from job analyses to demonstrate the relevance of the content (in the case of job knowledge or proficiency tests) or the construct (in the case of trait measures). Evidence of content validity alone may be acceptable for well-developed tests that consist of suitable samples of the essential knowledge, skills or behaviors composing the job in question. The types of knowledge, skills or behaviors contemplated here do not include those which can be acquired in a brief orientation to the job.

(b) Although any appropriate validation strategy may be used to develop such empirical evidence, the following minimum standards, as applicable, must be met in the research approach and in the presentation of results which constitute evidence of validity.

(1) Where a validity study is conducted in which tests are administered to applicants, with criterion data collected later, the sample of subjects must be representative of the normal or typical candidate group for the job or jobs in question. This further assumes that the applicant sample is representative of the minority population available for the job or jobs in question in the local labor market. Where a validity study is conducted in which tests are administered to present employees, the sample must be representative of the minority groups currently included in the applicant population. If it is not technically feasible to include minority employees in validation studies conducted on the present work force, the conduct of a validation study without minority candidates does not relieve any person of his subsequent obligation for validation when inclusion of minority candidates becomes technically feasible.

(2) Tests must be administered and scored under controlled and standardized conditions, with proper safeguards to protect the security of test scores and to insure that scores do not enter into any judgments of employee adequacy that are to be used as criterion measures. Copies of tests and test manuals, including instructions for administration, scoring, and interpretation of test results, that are privately developed and/or are not available through normal commercial channels must be included as a part of the validation evidence.

(3) The work behaviors or other criteria of employee adequacy which the test is intended to predict or identify must be fully described: and, additionally, in the case of rating techniques, the appraisal form(s) and instructions to the rater(s) must be included as a part of the validation evidence. Such criteria may include measures other than actual work proficiency, such as training time, supervisory ratings, regularity of attendance and tenure. Whatever criteria are used they must represent major or critical work behaviors as revealed by careful job analyses.

(4) In view of the possibility of bias inherent in subjective evaluations, supervisory rating techniques should be carefully developed, and the ratings should be closely examined for evidence of bias. In addition, minorities might obtain unfairly low performance criterion scores for reasons other than supervisors' prejudice, as, when, as new employees, they have had less opportunity to learn job skills. The general point is that all criteria need to be examined to insure freedom from factors which would unfairly depress the scores of minority groups.

(5) Differential validity. Data must be generated and results separately reported for minority and nonminority groups wherever technically feasible. Where a minority group is sufficiently large to constitute an identifiable factor in the local labor market, but validation data have not been developed and presented separately for that group, evidence of satisfactory validity based on other groups will be regarded as only provisional compliance with these guidelines pending separate validation of the test for the minority group in question. (See §1607.9). A test which is differentially valid may be used in groups for which it is valid but not for those in which it is not valid. In this regard, where a test is valid for two groups but one group characteristically obtains higher test scores than the other without a corresponding difference in job performance, cutoff scores must be set so as to predict the same probability of job success in both groups.

(c) In assessing the utility of a test the following considerations will be applicable:

(1) The relationship between the test and at least one relevant criterion must be statistically significant. This ordinarily means that the relationship should be sufficiently high as to have a probability of no more than 1 to 20 to have occurred by chance. However, the use of a single test as the sole selection device will be scrutinized closely when that test is valid against only one component of job performance.

(2) In addition to statistical significance, the relationship between the test and criterion should have practical significance. The magnitude of the relationship needed for practical significance or usefulness is affected by several factors, including:

(i) The larger the proportion of applicants who are hired for or placed on the job, the higher the relationship needs to be in order to be practically useful. Conversely, a relatively low relationship may prove useful when proportionately few job vacancies are available;

(ii) The larger the proportion of applicants who become satisfactory employees when not selected on the basis of the test, the higher the relationship needs to be between the test and a criterion of job success for the test to be practically useful. Conversely, a relatively low relationship may prove useful when proportionately few applicants turn out to be satisfactory;

(iii) The smaller the economic and human risks involved in hiring an unqualified applicant relative to the risks entailed in rejecting a qualified applicant, the greater the relationship needs to be in order to be practically useful. Conversely, a relatively low relationship may prove useful when the former risks are relatively high.

Sec. 1607.6 Presentation of validity evidence.

The presentation of the results of a validation study must include graphical and statistical representations of the relationships between the test and the criteria, permitting judgments of the test's utility in making predictions of future work behavior. (See §1807.5(c) concerning assessing utility of a test.) Average scores for all tests and criteria must be reported for all relevant subgroups, including minority and nonminority groups where differential validation is required. Whenever statistical adjustments are made in validity results for less than perfect reliability or for restriction of score range in the test or the criterion, or both, the supporting evidence from the validation study must be presented in detail. Furthermore, for each test that is to be established or continued as an operational employee selection instrument, as a result of the validation study, the minimum acceptable cutoff (passing) score on the test must be reported. It is expected that each operational cutoff score will be reasonable and consistent with normal expectations of proficiency within the work force or group on which the study was conducted.

Sec. 1607.7 Use of other validity studies.

In cases where the validity of a test cannot be determined pursuant to §1607.4 and §1607.5 (e.g., the number of subjects is less than that required for a technically adequate validation study, or an appropriate criterion measure cannot be developed), evidence from validity studies conducted in other organizations such as that reported in test manuals and professional literature, may be considered acceptable when: (a) The studies pertain to jobs which are comparable (i.e., have basically the same task elements), and (b) there are no major differences in contextual variables or sample composition which are likely to significantly affect validity. Any person citing evidence from other validity studies as evidence of test validity for his own jobs must substantiate in detail job comparability and must demonstrate the absence of contextual or sample differences cited in paragraphs (a) and (b) of this section.

Sec. 1607.8   Assumption of validity.

(a) Under no circumstances will the general reputation of a test, its author or its publisher, or casual reports of test utility be accepted in lieu of evidence of validity. Specifically ruled out are: assumptions of validity based on test names or descriptive labels; all forms of promotional literature; data bearing on the frequency of a test's usage; testimonial statements of sellers, users, or consultants; and other nonempirical or anecdotal accounts of testing practices or testing outcomes.

(b) Although professional supervision of testing activities may help greatly to insure technically sound and nondiscriminatory test usage, such involvement alone shall not be regarded as constituting satisfactory evidence of test validity.

Sec. 1607.9   Continued use of tests.

Under certain conditions, a person may be permitted to continue the use of a test which is not at the moment fully supported by the required evidence of validity. If, for example, determination of criterion-related validity in a specific setting is practicable and required but not yet obtained, the use of the test may continue: *Provided:* (a) The person can cite substantial evidence of validity as described in §1007.7 (a) and (b); and (b) he has in progress validation procedures which are designed to produce, within a reasonable time, the additional data required. It is expected also that the person may have to alter or suspend test cutoff scores so that score ranges broad enough to permit the identification of criterion-related validity will be obtained.

Sec. 1607.10   Employment agencies and employment services.

(a) An employment service, including private employment agencies, State employment agencies, and the U.S. Training and Employment Service, as defined in section 701(c), shall not make applicant or employee appraisals or referrals based on the results obtained from any psychological test or other selection standard not validated in accordance with these guidelines.

(b) An employment agency or service which is requested by an employer or union to devise a testing program is required to follow the standards for test validation as set forth in these guidelines. An employment service is not relieved of its obligation herein because the test user did not request such validation or has requested the use of some lesser standard than is provided in these guidelines.

(c) Where an employment agency or service is requested only to administer a testing program which has been elsewhere devised, the employment agency or service shall request evidence of validation, as described in the guidelines in this part, before it administers the testing program and/or makes referral pursuant to the test results. The employment agency must furnish on request such evidence of validation. An employment agency or service will be expected to refuse to administer a test where the employer or union does not supply satisfactory evidence of validation. Reliance by the test user on the reputation of the test, its author, or the name of the test shall not be deemed sufficient evidence of validity (see §1607.8(a)). An employment agency or service may administer a testing program where the evidence of validity comports with the standards provided in §1607.7.

Sec. 1607.11   Disparate treatment.

The principle of disparate or unequal treatment must be distinguished from the concepts of test validation. A test or other employee selection standard—even though validated against job performance in accordance with the guidelines in this part—cannot be imposed upon any individual or class protected by title VII where other employees, applicants or members have not been subjected to that standard. Disparate treatment, for example, occurs where members of a minority or sex group have been denied the same employment, promotion, transfer or membership opportunities as have been made available to other employees or applicants. Those employees or applicants who have been denied equal treatment, because of prior discriminatory practices or policies, must at least be afforded the same opportunities as had existed for other employees or applicants during the period of discrimination. Thus, no new test or other employee selection standard can be imposed upon a class of individuals protected by title VII who, but for prior discrimination, would have been granted the opportunity to qualify under less stringent selection standards previously in force.

Sec. 1607.12   Retesting.

Employers, unions, and employment agencies should provide an opportunity for retesting and reconsideration to earlier "failure" candidates who have availed themselves of more training or experience. In particular, if any applicant or employee during the course of an interview or other employment procedure claims more education or experience, that individual should be retested.

Sec. 1607.13   Other selection techniques.

Selection techniques other than tests, as defined in §1607.2, may be improperly used so as to have the effect of discriminating against minority groups. Such techniques include, but are not restricted to, unscored or casual interviews and unscored application forms. Where there are data suggesting employment discrimination, the person may be called upon to present evidence concerning the validity of his unscored procedures as well as of any tests which may be used, the evidence of validity being of the same types referred to in §§1607.4 and 1607.5. Data suggesting the possibility of discrimination exist, for example, when there are differential rates of applicant rejection from various minority and non-minority or sex groups for the same job or group of jobs or when there are disproportionate representations of minority and nonminority or sex groups among present employees in different types of jobs. If the person is unable or unwilling to perform such validation studies, he has the option of adjusting employment procedures so as to eliminate the conditions suggestive of employment discrimination.

Sec. 1607.14   Affirmative action.

Nothing in these guidelines shall be interpreted as diminishing a person's obligation under both title VII and Executive Order 11246 as amended by Executive Order 11376 to undertake affirmative action to ensure that applicants or employees are treated without regard to race, color, religion, sex, or national origin. Specifically, the use of tests which have been validated pursuant to those guidelines does not relieve employers, unions or employment agencies of their obligations to take positive action in affording employment and training to members of classes protected by title VII.

The guidelines in this part are effective upon publication in the FEDERAL REGISTER.

GUIDELINES ON DISCRIMINATION BECAUSE OF RELIGION

The EEOC's guidelines on religious discrimination, issued in 1967, outline the employer's obligation to reasonably accommodate the beliefs of employees. They read as follows:

TITLE 29—LABOR

Chapter XIV—Equal Employment Opportunity Commission

PART 1605—Guidelines on Discrimination because of Religion

OBSERVANCE OF THE SABBATH AND OTHER RELIGIOUS HOLIDAYS

By virtue of its authority under section 713 of the Civil Rights Act of 1964, 42 U.S.C. 2000e-12(b), the Equal Employment Opportunity Commission hereby amends §1605.1, Guidelines on Discrimination Because of Religion. This amendment becomes effective immediately and shall be applicable with respect to cases presently before or hereafter filed with the Commission. Section 1605.1 as amended shall read as follows:

Sec. 1605.1 Observation of the Sabbath and other religious holidays.

(a) Several complaints filed with the Commission have raised the question whether it is discrimination on account of religion to discharge or refuse to hire employes who regularly observe Friday evening and Saturday, or some other day of the week, as the Sabbath or who observe certain special religious holidays during the year and, as a consequence, do not work on such days.

(b) The Commission believes that the duty not to discriminate on religious grounds, required by section 703(a)(1) of the Civil Rights Act of 1964, includes an obligation on the part of the employer to make reasonable accommodation to the religious needs of employees and prospective employees where such accommodations can be made without undue hardship on the conduct of the employer's business. Such undue hardship, for example, may exist where the employee's needed work cannot be performed by another employee of substantially similar qualifications during the period of absence of the Sabbath observer.

(c) Because of the particularly sensitive nature of discharging or refusing to hire an employee or applicant on account of his religious beliefs, the employer has the burden of proving that an undue hardship renders the required accommodations to the religious needs of the employee unreasonable.

(d) The Commission will review each case on an individual basis in an effort to seek an equitable application of these guidelines to the variety of situations which arise due to the varied religious practices of the American people.

STATEMENT ON PREHIRE INQUIRIES

In 1968 the EEOC issued the following statement clarifying its position on prehire inquiries relating to prohibited basis of discrimination.

ISSUED BY THE EQUAL EMPLOYMENT OPPORTUNITY COMMISSION, JANUARY 13, 1966, AND AMENDED MAY 27, 1968.

Some state fair employment practice laws expressly prohibit inquiries on applications for employment concerning the applicant's race, color, religion or national origin, and state Commissions have determined that such direct inquiries, as well as the elicitation of indirect indicia, such as former name, past residences, names of relatives, place of birth, citizenship, education, work and military experience, organizational activities, references and photographs, may be unlawful.

Title VII of the Civil Rights Act of 1964 does not expressly prohibit pre-employment inquiries concerning a job applicant's race, color, religion or national origin. The legislative history of the statute is silent as to the Congressional intent on the subject.

Although Title VII does not make pre-employment inquiries concerning race, color, religion or national origin *per se* violations of law, the Commission's responsibility to promote equal employment opportunity compels it to regard such inquiries with extreme disfavor. Except in those infrequent instances where religion or national origin is a bona fide occupational qualification reasonably necessary for the performance of a particular job, an applicant's race, religion and the like are totally irrelevant to his or her ability or qualifications as a prospective employee, and no useful purpose is served by eliciting such information. The Commission is also mindful that such inquiries traditionally have been used to deprive individuals of employment opportunities and to discriminate in ways now proscribed by Title VII.

Accordingly, in the investigation of charges alleging the commission of unlawful employment practices, the Commission will pay particular attention to the use by the party against whom charges have been made of pre-employment inquiries concerning race, religion, color or national origin, or other inquiries which tend directly or indirectly to disclose such information. The fact that such questions are asked may, unless otherwise explained, constitute evidence of discrimination, and will weigh significantly in the Commission's decision as to whether or not Title VII has been violated.

Pre-employment inquiries which are made in conformance with instructions from, or the requirements of, an agency or agencies of the local, State, or Federal Government in connection with the administration of a fair employment practices program will not constitute evidence of discrimination under Title VII.

The Age Discrimination in Employment Act and Its Interpretive Bulletin

In 1967 Congress passed legislation prohibiting age discrimination and two years later the Department of Labor issued guidelines on its interpretation. The revised text of the law reads as follows:

Be it enacted by the Senate and House of Representatives of the United States of America in Congress assembled, That this Act may be cited as the "Age Discrimination in Employment Act of 1967".

STATEMENT OF FINDINGS AND PURPOSE

Sec. 2. (a) The Congress hereby finds and declares that—

(1) in the face of rising productivity and affluence, older workers find themselves disadvantaged in their efforts to retain employment, and especially to regain employment when displaced from jobs;

(2) the setting of arbitrary age limits regardless of potential for job performance has become a common practice, and certain otherwise desirable practices may work to the disadvantage of older persons;

(3) the incidence of unemployment, especially long-term unemployment with resultant deterioration of skill, morale, and employer acceptability is, relative to the younger ages, high among older workers; their numbers are great and growing; and their employment problems grave;

(4) the existence in industries affecting commerce, of arbitrary discrimination in employment because of age, burdens commerce and the free flow of goods in commerce.

(b) It is therefore the purpose of this Act to promote employment of older persons based on their ability rather than age; to prohibit arbitrary age discrimination in employment; to help employers and workers find ways of meeting problems arising from the impact of age on employment.

EDUCATION AND RESEARCH PROGRAM

(a) The Secretary of Labor shall undertake studies and provide information to ons, management, and the general public concerning the needs and abilities of rkers, and their potentials for continued employment and contribution to the ...omy. In order to achieve the purposes of this Act, the Secretary of Labor shall carry on a continuing program of education and information, under which he may, among other measures—

(1) undertake research, and promote research, with a view to reducing barriers to the employment of older persons, and the promotion of measures for utilizing their skills;

(2) publish and otherwise make available to employers, professional societies, the various media of communication, and other interested persons the findings of studies and other materials for the promotion of employment;

(3) foster through the public employment service system and through cooperative effort the development of facilities of public and private agencies for expanding the opportunities and potentials of older persons;

(4) sponsor and assist State and community informational and educational programs.

(b) Not later than six months after the effective date of this Act, the Secretary shall recommend to the Congress any measures he may deem desirable to change the lower or upper age limits set forth in section 12.

PROHIBITION OF AGE DISCRIMINATION

Sec. 4. (a) It shall be unlawful for an employer—

(1) to fail or refuse to hire or to discharge any individual or otherwise discriminate against any individual with respect to his compensation, terms, conditions, or privileges of employment, because of such individual's age;

(2) to limit, segregate, or classify his employees in any way which would deprive or tend to deprive any individual of employment opportunities or otherwise adversely affect his status as an employee, because of such individual's age; or

(3) to reduce the wage rate of any employee in order to comply with this Act.

(b) It shall be unlawful for an employment agency to fail or refuse to refer for employment, or otherwise to discriminate against, any individual because of such individual's age, or to classify or refer for employment any individual on the basis of such individual's age.

(c) It shall be unlawful for a labor organization—

(1) to exclude or to expel from its membership, or otherwise to discriminate against, any individual because of his age;

(2) to limit, segregate, or classify its membership, or to classify or fail or refuse to refer for employment any individual, in any way which would deprive or tend to deprive any individual of employment opportunities, or would limit such employment opportunities or otherwise adversely affect his status as an employee or as an applicant for employment, because of such individual's age;

(3) to cause or attempt to cause an employer to discriminate against an individual in violation of this section.

(d) It shall be unlawful for an employer to discriminate against any of his employees or applicants for employment, for an employment agency to discriminate against any individual, or for a labor organization to discriminate against any member thereof or applicant for membership, because such individual, member or applicant for membership has opposed any practice made unlawful by this section, or because such individual, member or applicant for membership has made a charge, testified, assisted, or participated in any manner in an investigation, proceeding, or litigation under this Act.

(e) It shall be unlawful for an employer, labor organization, or employment agency to print or publish, or cause to be printed or published, any notice or advertisement relating to employment by such an employer or membership in or any classification or referral for employment by such a labor organization, or relating to any classification or referral for employment by such an employment agency, indicating any preference, limitation, specification, or discrimination, based on age.

(f) It shall not be lawful for an employer, employment agency, or labor organization—

(1) to take any action otherwise prohibited under subsections (a), (b), (c), or (e) of this section where age is a bona fide occupational qualification reasonably necessary to the normal operation of the particular business, or where the differentiation is based on reasonable factors other than age;

(2) to observe the terms of a bona fide seniority system or any bona fide employee benefit plan such as a retirement, pension, or insurance plan, which is not a subterfuge to evade the purposes of this Act, except that no such employee benefit plan shall excuse the failure to hire any individual; or

(3) to discharge or otherwise discipline an individual for good cause.

STUDY BY SECRETARY OF LABOR

Sec. 5. The Secretary of Labor is directed to undertake an appropriate study of institutional and other arrangements giving rise to involuntary retirement, and report his findings and any appropriate legislative recommendations to the President and to the Congress.

ADMINISTRATION

Sec. 6. The Secretary shall have the power—

(a) to make delegations, to appoint such agents and employees, and to pay for technical assistance on a fee for service basis, as he deems necessary to assist him in the performance of his functions under this Act;

(b) to cooperate with regional, State, local, and other agencies, and to cooperate with and furnish technical assistance to employers, labor organizations, and employment agencies to aid in effectuating the purposes of this Act.

RECORDKEEPING, INVESTIGATION, AND ENFORCEMENT

Sec. 7. (a) The Secretary shall have the power to make investigations and require the keeping of records necessary or appropriate for the administration of this Act in accordance with the powers and procedures provided in sections 9 and 11 of the Fair Labor Standards Act of 1938, as amended (29 U.S.C. 209 and 211).

(b) The provisions of this Act shall be enforced in accordance with the powers, remedies, and procedures provided in sections 11(b), 16 (except for subsection (a) thereof), and 17 of the Fair Labor Standards Act of 1938, as amended (29 U.S.C. 211(b), 216, 217), and subsection (c) of this section. Any act prohibited under section 4 of this Act shall be deemed to be a prohibited act under section 15 of the Fair Labor Standards Act of 1938, as amended (29 U.S.C. 215). Amounts owing to a person as a result of a violation of this Act shall be deemed to be unpaid minimum wages or unpaid overtime compensation for purposes of sections 16 and 17 of the Fair Labor Standards Act of 1938, as amended (29 U.S.C. 216, 217): *Provided,* That liquidated damages shall be payable only in cases of willful violations of this Act. In any action brought to enforce this Act the court shall have jurisdiction to grant such legal or equitable relief as may be appropriate to effectuate the purposes of this Act, including without limitation judgments compelling employment, reinstatement or promotion, or enforcing the liability for amounts deemed to be unpaid minimum wages or unpaid overtime compensation under this section. Before instituting any action under this section, the Secretary shall attempt to eliminate the discriminatory practice or practices alleged, and to effect voluntary compliance with requirements of this Act through informal methods of conciliation, conference, and persuasion.

(c) Any person aggrieved may bring a civil action in any court of competent jurisdiction for such legal or equitable relief as will effectuate the purposes of this Act: *Provided,* That the right of any person to bring such action shall terminate upon the commencement of an action by the Secretary to enforce the right of such employee under this Act.

(d) No civil action may be commenced by any individual under this section until the individual has given the Secretary not less than sixty days' notice of an intent to file such action. Such notice shall be filed—

(1) within one hundred and eighty days after the alleged unlawful practice occurred, or

(2) in a case to which section 14(b) applies, within three hundred days after the alleged unlawful practice occurred or within thirty days after receipt by the individual of notice of termination of proceedings under State law, whichever is earlier.

Upon receiving a notice of intent to sue, the Secretary shall promptly notify all persons named therein as prospective defendants in the action and shall promptly seek to eliminate any alleged unlawful practice by informal methods of conciliation, conference, and persuasion.

(e) Sections 6 and 10 of the Portal-to-Portal Act of 1947 shall apply to actions under this Act.

NOTICE TO BE POSTED

Sec. 8. Every employer, employment agency, and labor organization shall post and keep posted in conspicuous places upon its premises a notice to be prepared or approved by the Secretary setting forth information as the Secretary deems appropriate to effectuate the purposes of this Act.

RULES AND REGULATIONS

Sec. 9. In accordance with the provisions of subchapter II of chapter 5 of title 5, United States Code, the Secretary of Labor may issue such rules and regulations as he may consider necessary or appropriate for carrying out this Act, and may establish such reasonable exemptions to and from any or all provisions of this Act as he may find necessary and proper in the public interest.

CRIMINAL PENALTIES

Sec. 10. Whoever shall forcibly resist, oppose, impede, intimidate or interfere with a duly authorized representative of the Secretary while he is engaged in the performance of duties under this Act shall be punished by a fine of not more than $500 or by imprisonment for not more than one year, or both: *Provided, however,* That no person shall be imprisoned under this section except when there has been a prior conviction hereunder.

DEFINITIONS

Sec. 11. For the purposes of this Act—

(a) The term "person" means one or more individuals, partnerships, associations, labor organizations, corporations, business trusts, legal representatives, or any organized groups of persons.

(b) The term "employer" means a person engaged in an industry affecting commerce who has twenty or more employees for each working day in each of twenty or more calendar weeks in the current or preceding calendar year: *Provided,* That prior to June 30, 1968, employers having fewer than fifty employees shall not be considered employers. The term also means (1) any agent of such a person, and (2) a State or political subdivision of a State and any agency or instrumentality of a State or a political subdivision of a State, and any interstate agency, but such term does not include the United States, or a corporation wholly owned by the Government of the United States.

(c) The term "employment agency" means any person regularly undertaking with or without compensation to procure employees for an employer and includes an agent of such a person; but shall not include an agency of the United States.[1]

(d) The term "labor organization" means a labor organization engaged in an industry affecting commerce, and any agent of such an organization, and includes any organization of any kind, any agency, or employee representation committee, group, association, or plan so engaged in which employees participate and which exists for the purpose, in whole or in part, of dealing with employers concerning grievances, labor disputes, wages, rates of pay, hours, or other terms or conditions of employment, and any conference, general committee, joint or system board, or joint council so engaged which is subordinate to a national or international labor organization.

(3) A labor organization shall be deemed to be engaged in an industry affecting commerce if (1) it maintains or operates a hiring hall or hiring office which procures employees for an employer or procures for employees opportunities to work for an employer, or (2) the number of its members (or, where it is a labor organization composed of other labor organizations or their representatives, if the aggregate number of the members of such other labor organization) is fifty or more prior to July 1, 1968, or twenty-five or more on or after July 1, 1968, and such labor organization—

(1) is the certified representative of employees under the provisions of the National Labor Relations Act, as amended, or the Railway Labor Act, as amended; or

(2) although not certified, is a national or international labor organization or a local labor organization recognized or acting as the representative of employees of an employer or employers engaged in an industry affecting commerce; or

(3) has chartered a local labor organization or subsidiary body which is representing or actively seeking to represent employees of employers within the meaning of paragraph (1) or (2); or

(4) has been chartered by a labor organization representing or actively seeking to represent employees within the meaning of paragraph (1) or (2) as the local or subordinate body through which such employees may enjoy membership or become affiliated with such labor organization; or

(5) is a conference, general committee, joint or system board, or joint council subordinate to a national or international labor organization, which includes a labor

---

[1] Prior to the Fair Labor Standards Amendments of 1974, the Act's definition of an "employment agency" excluded "an agency of a State or political subdivision of a State, except that such term shall include the United States Employment Service and the system of State and local employment services receiving Federal assistance."

organization engaged in an industry affecting commerce within the meaning of any of the preceding paragraphs of this subsection.

(f) The term "employee" means an individual employed by any employer except that the term "employee" shall not include any person elected to public office in any State or political subdivision of any State by the qualified voters thereof, or any person chosen by such officer to be on such officer's personal staff, or an appointee on the policymaking level or an immediate adviser with respect to the exercise of the constitutional or legal powers of the office. The exemption set forth in the preceding sentence shall not include employees subject to the civil service laws of a State government, governmental agency, or political subdivision.

(g) The term "commerce" means trade, traffic, commerce, transportation, transmission, or communication among the several States; or between a State and any place outside thereof; or within the District of Columbia, or a possession of the United States; or between points in the same State but through a point outside thereof.

(h) The term "industry affecting commerce" means any activity, business, or industry in commerce or in which a labor dispute would hinder or obstruct commerce or the free flow of commerce and includes any activity or industry "affecting commerce" within the meaning of the Labor-Management Reporting and Disclosure Act of 1959.

(i) The term "State" includes a State of the United States, the District of Columbia, Puerto Rico, the Virgin Islands, American Samoa, Guam, Wake Island, the Canal Zone, and Outer Continental Shelf lands defined in the Outer Continental Shelf Lands Act.

LIMITATION

Sec. 12. The prohibitions in this Act shall be limited to individuals who are at least forty years of age but less than sixty-five years of age.

ANNUAL REPORT

Sec. 13. The Secretary shall submit annually in January a report to the Congress covering his activities for the preceding year and including such information, data, and recommendations for further legislation in connection with the matters covered by this Act as he may find advisable. Such report shall contain an evaluation and appraisal by the Secretary of the effect of the minimum and maximum ages established by this Act, together with his recommendations to the Congress. In making such evaluation and appraisal, the Secretary shall take into consideration any changes which may have occurred in the general age level of the population, the effect of the Act upon workers not covered by its provisions, and such other factors as he may deem pertinent.

FEDERAL-STATE RELATIONSHIP

Sec. 14. (a) Nothing in this Act shall affect the jurisdiction of any agency of any State performing like functions with regard to discriminatory employment practices on account of age except that upon commencement of action under this Act such action shall supersede any State action.

(b) In the case of an alleged unlawful practice occurring in a State which has a law prohibiting discrimination in employment because of age and establishing or authorizing a State authority to grant or seek relief from such discriminatory practice, no suit may be brought under section 7 of this Act before the expiration of sixty days after proceedings have been commenced under the State law, unless such proceedings have been earlier terminated: *Provided,* That such sixty-day period shall be extended to one hundred and twenty days during the first year after the effective date of such State law. If any requirement for the commencement of such proceedings is imposed by a State authority other than a requirement of the filing of a written and signed statement of the facts upon which the proceeding is based, the proceeding shall be deemed to have been commenced for the purposes of this subsection at the time such statement is sent by registered mail to the appropriate State authority.

NONDISCRIMINATION ON ACCOUNT OF AGE IN FEDERAL GOVERNMENT EMPLOYMENT

Sec. 15. (a) All personnel actions affecting employees or applicants for employment (except with regard to aliens employed outside the limits of the United States) in military departments as defined in section 102 of title 5, United States Code, in executive agencies as defined in section 105 of title 5, United States Code (including employees and applicants for employment who are paid from nonappropriated funds), in the United States Postal Service and the Postal Rate Commission, in those units in the government of the District of Columbia having positions in the competitive service, and in those units of the legislative and judicial branches of the Federal Government having positions in the competitive service, and in the Library of Congress shall be made free from any discrimination based on age.

(b) Except as otherwise provided in this subsection, the Civil Service Commission is authorized to enforce the provisions of subsection (a) through appropriate remedies, including reinstatement or hiring of employees with or without backpay, as will effectuate the policies of this section. The Civil Service Commission shall issue such rules, regulations, orders, and instructions as it deems necessary and appropriate to carry out its responsibilities under this section. The Civil Service Commission shall—

(1) be responsible for the review and evaluation of the operation of all agency programs designed to carry out the policy of this section, periodically obtaining and publishing (on at least a semiannual basis) progress reports from each department, agency, or unit referred to in subsection (a);

(2) consult with and solicit the recommendations of interested individuals, groups, and organizations relating to nondiscrimination in employment on account of age; and

(3) provide for the acceptance and processing of complaints of discrimination in Federal employment on account of age.

The head of each such department, agency, or unit shall comply with such rules, regulations, orders, and instructions of the Civil Service Commission which shall include a provision that an employee or applicant for employment shall be notified of any final action taken on any complaint of discrimination filed by him thereunder. Reasonable exemptions to the provisions of this section may be established by the Commission but only when the Commission has established a maximum age requirement on the basis of a determination that age is a bona fide occupational qualification necessary to the performance of the duties of the position. With respect to employment in the Library of Congress, authorities granted in this subsection to the Civil Service Commission shall be exercised by the Librarian of Congress.

(c) Any person aggrieved may bring a civil action in any Federal district court of competent jurisdiction for such legal or equitable relief as will effectuate the purposes of this Act.

(d) When the individual has not filed a complaint concerning age discrimination with the Commission, no civil action may be commenced by an individual under this section until the individual has given the Commission not less than thirty days' notice of an intent to file such action. Such notice shall be filed within one hundred and eighty days after the alleged unlawful practice occurred. Upon receiving a notice of intent to sue, the Commission shall promptly notify all persons named therein as prospective defendants in the action and take any appropriate action to assure the elimination of any unlawful practice.

(e) Nothing contained in this section shall relieve any Government agency or official of the responsibility to assure nondiscrimination on account of age in employment as required under any provision of Federal law.

EFFECTIVE DATE[2]

Sec. 16. This Act shall become effective one hundred and eighty days after enactment, except (a) that the Secretary of Labor may extend the delay in effective date of any provision of this Act up to an additional ninety days thereafter if he finds that such time is necessary in permitting adjustments to the provisions hereof, and (b) that on or after the date of enactment the Secretary of Labor is authorized to issue such rules and regulations as may be necessary to carry out its provisions.

APPROPRIATIONS

Sec. 17. There are hereby authorized to be appropriated such sums, not in excess of $5,000,000 for any fiscal year, as may be necessary to carry out this Act.
Approved December 15, 1967.

INTERPRETIVE BULLETIN ON THE AGE DISCRIMINATION IN EMPLOYMENT ACT OF 1967

This bulletin sets forth the Department of Labor's interpretation of the Age Discrimination in Employment Act. It reads as follows:

Sec. 860.1   Purpose of this part.

This part is intended to provide an interpretive bulletin on the Age Discrimination in Employment Act of 1967 like Subchapter B of this title relating to the Fair Labor Standards Act of 1938. Such interpretations of this Act are published to provide "a practical guide to employers and employees as to how the office representing the public interest in its enforcement will seek to apply it" (Skidmore v. Swift & Co., 323 U.S. 134, 138). These interpretations indicate the construction of the law which the Department of Labor believes to be correct, and which will guide it in the performance of its administrative and enforcement duties under the Act unless and until it is otherwise directed by authoritative decisions of the Courts or concludes, upon reexamination of an interpretation, that it is incorrect.

Sec. 806.20   Geographical scope of coverage.

The prohibitions in section 4 of the Act are considered to apply only to performance of the described discriminatory acts in places over which the United States has sovereignty,

---

[2] The effective date of the provisions added by the Fair Labor Standards Amendments of 1974, which are shown in bold face type, was May 1, 1974. See section 29(a) of the Fair Labor Standards Amendments of 1974.

territorial jurisdiction, or legislative control. These include principally the geographical areas set forth in the definition of the term "State" in section 11(i). There, the term State is defined to include "a State of the United States, the District of Columbia, Puerto Rico, the Virgin Islands, American Samoa, Guam, Wake Island, the Canal Zone, and Outer Continental Shelf lands defined in the Outer Continental Shelf Lands Act." Activities within such geographical areas which are discriminatory against protected individuals or employees are within the scope of the Act even though the activities are related to employment outside of such geographical areas.

[34 F.R. 322, January 9, 1969]

Sec. 860.30 Definitions.

Considering the purpose of the proviso to section 7(c) of the Act as indicated in the reports of both the Senate and House Committees (see S. Rept. No. 723, 90th Cong., 1st Sess., and H. Rept. No. 805, 90th Cong., 1st Sess.) it was clearly the intent of Congress that the term "employee" in that proviso should apply to any person who has a right to bring an action under the Act, including an applicant for employment.

[34 F.R. 9708, June 21, 1969]

Sec. 860.50 "Compensation, terms, conditions, or privileges of employment.***"

(a) Section 4(a)(1) of the Act specifies that it is unlawful for an employer "to fail or refuse to hire or to discharge any individual or otherwise discriminate against any individual with respect to his compensation, terms, conditions, or privileges of employment, because of such individual's age;"

(b) The term "compensation" includes all types and methods of enumeration paid to or on behalf of or received by an employee for his employment.

(c) The phrase "terms, conditions, or privileges of employment" encompasses a wide and varied range of job-related factors including, but not limited to, job security, advancement, status, and benefits. The following are examples of some of the more common terms, conditions, or privileges of employment: The many and varied employee advantages generally regarded as being within the phrase "fringe benefits," promotion, demotion or other disciplinary action, hours of work (including overtime), leave policy (including sick leave, vacation, holidays), career development programs, and seniority or merit systems (which govern such conditions as transfer, assignment, job retention, layoff and recall). An employer will be deemed to have violated the Act if he discriminates against any individual within its protection because of age with respect to any terms, conditions, or privileges of employment, such as the above, unless a statutory exception applies.

[33 F.R. 12227, August 30, 1968]

Sec. 860.75 Wage rate reduction prohibited.

Section 4(a)(3) of the Act provides that where an age-based wage differential is paid in violation of the statute, the employer cannot correct the violation by reducing the wage rate of any employee. Thus, for example, in a situation where it has been determined that an employer has violated the Act by paying a 62-year-old employee a prohibited wage differential of 50 cents an hour less than he is paying a 30-year-old worker, in order to achieve compliance with the Act he must raise the wage rate of the older employee to equal that of the younger worker. Furthermore, the employer's obligation to comply with the statute cannot be avoided by transferring either the older or the younger employee to other work since the transfer itself would appear discriminatory under the particular facts and circumstances.

[34 F.R. 322, January 9, 1969]

Sec. 860.91   Discrimination within the age bracket of 40–65.

(a) Although section 4 of the Act broadly makes unlawful various types of age discrimination by employers, employment agencies, and labor organizations, section 12 limits this protection to individuals who are at least 40 years of age but less than 65 years of age. Thus, for example it is unlawful in situations where this Act applies, for an employer to discriminate in hiring or in any other way by giving preference because of age to an individual 30 years old over another individual who is within the 40–65 age bracket limitation of section 12. Similarly, an employer will have violated the Act, in situations where it applies, when one individual within the age bracket of 40–65 is given job preference in hiring, assignment, promotion or any other term, condition, or privilege of employment, on the basis of age, over another individual within the same age bracket.

(b) Thus, if two men apply for employment to which the Act applies, and one is 42 and the other 52, the personnel officer or employer may not lawfully turn down either one on the basis of his age; he must make his decision on the basis of other factors, such as the capabilities and experience of the two individuals. The Act, however, does not restrain age discrimination between two individuals 25 and 35 years of age.

Sec. 860.92   Help wanted notices or advertisements.

(a) Section 4(e) of the Act prohibits "an employer, labor organization, or employment agency" from using printed or published notices or advertisements indicating any preference, limitation, specification, or discrimination, based on age.

(b) When help wanted notices or advertisements contain terms and phrases such as "age 25 to 35," "young," "boy," "girl," "college student," "recent college graduate," or others of a similar nature, such a term or phrase discriminates against the employment of older persons and will be considered in violation of the Act. Such specifications as "age 40 to 50," "age over 50," or "age over 65" are also considered to be prohibited. Where such specifications as "retired person" or "supplement your pension" are intended and applied so as to discriminate against others within the protected group, they too are regarded as prohibited, unless one of the exceptions applies.

[34 F.R. 9708, June 21, 1969]

(c) However, help wanted notices or advertisements which include a term or phrase such as "college graduate," or other educational requirement, or specify a minimum age less than 40, such as "not under 18," or "not under 21," are not prohibited by the statute.

(d) The use of the phrase "state age" in help wanted notices or advertisements is not, in itself, a violation of the statute. But because the request that an applicant state his age may tend to deter older applicants or otherwise indicate a discrimination based on age, employment notices or advertisements which include the phrase "state age," or any similar term, will be closely scrutinized to assure that the request is for a permissible purpose and not for purposes proscribed by the statute.

(e) There is no provision in the statute which prohibits an individual seeking employment through advertising from specifying his own age.

Sec. 860.95   Job applications.

(a) The term "job applications," within the meaning of the record keeping regulations under the Act (Part 850 of this chapter), refers to all inquiries about employment or applications for employment or promotion including, but not limited to, résumés or other summaries of the applicant's background. It relates not only to preemployment inquiries but to inquiries by employees concerning terms, conditions, or privileges of employment as specified in section 4 of the statute. As in the case with help wanted notices or advertisements (see §860.92), a request on the part of an employer, employment agency, or labor organization for information such as "Date of Birth" or "State Age" on an employment application form is not, in itself, a violation of the Age Discrimination in Employment Act of 1967. But because the request that an applicant state his age may tend to deter older applicants or otherwise indicate a discrimination based on age, employment application forms which request such information in the above, or any similar phrase, will be closely scrutinized to assure that the request is for a permissible purpose and not for purposes proscribed by the statute. That the purpose is not one proscribed by the statute should be made known to the applicant, as by a reference on the application form to the statutory prohibition in language to the following effect: "The Age Discrimination in Employment Act of 1967 prohibits discrimination on the basis of age with respect to individuals who are at least 40 but less than 65 years of age."

[33 F.R. 12227, August 30, 1968]

(b) An employer may limit the active period of consideration of an application so long as he treats all applicants alike regardless of age. Thus, for example, if the employer customarily retains employment applications in an active status for a period of 60 days, he will be in compliance with the Act if he so retains those of individuals in the 40 to 65 age group for an equal period of consideration as those of younger persons. Further, there is no objection to the employer advising all applicants of the above practice by means of a legend on his application forms as long as this does not suggest any limitation based on age. If it develops, however, that such a legend is used as a device to avoid consideration of the applications of older persons, or otherwise discriminate against them because of age, there would then appear to be a violation of the Act. It should be noted that this position in no way alters the recordkeeping requirements of the Act which are set forth in Part 850 of this chapter.

[34 F.R. 9708, June 21, 1969]

Sec. 860.102 Bona fide occupational qualifications.

(a) Section 4(f)(1) of the Act provides that "It shall not be unlawful for an employer, employment agency, or labor organization * * * to take any action otherwise prohibited under subsections (a), (b), (c), or (e) of this section where age is a bona fide occupational qualification reasonably necessary to the normal operation of the particular business * * * "

(b) Whether occupational qualifications will be deemed to be "bona fide" and "reasonably necessary to the normal operation of the particular business," will be determined on the basis of all the pertinent facts surrounding each particular situation. It is anticipated that this concept of a bona fide occupational qualification will have limited scope and application. Further, as this is an exception it must be construed narrowly, and the burden of proof in establishing that it applies is the responsibility of the employer, employment agency, or labor organization which relies upon it.

(c) The following are illustrations of possible bona fide occupational qualifications.

(d) Federal statutory and regulatory requirements which provide compulsory age limitations for hiring or compulsory retirement, without reference to the individual's actual physical condition at the terminal age, when such conditions are clearly imposed for the safety and convenience of the public. This exception would apply, for example, to airline pilots within the jurisdiction of the Federal Aviation Agency. Federal Aviation Agency regulations do not permit airline pilots to engage in carrier operations, as pilots, after they reach age 60.

(e) A bona fide occupational qualification will also be recognized in certain special, individual occupational circumstances, e.g., actors required for youthful or elderly characterizations or roles, and persons used to advertise or promote the sale of products designed for, and directed to appeal exclusively to, either youthful or elderly consumers.

Sec. 860.103 Differentiations based on reasonable factors other than age.

(a) Section 4(f)(1) of the Act provides that "It shall not be unlawful for an employer, employment agency, or labor organization * * * to take any action otherwise prohibited under subsections (a), (b), (c), or (e) of this section * * * where the differentiation is based on reasonable factors other than age; * * * "

(b) No precise and unequivocal determination can be made as to the scope of the phrase "differentiation based on reasonable factors other than age." Whether such differentiations exist must be decided on the basis of all the particular facts and circumstances surrounding each individual situation.

(c) It should be kept in mind that it was not the purpose or intent of Congress in enacting this Act to require the employment of anyone, regardless of age, who is disqualified on grounds other than age from performing a particular job. The clear purpose is to insure that age, within the limits prescribed by the Act, is not a determining factor in making any decision regarding hiring, dismissal, promotion or any other term, condition or privilege of employment of an individual.

(d) The reasonableness of a differentiation will be determined on an individual, case by case basis, not on the basis of any general or class concept, with unusual working conditions given weight according to their individual merit.

(e) Further, in accord with a long chain of decisions of the Supreme Court of the United States with respect to other remedial labor legislation, all exceptions such as this must be construed narrowly, and the burden of proof in establishing the applicability of the exception will rest upon the employer, employment agency or labor union which seeks to invoke it.

(f) Where the particular facts and circumstances in individual situations warrant such a conclusion, the following factors are among those which may be recognized as supporting a differentiation based on reasonable factors other than age:

(1)(i) Physical fitness requirements based upon preemployment or periodic physical examinations relating to minimum standards for employment: *Provided, however,* That such standards are reasonably necessary for the specific work to be performed and are uniformly and equally applied to all applicants for the particular job category, regardless of age.

(ii) Thus, a differentiation based on a physical examination, but not one based on age, may be recognized as reasonable in certain job situations which necessitate stringent physical requirements due to inherent occupational factors such as the safety of the individual employees or of other persons in their charge, or those occupations which by nature are particularly hazardous: For example, iron workers, bridge builders, sandhogs, underwater demolition men, and other similar job classifications which require rapid reflexes or a high degree of speed, coordination, dexterity, endurance, or strength.

(iii) However, a claim for a differentiation will not be permitted on the basis of an employer's assumption that every employee over a certain age in a particular type of job usually becomes physically unable to perform the duties of that job. There is medical evidence, for example, to support the contention that such is generally not the case. In many instances, an individual at age 60 may be physically capable of performing heavy-lifting on a job, whereas another individual of age 30 may be physically incapable of doing so.

(2) Evaluation factors such as quantity or quality of production, or educational level, would be acceptable bases for differentiation when, in the individual case, such factors are shown to have a valid relationship to job requirements and where the criteria or personnel policy establishing such factors are applied uniformly to all employees, regardless of age.

(g) The foregoing are intended only as examples of differentiations based on reasonable factors other than age, and do not constitute a complete or exhaustive list or limitation. It should always be kept in mind that even in situations where experience has shown that most elderly persons do not have certain qualifications which are essential to those who hold certain jobs, some may have them even though they have attained the age of 60 or 64, and thus discrimination based on age is forbidden.

(h) It should also be made clear that a general assertion that the average cost of employing older workers as a group is higher than the average cost of employing younger workers as a group will not be recognized as a differentiation under the terms and provisions of the Act, unless one of the other statutory exceptions applies. To classify or group employees solely on the basis of age for the purpose of comparing costs, or for any other purpose, necessarily rests on the assumption that the age factor alone may be used to justify a differentiation—an assumption plainly contrary to the terms of the Act and the purpose of Congress in enacting it. Differentials so based would serve only to perpetuate and promote the very discrimination at which the Act is directed.

Sec. 860.104 Differentiations based on reasonable factors other than age—Additional examples.

(a) *Employment of Social Security recipients.* (1) It is considered discriminatory for an employer to specify that he will hire only persons receiving old age Social Security insurance benefits. Such a specification could result in discrimination against other individuals within the age group covered by the Act willing to work under the wages and other conditions of employment involved, even though those wages and conditions may be peculiarly attractive to Social Security recipients. Similarly, the specification of Social Security recipients cannot be used as a convenient reference to persons of sufficient age to be eligible for old age benefits. Thus, where two persons apply for a job, one age 56, and the other age 62 and receiving Social Security benefits, the employer may not lawfully give preference in hiring to the older individual solely because he is receiving such benefits.

(2) Where a job applicant under age 65 is unwilling to accept the number or schedule of hours required by an employer as a condition for a particular job, because he is receiving Social Security benefits and is limited in the amount of wages he may earn without losing such benefits, failure to employ him would not violate the Act. An employer's condition as to the number or schedule of hours may be "a reasonable factor other than age" on which to base a differentiation.

(b) *Employee testing.* The use of a validated employee test is not, of itself, a violation of the Act when such test is specifically related to the requirements of the job, is fair and reasonable, is administered in good faith and without discrimination on the basis of age, and is properly evaluated. A vital factor in employee testing as it relates to the 40–65-age group protected by the statute is the "test-sophistication" or "test-wiseness" of the individual. Younger persons, due to the tremendous increase in the use of tests in primary and secondary schools in recent years, may generally have had more experience in test-taking than older individuals and, consequently, where an employee test is used as the sole tool or the controlling factor in the employee selection procedure, such younger persons may have an advantage over older applicants who may have had considerable on-the-job experience but who due to age, are further removed from their schooling. Therefore, situations in which an employee test is used as the sole tool or the controlling factor in the employee selection procedure will be carefully scrutinized to ensure that the test is for a permissible purpose and not for purposes prohibited by the statute.

[34 F.R. 322, January 9, 1969]

(c) *Refusal to hire relatives of current employees.* There is no provision in the Act which would prohibit an employer, employment agency, or labor organization from refusing to hire individuals within the protected age group not because of their age but because they are relatives of persons already employed by the firm or organization involved. Such a differentiation would appear to be based on "reasonable factors other than age."

[34 F.R. 9709, June 21, 1969]

Sec. 860.105 Bona fide seniority systems.

Section 4(f)(2) of the Act provides that "It shall not be unlawful for an employer, employment agency, or labor organization * * * to observe the terms of a bona fide seniority system * * * which is not a subterfuge to evade the purposes of this Act * * * "

(a) Though a seniority system may be qualified by such factors as merit, capacity, or ability, any bona fide seniority system must be based on length of service as the primary criterion for the equitable allocation of available employment opportunities and prerogatives among younger and older workers. In this regard it should be noted that a bona fide seniority system may operate, for example, on an occupational, departmental, plant, or company wide unit basis.

(b) Seniority systems not only distinguish between employees on the basis of their length of service, they normally afford greater rights to those who have the longer service. Therefore, adoption of a purported seniority system which gives those with longer service lesser rights, and results in discharge or less favored treatment to those within the protection of the Act, may, depending upon the circumstances, be a "subterfuge to evade the purposes" of the Act. Furthermore, a seniority system which has the effect of perpetuating discrimination which may have existed on the basis of age prior to the effective date of the Act will not be recognized as "bona fide."

(c) Unless the essential terms and conditions of an alleged seniority system have been communicated to the affected employees and can be shown to be applied uniformly to all of those affected, regardless of age, it will also be regarded as lacking the necessary bona fides to qualify for the exception.

(d) It should be noted that seniority systems which segregate, classify, or otherwise discriminate against individuals on the basis of race, color, religion, sex, or national origin, are prohibited under Title VII of the Civil Rights Act of 1964, where that Act otherwise applies. Neither will such systems be regarded as "bona fide" within the meaning of section 4(f)(2) of the Age Discrimination in Employment Act of 1967.

[33 F.R. 12227, August 30, 1968]

Sec. 860.106 Bona fide apprenticeship programs.

Age limitations for entry into bona fide apprenticeship programs were not intended to be affected by the Act. Entry into most apprenticeship programs has traditionally been limited to youths under specified ages. This is in recognition of the fact that apprenticeship is an extension of the educational process to prepare young men and women for skilled employment. Accordingly, the prohibitions contained in the Act will not be applied to bona fide apprenticeship programs which meet the standards specified in §§521.2 and 521.3 of this chapter.

[34 F.R. 323, January 9, 1969]

Sec. 860.110 Involuntary retirement before age 65.

(a) Section 4(f)(2) of the Act provides that "It shall not be unlawful for an employer, employment agency, or labor organization * * * to observe the terms of * * * any bona fide employee benefit plan such as a retirement, pension, or insurance plan, which is not a subterfuge to evade the purposes of this Act, except that no such employee benefit plan shall excuse the failure to hire any individual * * * ." Thus, the Act authorizes involuntary retirement irrespective of age, provided that such retirement is pursuant to the terms of a retirement or pension plan meeting the requirements of section 4(f)(2). The fact that an employer may decide to permit certain employees to continue working beyond the age stipulated in the formal retirement program does not, in and of itself, render an otherwise bona fide plan invalid insofar as the exception provided in section 4(f)(2) is concerned.

(b) This exception does not apply to the involuntary retirement before 65 of employees who are not participants in the employer's retirement or pension program. It should be noted that section 5 of the Act directs the Secretary of Labor to undertake an appropriate study of institutional and other arrangements giving rise to involuntary retirement, and report his findings and any appropriate legislative recommendations to the President and to Congress.

[34 F.R. 9709, June 21, 1969]

Sec. 860.120   Costs and benefits under employee benefit plans.

(a) Section 4(f)(2) of the Act provides that it is not unlawful for an employer, employment agency, or labor organization "to observe the terms of * * * any bona fide employee benefit plan such as a retirement, pension, or insurance plan, which is not a subterfuge to evade the purposes of this Act, except that no such employee benefit plan shall excuse the failure to hire any individual * * * ." Thus, an employer is not required to provide older workers who are otherwise protected by the law with the same pension, retirement or insurance benefits as he provides to younger workers, so long as any differential between them is in accordance with the terms of a bona fide benefit plan. For example, an employer may provide lesser amounts of insurance coverage under a group insurance plan to older workers than he does to younger workers, where the plan is not a subterfuge to evade the purposes of the Act. A retirement, pension, or insurance plan will be considered in compliance with the statute where the actual amount of payment made, or cost incurred, in behalf of an older worker is equal to that made or incurred in behalf of a younger worker, even though the older worker may thereby receive a lesser amount of pension or retirement benefits, or insurance coverage. Further, an employer may provide varying benefits under a bona fide plan to employees within the age group protected by the Act, when such benefits are determined by a formula involving age and length of service requirements.

(b) Profit-sharing plans: Not all employee benefit plans but only those similar to the kind enumerated in section 4(f)(2) of the Act come within this provision and a profit-sharing plan as such would not appear to be within its terms. However, where it is the essential purpose of a plan financed from profits to provide retirement benefits for employees, the exception may apply. The "bona fides" of such plans will be considered on the basis of all the particular facts and circumstances.

(c) Forfeiture clauses in retirement programs: Clauses in retirement programs which state that litigation or participation in any manner in a formal proceeding by an employee will result in the forfeiture of his rights are unlawful insofar as they may be applied to those who seek redress under the Act. This is by reason of section 4(d) which provides that it "shall be unlawful for an employer to discriminate against any of his employees * * * because such individual * * * has made a charge, testified, assisted, or participated in any manner in an investigation, proceeding, or litigation under this Act."

[34 F.R. 9709, June 21, 1969]

The Equal Pay Act and Its Interpretive Bulletin

In 1963 Congress passed legislation prohibiting sex discrimination specifically in the area of wages, and the Department of Labor issued extensive guidelines on its interpretation.

THE EQUAL PAY ACT OF 1963

The Equal Pay Act of 1963 [subsection (d) of the Fair Labor Standards Act of 1938, as amended] prohibits sex discrimination in wages and was amended in 1972 to cover executive, administrative, and professional employees. The text reads as follows:

Sec. 3(d)(1) No employer having employees subject to any provisions of this section shall discriminate, within any establishment in which such employees are employed, between employees on the basis of sex by paying wages to employees in such establishment at a rate less than the rate at which he pays wages to employees of the opposite sex in such establishment for equal work on jobs the performance of which requires equal skill, effort, and responsibility, and which are performed under similar working conditions, except where such payment is made pursuant to (i) a seniority system; (ii) a merit system; (iii) a system which measures earnings by quantity or quality of production; or (iv) a differential based on any other factor other than sex: *Provided,* That an employer who is paying a wage rate differential in violation of this subsection shall not, in order to comply with the provisions of this subsection, reduce the wage rate of any employee.

(2) No labor organization, or its agents, representing employees of an employer having employees subject to any provisions of this section shall cause or attempt to cause such an employer to discriminate against an employee in violation of paragraph (1) of this subsection.

(3) For purposes of administration and enforcement, any amounts owing to any employee which have been withheld in violation of this subsection shall be deemed to be unpaid minimum wages or unpaid overtime compensation under this Act.

(4) As used in this subsection, the term "labor organization" means any organization of any kind, or any agency or employee representation committee or plan, in which em-

ployees participate and which exists for the purpose, in whole or in part, of dealing with employers concerning grievances, labor disputes, wages, rates of pay, hours of employment, or conditions of work.

INTERPRETIVE BULLETIN: EQUAL PAY FOR EQUAL WORK

This bulletin sets forth the Department of Labor's interpretation of the Equal Pay Act. It reads as follows:

INTRODUCTORY

Section 800.0.—General scope of the Fair Labor Standards Act.

The Fair Labor Standards Act, as amended, hereinafter referred to as the Act, is a Federal statute of general application which establishes minimum wage, overtime pay, child labor, and equal pay requirements that apply as provided in the Act. All employees whose employment has the relationship to interstate or foreign commerce which the Act specifies are subject to the prescribed labor standards unless specifically exempted from them. Employers having such employees are required to comply with the Act's provisions in this regard unless relieved therefrom by some exemption in the Act. Such employers are also required to comply with specified recordkeeping requirements contained in Part 516 of this chapter. The law authorizes the Department of Labor to investigate for compliance and, in the event of violations, to supervise the payment of unpaid wages or unpaid overtime compensation owing to any employee. The law also provides for enforcement in the courts.

Section 800.1.—Purpose of this part.

It is the purpose of this Part 800 to make available official interpretations of the Department of Labor with respect to the meaning and application of the equal pay provisions added to the Fair Labor Standards Act by the Equal Pay Act of 1963 (Public Law 88–38). The Equal Pay Act was enacted on June 10, 1963, for the purpose of correcting "the existence in industries engaged in commerce or in the production of goods for commerce of wage differentials based on sex". This law amends the Fair Labor Standards Act by adding a new section 6(d) to its minimum wage provisions.

Section 800.2.—Significance of official interpretations.

The interpretations of the law contained in this part are official interpretations of the Department of Labor with respect to the application under described circumstances of the provisions of law which they discuss. The ultimate decisions on interpretations of the Act are made by the courts. Court decisions supporting interpretations contained in this part are cited where it is believed they may be helpful. On matters which have not been determined by the courts, it is necessary for the Secretary of Labor and the Administrator to reach conclusions as to the meaning and the application of provisions of the law in order to carry out their responsibilities of administration and enforcement (*Skidmore* v. *Swift*, 323 U.S. 134). In order that these positions may be made known to persons who may be affected by them, official interpretations are issued by the Administrator on the advice of the Solicitor of Labor, as authorized by the Secretary (Reorg. Pl. 6 of 1950, 64 Stat. 1263; Gen. Ord. 45A, May 24, 1950, 15 F.R. 3290). As included in the regulations in this part, these interpretations are believed to express the intent of the law as reflected in its provisions and as construed by the courts and evidenced by its legislative history. They indicate the construction of the law which the Secretary of Labor and the Administrator believe to be correct and which will guide them in the performance of their duties under the Act unless and until they are otherwise directed by authoritative decisions of the courts or conclude, upon reexamination of an interpretation, that it is incorrect. References to pertinent legislative history are made in this part where it appears that they will contribute to a better understanding of the interpretations.

Section 800.3.—Reliance on interpretations.

On and after publication of this part in the Federal Register, the interpretations contained therein shall be in effect and shall remain in effect until they are modified, rescinded, or withdrawn. So long as they remain effective and are not modified, amended, rescinded, or determined by judicial authority to be incorrect, they may be relied upon as provided in section 10 of the Portal-to-Portal Act of 1947 (61 Stat. 84, 29 U.S.C. 251 et seq., discussed in Part 790 of this chapter). In addition, the Supreme Court has recognized that such interpretations of this Act "provide a practical guide to employers and employees as to how the office representing the public interest in its enforcement will seek to apply it" and "constitute a body of experience and informed judgment to which courts and litigants may properly resort to guidance". Further, as stated by the Court: "Good administration of the Act and good judicial administration alike require that the standards of public enforcement and those for determining private rights shall be at variance only where justified by very good reasons." (*Skidmore* v. *Swift*, 323 U.S. 134). This part supersedes and replaces the interpretations previously published in the Federal Register and Code of Federal Regulations as Part 800 of this chapter. Prior opinions, rulings, and interpretations and prior enforcement policies which are not inconsistent with the interpretations in this part or with the Fair Labor Standards Act as amended are continued in effect; all other opinions, rulings, interpretations, and enforcement policies on the subjects discussed in the interpretations in this part are rescinded and withdrawn.

Section 800.4.—Matters discussed in this part.

(a) This part primarily discusses the meaning and application of the equal pay provisions in section 6(d) of the Act. These provisions are discussed in some detail in Subpart B. The enforcement provisions applicable to the equal pay requirements are discussed in Subpart B, sections 800.164–800.166. In addition, section 800.5 et seq. of this subpart briefly consider or make reference to the guides for determining what interstate commerce activities will bring employees and employers within the basic coverage of the Act so that its equal pay requirements may apply. The meaning and application of other provisions of the Act are discussed only to make clear their relevance to the equal pay provisions and are not considered in detail in this part.

(b) The interpretations in this part provide statements of general principles applicable to the subjects discussed and illustrations of the application of these principles to situations that frequently arise. They do not and cannot refer specifically to every problem which may be met in the consideration of the provisions discussed. The omission to discuss a particular problem in this part or in interpretations supplementing it should not be taken to indicate the adoption of any position by the Secretary of Labor or the Administrator with respect to such problem or to constitute an administrative interpretation or practice or enforcement policy. Questions on matters not fully covered by this part may be addressed to the Administrator of the Wage and Hour Division, United States Department of Labor, Washington, D.C. 20210, or to any Regional Office of the Division.

(c) Interpretations published elsewhere in this title deal with such subjects as the general coverage of the Act (Part 776 of this chapter), methods of payment of wages (Part 531, Subpart C of this chapter), computation and payment of overtime compensation (Part 778 of this chapter), retailing of goods or services (Part 779 of this chapter), hours worked (Part 785 of this chapter), and child labor provisions (Part 1500 of this title). Regulations on recordkeeping are contained in Part 516 of this chapter, and regulations defining exempt bona fide executive, administrative, professional employees and outside salesmen are contained in Part 541 of this chapter. Regulations and interpretations on other subjects concerned with the application of the Act are listed in the table of contents to this chapter. Copies of any of these documents may be obtained from any office of the Wage and Hour and Public Contracts Divisions.

BASIC COVERAGE AND EXEMPTION PROVISIONS AFFECTING APPLICATION OF EQUAL PAY REQUIREMENTS

Section 800.5.—Basic coverage as related to the equal pay provisions.

The equal pay provisions neither extend nor curtail coverage of the Fair Labor Standards Act but simply place within the new requirements those employers and employees who were already subject to the Act's minimum wage requirements (H. Rept. No. 309, 88th Cong., 1st sess., p. 2). The nature of the employment coming within the basic or general coverage of the Act should therefore be clearly understood. The general coverage of the Act extends, and its requirements apply except as otherwise provided by a specific exemption, to every employee who is "engaged in commerce or in the production of goods for commerce" and every employee who is "employed in an enterprise engaged in commerce or in the production of goods for commerce" or "by an establishment" qualifying as such an enterprise, as specified and defined in the statute. What employees are so engaged or employed must be ascertained in the light of the definitions and delimitations set forth in the statute, giving due regard to authoritative interpretations by the courts and to the legislative history of the Act, as amended. In section 800.6 to 800.12, the employment which comes within this basic coverage is briefly outlined. For a more comprehensive discussion and a detailed explanation of the applicable principles, reference should be made to the interpretations on general coverage contained in Part 776 of this chapter.

Section 800.6.—General coverage of employees "engaged in commerce".

(a) The minimum wage provisions of the Act have applied since 1938, and continue to apply along with the new equal pay provisions, except as otherwise provided by specific exemptions in the Act, to employees "engaged in commerce". "Commerce" is broadly defined in section 3(b) of the Act. It includes both interstate and foreign commerce and is not limited to transportation across State lines, or to activity of a commercial character. All parts of the movement among the several States or between any State and any place outside thereof of persons or things, tangibles or intangibles, including communication of information and intelligence constitute movement in "commerce" within the statutory definition. This includes those parts of any such activity which take place wholly within a single State. In addition, the instrumentalities for carrying on such commerce are so inseparable from the commerce itself that employees working on such instrumentalities within the borders of a single State are, by virtue of the contribution made by their work to the movement of the commerce, "engaged in commerce" within the meaning of the Act.

(b) Consistent with the purpose of the Act to apply the Federal standards "throughout the farthest reaches of the channels of interstate commerce", the courts have made it clear that the employees "engaged in commerce" to whom coverage is extended include every employee employed in the channels of such commerce or in activities so closely related to such commerce as to be considered a part of it as a practical matter. See *Walling* v. *Jacksonville Paper Co.*, 317 U.S. 564; *Overstreet* v. *North Shore Corp.*, 318 U.S. 125; *Mitchell*

v. *Volmer*, 349 U.S. 427; *Mitchell* v. *Lublin*, 358 U.S. 207; see also *Borden Co.* v. *Borella*, 325 U.S. 679; and see the discussion, with other pertinent court decisions cited, in Part 776 of this chapter. Engaging "in commerce" includes activities connected therewith such as management and control of the various physical processes, together with the accompanying accounting and clerical activities. Thus, employees engaged in interstate or foreign commerce will typically include, among others, employees in distributing industries such as wholesaling or retailing who sell, transport, handle, or otherwise work on goods moving in interstate or foreign commerce as well as workers who order, receive, guard, pack, ship, or keep records of such goods; employees who handle payroll or personnel functions for workers engaged in such activities; clerical and other workers who regularly use the mails, telephone, or telegraph for communication across State lines; and employees who regularly travel across State lines while working. For other illustrations see Part 776 of this chapter.

Section 800.7.—General coverage of employees "engaged in * * * the production of goods for commerce".

(a) The minimum wage provisions of the Act also have applied since 1938, and continue to apply along with the new equal pay provisions, except as otherwise provided by specific exemptions in the Act, to employees "engaged in * * * the production of goods for commerce". The broad meaning of "commerce" as defined in section 3(b) of the Act has been outlined in section 800.6. "Goods" is also comprehensively defined in section 3(i) of the Act, and includes "articles or subjects of commerce of any character, or any part or ingredient thereof" not expressly excepted by the statute. The activities constituting "production" of the goods for commerce are defined in section 3(j) of the Act. These are not limited to such work as manufacturing but include handling or otherwise working on goods intended for shipment out of the State either directly or indirectly or for use within the State to serve the needs of the instrumentalities or facilities by which interstate or foreign commerce is carried on. See *United States* v. *Darby*, 312 U.S. 100; *Alstate Constr. Co.* v. *Durkin*, 345 U.S. 13. Employees engaged in any closely related process or occupation directly essential to such production of any goods, whether employed by the producer or by an independent employer, are also engaged, by definition, in "production". See section 800.8 and the detailed discussion in Part 776 of this chapter. Further, the courts have recognized that an enterprise producing goods for commerce does not accomplish the actual production of such goods solely with employees performing physical labor on them. Thus, in *Borden* v. *Borella*, 325 U.S. 679, it was held that employees engaged in the administration, planning, management, and control of the various physical processes together with the accompanying clerical and accounting activities are, from a productive standpoint and for purposes of the Act, "actually engaged in the production of goods for commerce just as much as are those who process and work on the tangible products" in the manufacturing plants or other producing facilities of the enterprise.

(b) Typically, but not exclusively, employees engaged in the production of goods for interstate or foreign commerce include those who work in manufacturing, processing, and distributing establishments, including wholesale and retail establishments, that "produce" (including handle or work on) goods for such commerce. This includes everyone employed in such establishments, or elsewhere in the enterprises by which they are operated, whose activities constitute "production" of such goods under the principles outlined in paragraph (a) of this section. Thus, employees who sell, process, load, pack, or otherwise handle or work on goods which are to be shipped or delivered outside the State either by their employer or by another firm, and either in the same form or as a part or ingredient of other goods, are engaged in the production of goods for commerce within the coverage of the Act. So also are the office, management sales, and shipping personnel, and maintenance, custodial, and protective employees who perform, as a part of the integrated effort for the production of the goods for commerce, services related to such production or to such goods or to the plant, equipment, or personnel by which the production is accomplished.

Section 800.8.—"Closely related" and "directly essential" activities.

As previously noted in section 800.7 an employee is engaged in the production of goods for interstate or foreign commerce within the meaning of the general coverage provisions of the Act even if his work is not an actual and direct part of such production, so long as he is engaged in a process or occupation which is "closely related" and "directly essential" to it. This is true whether he is employed by the producer of the goods or by someone else who provides goods or services to the producer. See in this connection *Kirschbaum* v. *Walling*, 316 U.S. 517, and *Mitchell* v. *Joyce Agency*, 348 U.S. 945, affirming 110 F. Supp. 918. A full discussion of "closely related" and "directly essential" work is contained in Part 776 of this chapter. Typical of employees covered under these principles are bookkeepers, stenographers, clerks, accountants, and auditors and other office and white-collar workers, and employees doing payroll, timekeeping, and time study work for the producer of goods; employees in the personnel, labor relations, safety and health, advertising, promotion, and public relations activities of the producing enterprise; work instructors for the producers; employees maintaining, servicing, repairing or improving the buildings, machinery, equipment, vehicles or other facilities used in the production of goods for commerce, and such custodial and protective employees as watchmen, guards, firemen, patrolmen, caretakers, stockroom workers and warehousemen; and transportation workers bringing supplies, materials, or equipment to the producer's premises, removing waste materials therefrom, or transporting materials or other goods, or performing such other transportation activities, as the needs of production may require. These examples are illustrative, rather than exhaustive, of the employees who are "engaged in the production of goods for commerce" by reason of performing activities closely related and directly essential to such production.

Section 800.9.—What goods are considered as produced for commerce.

Goods (as defined in 3(i) of the Act) are "produced for commerce" if they are "produced, manufactured, mined, handled or in any other manner worked on" in any State for sale, trade, transportation, transmission, shipment, or delivery, to any place outside thereof. Goods are produced for commerce where the producer intends, hopes, expects, or has reason to believe that the goods or any unsegregated part of them will move (in the same or in an altered form or as a part or ingredient of other goods) in interstate or foreign commerce. If such movement of the goods in commerce can reasonably be anticipated by the producer when the goods are produced, it makes no difference whether he himself or the person to whom the goods are transferred puts the goods in interstate or foreign commerce. The fact that goods do move in interstate or foreign commerce is strong evidence that the producer intended, hoped, expected, or had reason to believe that they would so move. Goods may also be produced "for commerce" where they are to be used within the State and not transported in any form across State lines. This is true where the use to which they are put is one which serves the needs of the instrumentalities or facilities by which interstate or foreign commerce is carried on within the State. These principles are discussed comprehensively in Part 776 of this chapter.

Section 800.10.—Coverage is not based on amount of covered activity.

The act makes no distinction as to the percentage, volume, or amount of activities of either the employee or the employer which constitute engaging in commerce or in the production of goods for commerce. (Mabee v. White Plains Publishing Co., 327 U.S. 128;

United States v. Darby, 312 U.S. 100.) As explained more fully in Part 776 of this chapter, the law is settled that every employee whose activities in commerce or in the production of goods for commerce, even though small in amount, are regular and recurring, is considered "engaged in commerce or in the production of goods for commerce". Also, under the definition in section 3(s) of the act, an enterprise described in any of the four numbered clauses of the subsection is an enterprise "engaged in commerce or in the production of goods for commerce" if, in its activities, some employees are so engaged, "including employees handling, selling, or otherwise working on goods that have been moved in or produced for commerce by any person".

[32 F.R. 2378, February 3, 1967]

Section 800.11.—"Enterprise" coverage.

The scope of the added coverage on an enterprise basis, which was provided by amendments to the Act, is determined with reference to the special definitions of the term "enterprise" in section 3(r) of the Act and of the term "enterprise engaged in commerce or in the production of goods for commerce" under section 3(s). Under these enterprise coverage provisions, if an enterprise or establishment is an "enterprise engaged in commerce or in the production of goods for commerce" as defined and delimited in section 3(s) of the Act, every employee employed in such enterprise or by such establishment is within the coverage of the minimum wage and the equal pay provisions, except as otherwise specifically provided by the Act. "Enterprise" coverage is discussed comprehensively elsewhere in this chapter. A detailed discussion of the statutory definition of "enterprise" and of enterprise coverage as it relates to enterprises which have retail or service establishments and as it relates to gasoline service establishments is contained in Part 779 of this chapter.

Section 800.12.—Exemptions from section 6 provided by section 13.

The equal pay provisions do not apply to employees exempted from the provisions of section 6 under any provision of section 13(a) of the act. The following employees are among those excluded if their employment fully satisfies all the statutory conditions for exemption: Bona fide executive, administrative, and professional employees, including academic administrative personnel and teachers in elementary and secondary schools, and outside salesmen, as defined in regulations (see Part 541 of this chapter); employees of certain retail or service establishments (see Part 779 of this chapter); employees of certain amusement or recreational establishments (see Act, sec. 13(a)(3)); employees of certain small newspapers (see Act, sec. 13(a)(8)); employees of motion picture theaters (see Act, sec. 13(a)(9)); switchboard operators of independent telephone companies which have fewer than 750 stations (see Act, sec. 13(a)(10)); employees on small farms and certain hand harvest workers paid piece rates (see Part 780 of this chapter).

[32 F.R. 2379, February 3, 1967]

Subpart B—The Equal Pay Provisions

THE STATUTORY PROVISIONS

Section 800.100.—Section 6(d) of the Act.

The Equal Pay Act of 1963 amended section 6 of the Fair Labor Standards Act by adding thereto a new subsection (d) as follows:

(d) (1) No employer having employees subject to any provisions of this section shall discriminate, within any establishment in which such employees are employed, between employees on the basis of sex by paying wages to employees in such establishment at a rate less than the rate at which he pays wages to employees of the opposite sex in such establishment for equal work on jobs the performance of which requires equal skill, effort, and responsibility, and which are performed under similar working conditions, except where such payment is made pursuant to (i) a seniority system; (ii) a merit system; (iii) a system which measures earnings by quantity or quality of production; or (iv) a differential based on any other factor other than sex: *Provided*, That an employer who is paying a wage rate differential in violation of this subsection shall not, in order to comply with the provisions of this subsection, reduce the wage rate of any employee.

(2) No labor organization, or its agents, representing employees of an employer having employees subject to any provisions of this section shall cause or attempt to cause such an employer to discriminate against an employee in violation of paragraph (1) of this subsection.

(3) For purposes of administration and enforcement, any amounts owing to any employee which have been withheld in violation of this subsection shall be deemed to be unpaid minimum wages or unpaid overtime compensation under this Act.

(4) As used in this subsection, the term "labor organization" means any organization of any kind, or any agency or employee representation committee or plan, in which employees participate and which exists for the purpose, in whole or in part, of dealing with employers concerning grievances, labor disputes, wages, rates of pay, hours of employment, or conditions of work.

Section 800.101.—Effective date of equal pay requirements.

(a) Section 4 of the Equal Pay Act of 1963 provides as follows with respect to the effective date of its amendments to the Fair Labor Standards Act:

Sec. 4. The amendments made by this Act shall take effect upon the expiration of 1 year from the date of its enactment: *Provided*, That in the case of employees covered by a bona fide collective bargaining agreement in effect at least 30 days prior to the date of enactment of this Act, entered into by a labor organization (as defined in section 6(d)(4) of the Fair Labor Standards Act of 1938, as amended), the amendments made by this Act shall take effect upon the termination of such collective bargaining agreement or upon the expiration of 2 years from the date of enactment of this Act, whichever shall first occur.

(b) Under the above provision, on and after June 11, 1965, the equal pay provisions are effective with respect to all employment subject to their terms. On and after June 11, 1964, these provisions were applicable to most such employment. However, their application was deferred as to employees covered by bona fide collective bargaining agreements, which were in effect on May 11, 1963, and which did not terminate until some date after June 11, 1964. As to employees covered by such agreements the provisions became effective on the termination date of the agreement or on June 11, 1965, whichever was the earlier date.

APPLICATION OF PROVISIONS IN GENERAL

Section 800.102.—Application to employers.

The prohibition against discrimination in wages on account of sex contained in section 6(d)(1) of the Act (see sec. 800.100) is applicable to every employer having employees subject to a minimum wage under the Act. The employer may not discriminate on the basis of sex against such employees in any establishment (see sec. 800.103) in which such employees are employed by him by paying them wages at rates lower than he pays employees of the opposite sex employed in the same establishment for work subject to the equal pay standard—that is, where equal work is performed by such employees and by employees of the opposite sex on jobs the performance of which requires equal skill, effort, and responsibility, and which are performed under similar working conditions. (See secs. 800.119–800.132.) The Act excepts from this general prohibition such differences between the wage rates for such work performed by men and women employed by the employer in the establishment as can be shown to be based on a factor or factors other than sex. (See secs. 800.140–800.151.) It is clear from the proviso included in section 6(d)(1) that where a wage rate differential in violation of the provision is paid, the violation cannot be corrected by reducing the wage rate of any employee.

Section 800.103.—Application to establishments.

The prohibition against discrimination in wages on account of sex contained in section 6(d)(1) of the Act applies "within any establishment" in which employees who must be paid a minimum wage under section 6 are employed by an employer. The term "establishment" as used in section 6(d)(1) has the same meaning as it has in section 13(a)(2) and elsewhere in the Act. (See sec. 800.108.) It should be kept in mind, in determining an employer's obligations under the equal pay provisions, that "employer" and "establishment" as used in these and other provisions of the Act are not synonymous terms. An employer may have more than one establishment in which he employs employees within the meaning of the Act. In such cases, the legislative history makes clear that there shall be no comparison between wages paid to employees in different establishments.

Section 800.104.—Application to employees.

As has been seen, there must be compliance by the employer with the equal pay requirements within any establishment in which employees subject to the Act's minimum wage provisions are employed by him. The Act's concern with wage discrimination by an employer on account of sex to the detriment of his employees who are subject to the minimum wage provisions is not limited either by its language or by its legislative history to those employees whose work is performed on the premises of their employer's establishment. The Act speaks of the employment of employees in the establishment rather than of their engagement in work there. Also, the legislative history of the Equal Pay Act makes it clear that coverage under the equal pay provisions is equal to that provided by the other provisions of section 6 of the Fair Labor Standards Act, and that those employers and employees who are subject to the minimum wage provisions will be subject to the new provisions on equal pay. (See S. Rept. No. 176, 88th Cong., 1st sess., p. 2; H. Rept. No. 309, 88th Cong., 1st sess., p. 2.) Congress clearly rejected the concept that the equal pay provisions apply only to work performed inside a physical establishment. Otherwise, those employees, subject to section 6 of the Act, would be incongruously deprived of equal pay protection simply because their work is performed away from the physical premises of the establishment in which they are employed. On the other hand, it is clear from the language of the Act that in each distinct physical place of business where employees of an employer work (including, but not limited to, the employer's own establishments), the obligation of the employer to comply with the equal pay requirements must be determined separately with reference to those of his employees who are employed in that particular establishment. Accordingly, where there are a number of distinct physical places of business in which an employer's employees are employed, compliance with the equal pay provisions must be tested within each establishment by comparing the jobs in which employees are employed in that establishment and the wages paid for work on such jobs when performed by employees of opposite sexes.

[31 F.R. 11720, Sept. 7, 1966, as amended at 32 F.R. 2379, February 3, 1967]

Section 800.105.—Employees not subject to provisions.

An employee may be employed in an establishment by an employer subject to the equal pay provisions, and yet not be protected by these provisions. Unless such an employee is one to whom the minimum wage provisions apply, the Act does not afford protection from a discrimination in wages based on sex between such employee and an employee of the opposite sex. This is true both with respect to employees who are not covered under section 6 and with respect to employees to whom section 6 cannot apply by reason of an express exemption in section 13(a). (See sec. 800.12.) More particularly, the equal pay standards have no application with respect to wages paid employees who are neither engaged in or in the production of goods for interstate commerce nor employed in an enterprise which is so engaged.

Section 800.106.—Application to labor organizations.

Section 6(d)(2) of the Act prohibits a labor organization, representing employees of an employer having employees subject to the minimum wage provisions of section 6, from engaging in acts that cause or attempt to cause the employer to discriminate against an employee in violation of the equal pay provisions. Agents of the labor organization are also prohibited from doing so. Thus, such a labor organization and its agents must refrain from strike or picketing activities aimed at inducing an employer to institute or maintain a prohibited wage differential, and must not demand any terms or any interpretation of terms in a collective bargaining agreement with such an employer which would require the latter to discriminate in the payment of wages contrary to the provisions of section 6(d)(1). Section 6(d)(2), together with the special provision in section 4 of the Equal Pay Act of 1963 allowing a deferred effective date for application of the equal pay provisions to employees covered by specified existing collective bargaining agreements (see sec. 800.101) are indicative of the legislative intent that in situations where wage rates are governed by collective bargaining agreements, unions representing the employees shall share with the employer the responsibility for ensuring that the wage rates required by such agreements will not cause the employer to make payments that are not in compliance with the equal pay provisions. Thus, where equal work is being performed within the meaning of the statute, a wage rate differential which exists between male and female employees cannot be justified on the ground that it is a result of negotiation by the union with the employer, for negotiation of such a discriminatory wage differential is prohibited under the terms of the equal pay amendment.

DEFINITIONS PERTINENT TO APPLICATION

Section 800.107.—"Employer", "employee", "employ" defined.

The Act provides its own definitions of "employer", "employee", and "employ", under which "economic reality" rather than "technical concepts" determines whether there is employment subject to its terms (Goldberg v. Whitaker House Cooperative, 366 U.S. 28; United States v. Silk, 331 U.S. 704; Rutherford Food Corp. v. McComb, 331 U.S. 722). An "employer", as defined in section 3(d) of the Act, "includes any person acting directly or indirectly in the interest of an employer in relation to an employee but shall not include the United States or any State or political subdivision of a State (except with respect to employees of a State, or a political subdivision thereof, employed (a) in a hospital, institution, or school referred to in the last sentence of subsection (r) of this section, or (b) in the operation of a railway or carrier referred to in such sentence) or any labor organization (other than when acting as an employer), or anyone acting in the capacity of officer or agent of such labor organization". An "employee" as defined in section 3(e) of the Act "includes any individual employed by an employer" and "employ", as used in the Act, is defined in section 3(g) to include "to suffer or permit to work". It should be noted, as explained in the interpretative bulletin on joint employment, Part 791 of this chapter, that in appropriate circumstances two or more employers may be jointly responsible for compliance with the statutory requirements applicable to employment of a particular employee.

[32 F.R. 2379, February 3, 1967]

Section 800.108.—Meaning of "establishment".

Although not expressly defined in the Act, the term "establishment" has a well settled meaning in the application of the Act's provisions. It refers to a "distinct physical place of business" rather than to "an entire business or enterprise" which may include several separate places of business. This is consistent with the meaning of the term as it is normally used in business and in government, is judicially settled, and has been recognized in the Congress in the course of enactment of amendatory legislation (Phillips v. Walling, 324 U.S. 490; Mitchell v. Bekins Van & Storage Co., 352 U.S. 1027; 95 Cong. Rec. 12505, 12579, 14877; H. Rept. No. 1453, 81st Cong., 1st sess., p. 25). Each physically separate place of business is ordinarily considered a separate establishment. For example, where a manufacturer operates at separate locations a plant for production of its goods, a warehouse for storage and distribution, several stores from which its products are sold, and a central office for the enterprise, each physically separate place of business is a separate establishment. Under certain circumstances, however, two or more portions of a business enterprise, even though located on the same premises and under the same roof, may constitute more than one establishment. This would ordinarily be the case only if these portions of the enterprise are both physically segregated and engaged in operations which are functionally separated from each other and which have separate employees and maintain separate records. The application of these principles is illustrated further and in more detail by the discussion in Part 779 of this chapter of the term "establishment".

[32 F.R. 2379, February 3, 1967]

Section 800.109.—"Labor organization" defined.

For purposes of application to labor organizations of the requirements of section 6(d) of the Act and the enforcement of such requirements under sections 16 and 17 (see sec. 800.166), section 6(d)(4) of the Act defines the term "labor organization" as meaning "any organization of any kind, or any agency or employee representation committee or plan, in which employees participate and which exists for the purpose, in whole or in part, of dealing with employers concerning grievances, labor disputes, wages, rates of pay, hours of employment, or conditions of work." This is the same definition of "labor organization" that is used in the Labor Management Relations Act, 1947, and will be applied in the same manner.

Section 800.110.—Meaning of "wages".

The term "wages" used in section 6(d)(1) of the Act is considered to have the same meaning it has elsewhere in the Act. As a general rule, in determining compliance with the equal pay provisions, the wages paid by the employer will be calculated pursuant to the same principles and procedures as have traditionally been followed in calculating such wages for purposes of determining compliance with the minimum wage provisions of the Act. Wages paid to an employee generally include all payments made to or on behalf of the employee as remuneration for employment. The provisions of section 7(e) of the Act under which some such payments may be excluded in computing an employee's "regular rate" of pay for purposes of section 7 do not authorize the exclusion of any such remuneration from the "wages" of an employee in applying section 6(d) of the Act. Thus, vacation and holiday pay, and premium payments for work on Saturdays, Sundays, holidays, regular days of rest, or other days or hours in excess or outside of the employee's regular days or hours of work, are remuneration for employment and therefore wage payments that must be considered in applying the equal pay provisions of the Act, even though not a part of the employee's "regular rate". On the other hand, payments made by an employer to an employee which do not constitute remuneration for employment are not "wages" to be compared for equal pay purposes under section 6(d) of the Act. Examples are payments related to maternity, and such reasonable payments for reimbursable expenses of traveling on the employer's business as are discussed in section 778.217 of this chapter.

[32 F.R. 2379, February 3, 1967]

Section 800.111.—Wage "rate".

The term wage "rate" used in section 6(d)(1) of the Act is considered to encompass all rates of wages whether calculated on a time, piece, job, incentive or other basis. The term includes the rate at which overtime compensation or other special remuneration is paid as well as the rate at which straight time compensation for ordinary work is paid. The term also includes the rate at which a "draw", advance, or guarantee is paid against a commission settlement.

Section 800.112.—Cost or value of non-cash items as included in wages.

The reasonable cost or fair value of certain perquisites, as provided in section 3(m) of the Act and Part 531 of this chapter is, by definition, a part of the wage paid to an employee for purposes of the Act. Section 3(m), in part provides that the wage paid to any employee includes "the reasonable cost, as determined by the Secretary of Labor, to the employer of furnishing such employee with board, lodging, or other facilities, if such board, lodging, or other facilities are customarily furnished by such employer to his employees". As an exception to this rule, section 3(m) provides the cost of board, lodging, or other facilities shall not be included as a part of the wage paid to any employee to the extent it is excluded therefrom under the terms of a bona fide collective-bargaining agreement applicable to the particular employee. A further provision of section 3(m) authorizes the Secretary "to determine the fair value of such board, lodging, or other facilities for defined classes of employees and in defined areas, based on average cost to the employer or to groups of employers similarly situated, or average value to groups of employees, or other appropriate measures of fair value." The statute directs that such evaluations, "where applicable and pertinent, shall be used in lieu of actual measure of cost in determining the wage paid to any employee". As explained in Part 531 of this chapter, it is the above provision of the Act which governs the payment, otherwise than in cash, of wages which the Act requires. Regulations under which the reasonable cost or fair value of such facilities furnished may be computed for inclusion as part of the wages required by the Act are also contained in Part 531 of this chapter.

[32 F.R. 23880, February 3, 1967]

Section 800.113.—Particular types of payments as wages.

In addition to the examples referred to in sections 800.110 through 800.112, some further illustrations of the types of payments that must be considered in computing wages and wage rates for purposes of the equal pay provisions may be helpful. The Act requires comparison of the wage rates paid for "work on jobs", which makes relevant all remuneration for employment and not just that portion which constitutes compensation for particular hours of employment or particular work done. Clearly this includes all payments that may be counted as part of the minimum wage rate per hour required under section 6 of the Act, all payments that are part of the employee's regular rate under section 7 of the Act, and all overtime premiums. It includes in addition, however, other payments (such as the holiday and vacation pay previously mentioned in section 800.110) for the employee's work on the job as a whole which may have no direct relation to particular hours or weeks of work; and the inclusion of such payments in the wages compared for equal pay purposes does not depend on whether they can be counted as a part of the wage rate per hour required under section 6 as a minimum wage or whether they constitute part of the regular rate of pay under section 7. In accordance with the foregoing principles, the wages to be considered in determining compliance with the equal pay provisions include, in addition to such payments as hourly and daily wages, sums paid as weekly, monthly, or annual salaries; wages measured by pieces produced or tasks performed; commissions, bonuses or other payments measured by production, efficiency, attendance, or other job-related factors, or agreed to be paid under the employment contract; standby and on-call pay; and extra payments made for hazardous, disagreeable, or inconvenient working conditions. These are illustrative, although not exhaustive, of the types of payments included, when part of the remuneration for employment, in the wages to be compared where employees of opposite sexes are employed in jobs subject to the equal pay standard. On the other hand, the "wages" which are compared for equal pay purposes do not include bona fide gifts or payments in the nature of gifts which would be excluded from the employee's regular rate under section 7(e)(1) of the Act and section 778.212 of this chapter. Likewise, sums paid as discretionary bonuses are not considered wages for equal pay purposes if such payments meet the requirements of section 7(e)(3)(a) of the Act and section 778.211 of this chapter. Study is still being given to some categories of payments made in connection with employment subject to the Act, to determine whether and to what extent such payments are remuneration for employment that must be counted as part of wages for equal pay purposes. These categories of payments include sums paid in recognition of services performed during a given period pursuant to a bona fide profit-sharing plan or trust meeting the requirements of Part 549 of this chapter or pursuant to a bona fide thrift or savings plan meeting the requirements of Part 547 of this chapter, and contributions irrevocably made by an employer to a trustee or third person pursuant to a bona fide plan for providing old-age, retirement, life, accident, or health insurance or similar benefits for employees. (See sections 778.214 and 778.215 of this chapter.)

[32 F.R. 2380, February 3, 1967]

EQUALITY OF PAY

Section 800.114.—"Male jobs" and "female jobs" generally.

(a) Wage classification systems which designate certain jobs as "male jobs" and other jobs as "female jobs" frequently specify markedly lower rates for the "female jobs". Because such a practice frequently indicates a pay practice of discrimination based on sex, where such systems exist a serious question would be raised as to whether prohibited wage differentials are involved. This position is consistent with that taken by the National War Labor Board which found such systems inherently discriminatory and explained that it is not consistent with the principle of equal pay for equal work to designate certain jobs as "female jobs" and other jobs as "male jobs" and on that ground alone establish rate differentials against the former and in favor of the latter. The Board held that the equal pay principle requires that proper rates be set for all jobs, based upon a fair objective evaluation of duties and functions, irrespective of the sex of the workers assigned to them (General Electric Co. and Westinghouse Electric Corp., Case No. 111–17208–D and 111–17209–D, Dec. 12, 1945).

[32 F.R. 2380, February 3, 1967]

It should be further noted that wage classification systems which designate certain jobs as "male jobs" and other jobs as "female jobs" may contravene Title VII of the Civil Rights Act of 1964 except in those certain instances where sex is a bona fide occupational qualification reasonably necessary to the normal operation of that particular business or enterprise (78 Stat. 241, 256).

[32 F.R. 5737, April 8, 1967]

(b) Section 6(d)(1) prohibits discrimination on the basis of sex in the payment of wages to employees "for equal work *on jobs*" which are equal under the standards which it provides (emphasis supplied). (See the discussion in section 800.119 et seq.) The legislative history of the Equal Pay Act expressly refers to the War Labor Board experience as furnishing a guide for testing "the relationship between jobs" and determining "equal work" and "equal skills" for purposes of a "practical" administration and application of the Act's "equal pay policy" (see, e.g., S. Rept. 176, 88th Cong. 1st sess., to accompany S. 1409; H. Rept. 309, 88th Cong. 1st sess., to accompany H.R. 6060). Some of the earliest cases confronting the War Labor Board on the application of the "equal pay for equal work" principle involved situations in which women were being hired to replace men as a result of the manpower shortages. The Board consistently ruled that the principle applied to these situations, as well as to situations where male and female employees performed the same work concurrently and interchangeably, and therefore that women assigned "to take the place of men" to perform substantially the same jobs "formerly performed by men" were entitled to the same rate of pay as the men whom they replaced. Rotary Cut Box Shook Industry, 12 W.L.B. Rept. 605, 606, 608; General Electric Co., and Westinghouse Electric Co., supra, at pp. 668–669, 677, 686.

(c) That the Equal Pay Act was intended to encompass situations of this kind is confirmed by the declared purposes and terms of the Act as well as by the legislative history. The statute is intended to eliminate sex as a basis for wage differentials between employees performing equal work on jobs within the establishment, and if the rates paid for the same jobs are lower when occupants of the jobs are of one sex than they are when the jobs are filled by employees of the opposite sex, such discrimination within the establishment is equally in violation of the statutory prohibition whether or not employees of both sexes are employed in such jobs at the same time. Accordingly, where an employee of one sex is hired or assigned to a particular job to replace an employee of the opposite sex, comparison of the newly assigned employee's wage rate with that of the replaced former employee is required for purposes of section 6(d)(1), whether or not the job is performed concurrently by employees of both sexes. For example, if a particular job which in the past has been performed by a male employee becomes vacant and is then filled by a female employee, it would be contrary to the equal pay requirement to pay the female employee a lower wage rate than was paid for the same job when performed by the male employee, even though employees of both sexes may not be performing the job at the same time. Payment of the lower wage rate in such circumstances is a prohibited wage differential. The same principle is involved if all employees of one sex are removed from a particular job (by transfer or discharge) so as to retain employees of only one sex in a job previously performed interchangeably or concurrently by employees of both sexes. If a prohibited sex-based wage differential had been established or maintained in violation of the Act when the same job was being performed by employees of both sexes, the employer's obligation to pay the higher rate for the job cannot be avoided or evaded by the device of confining the job to members of the lower paid sex. Compliance with the Act in such circumstances can be achieved only by increasing the wage rate to the higher rate paid for the job when performed by employees of the opposite sex.

[32 F.R. 2380, February 3, 1967]

Section 800.115.—Inequalities in pay that raise questions under the Act.

It is necessary to scrutinize with especial care those inequalities in pay between employees of opposite sexes which may indicate a pattern of discrimination in wage payment that is based on sex. Thus, a serious question would be raised where such an inequality, allegedly based on a difference in job content, is in fact one in which the employee occupying the job purportedly requiring the higher degree of skill, effort, or responsibility receives the lower wage rate. Likewise, because the equal pay amendment was designed to eliminate wage rate differentials which are based on sex, situations will be carefully scrutinized where employees of only one sex are concentrated in the lower grades of the wage scale, and where there does not appear to be any material relationship other than sex between the lower wage rates paid to such employees and the higher rates paid to employees of the opposite sex. Such concentrations in rate range situations may occur also where an employer follows a practice of paying a range of rates to newly hired employees. Differentials in entrance rates will not constitute a violation of the equal pay principle if the factors taken into consideration in determining which rate is to be paid each employee are applied equally to men and women. This would be true, for example, if all persons who have a parent employed by the firm are paid at the highest rate of the rate range whether they are men or women. However, if in a particular establishment all persons of one sex tend to be paid at the lowest rate of the range and employees of the opposite sex hired to perform the same work tend to be paid at the highest rate of the range, and if no specific factor or factors other than sex appear to be associated with the difference in pay, a serious question would be raised as to whether the pay practice involves prohibited wage differentials.

Section 800.116.—Equality and inequality of pay in particular situations.

(a) *Overtime work.* Because overtime premiums are a part of wages for purposes of the equal pay provisions, where men and women receive the same straight-time rates for work subject to the equal pay standards, but the men receive an overtime premium rate of twice the straight-time rate while the women receive only one and one-half times the straight-time rate for overtime, a prohibited wage rate differential is being paid. On the other hand, where male and female employees perform equal work during regular hours but employees of one sex only continue working overtime into another work period, work performed during this later period may be compensated at a higher rate where such is required by law or is the customary practice of the employer. However, in such a situation the payment of the higher rate to employees of one sex for all hours worked, including the non-overtime hours when they are performing equal work with employees of the opposite sex, would result in a violation of the equal pay provisions. If male and female employees are performing equal work in the establishment during regular hours but only some of these employees continue working into an overtime period, payment of a higher wage rate for the overtime worked would not be in violation of the equal pay standard so long as it were paid for the actual overtime hours worked by the employees, whether male or female.

(b) *Special assignments.* The fact that an employee may be required to perform an additional task outside his regular working hours would not justify payment of a higher wage rate to that employee for all hours worked. However, employees who are assigned a different and unrelated task to be performed outside the regular workday may under some circumstances be paid at a different rate of pay for the time spent in performing such additional duty provided such rate is commensurate with the task performed. For example, suppose a male employee is regularly employed in the same job with female employees in the same establishment in work which requires equal skill, effort, and responsibility, and is performed under similar working conditions, except that the male employee must carry money to a bank after the establishment closes at night. Such an employee may be paid at a different rate for the time spent in performing this unrelated task if the rate is appropriate to the task performed and the payment is bona fide and not simply used as a device to escape the equal pay requirements of the Act.

(c) *Vacation or holiday pay.* Since vacation or holiday pay is deemed to be remuneration for employment included in wages within the meaning of the Act, if employees of one sex receive vacation pay for a greater number of hours than employees of the opposite sex, a prohibited wage rate differential is being paid if their work is subject to the equal pay standard and the differential is not shown to come within any of the specified exceptions.

(d) *Contributions to employee benefit plans.* If employer contributions to a plan providing insurance or similar benefits to employees are equal for both men and women, no wage differential prohibited by the equal pay provisions will result from such payments, even though the benefits which accrue to the employees in question are greater for one sex than for the other. The mere fact that the employer may make unequal contributions for employees of opposite sexes in such a situation will not, however, be considered to indicate that the employer's payments are in violation of section 6(d), if the resulting benefits are equal for such employees.

(e) *Commissions.* The establishment of different rates of commission on different types of merchandise would not result in a violation of the equal pay provisions where the factor of sex provides no part of the basis for the differential. For example, suppose that a retail store maintains two shoe departments, each having employees of both sexes, that the shoes carried in the two departments differ in style, quality, and price, and that the male and female sales clerks in the one department are performing "equal work" with those in the other. In such a situation, a prohibited differential would not result from payment of a lower commission rate in the department where a lower price line with a lower markup is sold than in the other department where the merchandise is higher priced and has a higher markup, if the employer can show that the commission rates paid in each department are applied equally to the employees of both sexes in the establishment for all employment in that department and that the factor of sex has played no part in the setting of the different commission rates.

[31 F.R. 6770, May 6, 1966]

Sections 800.117–800.118.—[Reserved]

THE EQUAL PAY FOR EQUAL WORK STANDARD—GENERALLY

Section 800.119.—The job concept in general.

Section 6(d)(1) of the Act prohibits an employer from paying to employees of one sex wages at rates lower than he pays employees of the opposite sex for "equal work on jobs" described by the statute in terms of equality of the "skill, effort, and responsibility" required for performance and similarity of the "working conditions" under which they are performed. This descriptive language refers to "jobs". In applying the various tests of equality to the requirements for the performance of such jobs, it will generally be necessary to scrutinize the job as a whole and to look at the characteristics of the jobs being compared over a full work cycle. This will be true because the kinds of activities required to perform a given job and the amount of time devoted to such activities may vary from time to time. As the legislative history makes clear, the equal pay standard provided by the Act is designed to eliminate any wage rate differentials which are based on sex; nothing in the equal pay provisions is intended to prohibit differences in wage rates that are based not at all on sex but wholly on other factors. (See S. Rept. No. 176, 88th Cong. 1st sess., p. 4; H. Rept. No. 309, 88th Cong. 1st sess., p. 2.)

Section 800.120.—Effect of differences between jobs in general.

There is evidence that Congress intended that jobs of the same or closely related character should be compared in applying the equal pay for equal work standard (Daily Congressional Record, House, May 23, 1963, pp. 8686, 8698). Jobs that require equal skill, effort, and responsibility in their performance within the meaning of the Act are usually not identical in every respect (Daily Congressional Record, Senate, May 28, 1963, p. 9219). Congress did not intend that inconsequential differences in job content would be a valid excuse for payment of a lower wage to an employee of one sex than to an employee of the opposite sex if the two are performing equal work on essentially the same jobs in the same establishment. It will be remembered in this connection that the National War Labor Board (to the experience of which attention is directed in the Senate and House Committee Reports) developed a policy of ignoring inconsequential differences in job content in administering equal pay for equal work provisions (Brown & Sharp Manufacturing Co. Case No. 2228–D, Sept. 25, 1942). On the other hand, it is clear that Congress did not intend to apply the equal pay standard to jobs substantially differing in their terms and conditions. Thus, the question of whether a female bookkeeper should be paid as much as a male file clerk required to perform a substantially different job is outside the purview of the equal pay provisions. It is also clear that the equal pay standard is not to be applied where only men are employed in the establishment in one job and only women are employed in a dissimilar job. For example, the standard would not apply where only women are employed in clerk typist positions and only men are employed in jobs as administrative secretaries if the latter really require substantially different duties.

Section 800.121.—Job content controlling.

Application of the equal pay standard is not dependent on job classifications or titles but depends rather on actual job requirements and performance. For example, the fact that jobs performed by male and female employees may have the same total point value under an evaluation system in use by the employer does not in itself mean that the jobs concerned are equal according to the terms of the statute. Conversely, although the point values allocated to jobs may add up to unequal totals, it does not necessarily follow that the work being performed in such jobs is unequal when the statutory tests of the equal pay standard are applied. Job titles are frequently of such a general nature as to provide very little guidance in determining the application of the equal pay standard. For example, the job title "clerk" may be applied to employees who perform a variety of duties so dissimilar as to place many of them beyond the scope of comparison under the statute. Similarly, jobs included under the title "stock clerk" may include an employee of one sex who spends all or most of his working hours in shifting and moving goods in the establishment whereas another employee, of the opposite sex, may also be described as a "stock clerk" but be engaged entirely in checking inventory. Clearly, the equal pay standard would not apply where jobs require such substantially different duties, even though the job titles are identical. In other situations, including those which exist in the case of jobs identified by the general title "retail clerks", the facts may show that equal skill, effort, and responsibility are required in the jobs of male and female employees notwithstanding they are engaged in selling different kinds of merchandise. In all such situations, the application of the equal pay standard will have to be determined by applying the terms of the statute to the full factual situation.

Section 800.122.—General guides for testing equality of jobs.

(a) What constitutes equal skill, equal effort, or equal responsibility cannot be precisely defined. In interpreting these key terms of the statute, the broad remedial purpose of the law must be taken into consideration. The terms are considered to constitute three separate tests, each of which must be met in order for the equal pay standard to apply. In applying the tests it should be kept in mind that "equal" does not mean "identical" (Daily Congressional Record, Senate, May 28, 1963, p. 9219). Insubstantial or minor differences in the degree or amount of skill, or effort, or responsibility required for the performance of jobs will not render the equal pay standard inapplicable. On the other hand, substantial differences, such as those customarily associated with differences in wage levels when the jobs are performed by persons of one sex only, will ordinarily demonstrate an inequality as between the jobs justifying differences in pay. In determining whether job differences are so substantial as to make jobs unequal, it is pertinent to inquire whether and to what extent significance has been given to such differences in setting the wage levels for such jobs. Such an inquiry may, for example, disclose that apparent differences between jobs have not been recognized as relevant for wage purposes and that the facts as a whole support the conclusion that the differences are too insubstantial to prevent the jobs from being equal in all significant respects under the law.

(b) To illustrate, where employees of opposite sexes are employed in jobs in which the duties they are required to perform and the working conditions are substantially the same, except that an employee of one sex is required to perform some duty or duties involving a higher skill which an employee of the other sex is not required to perform, the fact that the duties are different in this respect is insufficient to remove the jobs from the application of the equal pay standard if it also appears that the employer is paying a lower wage rate to the employee performing the additional duties notwithstanding the additional skill which they involve. In other situations, where employees of opposite sex are employed in jobs which are equal in the levels of skill, effort, and responsibility required for their performance, it may be alleged that the assignment to employees of one sex but not the other of certain duties requiring less skill makes the jobs too different for comparison under the equal pay provisions. But so long as the higher level of skill is required for the performance of the jobs occupied by employees of both sexes, the fact that some of the duties assigned to employees of one sex require less skill than the employee must have for the job as a whole does not warrant any conclusion that the jobs are outside the purview of the equal pay standard. Such a conclusion would be especially inappropriate if the employees of the sex to whom the less skilled work was assigned received a higher rate of pay. There are, of course, situations in which a review of all the pertinent facts will clearly establish that the male and female employees in question are not performing equal work on jobs which are equal in their requirements of skill, effort, and responsibility, and which are performed under similar working conditions. Where it is clear that this is so, the existence or extent of a wage differential between employees of opposite sexes cannot of itself provide a basis for holding an employer liable for violations under the provisions of section 6(d) of the Act.

Section 800.123.—Determining equality of job content in general.

In determining whether differences in job content are substantial in order to establish whether or not employees are performing equal work within the meaning of the Act, the amounts of time which employees spend in the performance of different duties are not the sole criteria. It is also necessary to consider the degree of difference in terms of skill, effort, and responsibility. These factors are related in such a manner that a general standard to determine equality of jobs cannot be set up solely on the basis of a percentage of time. Consequently, a finding that one job requires employees to expend greater effort for a certain percentage of their working time than employees performing another job, would not in itself establish that the two jobs do not constitute equal work. Similarly, the performance of jobs on different machines or equipment would not necessarily result in a determination that the work so performed is unequal within the meaning of the statute if the equal pay provisions otherwise apply. If the difference in skill or effort required for the operation of such equipment is inconsequential, payment of a higher wage rate to employees of one sex because of a difference in machines or equipment would constitute a prohibited wage rate differential. Likewise, the fact that jobs are performed in different departments or locations within the establishment would not necessarily be sufficient to demonstrate that unequal work is involved where the equal pay standard otherwise applies. This is particularly true in the case of retail establishments, and unless a showing can be made by the employer that the sale of one article requires such a higher degree of skill or effort than the sale of another article as to render the equal pay standard inapplicable, it will be assumed that the salesmen and saleswomen concerned are performing equal work. Although the equal pay provisions apply on an establishment basis and the jobs to be compared are those in the particular establishment, all relevant evidence that may demonstrate whether the skill, effort, and responsibility required in the jobs at the particular establishment are equal should be considered, whether this relates to the performance of like jobs in other establishments or not.

Section 800.124.—Comparing "exempt" and "nonexempt" jobs.

Situations sometimes arise in which it is alleged that lower wages are being paid, in violation of the Act, to a nonexempt employee than to an exempt employee of the opposite sex for equal work on jobs said to be equal within the meaning of the Act. Usually it is necessary in such a case to scrutinize carefully the respective job requirements, working conditions, and pay arrangements before it is possible to reach an informed judgment as to the existence of any violation of the Act. To illustrate, suppose it is alleged that employees of opposite sexes are performing equal work within the meaning of the Act and that a wage discrimination on account of sex exists because one of such employees, but not the other, is paid the minimum compensation on a salary basis which is required for exemption as a bona fide executive or administrative employee and is treated by the employer as such an exempt employee under section 13(a)(1) of the Act and the regulations in 29 CFR Part 541. In such a case, regard must be had to the fact that the regulations define an employee employed in a bona fide executive or administrative capacity in terms of the coexistence of a number of factors, only one of which is the receipt of compensation in a specified minimum amount on a salary basis. The existence of all these factors must be verified to determine whether the employer is correct in treating the employee who receives such salary as exempt. Regard must also be had to the fact that an employee who qualifies for exemption, because all the factors required by the regulations coexist, may be required to work as many hours as the employer may be able to persuade him to work for the stated salary, without any necessity of compliance by the employer with the minimum wage, equal pay or overtime compensation requirements of the Act. This is important because the fact that another employee of the opposite sex doing similar work does not receive the salary requisite for an exemption under the regulations would not in all cases mean that such employee is being paid at a lower rate of pay. In fact, because the nonexempt employee must receive at least the minimum wage for every hour worked and the prescribed additional compensation at the specified multiple of the regular rate for every such hour in excess of the applicable maximum workweek, it is possible, depending on the length of the workweek, that the pay in the nonexempt job may exceed the salary paid in the exempt job for the identical number of hours worked. For these reasons, a comparison of exempt and nonexempt jobs requires careful examination of all the facts and does not lend itself to the application of any general rules.

EQUAL SKILL

Section 800.125.—Jobs requiring equal skill in performance.

The jobs to which the equal pay standard is applicable are jobs requiring equal skill in their performance. Where the amount or degree of skill required to perform one job is substantially greater than that required to perform another job, the equal pay standard cannot apply even though the jobs may be equal in all other respects. Skill includes consideration of such factors as experience, training, education, and ability. It must be measured in terms of the performance requirements of the job. If an employee must have essentially the same skill in order to perform either of two jobs, the jobs will qualify under the Act as jobs the performance of which requires equal skill, even though the employee in one of the jobs may not exercise the required skill as frequently or during as much of his working time as the employee in the other job. Possession of a skill not needed to meet requirements of the job cannot be considered in making a determination regarding equality of skill. The efficiency of the employee's performance in the job is not in itself an appropriate factor to consider in evaluating skill.

Section 800.126.—Comparing skill requirements of jobs.

As a simple illustration of the principle of equal skill, suppose that a man and a woman have jobs classified as typists. Both jobs require them to spend two-thirds of their working time in typing and related activities, such as proofreading and filing, and the remaining one-third in diversified tasks, not necessarily the same. Since there is no difference in the skills required for most of their work, whether or not these jobs require equal skill in performance will depend upon the nature of the work the employees must actually perform during this latter period to meet the requirements of the jobs. If it happens that the man, during the remaining one-third of the time, spends twice as much time operating a calculator as does the woman who prefers and is allowed to do most of the copying work required in the office, this would not preclude a conclusion that the performance of the two jobs requires equal skill if there is actually no distinction in the performance requirements of such jobs so far as the skills utilized in these tasks are concerned. Even if the man were required to do all of the calculating work in order to perform his job, it is not at all apparent that the jobs would require substantially different degrees of skill unless it should appear that operation of that calculator requires more training and can command a higher wage than the typing and related work performed by both the man and the woman, and that the work required to be done by the woman in the remaining one-third of the time requires less training and is recognized as commanding a lower wage whether performed by a man or a woman.

EQUAL EFFORT

Section 800.127.—Jobs requiring equal effort in performance.

The jobs to which the equal pay standard is applicable are jobs that require equal effort to perform. Where substantial differences exist in the amount or degree of effort required to be expended in the performance of jobs, the equal pay standard cannot apply even though the jobs may be equal in all other respects. Effort is concerned with the measurement of the physical or mental exertion needed for the performance of a job. Where jobs are otherwise equal under the Act, and there is no substantial difference in the amount or degree of effort which must be expended in performing the jobs under comparison, the jobs may require equal effort in their performance even though the effort may be exerted in different ways on the two jobs. Differences only in the kind of effort required to be expended in such a situation will not justify wage differentials.

Section 800.128.—Comparing effort requirements of jobs.

To illustrate the principle of equal effort exerted in different ways, suppose that a male checker employed by a supermarket is required to spend part of his time carrying out heavy packages or replacing stock involving the lifting of heavy items whereas a female checker is required to devote an equal degree of effort during a similar portion of her time to performing fill-in work requiring greater dexterity—such as rearranging displays of spices or other small items. The difference in kind of effort required of the employees does not appear to make their efforts unequal in any respect which would justify a wage differential, where such differences in kind of effort expended to perform the job are not ordinarily considered a factor in setting wage levels. Further, the occasional or sporadic performance of an activity which may require extra physical or mental exertion is not alone sufficient to justify a finding of unequal effort. Suppose, however, that men and women are working side by side on a line assembling parts. Suppose further that one of the men who performs the operations at the end of the line must also lift the assembly, as he completes his part of it, and places it on a waiting pallet. In such a situation, a wage rate differential might be justified for the person (but only for the person) who is required to expend the extra effort in the performance of his job, provided that the extra effort so expended is substantial and is performed over a considerable portion of the work cycle. However, a serious question would be raised about the bona fides of a wage differential if it is paid to a male employee who is otherwise performing equal work with female employees on the basis that the male is required to do some heavy lifting, unless a similar distinction in wage rates is made in the establishment as between male employees only where some do heavy lifting and others do not. In general, a wage rate differential based on differences in the degree or amount of effort required for performance of jobs must be applied uniformly to men and women. For example, if all women and some of the men performing a particular type of job do not perform heavy lifting, and some men do, payment of a higher wage rate to all of the men than to the women would constitute a prohibited wage rate differential if the equal pay provisions otherwise apply.

EQUAL RESPONSIBILITY

Section 800.129.—Jobs requiring equal responsibility in performance.

The jobs to which the equal pay standard applies are jobs in the performance of which equal responsibility is required. Responsibility is concerned with the degree of accountability required in the performance of the job, with emphasis on the importance of the job obligation. Differences in the degree of responsibility required in the performance of otherwise equal jobs cover a wide variety of situations. The following illustrations in section 800.130, which are by no means exhaustive, may suggest the nature or degree of differences in responsibility which will constitute unequal work.

Section 800.130.—Comparing responsibility requirements of jobs.

(a) There are many situations where one employee of a group performing jobs which are equal in other respects is required from time to time to assume supervisory duties for reasons such as the absence of the regular supervisor. Suppose, for instance, that it is the employer's practice to pay a higher wage rate to such a "relief" supervisor with the understanding that during the intervals in which he performs supervisory duties he is in training for a supervisory position. In such a situation, payment of the higher rate to him might well be based solely on the additional responsibility required to perform his job and the equal pay provisions would not require the same rates to be paid to an employee of the opposite sex in the group who does not have an equal responsibility. There would clearly be no question concerning such a wage rate differential if the employer pays the higher rate to both men and women who are called upon from time to time to assume such supervisory responsibilities.

(b) Other differences in responsibilities of employees in generally similar jobs may require similar conclusions. Sales clerks, for example, who are engaged primarily in selling identical or similar merchandise may be given different responsibilities. Suppose that one employee of such a group (who may be either a man or a woman) is authorized and required to determine whether to accept payment for purchases by personal checks of customers. The person having this authority to accept personal checks may have a considerable additional degree of responsibility which may materially affect the business operations of the employer. In this situation, payment of a higher wage rate to this employee would be permissible.

(c) On the other hand, there are situations where one employee of the group may be given some minor responsibility which the others do not have (e.g., turning out the lights in his department at the end of the business day) but which is not of sufficient consequence or importance to justify a finding of unequal responsibility. As another example of a minor difference in responsibility, suppose that office employees of both sexes work in jobs essentially alike but at certain intervals a male and female employee performing otherwise equal work within the meaning of the statute are responsible for the office payroll. One of these employees may be assigned the job of checking time cards and compiling the payroll list. The other, of the opposite sex, may be required to make out paychecks, or divide up cash and put the proper amounts into pay envelopes after drawing a payroll check. In such circumstances, although some of the employees' duties are occasionally dissimilar, the difference in responsibility involved would not appear to be of a kind that is recognized in wage administration as a significant factor in determining wage rates. Under such circumstances, this difference would seem insufficient to justify a wage rate differential between the man's and the woman's job if the equal pay provisions otherwise apply.

SIMILAR WORKING CONDITIONS

Section 800.131.—Jobs performed under similar working conditions.

In order for the equal pay standard to apply, the jobs must be performed under similar working conditions. It should be noted that the statute adopts the flexible standard of similarity as a basis for testing this requirement. In determining whether the requirement is met, a practical judgment is required in the light of whether the differences in working conditions are the kind customarily taken into consideration in setting wage levels. The mere fact that jobs are in different departments of an establishment will not necessarily mean that the jobs are performed under dissimilar working conditions. This may or may not be the case.

Section 800.132.—Determining similarity of working conditions.

Generally, employees performing jobs requiring equal skill, effort, and responsibility are likely to be performing them under similar working conditions. However, in situations where some employees performing work meeting these standards have working conditions substantially different from those required for the performance of other jobs the equal pay principle would not apply. For example, if some sales persons are engaged in selling a product exclusively inside a store and others employed by the same establishment spend a large part of their time selling the same product away from the establishment, the working conditions would be dissimilar. Also, where some employees do repair work exclusively inside a shop while others employed by the shop spend most of their time doing similar repair work in customers' homes, there would not be similarity in working conditions. On the other hand, slight or inconsequential differences in working conditions that are essentially similar would not justify a differential in pay. Such differences are not usually taken into consideration by employers or in collective bargaining in setting wage rates.

Sections 800.133–800.139.—[Reserved]

EXCEPTIONS TO EQUAL PAY STANDARD

Section 800.140.—The specified exceptions.

Section 6(d)(1) of the Act provides three specific exceptions and one broad general exception to its general standard requiring that employees doing equal work be paid equal wages, regardless of sex. Under these exceptions, where it can be established that a differential in pay is the result of a wage payment made pursuant to a seniority system, a merit system, a system measuring earnings by quantity or quality of production, or that the differential is based on any other factor other than sex, the differential is expressly excluded from the statutory prohibition of wage discrimination based on sex. The legislative intent was stated to be that any discrimination based upon any of these exceptions shall be exempted from the operation of the statute. These exceptions recognize, as do the reports of the legislative committees, that there are factors other than sex that can be used to justify a wage differential, even as between employees of opposite sexes performing equal work on jobs which meet the statutory tests of equal skill, effort, and responsibility, and similar working conditions. (See H. Rept. No. 309, S. Rept. No. 176, 88th Congress 1st sess.)

Section 800.141.—Establishing application of an exception.

(a) The facts necessary to establish that a wage differential has a basis specified in any of the foregoing exceptions are peculiarly within the knowledge of the employer. If he relies on the excepting language to exempt a differential in pay from the operation of the equal pay provisions, he will be expected to show the necessary facts. Thus, such a showing will be required to demonstrate that a payment of wages to employees at a rate less than the rate at which he pays employees of the opposite sex is based on a factor other than sex where it appears that such payments are for equal work on jobs the performance of which requires equal skill, effort, and responsibility, and which are performed under similar working conditions within the meaning of the statute. After careful examination of the legislative history and the judicial precedents, this is believed to be the most reasonable construction of the law and the one which will be approved by the courts. However, because there is some legislative history that could support a different view, the reasons for reaching the foregoing conclusions are explained in some detail in paragraph (b) of this section.

(b) The legislative history of the Equal Pay Act amendments to the Fair Labor Standards Act includes some statements in the House debate, by a member of the House committee who was an active sponsor of the legislation in the form approved by the committee, expressing a view differing from that stated in paragraph (a) of this section. The opinion expressed in these statements appears to be that the burden of establishing a prima facie case of violation of the equal pay provisions includes not only a showing of the facts necessary to establish a failure to comply with the Act's general standard, but also a showing that no facts exist that could bring the wage differential within an exception. In this view, the employer would not have to show facts necessary to prove the exception as an affirmative defense (Daily Congressional Record, House, May 23, 1963, p. 8698). But if the exceptions are intended to have an exempting effect, as was indicated by House committee spokesmen (H. Rept. No. 309, 88th Cong., 1st sess., p. 3; statement of Subcommittee Chairman Thompson, Daily Congressional Record, House, May 23, 1963, p. 8685), it seems plain that a view such as that expressed above is not consistent with the general rule established by the courts that the application of an exemption under this Act is a matter of affirmative defense and the employer urging such an exemption has the burden of showing that it applies. (See *Phillips* v. *Walling*, 334 U.S. 490; *Arnold* v. *Kanowsky*, 361 U.S. 388; *Walling* v. *General Industries Co.*, 330 U.S. 545; *Mitchell* v. *Kentucky Finance Co.*, 359 U.S. 290.) On balance, it would be difficult to conclude from the legislative history that it was the intent of Congress to supersede this established rule by applying a different rule to these provisions than to other exemptions from section 6 or 7. The House committee report emphasized that the "now familiar system of * * * administration, and enforcement, * * * will be utilized fully to complement the new provision" and many statements in the legislative debates as well as the report of the Senate committee further indicate a well-understood legislative intent to apply and enforce the equal pay provisions in a manner consistent with the familiar procedures traditionally followed under the Act in the administration and enforcement of its labor standards. (H. Rept. No. 309, S. Rept. No. 176, 88th Cong. 1st sess.; Daily Congressional Record, House, May 23, 1963, pp. 8692, 8705; Daily Congressional Record, Senate, May 28, 1963, pp. 9219-9220). Also pertinent is the understanding expressed by the House sponsors that a "bona fide program" that "does not discriminate on the basis of sex will serve as a valid defense to a charge of discrimination" (H. Rept. No. 309, 88th Cong. 1st sess.; Daily Congressional Record, House, May 23, 1963, p. 8685) and the clarifying remarks of the subcommittee chairman managing the House-passed legislation in the Senate, who said: "The employer's defense, if it is based on an employer's plan, must be a bona fide one; and the burden of demonstrating the legitimacy of that defense will rest upon the employer." (Daily Congressional Record, Senate, May 28, 1963, p. 9219). On review of the legislative history as a whole, therefore, the most reasonable conclusion appears to be that the position expressed in paragraph (a) of this section is the better view, and that it is consistent with the legislative intent to consider the statutory exceptions, like other exemptions from section 6, as matters of affirmative defense and to require an employer who believes he comes within them to show facts establishing that this is so.

Section 800.142.—Sex must not be a factor in excepted wage differentials.

While differentials in the payment of wages are permitted when it can be shown that they are based on a seniority system, a merit system, a system measuring earnings by quantity or quality of production, or on any other factor other than sex, the requirements for such an exception are not met unless the factor of sex provides no part of the basis for the wage differential. If these conditions are met, the fact that application of the system for measuring earnings results in higher average earnings for employees of one sex than for employees of the opposite sex performing equal work would not constitute a prohibited wage differential. However, to come within the exempting provisions, any system or factor of the type described pursuant to which a wage rate differential is paid must be applied equally to men and women whose jobs require equal skill, effort, and responsibility, and are performed under similar working conditions. Any evaluation, incentive, or other payment plan which establishes separate and different "male rates" and "female rates" without regard to job content will be carefully examined to determine if these rate differentials are based on sex in violation of the equal pay requirements.

Section 800.143.—Establishing absence of sex as a factor.

A showing that a wage differential is based on a factor other than sex, so as to come within one of the exceptions in section 6(d)(1), may sometimes be incomplete without a showing that there is a reasonable relationship between the amount of the differential and the weight properly attributable to the factor other than sex. To illustrate, suppose that male clerks who work 40 hours each week and female clerks who work 35 hours each week are performing equal work on jobs the performance of which requires equal skill, effort, and responsibility, and which are performed under similar working conditions. If they are paid weekly salaries for this work, a differential in the amounts could be justified as based on a difference in hours of work, a difference based on a factor other than sex which the chairman of the House subcommittee stated would "be exempted under this act." (Daily Congressional Record, House, p. 8685, May 23, 1963.) But if the difference in salaries paid is too great to be accounted for by the difference in hours of work, as where the male clerks are paid $90 for their 40-hour week (equal to $2.25 an hour) and the female clerks receive only $70 for their 35-hour week (equal to $2.00 an hour), then it would seem necessary to show some other factor other than sex as the basis for the unexplained portion of the wage differential before a conclusion that there is no wage discrimination based on sex would be warranted. To illustrate further, a compensation plan which provides for a higher rate of commission, "draw", advance or guarantee for sales employees of one sex than for employees of the opposite sex performing "equal work" would be in violation of the equal pay provisions of the Act unless the employer can establish that the differential in pay is pursuant to a seniority system, a merit system, or a system measuring earnings by quantity or quality of production, or is based on any other factor other than sex. A compensation plan which provides for a "draw" based on a percentage of each employee's earnings during a specified prior period would not be in violation of the equal pay provisions of the Act if the plan is applied equally to men and women. However, for all men to receive a higher draw, because it is the employer's experience that men generally earn more in commissions than women, would not be sufficient indication that the differential is based on a factor other than sex.

Section 800.144.—Excepted "systems".

The exceptions for a seniority "system", a merit "system", and a "system" for measuring earnings by quantity or quality of work are not restricted to, although they include, formal systems or systems or plans that are reduced to writing. Such formal or written systems or plans may, of course, provide better evidence of the actual factors which provide a basis for a wage differential, but any informal or unwritten system or plan which can be shown to provide the basis for differentials in wage rates because of seniority, merit, or quantity or quality of production may qualify under the statutory language if it can be demonstrated that the standards or criteria applied under it are applied pursuant to an established plan the essential terms and conditions of which have been communicated to the affected employees.

Section 800.145.—Application of exceptions illustrated, in general.

When applied without distinction to employees of both sexes, shift differentials, incentive payments, production bonuses, performance and longevity raises and the like will not result in equal pay violations. For example, in an establishment where men and women are employed on a job, but only men work on the night shift for which a night shift differential is paid, such a differential would not be prohibited. However, the payment of a higher hourly rate to all men on that job for all hours worked because some of the men may occasionally work nights would result in a prohibited wage differential. The examples (in the sections following) illustrate a few applications of the exception provisions.

Section 800.146.—Examples—"red circle" rates, in general.

The term "red circle" rates describes certain unusual, higher than normal, wage rates which are maintained for many reasons. An example of the use of a "red circle" rate might arise in a situation where a company wishes to transfer a long-service male employee, who can no longer perform his regular job because of ill health, to different work which is now being performed by women. Under the "red circle" principle the employer may continue to pay the male employee his present salary, which is greater than that paid to the women employees, for the work both will be doing. Under such circumstances, maintaining an employee's established wage rate, despite a reassignment to a less demanding job, is a valid reason for the differential even though other employees performing the less demanding work would be paid at a lower rate, since the differential is based on a factor other than sex. However, where wage rate differentials have been or are being paid on the basis of sex to employees performing equal work, rates of the higher paid employees may not be "red circled" in order to comply with the Act. To allow this would only continue the inequities which the Act was intended to cure.

Section 800.147.—Examples—temporary reassignments.

For a variety of reasons an employer may require an employee, for a short period, to perform the work of a job classification other than the employee's regular classification. If the employee's rate for his regular job is higher than the rate usually paid for the work to which he is temporarily reassigned, the employer may continue to pay him the higher rate, under the "red circle" principle. For instance, an employer who must reduce help in a skilled job may transfer employees to less demanding work without reducing their pay, in order to have them available when they are again needed for their former jobs. Although employees traditionally engaged in performing the less demanding work would be paid at a lower rate than those employees transferred from the more skilled jobs, the resultant wage differential would not constitute a violation of the equal pay provisions since the differential is based on factors other than sex. This would be true during the period of time for which the "red circle" rate is bona fide. (See sec. 800.146.) Temporary reassignments may also involve the opposite relationship of wage rates. Thus, an employee may be required, during the period of temporary reassignment, to perform work for which employees of the opposite sex are paid a higher wage rate than that paid for the duties of the employee's regular job classification. In such a situation, the employer may continue to pay the reassigned employee at the lower rate, if the rate is not based on quality or quantity of production, and if the reassignment is in fact a temporary one. If a piece rate is paid employees of the opposite sex who perform the work to which the employee in question is reassigned, failure to pay that employee the same piece rate paid such other employees would raise questions of discrimination based on sex. Also, failure to pay the higher rate to the reassigned employee after it becomes known that the reassignment will not be of a temporary nature would raise a question whether sex rather than the temporary nature of the assignment is the real basis for the wage differential. Generally, failure to pay the higher rate for a period longer than one month will raise questions as to whether the reassignment was in fact intended to be a temporary one.

Section 800.148.—Examples—training programs.

Employees employed under a bona fide training program may, in the furtherance of their training, be assigned from time to time to various types of work in the establishment. At such times, the employee in training status may be performing equal work with nontrainees of the opposite sex whose wages or wage rates may be unequal to those of the trainee. Under these circumstances, provided the rate paid to the employee in training status is paid, regardless of sex, under the training program, the differential can be shown to be attributable to a factor other than sex and no violation of the equal pay standard will result. Training programs which appear to be available only to employees of one sex will, however, be carefully examined to determine whether such programs are, in fact, bona fide. In an establishment where a differential is paid to employees of one sex because, traditionally, only they have been considered eligible for promotion to executive positions, such a practice, in the absence of a bona fide training program, would be a discrimination based on sex and result in a violation of the equal pay provisions, if the equal pay standard otherwise applies.

Section 800.149.—Examples—"head of household".

Sometimes differentials in pay to employees performing equal work are said to be based on the fact that one employee is head of a household and the other, of the opposite sex, is not. In general, such allegations have not been substantiated. Experience indicates that where such factor is claimed the wage differentials tend to be paid to employees of one sex only, regardless of the fact that employees of the opposite sex may bear equal or greater financial responsibility as head of a household or for the support of parents or other family dependents. Accordingly, since the normal pay practice in the United States is to set a wage rate in accordance with the requirements of the job itself and since a "head of household" or "head of family" status bears no relationship to the requirements of the job or to the individual's performance on the job, the general position of the Secretary of Labor and the Administrator is that they are not prepared to conclude that any differential allegedly based on such status is based on a "factor other than sex" within the intent of the statute.

Section 800.150.—Examples—temporary and part-time employees.

The payment of different wage rates to permanent employees than to temporary employees such as may be hired during the Christmas season would not necessarily be a violation of the equal pay provisions even though equal work is performed by both groups of workers. For example, no violation would result where payment of such a differential conforms with the nature and duration of the job and with the customary practice in the industry and the establishment, and the pay practice is applied uniformly to both men and women. Generally, employment for a period longer than one month will raise questions as to whether the employment is in fact temporary. Likewise, the payment of a different wage to employees who work only a few hours a day than to employees of the opposite sex who work a full day will not necessarily involve noncompliance with the equal pay provisions, even though both groups of workers are performing equal work in the same establishment. No violation of the equal pay standards would result if, for example, the difference in working time is the basis for the pay differential, and the pay practice is applied uniformly to both men and women. However, if employees of one sex work 30 to 35 hours a week and employees of the other sex work 40 to 45 hours, a question would be raised as to whether the differential is not in fact based on sex since different rates for part-time work are usually for workweeks of 20 hours or less.

Section 800.151.—Examples—employment cost factors.

A wage differential based on claimed differences between the average cost of employing the employer's women workers as a group and the average cost of employing the men workers as a group does not qualify as a differential based on any "factor other than sex," and would result in a violation of the equal pay provisions, if the equal pay standard otherwise applies. To group employees solely on the basis of sex for purposes of comparison of costs necessarily rests on the assumption that the sex factor alone may justify the wage differential—an assumption plainly contrary to the terms and purpose of the Equal Pay Act. Wage differentials so based would serve only to perpetuate and promote the very discrimination at which the Act is directed, because in any grouping by sex of the employees to which the cost data relates, the group cost experience is necessarily assessed against an individual of one sex without regard to whether it costs an employer more or less to employ such individual than a particular individual of the opposite sex under similar working conditions in jobs requiring equal skill, effort, and responsibility.

[31 F.R. 2657, Feb. 11, 1966]

RELATION TO OTHER LAWS

Section 800.160.—Relation to other equal pay laws.

The provisions of various State or other equal pay laws may differ from the equal pay provisions set forth in the Fair Labor Standards Act. There is also other Federal legislation which deals broadly with discrimination by employers against individuals because of sex, including discrimination on such grounds with respect to compensation for employment (see Civil Rights Act of 1964, 78 Stat. 241, Title VII). Where any such legislation and the equal pay provisions of the Fair Labor Standards Act both apply, the principle established in section 18 of the latter Act will be controlling. No provisions of the Fair Labor Standards Act will excuse noncompliance with any State or other law establishing equal pay standards higher than the equal pay standards provided by section 6(d) of the Fair Labor Standards Act. On the other hand, compliance with other applicable legislation will not excuse noncompliance with the equal pay provisions of the Fair Labor Standards Act.

Section 800.161.—Higher State minimum wage.

State laws providing minimum wage requirements may affect the application of the equal pay provisions of the Fair Labor Standards Act. If a higher minimum wage than that required under the Act is applicable to a particular sex pursuant to State law, and the employer pays the higher State minimum wage to male or female employees, he must also pay the higher rate to employees of the opposite sex for equal work in order to comply with the equal pay provisions of the Act.

Section 800.162.—Overtime payments required by State law.

The application of the equal pay provisions of the Act may also be affected by State legal requirements with respect to overtime pay. If as a result of a State law, female employees in an employer's establishment are paid overtime premiums for hours worked in excess of a prescribed maximum in any workday or workweek, the employer must pay male employees performing equal work in such establishment the same overtime premiums when they work such excess hours, in order to comply with the equal pay provisions of the Fair Labor Standards Act. This would be true even though both the male and the female employees performing equal work are otherwise qualified for exemption from the overtime pay requirements of section 7 of the Fair Labor Standards Act. It would not be true, however, unless the overtime requiring the premium pay is actually being worked by the women.

Section 800.163.—Other laws not applying equally to employment of both sexes.

In making a determination as to the application of the equal pay provisions of the Fair Labor Standards Act, legal restrictions in State or other laws upon the employment of individuals of a specified sex, with respect to such matters as hours of work, weight-lifting, rest periods, or other conditions of such employment, will not be deemed to make otherwise equal work unequal or be considered per se as justification for an otherwise prohibited differential in wage rates. For example, under the Act, the fact that a State law limits the weights which women are permitted to lift would not justify a wage differential in favor of all men regardless of job content. The Act would not prohibit a wage differential paid to male employees whose weight-lifting activities required by the job involve so significant a degree of extra effort as to warrant a finding that their jobs and those of female employees doing similar work do not involve equal work within the meaning of the Act. However, the fact that there is an upper limit set by State law on the weights that may be lifted by women would not justify a wage differential to male employees who are not regularly required to lift substantially greater weights or expend the extra effort necessary to make the jobs unequal. The requirement of equal pay in such situations depends on whether the employees involved are actually performing "equal work" as defined in the Act, rather than on legal restrictions which may vary from State to State.

ENFORCEMENT

Section 800.164.—Investigations and compliance assistance.

The Wage and Hour Division is charged with the administration of the Fair Labor Standards Act, including the equal pay provisions. Investigations under the Act will therefore include such inquiry as may be necessary to obtain compliance with the equal pay provisions in cases where they are applicable. As provided in section 11(a) of the Act, authorized representatives of the Division may investigate and gather data regarding the wages, hours and other conditions and practices of employment. They may enter establishments and inspect the premises and records, transcribe records, and interview employees. They may investigate whatever facts, conditions, practices, or matters are considered necessary to find out whether any person has violated any provisions of the Act or which may aid in enforcement of the Act. Wage-Hour investigators will advise employers regarding any changes necessary or desirable regarding payroll, recordkeeping and other personnel practices which will aid in achieving and maintaining compliance with the law. Complaints, records, and other information obtained from employers and employees are treated confidentially.

Section 800.165.—Recordkeeping requirements.

Records required to be kept by employers having employees subject to the equal pay provisions under section 6(d) of the Act are set forth in sections 516.2, 516.6, and 516.29 of this chapter.

Section 800.166.—Recovery of wages due; injunctions; penalties for willful violations.

(a) Pursuant to section 6(d)(3) of the Act, wages withheld in violation of the equal pay provisions have the status of unpaid minimum wages or unpaid overtime compensation under the Fair Labor Standards Act. This is true both of the additional wages required by the Act to be paid to an employee to meet the equal pay standard, and of any wages that the employer should have paid an employee whose wages he reduced in violation of the Act in an attempt to equalize his pay with that of an employee of the opposite sex performing equal work, on jobs subject to the equal pay standards.

(b) The following methods are provided under sections 16 and 17 of the Act for recovery of unpaid wages: The Administrator of the Wage and Hour Division may supervise payment of the back wages and, in certain circumstances, the Secretary of Labor may bring suit for back pay upon the written request of the employee. The employee may sue for back pay and an additional sum, up to the amount of back pay, as liquidated damages, plus attorney's fees and court costs. The employee may not bring suit if he has been paid back wages under supervision of the Administrator, or if the Secretary has filed suit to collect the wages. The Secretary may also obtain a court injunction to restrain any person from violating the law, including the unlawful withholding by an employer of proper compensation. A 2-year statute of limitations applies to the recovery of unpaid wages, except that an action on a cause of action arising out of a willful violation may be commenced within 3 years after the cause of action accrued.

[32 F.R. 2381, February 3, 1967]

(c) Willful violations of the Act may be prosecuted criminally and the violator fined up to $10,000. A second conviction for such a violation may result in imprisonment.

(d) The equal pay provisions are an integral part of section 6 of the Act, violation of any provision of which by any person, including any labor organization or agent thereof, is unlawful, as provided in section 15(a) of the Act. Accordingly, any labor organization, or agent thereof, who violates any provision of section 6(d) of the Act is subject to injunction proceedings in accordance with the applicable provisions of section 17 of the Act. Any such labor organization, or agent thereof, who willfully violates the provisions of section 15 is also liable to the penalties set forth in section 16(a) of the Act.

APPENDIX FOUR

The 706 Agencies

The 706 agencies, so called for their authorization under Section 706(d) of Title VII, are those state or local government bodies designated (as of October 29, 1976) to investigate and remedy EEOC complaints. The designated 706 Agencies are:

Alaska Commission for Human Rights
Alexandria Human Rights Office
Allentown Human Relations Commission
Arizona Civil Rights Division
Baltimore Community Relations Commission
Bloomington Human Rights Commission
California Fair Employment Practices Commission
Charleston Human Rights Commission
Colorado Civil Rights Commission
Connecticut Commission on Human Rights and Opportunities
Dade County Fair Housing, and Employment Commission
Delaware Department of Labor
District of Columbia Office of Human Rights
East Chicago Human Relations Commission
Evansville (Indiana) Human Relations Commission
Fairfax County Human Rights Commission
Fort Wayne (Indiana) Metropolitan Human Relations Commission
Gary Human Relations Commission
Idaho Commission on Human Rights
Illinois Fair Employment Practices Commission
Indiana Civil Rights Commission
Iowa Commission on Civil Rights
Kansas Commission on Civil Rights
Kentucky Commission on Human Rights
Madison (Wisconsin) Equal Opportunities Commission
Maine Human Relations Commission
Maryland Commission on Human Relations

Massachusetts Commission Against Discrimination
Michigan Civil Rights Commission
Minneapolis Department of Civil Rights
Minnesota Department on Human Rights
Missouri Commission on Human Rights
Montana Commission for Human Rights
Montgomery County Human Relations Commission
Nebraska Equal Opportunity Commission
Nevada Commission on Equal Rights of Citizens
New Hampshire Commission for Human Rights
New Jersey Division on Civil Rights, Department of Law and Public Safety
New York City Commission on Human Rights
New York State Division of Human Rights
Ohio Civil Rights Commission
Oklahoma Human Rights Commission
Omaha Human Relations Department
Oregon Bureau of Labor
Pennsylvania Human Relations Commission
Philadelphia Commission on Human Relations
Pittsburgh Commission on Human Relations
Rhode Island Commission for Human Rights
Rockville (Maryland) Human Rights Commission
St. Paul Department of Human Rights
Seattle Human Rights Commission
Springfield (Ohio) Human Relations Department
South Bend (Indiana) Human Rights Commission
South Carolina Human Affairs Commission
South Dakota Human Relations Commission
Tacoma Human Rights Commission
Utah Industrial Commission
Vermont Attorney General's Office, Civil Rights Division
Virgin Islands Department of Labor
Washington State Human Rights Commission
West Virginia Human Rights Commission
Wheeling Human Rights Commission
Wichita Commission on Civil Rights
Wisconsin Equal Rights Division, Department of Industry, Labor and Human Relations
Wyoming Fair Employment Practices Commission.

The designated Notice Agencies are:

Arkansas Governor's Committee on Human Resources
Florida Commission on Human Relations
Georgia Governor's Council on Human Relations
Montana Department of Labor and Industry
North Dakota Commission on Labor
Ohio Director of Industrial Relations
(Sec. 713(a), 78 Stat. 265 (42 U.S.C. Sec. 2000e–12(a)).)

This amendment is effective in October 29, 1976.

Index

330

INDEX